The Indestructible Jews

*An action-packed journey
through 4,000 years of history*

———◆———

MAX I. DIMONT

A NEW REVISED EDITION

Ⓞ

A SIGNET BOOK

NEW AMERICAN LIBRARY

TIMES MIRROR

Library of Congress Catalog Card Number: 70-136602

This is a reprint of a hardcover edition published
by The New American Library, Inc. in association
with The World Publishing Company. The hardcover
edition was published simultaneously in Canada
by George J. McLeod, Ltd., Toronto.

Published by arrangement with Max I. Dimont

SIGNET TRADEMARK REG. U.S. PAT. OFF. AND FOREIGN COUNTRIES
REGISTERED TRADEMARK—MARCA REGISTRADA
HECHO EN CHICAGO, U.S.A.

SIGNET, SIGNET CLASSICS, SIGNETTE, MENTOR AND PLUME BOOKS
*are published by The New American Library, Inc.,
1301 Avenue of the Americas, New York, New York 10019*

FIRST PRINTING, APRIL, 1973

    3 4 5 6 7 8 9 10 11

PRINTED IN THE UNITED STATES OF AMERICA

THE PATH THROUGH TIME

From a simple faith bound to priests to a universal ethic fashioned by prophets . . . from a tribe of shepherds to a people to be found in every corner of the globe . . . from the brink of extinction in the gas chambers to the position of potential saviors of all humankind . . .

Such has been the path followed by the Jewish people through their four-thousand-year history. For as Max I. Dimont brilliantly demonstrates in this fascinating book, the long travails and migrations of the Jews have not been the aimless wanderings of a persecuted people —but instead a constant progression toward a goal of preserving man's last and best hope of survival.

THE INDESTRUCTIBLE JEWS is a work of homage to a great past. Even more, it is a work of shining hope for the future.

"Dimont makes Jewish history read like an adventure story." —COMMENTARY LIBRARY

"The Jew in his proud and proper role as the bearer of culture and morality . . . fascinating reading." —ST. LOUIS POST-DISPATCH

"Dramatic, effective, and convincing. . . ." —AMERICAN JEWISH WORLD

"Readers who enjoyed Jews, God and History *will be happy that Dimont has surfaced again. . . ."* —NEW YORK TIMES BOOK REVIEW

Other SIGNET and MENTOR Books
You Will Want to Read

CONTENTS

inject the world with their concepts of ethics, justice, and brotherhood of man.

Time Span. From Jesus to Ben-Gurion

ACT III

THE PARADOX OF THE DIASPORA: Israel, the World, and the Brotherhood of Man *418*

In which the Jews, standing in the lobby of history, ask themselves if they have been the victims of a grand illusion or in the pursuit of a divine mission, and speculate on their own and the world's possible destiny in the coming third act.

Time Span: From Ben-Gurion to the Messiah

The Paradox of the Diaspora

A FABLE OF OUR TIMES:

On the wall of a subway station in
New York someone had scrawled:

> *"God is dead."*
> *Nietzsche*

Someone else had crossed it out and
scrawled underneath:

> *"Nietzsche is dead."*
> *God*

PREFACE

For all too long, Jews and Christians have distorted Jewish history with so many pious frauds and smothered it with so much pious mythology that at times it has been difficult for scholar or layman to perceive its real grandeur.

It was not always thus. The Old Testament, most of it unequaled for sheer narrative skill, gives us an entirely different picture of Jewish history—proud, grand, and dynamic. It is also the first historical record, in the modern sense of the word, so accurate that an archaeologist can go to where the Bible said things happened and find the evidence.

The Greeks and Romans patterned their historical writings on the Jewish idea of history as a continuous biography of a people. But with the decline of Greece and the fall of Rome, the writing of objective history disappeared for close to a thousand years.

After the Renaissance it became the fashion in Church circles to denigrate Jewish history in order to ennoble the Christian view of things, thus reducing Jewish history to a meaningless, minor footnote. In ghetto circles, it became fashionable to count dead Jews in order to enhance Jewish suffering, thus reducing Jewish history to a meaningless, boring dirge.

In the nineteenth century, with the era of the German Enlightenment (*Aufklärung*), so-called scientific Judaism was born. A more apt phrase would be "public-relations

Judaism." In their eagerness to portray Jews to Christians as nice, tolerant, taxpaying citizens, German Reform Jewish scholars began to suppress anything they thought was unfavorable to the Jews. In their works, the Jew emerged as an innocent *schnook*, constantly pushed by predatory Christians to the slaughter-bench of history. Retroactively, they conferred the crown of martyrdom on Jews all the way back to Abraham.

With the twentieth century, scholars at last began to discard the stereotypes of Church, ghetto, and apologetes. Modern scholars—both Jewish and Christian—began to reexamine Jewish history with new, objective, critical eyes. Jewish scholars especially began to arm themselves with general world history, religious and secular. They let the facts fall where they would, and as obscuring myths were discarded, Jewish history was revealed in a new light.

Facts in themselves, however, have no intrinsic worth other than that they happened. Meaning can come only after facts have been sifted through the human mind and clothed with value. One need only read the contradictory accounts of the Reformation by Catholic and Protestant scholars to appreciate the difference interpretation makes. Though all may agree on dates, names, events, they may all disagree as to their meaning and relative importance. Yet such divergences of opinion are essential, for an important task of the historian is to render a moral judgment.

There is also a presumption among many scholars that responsible thought can be expressed only in "scholarly" language. But thought should not hide its meaning in turgid sentences. History is too important to be smothered by obscure writing. Scholarship does not die with lucidity, or vanish in the warmth of a smile. We hold there is nothing unscholarly in writing in the American vernacular. Nor should one hesitate to employ an apt cliché which, like a metaphor in poetry, can give instant understanding.

The reader who glances through the bibliography will note the general omission of works by Jewish historians of yesteryear whose writings so greatly contributed to the popular concept of Jewish history as a saga of specialized suffering. Rather, we have emphasized the works of modern scholars who have cleared paths through a jungle of otherwise meaningless facts. If this author's vision of Jewish history extends beyond the customary horizons, it is because he stands on the shoulders of this new breed of scholars who have pioneered in the new historiography.

It is now my distinct privilege to express grateful thanks to four St. Louis scholars who read my book in its manuscript form and rendered valuable critical appraisals: Dr. Julius Nodel, Rabbi, Congregation Shaare Emeth, for his firm guidance of this work through the pitfalls of Jewish theology; Dr. Jalo E. Nopola, D.D., on the editorial staff of a publishing house of religious works, for his firm guidance of this work through the pitfalls of Christian theology; Dr. Alexander C. Niven, Associate Professor of History, Meramec Community College, for his critical readings of all passages pertaining to Russian and French history; and F. Garland Russell, Jr., historian and attorney, for his critical evaluation of all sections dealing with Greek, Roman, and European history. This does not mean that these scholars agree with all my interpretations. It is said that "To err is human but to persist diabolical." If there are errors in these spheres, it is not because I was not warned but because I persisted in not heeding them.

And lastly my gratitude to three individuals—to my friend N. Gordon LeBert, my wife Ethel, and my daughter Gail. Gordon's expertise in editorial work, so essential to the writing of *Jews, God, and History*, was invaluable in the writing of this work. My wife Ethel read each successive draft of the manuscript, rendering valuable criticisms and suggestions. And to my daughter, Mrs. Michael Goldey, an editor of a competitive publishing company, I pay tribute for having read and critiqued so discerningly her father's manuscript.

ACT I

THE MANIFEST DESTINY

*Patriarchs, Prophets, and
The Jewish Predestination Drama*

(TIME SPAN: FROM ABRAHAM TO JESUS)

PROGRAM NOTE

Prescription For Survival

Jewish history consists of a unique series of events—accidental or purposive—which have had the practical effect of preserving the Jews as Jews in an "exile" to fulfill their avowed mission of ushering in a brotherhood of man. Whether this mission was initiated by God or retroactively attributed to God by the Jews themselves in no way alters our thesis of a Jewish manifest destiny. We contend that this exile is not a punishment for sins, but a key factor in Jewish survival. Instead of having doomed the Jews to extinction, it funneled them into freedom.

The unique flow of the Jewish saga is often lost sight of because it is obscured by the artificial plateaus of history known as ancient, medieval, and modern. But if we were to view history as the ebb and flow of civilizations shaped by the clash of ideas, rather than see it as the rise and fall of empires shaped by fortunes of war, we would perceive a more meaningful unfolding of Jewish destiny. To behold such a total panorama of Jewish history as it flows within the context of world history, let us step outside the usual chronological anchorage of events and survey the past from a different frame of reference.

From this new vantage point, we will behold world history not as a succession of dynasties but as tidal waves of civilizations. We will see the Akkadian-Sumerian city-states and the Egyptian kingdom sweep in on the shores of the planet Earth, followed by the emergence of the Baby-

17

lonian and Assyrian empires. These in turn are inundated
by the Persian tidal wave of success. Persia is washed away
by the Greek idea, and the Greeks are then engulfed by
the legions of Rome. Next, the Byzantine and Islamic
civilizations flood over the shores of history, and feudalism
rises in Europe. Finally, we will see the Modern Age wade
in on the stilts of capitalism and industrialism.

But where are the Jews? We have raced through 5,000
years of history and not beheld a single one. We know
they are there, somewhere, so we look again, more closely
this time, and we do see them, but in a most peculiar position. They are riding cultural surfboards on the crests of
these tidal waves, precariously bobbing up and down with
the rising and falling fortunes of these civilizations.

If we focus the lens of history on this phenomenon, we
behold another unique sight. After the flow of a civilization has reached its high point, we see it slowly ebb and
ultimately sink into the depths of historical oblivion. And
we see the Jews in that civilization go down with it. But
whereas each sunken civilization remains submerged, the
Jews emerge time and again from seeming doom, riding
the crest of a new civilization rolling in where the old one
once flowed.

We see the Jews make their first appearance in history in
the Babylonian world, about 2000 B.C. When the Babylonian state disappears, the Jews make their entry in the
Persian Empire. As the Persian world disintegrates, they
announce their debut in the Hellenic drawing room. When
Rome conquers the "world," they settle in western Europe,
helping the Romans carry the banners of business enterprise into barbaric Gaul. When the star of Islam rises, the
Jews rise with it to a golden age of intellectual creativity.
When feudalism settles over Europe, they open shop as its
bankers and scholars. And when the Modern Age struts in,
we find them sitting on the architectural staff shaping it.

What can we make of these events? Are they mere accidents of history? Are they but meaningless facts, a series
of causes and effects without a definite design? Or does this
improbable succession of events have a predetermined purpose? If so, who drafted such a blueprint? God? Or the
Jews themselves?

The answer depends not only on faith but on how one views history. Voltaire, representing the rationalist view, saw history as "little else than a picture of human crimes and misfortunes." Jews, representing the humanistic view, attempted to invest history with a moral purposiveness. Therefore it was not survival for its own sake that guided them through the obstacle course of their history. They never jettisoned their ideology even in the hour of peril. What the Jews themselves have thought of their destiny has shaped their history more profoundly than did events. And in the end their unique way of thinking about themselves produced three pronounced and fundamental differences between Jewish history and the history of other peoples.

First, there have been twenty to thirty civilized societies in the history of mankind, the number depending on how one defines a civilization. The usual life span of a civilization as a culture-producing entity has been 500 to 1,000 years. Then the civilization has either stagnated or disintegrated. The Jews are seemingly the only exception to this "rule."

Second, the moment a people lost its country through war or some other calamity, that people either disappeared as an ethnic entity or regressed into a meaningless existence. The Jews, however, though conquered time and again, though exiled from their homeland, did not die out. Against the odds of history, they survived for 2,000 years without a country of their own.

Finally, no people except the Jews has ever managed to create a culture in exile. The Jews, however, in exile created not just one but six different cultures, one in each of the six major civilizations within which their history flowed.

When we stated that the normal life span of a civilization is but 500 to 1,000 years, we were not speaking of survival in a biological sense. In such a sense, the modern Greeks are the descendants of Homer's heroes just as much as the modern Jews are the descendants of the biblical Abraham. We are referring to the continuity of those ideas that spark a culture. When that continuity is disrupted, the culture dies. In such a sense, the Greeks today are no longer of the same culture as the Greeks of Homer's time, and the Egyptians today are not of the same culture as the Egyptians of the time of the pharaohs. But the Jews today are still of the same "culture" and the same people as the Jews of yesteryear. They represent a continuum of ideas that extends unbroken 4,000 years back into history, back to Abraham.

Why is Jewish history so different? Why are the Jews seemingly indestructible? Why were they able to survive where others did not? Why were they able to create new cultures in alien civilizations, whereas others were not?

Is there an element in Jewish history which exempts it from the normal historical process of decay? Was it guided by a Divinity, or did the Jews shape their own destiny? Have historians perhaps obscured the past with too many irrelevant facts?

Consonant with our thesis that Jewish history consists of an onslaught of ideas that toppled empires and ushered in a new world thought, we must discard the usual stereotypes of Jewish history, free it from the shackles imposed on it by friend and foe, and demonstrate not only the source of its indestructibility but also the nature of its vitality. Instead of viewing Jewish history as the unfolding of political events manipulated by man, let us view it as the unfolding of a manifest drama motivated by ideas.

Let us suppose that a playwright, some 4,000 years ago, decided to draft a play about a people whose task would be to bring about an ultimate brotherhood of man. What are some of the difficulties that dramatizing such a unique theme would pose?

First, our mythical playwright would have to choose a people for his mission, and then he would have to embed the message so deeply into their collective consciousness that it would not be forgotten throughout the centuries it would take to accomplish such an ambitious task. He would have to think up ways and means of ensuring the survival of his chosen messenger-people. He would also have to think of some method whereby they could come into contact with all the nations on earth in order to accomplish their mission.

Now let us suppose that to solve this dual problem our

playwright conceived of a special exile, which would not only ensure his chosen people the means of coming into contact with the nations of the world but at the same time also establish the condition for their continuous survival. Instead of beginning with an already existing people whom he would have to reeducate, he would begin with a "clean slate," on which he could inscribe the mission. Instead of choosing an entire people all at once, he would begin with one man and his family, whom he then could make the progenitor of his chosen people. Each generation would pass on to its children the sacredness of the mission. The families would grow into tribes, the tribes into a nation, and this nation would be dispersed among the people of the world. As brotherly love cannot be imposed by the sword but must be accepted by the mind, there would be no point in our playwright's providing his chosen people with a retinue of brilliant generals to conquer the world. He would have to endow them with a panoply of great prophets who would inspire the ideas for conquering men's minds.

Whether by blind accident, human choice, or divine design, the first 2,000 years of Jewish history seem to constitute just such a succession of fortuitous circumstances that develop into a "training program" for survival in a coming exile. Curiously enough, the second 2,000 years of Jewish history does institute an exile for the Jews in which they are seemingly unhinged from the historical process of cultural decay. And there are indications that in the future third 2,000 years of Jewish history the Jewish idea of a universal brotherhood may be the only antidote to the anxieties generated by man's indiscriminate destruction of the ecological balance of the world and the concentration of atomic power in his hands.

No dramatist could have devised a better sequence of events than that which actually happened. We are not concerned with whether what took place was an accidental sequence or a manipulated series, or whether it was God Himself who blueprinted both. We are impressed by the fact that whichever viewpoint one chooses in no way alters the fascinating, incredible succession of events themselves. Though history regrettably has not provided us with such a dramatist, it has bequeathed us a sixteenth-century Jewish kabalist, a mystic philosopher named Isaac Luria, whose ideas constitute a perfect outline for such a drama.

Facts about Luria are meager. Born in Jerusalem in 1534, and educated in Egypt, he was buried in Palestine in 1572. According to pious legends, Luria immersed himself in the Kabala at the age of six, acquiring his kabalistic wisdom in cheerless, bleak, one-room schools, which today would be considered unfit for the culturally deprived. His learning soon earned him a reputation as a saint. But Luria lived the life of an ascetic on weekdays only. On the Sabbath he came home to his wife, and sired a brood of children.

Like Jesus, Luria wrote nothing down; he merely taught. Just as we have to depend on Mark, Matthew, Luke, and John for what Jesus said, so we have to depend on the disciples of Luria for what he said. The kabalistic teachings by Luria's apostles made a tremendous impact not only on Jewish life but on Christian thought.

Luria, according to his disciples, developed a remarkable theory of the evolution of mind, matter, and history—a philosophy of the exile and the redemption of man that can be interpreted on many levels. Stripped of its metaphysical language, Luria states that all matter, thought, and human experience pass through three stages, or cycles.

The first stage Luria called the *tzimtzum,* the "contraction," that is, the "thesis" of history, or, the "statement." This first stage is a cosmic drama that ushers in world history and the special role of the Jews. Here Luria saw a twofold action taking place. As God brings all the dissident elements of Jewish history into a thesis of world history, God also simultaneously withdraws Himself from that which he has created and retreats into an exile within Himself.

The second stage, Luria called *shevirat ha'keilim,* the "breaking of the vessels." This would be the "antithesis," that is, the "counter-statement." In this phase, everything that had been brought together in the first stage is shattered, and the Jews are strewn as "exiled lights" over the face of the earth. Now both Jews and God are in "exile." This second stage is a "cosmological drama that determines man's place in it."[1]

The third stage Luria called the *tikkun*, the "restoration." Again, in Hegelian terminology this would be the "synthesis," the joining of the statement and the counterstatement into a new, higher concept. In this stage, all that was shattered in the second is unified into a new, greater, and final totality. "The process of *tikkun* . . . corresponds to the process of mundane history. The metahistorical process and . . . the religious act of the Jews, prepare the way for the final restitution of all the scattered and exiled lights. The redemption of Israel concludes the redemption of all things."[2]

We propose, in this book, to present the idea of Jewish history dramatically, by transposing Luria's three stages into three acts, each act 2,000 years long. We shall fit the 4,000-year history of the Jews into the first two acts. Then we will permit ourselves to speculate about Jewish and world destiny in the subsequent 2,000 years—the third act.

Our first act, extending in time from Abraham to Jesus, will serve to prepare the Jews emotionally and intellectually for survival in a Diaspora. Our second act, extending in time from Jesus to Ben-Gurion, will show the Jews strewn as "exiled lights" throughout the Diaspora in order to accomplish their mission. Our third act, extending in time from Ben-Gurion to 2,000 years into the future, will usher in the final accomplishment of the Jews—the messianic age of man on earth.

The first 2,000 years of Jewish history that comprise our first act will proceed like a Greek predestination drama, with God seemingly the author and divine director. But whereas in a Greek predestination drama the characters are not aware of their ultimate destiny as they are pathetically driven toward it by remorseless gods, the participants in our Jewish predestination drama are told in advance what their roles are to be. Stoically, heroically, they act out these roles, even when aware of an ultimate tragedy awaiting them personally, always believing firmly

---

[1]Gershom G. Scholem: *Major Trends in Jewish Mysticism.*
[2]*Ibid.*

in the grandeur of the final destiny of the Jews themselves.

The ideas contained in the first act profoundly affect not only Jewish history but world history. These ideas successively shape Jewish character and Jewish destiny. They free the Jews from time and space, train them for world citizenship, and shape them for survival in their great exile in the first century A.D. Though the people in this first act are insignificant in numbers, they cast a giant shadow before them. Our stage is the world, and our audience its inhabitants.

FROM ABRAHAM TO JESUS

Pre-History

1,000,000 B.C.	Future man begins his descent from trees.
100,000 B.C.	Neanderthal man, first true species of *homo sapiens*, appears.
30,000 B.C.	Asia's Neanderthal man invades European continent and exterminates Cro-Magnon "pre-man," the only "native" produced by Europe.

History Begins

	World History	Biblical History
10,000 B.C.	Three Semitic migrations from Sinai to Palestine, Mesopotamia, and	

Egypt spark the world's first civilizations.
Neolithic revolution changes man from a food hunter to a food producer.

7500   Jericho, first known city in history of man, founded.

5000   Age of the Semites begins (5000 to 500 B.C.).
Mesopotamia springs into history with the city-states of Sumer and Akkad.
Beginnings of pictographic writing.

Creation: 3760 B.C.
Cain kills Abel: 3631 B.C.

3500 to 3000   Sumerians appear from "nowhere," act as catalytic agent that brings the Semitic civilizations to a simmer.

3000 to 2500   Bronze Age introduced in Mesopotamia.
Egypt makes her debut in history; leaps from infancy to maturity in two centuries. First dynasty of Ur. Crete invaded by West Semites who lay

foundations for her
Early Minoan
culture (2700 to
2000). Canaanites
ensconced in
Palestine. Neolithic
civilization
introduced to
European mainland
by a new wave of
Asiatic invaders.

2500
to
2000

King Sargon I drives
out Sumerians; fuses
Sumer and Akkad
into world's first
empire; ushers in a
new age of science,
mathematics, and
astronomy. A
"non-Greek,"
Helladic culture
appears in Greece.

The Flood: 2104 B.C.

Jewish History

Scene 1: 2000–1300

2000
to
1800

Mycenean, or
Achean, tribes from
Asiatic mainland
(first historic
Greeks), invade
Greece via Balkans.
Asiatic
"Villanovians"
invade Northern
Italy. Hammurabi
forges Babylonian
Empire. Hittites
establish their first
power structure.

Jewish history begins
with entry of Abram
(later Abraham), a
75-year-old *goy* who
reveals a new concept
of God.

The Middle Kingdom period in Egyptian history. Crete enters its Middle Minoan cultural stage (2000 to 1650).

1800 to 1600	Semites invent the alphabet. Cretans introduce Linear A. Hyksos invade Egypt (*circa* 1750); establish own dynasty. Assyria rises to power; Hittites attain empire status. First Amorite dynasty in Babylon.	Age of Patriarchs. Joseph settles in Egypt. Jews settle in land of pharaohs—or are swept into it with invasion of Hyksos.
1600 to 1400	Late Minoan culture (1650–1050) in Crete; Linear B appears. Hyksos expelled (1550). Egypt leaps to new cultural life under Tuthmosis III and Amenhotep III. First Egyptian invasions of Palestine and Syria.	Jews enslaved by Egyptians, probably around 1500, after expulsion of Hyksos.

Scene 2: 1300–1200

1400 to 1200	Religious revolution of Amenhotep IV (Ikhnaton) around 1350. Mycenean invaders reach Peloponnesus and are baptized into	An 85-year-old sheepherder named Moses leads Jews out of Egypt; gives them the *Torah* as an instrument of the future liberation of man.

Minoan culture.
Downfall of Crete.
Ramses II signs
treaty with Hittites.

Scene 3: 1200–900

| 1200 to 1000 | Agamemnon invades Phrygia. Fall of Troy (*circa* 1200). Dorian tribes from Asia invade Greece, exterminate the Myceneans. Dark age settles over Greece. Egyptian empire period ends with Ramses III. Babylonia and Assyria start flexing their conquest muscles. | Joshua invades Canaan. Fall of Jericho (*circa* 1200). Philistines penetrate Palestine. A two-century age of darkness settles over Jewish history under Judges (1200–1000). First Jewish kingdoms under David and Solomon. Concept of no divine rights of kings evolved. |
| 1000 to 800 | Greece recovers from her dark age. Period of chaos in Egypt under Libyan dynasties. Assyria extends her empire to dominant position. Carthage founded by Semitic Phoenicians. Asiatic Etruscans invade Italy. | Solomon's realm ripped apart into Kingdoms of Israel and Judah upon his death (922). Davidic dynasty continues rule in Judah. |

Scene 4: 900–600

| 800 to 600 | Homer composes *Iliad* and *Odyssey*. City-states arise in Greece. Doric and | Assyrians invade Kingdom of Israel, destroy its capital, and deport |

Ionic orders evolved.
Height of Etruscan
power. Rome is
founded. Assyrians
march to summit of
power but after
conquest of Israel
are given death
blow by resurgent
Babylonians.

the people (722).
Babylonians vanquish
Assyria and threaten
Judah, which averts
disaster by paying
tribute. King Josiah
unites Jews of Judah
with canon and
charisma.

Scene 5: 800–500

600
to
500

Babylonians destroy
Kingdom of Judah
and rule the Near
East (612–538).
Persia enters history
with Cyrus I;
Babylonia is
conquered and
Persia rules the
Near East (538–
332). End of the
five-millennia
Semitic cultural
overlordship. Age of
Solon and
Pythagoras in
Greece.

Age of prophecy. Amos
and Hosea first
Prophets in Israel.
Isaiah appears in Judah;
voice of Jeremiah
heard during reign of Josiah.
Babylonians sack
Jerusalem (584) and
banish its people.
Deported Jews in
Babylon convert their
exile into the world's
first "Diaspora."

Scene 6: 500–300

500
to
300

The
Hellenic
Age

Classical, name-
dropping period of
Greek history—the
age of the heavy
intellectual artillery
from Sophocles to
Aristotle and the
Golden Age of
Pericles.

Jews under political
rule of Persians and
business influence of
Greeks. Edict of Cyrus
permits Babylonian
Jews to return to
Jerusalem. First
Zionade under
Zerubbabel. Temple

Peloponnesian War. Three Samnite Wars make Romans master of Italy. Decline of Athens. Philip of Macedonia leads Greek States, and his son, Alexander the Great, conquers the Persian Empire (332), ushering in the Age of Hellenism, the international brand of Hellenic civilization. Alexander's empire split into Seleucid and Ptolemaic kingdoms after his death.

rebuilt. Second Zionade under Ezra. Nehemia made governor of Jerusalem. Jewish nationalism introduced. The Books of Moses canonized. Jews come under political rule and intellectual sway of the Greeks with Alexander's conquest of Persian Empire.

Scene 7: 300 B.C.–100 A.D.

300 B.C. to 1 A.D. The Hellenistic Age	Decline of Greece as a culture producer. The age of Epicurus, Euclid, Archimedes— intellectual giants born outside Greece. Arcases founds Parthian Kingdom (249). Rome bursts into world prominence with Three Punic Wars that make her master of Spain and	Jews catapulted into Ptolemaic Empire, then wrested by Seleucids into their political orbit. Win freedom after Maccabean revolt, establish state of Judea, and found Hasmonean dynasty. Judeans transformed from biblical Jews into Hellenistic Jews under impact of Greek thought. First Essene communities formed.

North Africa. Greece annexed as Roman province after Four Macedonian Wars. Three Mithridatic Wars spell doom of Seleucid Kingdom (64). Ptolemaic Empire ends with Roman conquest of Egypt (30 B.C.). Octavian becomes emperor of Rome.

Ministry of the Teacher of Righteousness (104–53? B.C.). Jesus born (4 B.C.).

1 A.D. to 100

Gaul and Britain conquered by Rome, which envisions Europe as one continental community. Reigns of Nero, Vespasian, and Titus. Christians viewed as subversives by Romans and persecuted.

Rule of Roman Procurators in Judea. Jesus crucified. Ministry of Paul. Jews stage revolt against Rome; Jerusalem is gutted; Masada stormed; Jews enslaved and exiled.

SCENE 1

The Intellectual Conception

As the curtain goes up on the first scene of our first act, the spotlight is on one man—a pagan, a goy, a non-Jew. It is Abraham, a seventy-five-year-old Babylonian lost deep in the heart of present-day Turkey. The time is 4,000 years ago. The place is Haran, an insignificant but—as we shall see—not a God-forsaken spot on the globe.

Adam and Eve, Cain and Abel, Noah and his sons—none are Jews. They are all pagans. Biblical history from the Creation and the Flood through the Tower of Babel —all is but a vast panoramic background for the entry of Abraham, the first Jew in history.[1]

It cannot be said that the world was waiting for Abraham; the world could not have cared less. But after Abraham's arrival the world changed, because of the religious revolution he fathered.

The world before Abraham had taken a long time in shaping up. Man's descent from the trees to a seat in a spacecraft took over a million years. For 90 percent of this time span, he was a tailless, hairy, two-legged beast, wielding a club for a living and dwelling in a cave with wall-to-wall dirt floors. Around 100,000 years ago, this two-legged caveman entered his "Stone Age." He now

---

[1] The Bible calls him a Hebrew. Although the Bible uses the term "Hebrew" or "Israelite" for the Jews, we shall use the modern term "Jew" throughout this work.

held mastery over other animals, not only with his cunning brain and dexterous hands, but with new, sophisticated weapons made of stones tied to sticks. After about 90,000 years of this borderline existence, man stood on the threshold of his first cultural revolution, the Neolithic Age, extending from about 10,000 to 3000 B.C. Pottery was introduced, animals were domesticated, agriculture was invented. Stable village life developed, and man's first cities cropped up.

The second cultural revolution was the Bronze Age, from about 3000 to 1200 B.C., when man learned how to fuse copper with tin to create his first alloy, bronze. He could now exchange his ancestral stone tools for tools of metal, which paved the way for more deadly warfare and more complex village life.

The third revolution was the development of pictographic and cuneiform writing, which, around 1700 B.C., culminated in the creation of an alphabet. Writing ushered in man's first age of literature, opened the mind to science, and paved the way for the first formation of a state, with men living as a unified people under one law and one ruler.

The fourth revolution was Abraham's religious innovation—monotheism. His concept was based on the proposition that it is not man who makes God but God who makes man. This proposition was destined to topple empires, conquer men's minds, and create new world civilizations.

Though men began descending from the trees at about the same time all over the world independently of one another, a spontaneous transition from cave to civilization took place only in those two small wedges of the globe we know as Palestine and Mesopotamia. From here the gospel of civilization was carried to the rest of the world. The Bronze Age, pictographic and cuneiform writing, the alphabet, the monotheistic-religious revolution, the subsequent Iron Age were all conceived in this small Palestinian-Mesopotamian womb and nurtured by a small group of people speaking that group of linguistically related languages we now call Semitic. In the four and a half millennia between 5000 and 500 B.C., when the Semitic peoples were the intellectual overlords of the world, the people of Europe still lived in a cultural "Stone Age." The refinements of the Neolithic revolution did not reach them until a millennium later, when Semites on the move introduced these innovations to them.

Who were these talented Semites to whom the world owes such a great debt? Until recently, we knew very little about their origins. Now, thanks to the modern sciences of archaeology and linguistics, we have more factual information about the entry of the Semites on the world scene.

The most current view is that sometime before 10,000 B.C., a group of people speaking a Semitic language and living in the vicinity of the Sinai Peninsula began a three-pronged migration. One prong pushed its way northeast into Palestine and Mesopotamia, becoming the progenitors of the Babylonians and Assyrians. The second migrated south into Egypt, giving rise to the Egyptian civilization.[2] The third, undulating west along the Mediterranean shore of Africa, got off to a bad start. History lost sight of this branch until the ninth century B.C., when Semitic Phoenicians founded Carthage, which was destroyed by the Romans in the Third Punic War (146 B.C.). There was a later migration, around 2000 B.C., when Semites from the Palestinian area settled the island of Crete, where they founded the Minoan civilization.

The spade of the archaeologist has unearthed evidence that history began at Jericho in 7500 B.C. and not at Sumer in 3500 B.C. From all evidence, civilization developed by giant strides in the Jordan Valley before it took hold in the Mesopotamian triangle. For 2,000 years before Sumer and Akkad, Jericho was a flourishing city, fortified with a stone wall surrounded by a moat, with brick and stone houses, streets, and running water, whose inhabitants knew of

---

[2]The ancient Egyptians were a Hamito-Semitic people. The people living in Egypt today have ethnically and racially little in common with the ancient Egyptians because of the massive intermixtures of races, peoples, and tongues that have taken place in the past 2,000 years as Egypt was raped, ravaged, and defiled in an unending succession of wars and conquests by Greeks, Romans, Mohammedans, Crusaders, Nubians, Turks, and Englishmen.

animal domestication, agriculture, crop rotation, and irrigation.

Unaccountably, this Jordanian civilization had disappeared by 4000 B.C., but by that time history had already focused its lens on Mesopotamia. We do not know in which century or in what language which people greeted the invading Semites from Sinai. We do know that the Akkadians, the first people identified as Semites in Mesopotamia, had settled there as early as 8000 B.C. and had perhaps even founded the city of Akkad, which bears their name.

Around 3500 B.C., an enigma of history took place. Seemingly from "nowhere" came a roundheaded, non-Semitic, non-Aryan people we now call the Sumerians, who conquered the area around the already existing city of Sumer in Lower Mesopotamia and imposed their Mongolian-type agglutinating language on its Semitic-speaking inhabitants. The Sumerians apparently acted as a catalyst in bringing the already developing native civilization to a simmer. A millennium later, the Akkadian King Sargon I drove out the Sumerians, and soon thereafter the Sumerians vanished from history as suddenly as sin on the Day of Atonement.

Sargon I, fathered by a mortal man, born of a virgin mother, abandoned by both in a basket of reeds to float to death down the Euphrates, was saved by that poor but honest couple of myth who rescue heroes in postnatal distress. Brought up as a gardener by his foster father, Akki, and surviving a love affair with the goddess Ishtar, black-bearded, gimlet-eyed Sargon I fought his way to the top of the Mesopotamian world and fused Akkad and Sumer into the world's first empire. Under his ruthless, capable, and enlightened leadership, the Semitic civilizations received new impetus. The Semitic languages reasserted themselves, and science, especially mathematics and astronomy, reached new heights. This then was the Semitic world that gave birth to Abraham sometime between the twentieth and nineteenth centuries B.C.

Abraham enters history unobtrusively at the age of seventy-five. The Bible wastes no words in introducing him. With no explanation, Abraham's aged parents pull up

stakes in Ur in Babylonia and head for Canaan. When the
family reaches Haran, the father dies, and Abraham has
his first encounter with God.

In this first encounter of God with man—of Jehovah
with Abraham—it is God who proposes a Covenant with
Abraham. If Abraham will do as God bids him, then God
will make Abraham's descendants His Chosen People and
will fashion them into a great nation. God does not, at
this time, reveal His purpose.

God stipulates but one commandment and gives but one
promise. The commandment is—all males of His future
Chosen People must be circumcised as a sign of their
"chosenness." The promise is—the Land of Canaan.

God does not say how long it will take to fulfill the
promise or how it will come about. Nor does God tell
His Chosen People that they will be better than others.
The inference is that they are to be different and that
they are to be set apart for a mission. There is no
chauvinism here, no superiority complex. How this uniqueness and this nationhood are to be brought about—
whether by the sword, or the book, or both—is not made
known at this time. No other commandments are spelled
out. God has now, however, chosen His messenger, and
the action of our drama can begin.

In spite of the indefiniteness of the Covenant, momentous consequences grew out of this new, bold concept
of God. Because the God of Abraham has no ancestry,
there is a total absence of mythological stories of His
origin. Because He is immortal, there can be rebellion
against His commandments but not against His life. Because creation in the Jewish view is not a result of
sexuality, as in all pagan religions, the Jewish concept of
the creation of heaven and earth, of flora and fauna, is
consonant with the scientific idea of natural evolution.
Substitute a "million years" where Genesis says "a day"
in the Creation story, and we have the same evolutionary
sequence in Genesis that we have in Darwin's theory.
Because the God of Abraham is above sexuality, the Jews
did not have to provide Him with a playmate as did the
pagans for their gods. Pagans learned to respect the God of
the Jews, who did not sneak into the beds of other men's

wives as did Egyptian, Greek, and Roman gods. And because the God of Abraham acts with a moral purpose and a preconceived plan, He is not a capricious God who acts on a day-to-day basis. The Jews know what God expects of them and can therefore make long-range plans.

That concepts of one's God do create moral outlooks in man can be illustrated by comparing the story in Genesis of the binding of Isaac by his father Abraham to the story in the Iliad of the sacrifice of Iphigenia by her father Agamemnon.

In the Genesis story, Abraham stands to gain nothing by sacrificing his son Isaac. God promises him no favors. Faith carries Abraham to Mount Moriah; hope sustains him. Faith makes him heroic; hope makes him human. The sacrifice is never consummated; an angel stays his hand, and a sacrificial lamb is substituted for Isaac. Through this story the Jews learned that God does not want human sacrifice, not even as an act of faith, just as fifteen centuries later the Jews were to learn through their Prophets that God does not even want animal sacrifice, but that he can be approached through prayer, humility, and good deeds.

In the Iliad story, an oracle advises Agamemnon, commander of the Greek forces, that only by sacrificing his daughter Iphigenia as atonement for a trifling crime he has committed will the gods give him the wind he needs to set sail for Troy. Agamemnon cuts her throat but she is whisked away, still alive, by the goddess Artemis, not as a moral lesson for man, but to consecrate Iphigenia as a priestess in the temple of Artemis, where she is taught to prepare victims for sacrifice.

An interplay of Jewish and pagan themes in the Isaac and Iphigenia stories cast their shadows over Christianity. As Isaac carried the wood for his sacrificial altar on his shoulders to Mount Moriah, so Jesus carried the cross for his crucifixion on his shoulders to Mount Golgotha. Jesus expected a Jewish ending but got a pagan one. Just as Abraham looked to heaven for God's grace to stay his hand, so Jesus looked to heaven for God's grace to stay the hand of fate. But as Jews did not write this script, there was no grace for Jesus. He died with a prayer from

the Psalms (22:2) on his lips: *"Eli, Eli lama sabachtani"*—
My God, My God, why hast Thou forsaken me?[3]

Once monotheism had been launched, there was no
going back for the Jews. The first three generations springing from the seed of Abraham did not look upon themselves as nomads, but saw themselves as proud heirs to
the Promised Land, superbly confident of the fulfillment of
their destiny.

Before ringing down the curtain on this first scene, however, we need to make one last observation on the nature
of Jewish monotheism. Its basic idea is "pure." It has no
roots, no antecedents in paganism or in anything that
existed previously. By one stroke of the Jewish imagination
all idols were done away with, not by conquest but by a
simple dismissal. The idea of monotheism affected not only
the destiny of the Jews but also the destiny of man. This
Jewish concept of monotheism was to give rise to new
cultures and create new art forms. It was to create a vast
new literature, destined to affect the world outlook of man.
As pagan empires crumbled, the Jewish idea of God prevailed. And, as the Jews saw their ideas triumph, their belief that events in their history were not haphazard but
evidence of their own manifest destiny was strengthened.

It is this concept of deity that shapes the Jewish
character and sets the Jews apart from the pagan world.
From this concept Jewish history is born. The first re-
quirement for conditioning the Jews for their future mission was met by their acceptance of monotheism.

[3]Jesus, who, like his fellow Jews, spoke Aramaic, the lingua franca
of that century among the Jews, prayed in that language, as was
the custom, using the Aramaic word *sabachtani* for the Hebrew
word *asavtani* in the Psalms. See Matthew 27:46 and Mark 15:34.

SCENE 2

The Double Revelation

THE ATON CULT

The setting for our second scene shifts from Mesopotamia to Egypt; the time drifts from 1800 to 1300 B.C. When the scene begins, the Jews are slaves; when it ends, the Jews will be free men. Before our scene begins, however, let us familiarize ourselves with the background of the events about to happen.

Around 2800 B.C., something incredible happened in Egypt. She leaped from infancy to maturity, skipping a cultural puberty period. By 2500 B.C. we are confronted with a full-blown civilization, surpassing in art, literature, and political unity anything that had been achieved in Mesopotamia, her tutor state.

But, because Egypt achieved her cultural summit early, subsequent generations were unable to improve on the original model. Having begun at the top, Egypt repeated her first experience over and over again. In spite of her precociousness, she never developed any further ideas of her own. The world has inherited nothing of consequence directly from Egypt. She had no written law, no political theories, no wealthy merchant class to give the state versatility. Hers was a priest-ridden culture in which a vast feudal officialdom of scribes, soldiers, and bureaucrats squatted like parasites on the backs of an exploited peasantry. From the First Dynasty in 2800 B.C. until the Thirtieth Dynasty in 400 B.C., except for her periods of captivity, Egypt remained a nation apart, isolated, parochial, living upon her past inheritance until she faded out of history. Her longevity was not due to inner resilience; it was an accidental attribute of her isolated geography on the fringe of the then civilized world. It was in this land of pharaohs and pyramids that the Jews arrived in the first half of the second millennium B.C.

After Abraham and his three generations of descendants —Isaac, Jacob, and the twelve sons of Jacob—had wandered back and forth between the Euphrates and the Nile, the Bible states that a portion of these nomadic Jews settled in Egypt at the invitation of one of the pharaohs. Many historians maintain that the Jews were swept into Egypt with the invading Hyksos—bands of Semitic warriors who ruled Egypt for two centuries (1750–1550).

The exact date of the Jewish debut in Egypt is still as much up in the air as the exact date of the Jewish exodus. The latest, most authoritative guess is that fate took the Jews into Egypt sometime between 1700 and 1400 B.C., and that Moses led them out of their subsequent enslavement sometime between 1300 and 1250 B.C.

The Jews in Egypt, however, were not slaves in the classic sense of the word. They were not sold on the auction block as slaves were sold in the United States. Nor were they regarded as chattel having no rights. On the contrary, their status was more like that of indentured servants working on vast government building projects alongside other enslaved peoples. The Jews had a right to exist as a community, to live according to their own laws, to practice their own religion, and to worship their one invisible God—until the time of the Exodus. Then, it seems, something happened in Egypt to change the political climate.

Around 1350 B.C. a religious revolution shook the land of the pyramids. A new pharaoh, Amenhotep IV, who later changed his name to Ikhnaton, abolished Egypt's polytheism, the belief in many gods, substituting the cult of one sun-god, whom he named Aton. The people were afraid of this innovation. How could only one god protect them, when all their many gods were inadequate? The priests were incensed. This new, over-simplified mode of worship threatened their entire hierarchy and power structure. Soon a religious counterrevolution took place, aided by the fortuitous death of Ikhnaton at the age of thirty. His beautiful wife Nefertiti (his sister whom he had married at the age of twelve when she was ten) tried to keep the new cult alive.[1] But Nefertiti was assassinated, the new god Aton was deposed from his man-made celestial throne, and the old gods with their animal heads were reinstated in their familiar places.

In the aftermath of this religious ferment and chaos, sometime during the reign of Ramses II (1292–1225 B.C.), the Jewish Exodus took place under the leadership of Moses, an Egyptian priest or prince who "converted" to Judaism, according to some scholars. They theorize that it was Ikhnaton who "invented" monotheism and that it was an Egyptian Moses who packaged it for export in the same way Jesus "invented" Christianity and Paul packaged it for export. This theory suggests that just as Paul went out and proselytized among the pagans when he found that the Jews would not buy the new religion of Christ, so Moses went out and proselytized among the Jews because the Egyptians would not buy the new religion of Aton. And just as Paul promised freedom for Roman slaves in the life hereafter if they accepted his Christianity, so Moses, the theory goes, promised the Jewish slaves in Egypt freedom in this world if they accepted his "Atonism."

Proponents of this view contend that several centuries after the Aton cult had become the established Jewish religion, Jewish priests eradicated from it all vestiges of Moses' Egyptian past and gave him Jewish antecedents. As a final retouching, to give the concept greater authenticity, these priests are supposed to have retroactively conferred the idea of monotheism all the way back to Abraham.

This theory seems logical and would be reasonable if

[1] Ikhnaton's conjugal chores were literally a family affair, for he was married not only to his sister Nefertiti but also to his mother Tye. A most interesting book on the subject is Immanuel Velikovsky's *Oedipus and Ikhnaton,* in which he persuasively holds that Ikhnaton was the prototype for Sophocles' Oedipus, just as a real Danish prince was the prototype for Shakespeare's Hamlet.

only the scanty facts available supported it. But it is more plausible that the descendants of Abraham brought their monotheism into Egypt with them, as stated in the Bible, and that they lived and practiced their monotheistic religion in Egypt for three centuries prior to the reign of Ikhnaton. It is even more plausible that it was Ikhnaton who received his "monotheistic" concept of Aton from the captive Jews, and not vice versa. The Jews actively engaged in proselytizing, for we read in the Old Testament that a "mixed multitude" accompanied them in their Exodus from Egypt. Does it not seem more probable that just as in the Roman Empire the slave religion of the Christians percolated its way up Roman ranks until finally Emperor Constantine himself was converted, so too in the Egyptian Empire the slave religion of the Jews percolated its way up Egyptian ranks until King Ikhnaton was "converted"? But whereas Constantine's Christian takeover of the Roman Empire was successful, Ikhnaton's attempt at a "monotheistic" takeover of the Egyptian Empire failed.

Perhaps we have another historical parallel. Just as Spain in the fifteenth century A.D. was worried about the role the Jewish idea of religious freedom played in undermining Spain's monolithic Church, so, too, Ramses II in the thirteenth century B.C. may have been worried about the role Jewish monotheism played in undermining Egypt's monolithic idolatry. If so, then the Exodus from Egypt could have been an expulsion, as in Spain. This would speak well for the ancient Egyptians, who, rather than commit wanton murder, as the Germans did in 1942, expelled the Jews, as did the Spaniards in 1492.

Do we have a hint of such a possible expulsion in the Book of Exodus? Here it is stated that time and again the pharaoh wanted to let the Israelites go, but that time and again God hardened Pharaoh's heart, forcing him to change his mind. These Biblical passages could be the literary seams that show where a later Jewish exodus theme was stitched over an earlier Egyptian expulsion order.

Whether it was a final expulsion by order of the pharaoh or an exodus under the aegis of God, it was a blessing that the Jews left Egypt when they did. Had they remained there, they would most probably have been engulfed by the counterrevolutionary wave of polytheism that swept Egypt. Jewish monotheism might have perished and Jewish history died stillborn.

Unfortunately, facts about Moses are as few as legends are plentiful. The biblical tale of his birth parallels that of the legendary tale of the birth of Sargon I. However, the priggish Jews not only denied their hero Moses a virgin birth but endowed him with properly married parents. Like Sargon's unwed mother, Moses' married mother placed her infant son in a basket of reeds to drift down the Nile. But unlike Sargon's mother, who wanted the death of her child, Moses' mother wanted to save her child from the wrath of a pharaoh who had decreed that all Hebrew male children were to be slain, because he feared a future Hebrew takeover. The Bible tells us that Moses is found by Pharaoh's daughter who brings him up as a prince in the royal court, an account which may substantiate the hypothesis that Moses was an Egyptian prince.

When Moses grows up, he is unaccountably drawn to the Hebrews toiling in Pharaoh's brick yards. One day he slays an Egyptian taskmaster for beating a Hebrew worker and flees for his life to Midian. Here Moses, the founder of historic Judaism, marries a *shiksa*, a pagan maiden, the daughter of a Midianite priest. He tends his father-in-law's sheep for forty years, until, like Abraham before him, he has his first encounter with God. Moses is eighty years old when God commands him to return to Egypt to lead the Jews to freedom.

Whether Moses was Hebrew, Israelite, Midianite, or Egyptian[2] matters little. What matters is that Moses became the hero of Jewish history. It is of interest to note, however, that if Moses did live to 120 years, as stated in the Bible, and if he was eighty years old when he led the Jews out of Egypt, he could have been a youth at the court of Ikhnaton at the time that the Aton revolution took place. If Moses did witness that religious revolution,

---

[2] For a fascinating account of a hypothetical Egyptian origin of Moses, the interested reader is referred to Sigmund Freud's *Moses and Monotheism*. A condensation of this view appears in this author's book *Jews, God and History*.

and was inspired by it, he revised it fundamentally. Ikhnaton's Aton religion was merely one of form. Moses' monotheism was one of social, ethical, and moral precepts. He made religion a way of life, not a mere mode of worship.

If we are dealing with a double revelation, if the Egyptians were the first "monotheists," so much the worse for their not having seized the initiative, and for allowing the Jewish revelation to surpass theirs. If Moses was not a Jew, let us give the Jews credit for possessing the genius to acknowledge him and the courage to undertake the great task demanded by him.

The racial origins of Moses are of little importance. What is crucial are the ideas he proclaimed, who accepted them, and what was done with them. His historic task in this second scene will be to resuscitate Abraham's idea of monotheism and to enlarge its frontiers. It is Moses who will flesh out the skeleton of God's Covenant with Abraham.

THE SINAI MAGNA CARTA

The curtain now rises on our second scene and the spotlight is again on one man, Moses, the Prophet, whom the Jews, even as they proclaim his greatness, refuse to enshrine.

At the site of the burning bush, God selects Moses to free the Jews from bondage. At Mount Sinai, God commands Moses to free man through the instrument of the Torah (the Hebrew name for the Five Books of Moses). There is no formal emancipation proclamation. The revelation does not take place at night; the Torah is given to all in the light of day, an open Covenant openly arrived at.

There are no shrines at Mount Sinai to commemorate this momentous event. Christians journey to Bethlehem to pay homage to Jesus. Muslims journey to Mecca to pay homage to Mohammed. But no Jew journeys to Sinai to pay homage to Moses. Not the place, not the man, but the *idea*, the Torah itself, is what the Jews enshrine. The

Torah, here used to mean the Five Books of Moses, is a written code of law that spells out new relationships of man to man, man to the state, and man to God.

The concept of justice based on a written code of law is a Semitic innovation. The earliest such codes thus far known are the Code of Nammu, written in Sumerian about 2000 B.C., and the Code of Bilalama, written in Akkadian a century later. Both, however, are based on an earlier, still undiscovered prototype. The codes of Nammu and Bilalama were incorporated into the Code of Hammurabi in 1800 B.C. The Greeks had no written laws until the time of Lycurgus (about 700 B.C.), who, according to Greek legend, went to Semitic Crete to study its ideas of written law. A written, judicial code was totally unknown to the Egyptians until 300 B.C.

To see how radically Semitic law generally, and Mosaic Law specifically, departed from the legal concepts of previous societies, and how much it influenced the judicial thinking of the future, let us examine six specific aspects of man's relations to man and the state as delineated in the Torah; namely, *lex talion*, individual rights, slavery, torture, harlotry, and sex.

Lex talion—the Roman name for the law of retaliation, an eye for an eye, a tooth for a tooth, a wound for a wound—has all too often been portrayed as a barbarous practice. Far from being barbarous, it was a "law of restraint." It was man's first step toward modern concepts of justice. In essence, it substituted public law for private vengeance, and served to prevent punishment in excess of the crime committed—the offender could not be made to pay for one eye with two. This limitation of punishment imposed by *lex talion* led to the next step of paying compensation in money. We find this Semitic concept already embodied in earliest Mosaic Law.

Compare this early Semitic legal system to that of the early Anglo-Saxons. While the Jews in the days of King David in 1000 B.C. had fully formalized civil laws, the Anglo-Saxons in 1000 A.D. still practiced ordeal by fire and trial by combat. These Anglo-Saxon legal notions, which had no counterpart among the ancient Semites, held that innocence would be established if the accused survived walking through fire and that truth was on the side of the victor in an armed combat between two litigants. As those who were roasted alive or slain in trial-combat never appealed their cases, it was natural for Anglo-Saxon intellectuals to deduce that divine justice had prevailed. ·

The laws in the Torah regarding man's relations to man constitute mankind's first "bill of rights." These laws boldly assert that man's freedom is his supreme right. He has the right to personal liberty, free speech, and private property. His life and person are inviolate. Charges against him must be made in open court, where he has a right to confront his accusers and to defend himself. A century before Jesus, the Jews added yet another innovation, the right to cross-examine a witness, so movingly illustrated in "Susanna and the Elders," one of the tales in the Apocrypha. This right was not incorporated into the legal kit of the world until the Modern Age.

The Torah recognizes no class distinctions before the law. When it comes to justice, there is no difference between patrician and plebeian, between the propertied and propertyless, as in pagan law. In Babylonian law, for instance, if a nobleman killed a serf, he was given a slight fine; if the reverse took place, the killer received a death sentence. Under Jewish law, murder is murder no matter who commits it against whom, and the punishment is the same for all offenders—rich man, poor man, aristocrat, or peasant. The Torah goes out of its way to forbid the cursing of the blind, the deaf, and the dumb, because of their helplessness. It was not Jesus who first said "Love thy neighbor as thyself." He merely quoted the Torah (Leviticus 19:18).

Slaves in ancient Israel were treated more humanely than slaves in the United States in 1800 A.D. Laws applying to freemen also applied to slaves, who had to be set free after seven years of servitude. Slave-trading, as practiced by Christians until the nineteenth century A.D., was unthinkable to the Jews a millennium before Jesus. Kidnapping a Jew or a Gentile, a white man or black man into slavery was an offense punishable by death. If a slave fled his master from one state to another, he could not be returned. Contrast this attitude to the Dred Scott decision of 1857, which held that a slave who had fled his master was simply a strayed piece of property that had to be returned.

Though we find much violence in early Jewish history, we find no evidence of torture in the Old Testament. The days of the Judges were violent; the purges and counter-purges instituted by the kings of Judah and Israel were bloody. But nothing in pre-Christian Jewish history compares to the agonizing tortures that fill the twenty centuries from Jesus to Hitler.[3] Such medieval refinements as pouring molten lead into ears, pulling out tongues with red-hot irons, roasting children to a brown crisp over slow fires, disemboweling pregnant women, flaying people alive had no counterpart in Jewish history.

Neither the pagan idea of harlotry as a divine duty or the Christian idea of sex as a satanic sin ever gained a foothold in Jewish thinking. Though pagan society banned incest and adultery and valued chastity in its brides, it offered nothing like the direct command of Leviticus (19:29): "You shall not defile your daughter by causing her to be a harlot." Equally adamantly, the Torah forbids the religious prostitution so popular among the pagans, especially the Greeks.

Though they looked upon harlotry with abhorrence and held chastity in high esteem, the Jews thought of sexual desire as normal but felt that it should be fulfilled within the marriage institution only. Taking into account that sexual transgressions would occur, the Mosaic Code also provided for the welfare of children born out of wedlock. Such children were regarded as legitimate and could not be disinherited, with one exception—children born to parents who could not marry legally, such as one partner

---

[3]Not even the Gospel writers claim that Jesus was tortured by the Jews. Compare even the distorted Gospel versions of Jewish court procedure in the first century A.D. to that of the British in the seventeenth century as revealed in a letter by Francis Bacon, who was not only a philosopher but also attorney general for King James I: "Peacham [a Puritan clergyman accused of treason] was examined before torture, in torture, between torture, and after torture; nothing could be drawn from him, he still persisting in his obstinate and inexcusable denials of former answers."

already married, or couples related by blood. Divorce laws were more liberal at the time of Moses than in Edwardian England. However, homosexuality, enshrined by Plato as the noblest form of love, was viewed with distaste by the less effete Jews, earning them the contempt of the Greeks for being so uncultured as to view pederasty as a criminal offense.

Although the Mosaic Laws pertaining to man's relations to man and man's relations to the state provided the Jews with a workable framework to govern themselves, it was the ideas in the Torah pertaining to man's relations to God which assisted the Jews most in carrying out their larger mission.

By making God spiritual instead of material, the Jews were free to speculate on the nature of God Himself. This permitted them to attain a higher concept of deity than was possible for the pagans. The Greeks, who attained great artistry in making statues of gods, remained naïve children in their concepts of God. Having a spiritual God rather than gods in stone gave the Jews a feeling of intellectual superiority. Though they were a marginal minority in every society, they were nonetheless superbly confident that their ideas, their ethics, and their morals, which stemmed from God, were superior to those of the dominant majorities among whom they resided.

Some historians argue that biblical accounts from Abraham to Moses were not written until a thousand or more years after their supposed occurrence; that these ideas also constitute a double revelation, attributed retroactively first to Moses and then to Abraham in order to give Jewish history a continuity with a past it did not have. If that is so, then the Jews picked a humble past for themselves, considering that they could have chosen something more glorious. With hindsight, one can always create a nobler ancestry for oneself.

If the Jews did invent their own past, why did they choose this particular myth? Psychoanalysts claim that the myths people create about themselves are more indicative of their true character than their actual history, that myths constitute the authentic psychic autobiography of a people. If so, it would be interesting and instructive to compare the concepts the Greeks, Romans, Germans, and Jews wove about themselves with their mythologies.

Conceiving gods in their own image, the Greeks attributed their origin to Zeus, a god who spent most of his time spawning a succession of bastards with other men's wives, whom he either raped or put in a family way through cunning. Disguised as a swan, he inserted a "fruit" in the womb of Leda; hiding in a shower of gold, he impregnated Danae; "touching" Io under the pretext of helping her, he got her heavy with child. In fact, Mount Olympus and ancient Greece seem to be well-inhabited by the illegitimate by-products of his busy phallus. Ancient Greek moral history comes close to being but a recapitulation of the immoral behavior of this Greek deity.

The Romans also created a personalized mythology consistent with their subsequent history. They conceived of themselves as the descendants of Romulus and Remus, womb-mates of a seduced vestal virgin, who were weaned at the teats of a wolf. After slaying Remus, brother Romulus invited the Sabines to a feast where he and his armed cohorts drove off the trusting unarmed Sabines and then raped their helpless wives and daughters. The descendants of this bacchanalian revelry, a by-product of lust and trickery, became the Roman people.

The process of selecting a mythology to fit a people's psychic personality was not peculiar to ancient times. Adolf Hitler, looking for a mythology to fit the new German state, rejected Christianity as a Jewish disease. In its place he chose a mythology that mirrored his new state —that of the Teutonic gods of pre-Christian Germany—a motley crew of illiterate, mead-swilling, lecherous murderers, whose chief pastimes were cheating, raping, and killing. General Eric von Ludendorff, German World War I hero and one of Hitler's earliest supporters, stated the Teutonic creed succinctly: "I hate Christianity because it is Jewish, because it is international, and because in a cowardly fashion it preaches peace on earth."

The Jews conceive of man as created in the image of God, a little below the angels but far above the beast. As believers in a just, merciful God, the Jews strive for those qualities with a firm belief in the infinite perfectibility of man. They were first humbled in slavery, after which they were deemed worthy to receive God's commandments. Instead of hiding the fact that they were once slaves, the Jews elevate the Exodus into a sacred Passover feast, at which time they proclaim that freedom is God-given to all men, and invite the world to partake of the food and the wine at their table in this celebration of freedom for all.

There are historians who attempt to derogate the Jewish past by showing how deeply its ideas are rooted in the pagan world. They show, for instance, how the story of the Flood stems from the Babylonian Gilgamesh Epic, or how much the Mosaic Code parallels the Hammurabi Code. This is true. But to say that the Jews adapted a pagan idea is not the same as saying that the Jewish achievement is pagan.

As an example of how different civilizations can borrow from the same source, and yet come up with different ethics, consider the case of the Greeks and Jews borrowing from the Canaanites. The Canaanites mated people with cattle in an imitative fertility rite. The Greek reaction to this practice is reflected in their legend of Pasiphae, wife of King Minos, who, after a love affair with a bull (catered by Daedalus), gave birth to the Minotaur, half bull and half human. The Jews, instead of enshrining such exotic erotica in their literature, forbade sodomy as a defilement of the human spirit.

The stories of the giving of the law to Moses and to Minos are both based on the same Canaanite prototype, say archaeologists. According to the Bible, God gave the Law to Moses on a holy mountain in the Sinai Peninsula, the master craftsman Bezalel assisting him in building the tabernacle. According to Greek legend, Zeus gave Minos the law on the holy mountain on the Island of Crete, the master craftsman Daedalus assisting him in building the labyrinth. Though similar in their externals, Jewish and Greek laws are vastly different in spirit.

The greatness of the Jewish achievement lies not in the source material, but in what the Jews did with it. Just as one cannot dull the greatness of Shakespeare by showing that Hamlet, Othello, and Macbeth were derived from Danish, Italian, and Scottish sources, we cannot denigrate the greatness of the Old Testament by pointing out some of its pagan origins. Just as the genius of Shakespeare lay in his ability to take an ordinary story and invest it with the stuff that makes literature immortal, so the genius of the Jews lay in their ability to take ordinary legends and invest them with a universal ideology that makes a people indestructible.

If Jewish history is to evolve into a manifest destiny, then we would expect that the giving of the Torah would in some way serve the Jews to attain such a predetermined goal. Indeed, we do note a curious aspect in the central theme of this second scene, a complete reversal of the normal historical process. In the history of all other people, first comes the state, and then comes the law, evolving from the conduct of the people in that state. So, for instance, first came the Babylonian state, then Hammurabi's Code of Law. The same holds true with the Greeks and Romans. This is not so, however, with the Jews. First came the Torah, the Law to shape the future Jewish state, and 200 years later the state. This Mosaic Magna Carta saved the Jews from straying into detours and oblivion, and prepared them for their special statehood to come in the next scene of our drama.

SCENE 3

Kings Without Divine Crowns

In our first scene, a Babylonian patriarch with one foot in the grave hit the conversion trail to Haran, where he had a revelation that he was to become the progenitor of a Chosen People who would be set apart spiritually with a new concept of God. As a result, the world received monotheism. In our second scene, an octogenarian sheep-herder took over the fate of this Chosen People and set them apart ideologically with a new code of law. As a result, the world received an outline for constitutional government. In our third scene, this Chosen People will be set apart physically with a state of their own. As a result, the world will receive a unique concept of nationhood.

Joshua is the first main character to appear in this scene. After the death of Moses, it becomes his task to finish what Moses had begun. Jewish legend-makers portray Joshua as a dolt who, as soon as Moses dies, forgets the main commandments of the Torah and misquotes the rest. In their accounts, he fumbles all his assignments and suc-ceeds only because God bails him out—a most cavalier way of treating the "George Washington" of their country, for it is under Joshua's leadership that the successful in-vasion of Canaan takes place. He proves to be a brilliant general who, in three swift campaigns, overcomes the fortified cities of Jericho and Hazor and defeats the coali-tion of armies set against him by local kings.

Once they gained a foothold in Canaan under Joshua,

the Jews divided the country among the members of the Confederacy of Twelve Tribes formed by Moses at Sinai. Each tribe was autonomous within its own parcel of land, the Elders in each tribe dispensing justice within it. But superimposed upon the authority of the Elders was the authority of "inspired men"—the Judges.

This system of Judges was to lead first to the Jewish concept of kingship, then to the idea of prophecy, and finally to the innovation of messiahship. But the system had one fatal weakness. Since the Judges held inspiration from God on a "lend-lease" basis, this inspiration manifested itself only sporadically, whenever God chose to send an inspired man.

For close to two centuries the Jews struggled with this system. The tribes were convinced that in times of national crisis an inspired person would arise to save them from peril. It never occurred to them that such an inspired person might not appear when most needed, and they were so convinced of it that no successor was ever provided for. The crisis, they felt, would create their deliverer.

This conviction is still alive today among a small pious sect of Jews who believe that the coming of the true messiah will be made known to all Jews by a body of men known as the *Lamed Vovnicks*, the "Thirty-Six" (from the Hebrew letter "L," *Lamed*, and "V," *Vov*, each letter in the Hebrew alphabet having a numerical value). This sect holds that there exists at all times thirty-six Jews chosen by God who will recognize instantly the true messiah when he arrives, and make that announcement simultaneously but independently of each other, thus authenticating the messiah.

Roughly speaking, the time of Joshua and the Judges (1200–1000 B.C.), the "heroic age" of Jewish history, corresponds to the heroic age of the Greeks, with the siege and fall of Jericho corresponding in time and spirit to the siege and fall of Troy.

To the consternation of orthodox Jews, who maintain that the Bible stories have no antecedents in paganism, and to the horror of Anglo-Saxon Grecophiles, who maintain that Hellenic literature has no antecedents in Judaism, recent scholarship has shown that both the Bible and the

Iliad are related by common origins to Canaanite literature. Just as in the Iliad, gods came to the aid of their favorite heroes—Ajax, Achilles, Agamemnon—so in the Book of Judges, prophets came to the aid of their favorite heroes— Deborah, Gideon, Samson. The author of the Iliad views with compassion the agony of a foe, as in the case of Andromache, waiting with anguished heart for the return of her husband Hector, who lies dead with his feet tied to the chariot of Achilles. Similarly, the author of Judges views with compassion Sisera's mother, waiting with anguished heart for the return of her son, who lies dead in the tent of Yael with a spike through his temple.

But though there are similarities in the lives of the people who color the pages of both the Iliad and the Bible, there are differences in stress. Whereas the Greek myth-makers glorify their warrior chiefs into heroes, Jewish legend-makers drop their warrior Judges down a peg or two, refusing to upgrade such barbarous illiterates into heroes. Whereas brainless Agamemnon, cruel Achilles, and deceitful Odysseus are extolled in Greek verse and prose, Jewish legend-makers reduce such heroines as Deborah and such heroes as Samson to petty warriors with more brawn (and in the case of Deborah, more beauty) than brains. Jewish legend-makers, acutely aware of Deborah's beauty, wanted it made plain that she dispensed her prophecies in the open, "for it was not becoming that men should visit a woman in her house." Barak, her intrepid general and probably her lover, who sounds and acts like Agamemnon, is referred to as an "ignoramus."[1] Samson's "Achilles heel" was a pre-Freudian displacement from below to above: the rabbis attributed his downfall to his vulnerable passion. For a night with Delilah, he paid with the "castration" of his eyes.

After 200 years of struggle, the system of Judges drifts toward its inevitable end. Even God, it seems, is disgusted with the results, for He commands Samuel, the last of the

[1]Jewish legend-makers, acutely embarrassed at the prospect of having a prophetess who also practiced a little adultery, state that Barak was her husband. Unfortunately, the Bible states Deborah was the wife of Lapidoth. To get around this, the legends have it that Barak and Lapidoth were one and the same person.

Judges, to find a suitable ruler for the Jews, and to anoint him king of all the people. With the anointment of Saul as the first king of Palestine, the way is at last paved for the world's first kingship without divine rights.

In pagan kingdoms, all rulers were either the descendants of gods, married to the offspring of gods, or kissing cousins to gods. Pharaoh was a descendant of the god Ra. The Babylonian and Assyrian kings were blood relatives of gods, and some even had the distinction of being suckled at the breast of virgin goddesses. Most Greek kings of legends were the illegitimate spawn of gods out for an evening of fun.

The Jews rejected such claptrap. Though the Jewish monarchy itself was modeled after those of pagan nations, the Torah provided the Jewish concept of kingship with an entirely different framework. The Jewish king had no antecedents in heaven. He was neither the son of God, nor a cousin of God, and no divine origins were ever attributed to him. Though Jewish kings were to commit all kinds of transgressions, none ever thought of claiming himself of divine essence.

The Jewish king had no priestly functions as did pagan kings, and was in no way connected with the priesthood, though in the Maccabean period some kings tried to combine the offices of king and priest into one. In Judaism, the Jewish king was subject to the laws of the Torah, just as the President of the United States is subject to the laws of the Constitution. The Jews, in essence, introduced the concept of constitutional monarchy without divine rights of kings. Europe did not catch up with this idea until after Cromwell and after the French Revolution. The kings were beheaded, and that put an end to their divine rights.

Historians can—and do—cite incident after incident in the Old Testament showing Jewish kings arrogating unto themselves despotic power. Jewish kings, being as mortal and human as any kings in history, sinned, but not with the consent of God.

Two Bible stories serve as excellent examples. One morning King David beheld from the rooftop of his house a beautiful woman bathing. She was Bathsheba, the wife of Uriah, a Hittite, one of David's mercenary generals.

King David seduced Bathsheba and sent Uriah to his death in battle. The point in this story is not that David acted like an Oriental despot, but that the Prophet Nathan dared to denounce him publicly for his deed without David's daring to retaliate.

The story of Naboth's vineyard illustrates the Jewish concept of individual freedom of life, liberty, and property. Naboth, a private citizen in the days of King Ahab (869–850), owned a vineyard next to the king's property. King Ahab coveted it, but as Naboth refused to sell, the king could do nothing. Ahab's wife, the Sidonite princess Jezebel, whose pagan background contained no such nonsense as rights of individuals, conspired to have Naboth stoned to death so that his property would be forfeited to the crown (as in feudal English law). The Prophet Elijah, however, protested publicly against this outrage. Pointing an accusing finger at the king, he cries out, "In the place where the dogs licked up the blood of Naboth shall dogs lick your own blood." People did not talk like this to pope or emperor in Europe until the eighteenth century A.D., when the revolutions sweeping Europe gave the common man the rights the Torah had given the Jews 2,500 years previously.

Christian historians also point to numerous passages in the Old Testament that seemingly discredit the nobility of its ideas. So, for instance, many point out the jungle life that prevailed during the two centuries of the Judges, citing the passage in the Bible (Judges 21:25) "There was no king in Israel; every man did that which was right in his own eyes."

This passage does indeed indicate that the "message" was forgotten quite often in the days of the Judges. But it does not mean it was destroyed. The Jewish philosopher Abraham J. Heschel defines the Jew as a messenger of God who now and then forgets his message. One could write a book (and books have been written) on the racial hatreds and bigotry that have flourished in the United States; yet by and large, the United States was and still is the world's most liberal democratic country. So too one must judge lapses from the Jewish norm of history against the total Jewish achievement.

With the establishment of the Jewish state in the tenth century B.C., the third scene is over. The previously nomadic Jews have now been doubly fenced in—by a national boundary of the state and by the moral-legal constitution of the Torah. The former, as with all other nations, will serve to mold the Jews into an identifiable national entity. The latter will serve to hold them within the bounds of Judaism should the state fall and the Jews be scattered.

These are but the first exploratory steps—or first fortuitous accidents—in their training program. Soil and faith must now be united in an indissoluble bond of promise and fulfillment so that even if the Jews lose their land, they will never lose hope of regaining it. Palestine must be made to serve as a beckoning symbol of strength and unity even as history will fling the Jews physically farther and farther away from Zion. The foundation for a duality in the Jewish soul—the national and the universal—has been laid.

SCENE 4

Canon and Charisma

When the curtain goes up on the fourth scene, a thousand
years have slipped by since the confrontation of Abraham
and God. Has the time come for the Jews to be exiled
into the world at large to fulfill the mission history has in
store for them? Are the concepts of Torah, Covenant, and
monotheism sufficient preparation to hold them together
in a world Diaspora if they should be dispersed at this
point in their history? If there is a Divine Director over-
seeing the action of our drama, can He at this time risk a
dry-run exile to test the efficacy of His training program?
What if the test should fail? There would then no longer
be a Chosen People, and the illusion of a Jewish manifest
destiny would come to an ignoble end. Fortunately, history
hands the Jews a solution to their problem.

The Jewish kingdom founded by King David had
achieved a short-lived brilliance under his rule and that of
his successor, Solomon. But after the death of Solomon
(922 B.C.), strife developed between King Rehoboam,
his son, and General Jeroboam, insurgent leader of the
ten northern tribes of Israel. The ensuing civil war ripped
Palestine into the Kingdom of Judah (ruled by Rehoboam
and his descendants of the house of King David) and
into the Kingdom of Israel (ruled by Jeroboam and a
succession of different dynasties). Now, if a first test with
one kingdom should fail, there would still be a second
chance with the Jews in the other kingdom.

The first test of Jewish ability to survive in an exile came toward the end of the eighth century B.C., when a new power, the lean, hook-nosed Assyrians, set out on the path of conquest. In that century they vanquished Babylonia and invaded Israel. To their surprise, Israel was not the pushover they had expected. It was a prolonged and bitter fight. But after inflicting several humiliating defeats on the mighty Assyrians, the Kingdom of Israel finally fell in 722, its capital Samaria destroyed after a three-year siege. In a final onslaught, Israel was devastated, her political institutions smashed, and most of her population, composed of ten of the twelve tribes, deported.

Without a state, without military power, and without political organization, the people of Israel soon forgot their monotheism, their Covenant, and their Torah. Not only did the Kingdom of Israel cease to exist, but within a century its exiled people vanished from history as an identifiable ethnic unit through paganism and intermarriage. If the defeat of Israel was meant to be a test of Jewish ability to survive in exile, it failed miserably.

The very existence of the Chosen People was in jeopardy. Of the original twelve tribes, only two were left in the Kingdom of Judah. Although she was saved from the fate that had befallen the Kingdom of Israel by a combination of miracle, luck, and judicious payment of a huge annual tribute to the Assyrians, Judah was nevertheless in a pathetic plight. The poor were oppressed by the rich. King after king was assassinated as plot succeeded political counterplot. The last two tribes of the Jewish people were in danger not only of vanishing out of history at the hands of a ruthless enemy at the frontier, but of fading out of Judaism at the bosom of the foreign bride in the bedroom. The will to survive as Jews was being diluted by intermarriage with pagan maidens who, along with their dowries, introduced pagan religious cults into their new Jewish homes.

If the Jews in the Kingdom of Judah receive no more effective preparation for survival in exile than the Jews in the Kingdom of Israel, what will happen to their dream of a brotherhood of man if they too are flung into an exile at the next spin of history's wheel of fate? The enemy, whoever it might be, would surely smash the political structure of Judah just as the Assyrians had smashed the political structure of Israel. In such an eventuality, some other form of cohesive power would be needed to hold the Jews of Judah together as an ethnic entity or they would disintegrate as the Jews of Israel had. If blind chance motivates Jewish history, obviously better luck is needed, but if a divine will directs the action, then a more effective training program is called for.

With a fine sense of timing, our Cosmic Director, or history itself, comes to the aid of the Kingdom of Judah. In her hour of crisis, Judah has the good fortune to inherit a resourceful king named Josiah, who had ascended the throne in 638 B.C. It is to him that our Divine Director presents the fourth script—a prescription for a religious shock-treatment and a program for social psychotherapy.

Though much happened during Josiah's thirty-year reign, his metahistoric function was to fuse the Jews into a cohesive unity, willing to obey not out of fear of physical reprisal but out of an inner, self-imposed discipline. This he did with "canon" and "charisma." He was unaware, of course, that not until centuries later would theologians and sociologists coin these names for his actions, just as he was unaware that he had created two essential tools for survival in a future exile. The issue, as King Josiah saw it, concerned not only the very life and death of the Kingdom of Judah but the very existence of the Jews as Jews. Only a return to first principles, to Moses and the Torah, could save his nation and his people. He decided to redistribute the wealth more justly, and to purge his realm of idols.

By a rare coincidence, according to the biblical version (II Chronicles 34 and II Kings 22–23), King Josiah's paymaster arrived with wages for workers renovating the Temple in Jerusalem at just the moment an accidental but momentous discovery was made. Hidden in a secluded and forgotten niche, the High Priest Hilkiah had found what orthodox Jews claim is the complete Pentateuch, the Five Books of Moses, and what modern scholars claim was merely an archaic manuscript of Deuteronomy.

The story of the discovery spread like wildfire throughout Jerusalem, throughout the land, and beyond the borders of Judah. To make certain of the authenticity of the manuscript, Josiah consulted the Prophetess Huldah, who readily confirmed its genuineness. It might seem amazing that he should have retained a third-rate Prophetess like Huldah when one of the greatest of Prophets, Jeremiah, was right at his elbow. But a careful reading of the Book of Jeremiah (VII:8) makes us realize why King Josiah did not consult him. Jeremiah considered the "Book of the Law" discovered in the Temple a deceitful forgery by scribes.[1]

After receiving the go-ahead signal from Huldah, King Josiah dramatically proclaimed that a book written by Moses had been found in the Temple. A religious renaissance swept the nation and carried with it Josiah's reform bills. Imported pagan priests were slain. Domestic worshipers of the Baal and Astarte cults risked the same fate if caught. Necromancers, sorcerers, and mediums—both the imported and the domestic varieties—along with their teraphim and divination rods were purged from the land.[2] All worship was centralized in the Temple. The use of "high places" as centers for decentralized "family-worship" was banned. In their stead, Josiah introduced the Passover Service, celebrating the Exodus from Egypt and man's freedom from slavery, a festival that has become a foundation stone of Judaism.

Josiah's sanctification of Deuteronomy introduced a new concept, something the world was to call "canonization," from the Greek word *canon,* meaning "rule" or "standard." In this instance, a "book" was made the "word" of God.

---

[1]The King James and Masoretic translations are euphemistic. For a clear intent of Jeremiah's words, see the Revised Standard Version which translates verse VII:8 as "But, behold, the false pen of the scribes has made it into a lie."

[2]Other times, other customs! One wonders what would have happened to Abraham, Isaac, and Jacob, and their wives and concubines, all of whom had their own household teraphim. These teraphim were images of lesser domestic deities used principally for divination. Some scholars believe that possession of them indicated inheritance rights, which is why Rachel stole the teraphim from her father's house when she left with her husband Jacob.

To paraphrase St. John, though in the beginning there had been spirit, the Jews made the spirit the Word, and the Word was God.

This innovation was to have universal repercussions. The sanctification of Deuteronomy paved the way for the future successive canonization of three great religious documents—the Old Testament of the Jews, the New Testament of the Christians, and the Koran of the Mohammedans. In this century, we are beholding the "canonization" of yet a fourth document, that of Karl Marx's *Das Kapital*, the "bible" of the communists. All four are essentially Semitic documents which have changed or shaped the world more profoundly than any other documents or ideas in the history of man.

The second effect of Josiah's sanctification of Deuteronomy was the establishment of charismatic power among the Jews. Whereas political power originates in an institution that has the physical means of enforcing its will, charismatic power relies on the inherent prestige of the office itself for obedience. Charismatic power is possible only when people voluntarily submit themselves to the will of that office, even to the point of dying in its defense.

The Jews have now been equipped with the essential armor of canon and charisma to cope with future challenges. But one other item is needed for them to be fully prepared, programmed, and preconditioned for the ordeal ahead—the message. This is the job of the Prophets, whose voices we can now hear thundering offstage.

SCENE 5

The Voice of the Prophets

Art and literature are the windows which permit the cultural voyeur to peer into the soul of a civilization. We perceive the emotional soul of Christianity through its artists, and the intellectual soul of Judaism through its Prophets. Just as Leonardo da Vinci, Michelangelo, and Raphael created an immortal Christian culture with paint and stone, so Hosea, Isaiah, and Jeremiah created an immortal Jewish culture with words and ideas. But whereas Christian art produced a unity in the Christian soul, Jewish prophetic thought produced a duality in Jewish life.

In the first four scenes of our drama, Jewish history consisted of an external clash between paganism and monotheism. In this our fifth scene, Jewish history becomes an internal clash between Jewish nationalism and Jewish universalism. This tension, introduced by the Prophets, transforms Judaism from a religion of rest to a religion of movement.

When our scene begins, we have a feeling of *dejà-vu*—that we have witnessed these events before. The Babylonians are preparing to storm the Kingdom of Judah just as in the previous scene the Assyrians stormed the Kingdom of Israel. The Assyrian assault had been successful. The Jews in the Kingdom of Israel had been exiled, and within a century had vanished from history. Now a Babylonian Damoclean sword of exile hangs over the heads of the

Jews in Judah. Will their fate be as disastrous as that of the Jews of Israel?

What has happened? Toward the twilight of the sixth century, after the death of King Josiah, the Babylonians were once again on the march for empire. Invading Assyria, they sacked its capital Nineveh (612 B.C.), trounced the Egyptians at the battle of Carchemish (605 B.C.), and held out the collection plate of tribute to Judah. Judah did the only sensible thing she could. She paid.

Injudiciously, however, Judah invited the wrath of giant Babylonia when her people became divided on the question of whether to continue to pay tribute and buy peace, or to stop paying and incite war. The Jews decided to strike for freedom, and almost succeeded. It took three Babylonian campaigns to subdue militant Judah. The first was disastrous for the Babylonians. During the second (597 B.C.), the Babylonians stormed Jerusalem and deported the rich. After the third uprising, the Babylonians devastated the land and deported another segment of Jews. Now there was no longer a Jewish kingdom.

If we were dealing with ordinary history rather than preordained history, we would expect Judah and its people to vanish, just as the Sumerians, Elamites, Kassaites, Hurrians, and Hittites had vanished before the fall of Israel. Such is not to be the case with the Jews of Judah, however. For whatever reasons one wishes to ascribe, the destiny of Judah takes an entirely different course. In the boiling cauldron of history, the Kingdom of Judah evaporates as a political power. But the Jews of Judah remain as a great moral force, destined to conquer the world, not with the sword but with their ideas. Behind these political events are ideological currents generated by the Prophets.

The Age of the Prophets coincides with that 300-year span of time (750–450 B.C.) when the destruction of Jews and Judaism seemed inevitable. We must, therefore, resort to a metahistoric view of how Prophets and history mingled to create Jewish destiny. Unable to bend history their way, the Prophets instead molded the Jews in such a fashion that they would bend with history. Thus the Jews were not swept into oblivion by the political forces that drastically rearranged the balance of power of the ancient world.

If the Jews are to fulfill their manifest destiny, they must survive as Jews in an exile in the Gentile world for whatever length of time it may take. History, therefore, must provide a Jewish nationalist center in Palestine for the preservation of the identity of the messenger, and Jewish universalist centers in the world at large for the propagation of the message.

Fortunately, with the Prophets we do indeed see the emergence of two such centers of Judaism—one universalist in outlook, created for Jews who will live voluntarily in exile, the other nationalist in outlook, created for Jews who will return time and again to Jerusalem to reaffirm their ties with Zion.

It is uncanny how the Prophets appear at precisely that stage in history when they are absolutely essential to the survival of the Jewish grand illusion. Even before the Assyrians storm the gates of the Kingdom of Israel, we hear the voices of the first two Prophets. We hear the contemporary Prophets Amos and Hosea (both of whom started their public careers as Prophets around 785 B.C.) espousing their opposite but equally necessary doctrines of survival—Amos preaching universalism and Hosea preaching nationalism. Though they begin their exhortations sixty years before the exile of the Jews in the Kingdom of Israel, their words come too late to have any effect. As we have seen, the Jews of Israel disappear after the fall of their kingdom.

After the fall of Israel, the center of prophecy shifts to Judah, where the voices of other Prophets first take up the universalist refrain of Amos, and later the nationalist tune of Hosea. This time, anticipating an exile for the Jews of Judah, the universalist Prophets outline a workable blueprint for survival. As they exhort about the exile to come, they also predict a return which this time will materialize.

We come now to an unresolved question. Do new political situations create new ideas, or do new ideas create new political situations? Ideas are like plagues—once they infect men, no sword can eradicate them. Unlike conquerors, who need huge armies and much bloodshed to capture enemy lands, ideas need but small bands of zealots to hold men's minds. Good arguments can be made for either view of this prophetic period in Jewish history, for men, Prophets, and events swiftly followed one another. Either view is valid, depending on whether one begins with a Prophet or with an event. Whether we see our play as divinely created or man-made, all the pieces fit.

Though it was the Prophet Amos, the humble sheepherder from Tekoa, who in five fiery sermons of doom forged the first universalist framework for prophetic philosophy, it was his contemporary Isaiah, the greatest of Jewish Prophets, who became the chief architect of Jewish universalism.[1] Just as Abraham was the founder of the Chosen People, just as Moses was the man who gave the Jews the Law, so it was Isaiah who gave the Jews their universalist message of a future brotherhood of man to carry to the nations of the world.

The personalities of Isaiah and Hosea reflect their philosophies. Isaiah, the aristocrat, prominent in public affairs, an intimate of kings, stands for political messianism, for a worldwide Jewish ethic for mankind—in short, ethical universalism. Hosea, the humble man of the people, married to the prostitute Gomer, Jesus-like in his forebearance for her transgressions, stands for religious messianism, for a Jewish humanism tied to Jewish soil—in short, humanistic nationalism.

Taking their cues from Hosea and Isaiah, other Prophets hammered away at these themes of the nationalist concept of the election of Israel versus the universalist concept of the brotherhood of man. Here we are again confronted with an uncanny coincidence. Whereas prior to the exile

[1]Scholars generally divide the Book of Isaiah into two parts. Chapters 1–39 are ascribed to the "First Isaiah," written before the Babylonian exile, and Chapters 40–66 are ascribed to the "Second" or "deutero-Isaiah," written during the Babylonian exile. Some scholars think that the First Isaiah was nationalist and the Second Isaiah universalist, but most think the First Isaiah foreshadows the Second. Such Chapters as 2 and 11, far from being nationalist, preach a lofty universalism which is later taken up by the Second Isaiah.

of the Jews into Babylon the Prophets generally moved from Hosea's nationalism toward Isaiah's universalism, after the return of the Jews from Babylonian exile other Prophets reversed the trend, and moved from Isaiah's ideological expansionism back to Hosea's nationalist particularism.

Midway, both historically and ideologically, the voice of the Prophet Jeremiah rises, preaching a blend of nationalism and universalism. Unable to make up his mind which ideology to embrace, Jeremiah thunders the gospel of Hosea in one chapter and the doctrine of Isaiah in the next. Tied as he was by love to the land of Zion, Jeremiah nevertheless understood the meaning of the shadow Babylon cast over Judah. He knew the fate that had befallen the people of Israel. He knew that if the Jews of Judah failed to create universal goals they would disappear as surely as the Jews of Israel had disappeared.

Jeremiah thus swung between emotion and intellect. Even after the fall of Judah, he was not certain which course of action to take—whether to accompany the Jews trudging the captivity road to Babylon, or flee to Egypt, which offered political asylum. His friends made the decision for him by literally carrying him to Egypt even as he protested he wanted to go to Babylon.

It is doubtful whether the Prophets themselves realized the impact their ideas were destined to have on their people. Yet the concepts they preached paved the way for a new mode of thought, a new way of worship, and a new concept of life—all destined to be practiced in the coming exile, not in the homeland.

The Prophets contended that justice and morality were superior to priestly cults, that God wanted not rituals but higher ethical standards. They had the vision and the courage to proclaim that God abhorred sacrifice, if it was an end in itself, that the real sin was perversion of justice. It is remarkable that they were not stoned to death for utterances such as these in an age when priesthood, ritual, and sacrifice were the essence of Judaism. What would have happened had Christian cardinals preached a comparable doctrine during the Middle Ages—that Jesus did not want confessions or Mass, that genuflections to statues in the image of Christ were an abomination unto God, that what Jesus wanted was higher moral and ethical standards from man? They would have been burned alive as were Huss and Savonarola.

Ideas, not deeds, dominate our fifth scene. The words of the universalist Prophets free the Jews from the limitations of time and space; they show the Jews how to convert their former static, cultic rites into dynamic, universal forms. They give the Jews a reason to remain Jews in exile, and a purpose for their fate.

When the cohorts of Nebuchadnezzar swoop down from Babylonia and haul them into captivity, the Jews of Judah are spiritually prepared. With the charismatic power imbued into them by the canonized book of Deuteronomy, and with the ideas supplied them by their Prophets, the Jews of Judah, unlike the Jews of Israel, possess the will and the tools to survive in exile as Jews.

Under the impetus of these prophetic guidelines, the exiled Jews of Judah innovated two ideas on Babylonian soil which have become universal possessions of mankind. Instead of a Temple for a priesthood cult, they built synagogues for popular devotion, and instead of sacrifice, they offered prayer. The synagogue became the prototype for the church and the mosque, and institutionalized prayer became the universal mode of worship.

Thus freed from priesthood, Temple, and sacrifice, the Jews could set up synagogues anywhere, and through prayer communicate directly with God without an intermediary priesthood. Survival of Judaism in exile had been assured.

The Prophets said one thing more, however, most crucial in terms of the thesis of our drama. The Jews, they said, must, by their conduct, their ethics, their concepts of man, life, and God, set an example for the rest of mankind. The ritual commandments of Judaism were for Jews only, but the Judaic spiritual message was universal.

Historically speaking, the Prophets turned political defeat into spiritual victory by transforming politics into ideology. Their ideas built a bridge for the Jews to escape from a crumbling political kingdom into the enduring fortress of the coming Diaspora. The Prophets preached of victory through surrender of the body and resistance of the spirit. In a political sense they were appeasers, but in a spiritual sense they understood men better than did kings. They foresaw that one day the hand that wielded the sword would wither, whereas the mind that spun ideas would never die. They channeled all ideas of the Jewish past into one river with two currents flowing in the same direction, separated time and again in midstream by islands of dissension, but always destined to merge again.

Thus the Prophets sowed the seeds for two ideas of Judaism. One is an ideological, universalist Judaism for export in the Diaspora, for the world at large. The other is a humanistic, nationalist Judaism for domestic consumption in Zion, for Jews. Consonant with our Lurianic theme that the redemption of Israel will herald the redemption of man, these two prophetic currents of Judaism should one day flow into a synthesis of Jewish history with world history.

Through the centuries, the pendulum of Jewish history is destined to swing between these two prophetic concepts of humanistic nationalism and ideological universalism. As the pendulum swings toward Hosea's religious messianism, it will give rise to new religious sects which will subordinate the universal message of Judaism for their private brands of salvation. As the pendulum swings to the opposite side of its arc, toward Isaiah's political messianism, it will activate new ideologies whose proponents will not forget the universal content of the message.

The framework of the future has been cast. The Prophets have paved a survival road for Jewish destiny to march side by side with world history. But along the way lurks the inherent danger that the Jews might disappear prematurely in the new universality created by the universalist Prophets. Providing a blueprint for preserving the Jews as Jews, at least until their mission is fulfilled, will be the function of a team of nationalist zealots, about to make its debut in our next scene.

SCENE 6

The Call to Nationalism

While waiting for our next scene to begin, let us briefly review the adventures of the Jews in Babylonian captivity, and then assess their historical condition against the backdrop of the new political forces about to alter the balance of power in the ancient world.

Though Assyrians and Babylonians were ruthless in battle, they, like other Semitic powers of that era, did not desecrate cemeteries, destroy crops, and exterminate vanquished populations as a calculated policy of state. These were policies instituted by the Romans and continued by Huns, Mongolians, and Christians. The ancient Semitic theory of conquest was to fragmentize a conquered nation and then disperse the segments throughout the empire to prevent a future unification and subsequent uprisings against the conquerors. Though the vanquished could retain their own gods and cults, they were nevertheless absorbed within a century or so by the host civilization through intermarriage instead of extermination by torture. This, as we saw, happened to the Jews of the Kingdom of Israel. After they were dispersed throughout the Assyrian Empire they simply disappeared into the general population. One would expect the same fate to befall the Jews of Judah, once the Babylonians carted them off into exile. But nothing went as planned.

By advising Nebuchadnezzar to deport the flower of Judah's aristocrats and intellectuals to the four corners of the empire, Babylonian policy-makers relied heavily on precedent. They reasoned that Judah would be so weakened that she would never again rise as an independent power to threaten Babylonian rule, and that in captivity the Jews would be assimilated into the general population. They were unaware of the charismatic guidelines implanted in the Jews by the Josianic reforms and the survival ideas generated by the Prophets which would nullify this normal process of assimilation.

Babylonian trade routes guided the venturesome Jews throughout the then-known world, transforming them from "parochial men" into cosmopolitan citizens. Their commercial trading outposts became centers for thriving Jewish communities. In the libraries of Babylon, intellectual Jews found a new world of new ideas. Within five decades, exiled Jews bobbed to the surface of the top echelons of Babylonian society, in business enterprises, in the scholastic world, in court circles. They became leaders in commerce, men of learning, advisors to kings. But they remained Jews.

The greatness that was Babylon was destined to decline and disappear. The 5,000-year luck of the Semites was running out. A new man of the hour, Cyrus, was on the march for empire. In 536 B.C., after barely fifty years enjoyment of the spoils of victory, Babylonia was vanquished by Cyrus, and the Persian Empire was born. With it a new era of history, the Age of the Aryans,[1] was ushered in. The Semitic world supremacy was over.

The racist concept of "Aryan" connotes a tall, blond, blue-eyed, pure-blooded Nordic speaking a Germanic language. Alas, anthropologists have failed to keep pace with modern racists. The Aryans are not a Nordic but an Asian people, a subdivision of the white race that embraces two distinct language groups widely separated by distance. One is the Semitic, originating in the vicinity of the Sinai Peninsula, already discussed. The other is the

---

[1] "Aryan" is an Iranian word, used by the Asiatic Iranians as a term to distinguish themselves from other people, from non-Iranians, just as the Jews in biblical days referred to themselves as "Hebrews," to distinguish themselves from all other people, that is, from the Goyyim, the non-Jews.

Aryan, originating in central Asia, also the birthplace of the Mongolian language group.

Aryan-speaking Asiatics migrated west, in three distinct waves. Before 2000 B.C., one group penetrated into the Balkans, and under the name of Achaeans became the forerunners of the Greeks. A second group, after 2000 B.C., crossed the mountains between the Caspian and Black seas, settling in northern India and the Anatolian plains under the respective names of Hindus and Hittites. A third, after 1500 B.C., invaded the lands northwest of Mesopotamia, becoming known as Medes and Persians.

The Medes and the Persians were related not only racially and linguistically but by marriage. The Kingdom of Media, patched together in the late seventh century B.C. by King Cyaxares from spin-off parts of the dying Assyrian Empire, was inherited by his son Astyages, who has two claims to fame—he invented trousers for men, and he was the grandfather of the man who deposed him, Cyrus, founder of the Persian Empire.

One by one, Cyrus conquered the small, semi-independent satellites fringing the Babylonian Empire, and in 538 B.C., the capital city of Babylon surrendered without the shot of an arrow. His son Cambyses added Egypt to the realm, and the Persian Empire, the largest the world had known till that time, reached from the Caucasus to the Indian Ocean, from the Indus River to the Mediterranean. This shift in power politics flung the Jews from the crumbling world of Semitic civilization into the rising orbit of Aryan history.

The Persians, however, were Aryans in language only; the core of their civilization was still Semitic. They introduced no new concepts and exerted no new influence on world thinking. They lived on Semitic antecedents, and served historically only as a conveyor belt to a future intellectual Aryan takeover by the Greeks.

Emperor Cyrus was an enlightened ruler who forged the heterogenous nations he had conquered into a unified empire through the exercise of tolerance. He viewed all gods and religions as equal. Under his benevolent rule art flourished, trade and commerce grew, intellect languished, and Persia became a materialistic wonderland. He also proclaimed that all exiled peoples in his vast realm, including the Jews, would be permitted to return to their respective homelands if they wished. This placed the Jews on the horns of a dilemma. If all exiled Jews return to Jerusalem, the Diaspora framework established in the Babylonian exile will collapse and the election of the Chosen People will be rendered meaningless. If, on the other hand, no Jews return to Jerusalem, our drama will also be rendered meaningless, for then there will be no Zion to hold the Jews within the orbit of Judaism. For a while it looked as if our drama would collapse for the second reason—no Jews rushed to reestablish a national home base for a Jewish manifest destiny.

The decree of Cyrus created mixed emotions, and the Jews failed to greet his generosity with the grandiloquent words of the Second Isaiah: "Thus says the Lord to his anointed, to Cyrus, whose right hand I have grasped . . . He shall build my city and set my exiles free" (Isaiah 45:1 and 13). Though wealthy Babylonian Jews were willing to finance one-way tickets for those who wanted to return to Judah, there were few takers. There was little danger of the Diaspora being abandoned. There was considerable danger of Jerusalem staying deserted. But again the totally unexpected happened. A few zealots, imbued with the sense of a Jewish manifest destiny, seized Jewish history and bent it to their will.

Just as European Christians in the Middle Ages instituted eight Crusades to wrest Jerusalem from the infidels who had begun to settle there after its destruction by Titus, so a few Babylonian Jews in the Persian Empire instituted two Zionades to wrest Jerusalem from the pagans who had begun to settle there after its destruction by Nebuchadnezzar. But whereas the Christians came with naked swords and unfurled banners of Christ, the Jews came with canonized Scripture and an unfulfilled Covenant with God.

The first Zionade, created several years after the edict of Cyrus, eventually proved as unsuccessful as all eight medieval Crusades. Never before had such a motley army of *asafsuf*—the undigestibles of Jewish-Babylonian society —had such august leadership: two princes of the House of

David, Sheshbazzar[2] and Ze
Priest, Jeshua. It was not lo
motivated them but ambition. S
both had an eye on the vacant thro
had visions of becoming the High Pr
Jeshua survived the suspicions of the
his ambitions. Yet it was under the ns
triumvirate that the rebuilding of the Tenegun.
Completed in 515 B.C., it must have been y affair,
architecturally no more imposing-looking thn a small-
town Moolah Temple, for even the Prophet Haggai complained it was a depressing sight.

Neither Zionade nor Temple helped. In one hundred
years no more than 42,000 Jews returned to resettle Judah.
Political ambition obscured ideological vision. Zeal vanished, organization crumbled, goals were lost. When disquieting rumors of this sorry state of affairs reached
wealthy Jews in Babylon, they found a wonderful excuse
for doing nothing by disbelieving the rumors. Jerusalem
and the surrounding territory sank back into its former
torpor, squalor, and paganism.

If this degeneration of Judah continued, if Jerusalem
were allowed to fade out of Jewish consciousness, there
would be no meaning left for exiled Jews to exist as Jews.
Dying memories and tempting assimilation would hurl
them out of Jewish history, their Covenant dead, their
great task unfulfilled. What centrifugal force would hold
them within the orbit of Judaism? The times cried out for
a new Zionade. But who would lead it?

It is at this point that the curtain rises on the action
in our sixth scene, on a team of two nationalists, a priest
named Ezra and an aristocrat named Nehemiah, who,
together, will create a new age for the Jews. With their
entry, in the middle of the fifth century B.C., the era of
prophecy is over. The time has come to transubstantiate
prophetic ideology into practical politics. Where the function of the Prophets had been to universalize the Jewish

[2]Some scholars suspect that Sheshbazzar is a cryptogram for
Zerubbabel and that Sheshbazzar and Zerubbabel were one and the
same person.

God and give mankind a universal ethic, the
...ion of Ezra and Nehemiah will be to formulate ideas
at will preserve the Jews as Jews. It almost seems as if
God is afraid that the Jews might prematurely disappear
into the universality created by the Prophets. Ezra and
Nehemiah must remind the Jews that before they disappear
into such a prophetic universality, they first have a mission
to fulfill.

The Bible is maddeningly silent about Ezra, the zealot,
enshrined in the minds of Orthodox Jews as the "second
Moses." Prudently, however, as if realizing that though
he was as intractable as the Torah he was not as wise, that
though he did save Judaism he was nothing but a chauvinist, the Jews have not conferred "prophethood" on Ezra.
Even legend-makers have shied away from attributing to
him the accolades usually reserved for heroes. His father
is made neither king nor carpenter.

The Bible states that Ezra was a scribe in the court
of the Persian King Artaxerxes in his summer capital city
of Susa. It is here that he hears of the plight of the Jews
and the sad state of Judaism in Jerusalem. He successfully
petitions the king to let him organize a second Zionade,
which proves successful beyond all legitimate expectations.

This second Zionade was not a mass movement. The
Bible gives the number of true believers heeding Ezra's
call as 1,760 souls. But what it lacked in numbers it made
up in spirit. From Susa to Judah with his mini-host of
volunteer redeemers marched Ezra, bent on reviving the
Torah in Zion. But when they arrived in the Promised
Land their eyes confirmed the tragic truth their ears had
refused to believe in Susa. Judah was waste and Jerusalem
barren, and Zion, their Zion, in shambles.

Nehemiah now enters the scene. The Bible tells us even
less about him than about Ezra. It merely identifies him
as an aristocrat who served as cupbearer to the king of
Persia, once again indicating the high status of Jews in
the Persian Empire. Nehemiah also petitions the king to
permit him to go to Jerusalem, and off he goes, not at
the head of a Zionade, but by himself, as the newly appointed governor of Jerusalem. The team of Ezra and

David, Sheshbazzar[2] and Zerubbabel, and a Zadokite High Priest, Jeshua. It was not love of the lower classes that motivated them but ambition. Sheshbazzar and Zerubbabel both had an eye on the vacant throne of Judah, and Jeshua had visions of becoming the High Priest of Jerusalem. Only Jeshua survived the suspicions of the Persians to realize his ambitions. Yet it was under the leadership of this triumvirate that the rebuilding of the Temple was begun. Completed in 515 B.C., it must have been a sorry affair, architecturally no more imposing-looking than a small-town Moolah Temple, for even the Prophet Haggai complained it was a depressing sight.

Neither Zionade nor Temple helped. In one hundred years no more than 42,000 Jews returned to resettle Judah. Political ambition obscured ideological vision. Zeal vanished, organization crumbled, goals were lost. When disquieting rumors of this sorry state of affairs reached wealthy Jews in Babylon, they found a wonderful excuse for doing nothing by disbelieving the rumors. Jerusalem and the surrounding territory sank back into its former torpor, squalor, and paganism.

If this degeneration of Judah continued, if Jerusalem were allowed to fade out of Jewish consciousness, there would be no meaning left for exiled Jews to exist as Jews. Dying memories and tempting assimilation would hurl them out of Jewish history, their Covenant dead, their great task unfulfilled. What centrifugal force would hold them within the orbit of Judaism? The times cried out for a new Zionade. But who would lead it?

It is at this point that the curtain rises on the action in our sixth scene, on a team of two nationalists, a priest named Ezra and an aristocrat named Nehemiah, who, together, will create a new age for the Jews. With their entry, in the middle of the fifth century B.C., the era of prophecy is over. The time has come to transubstantiate prophetic ideology into practical politics. Where the function of the Prophets had been to universalize the Jewish

---

[2]Some scholars suspect that Sheshbazzar is a cryptogram for Zerubbabel and that Sheshbazzar and Zerubbabel were one and the same person.

concept of God and give mankind a universal ethic, the function of Ezra and Nehemiah will be to formulate ideas that will preserve the Jews as Jews. It almost seems as if God is afraid that the Jews might prematurely disappear into the universality created by the Prophets. Ezra and Nehemiah must remind the Jews that before they disappear into such a prophetic universality, they first have a mission to fulfill.

The Bible is maddeningly silent about Ezra, the zealot, enshrined in the minds of Orthodox Jews as the "second Moses." Prudently, however, as if realizing that though he was as intractable as the Torah he was not as wise, that though he did save Judaism he was nothing but a chauvinist, the Jews have not conferred "prophethood" on Ezra. Even legend-makers have shied away from attributing to him the accolades usually reserved for heroes. His father is made neither king nor carpenter.

The Bible states that Ezra was a scribe in the court of the Persian King Artaxerxes in his summer capital city of Susa. It is here that he hears of the plight of the Jews and the sad state of Judaism in Jerusalem. He successfully petitions the king to let him organize a second Zionade, which proves successful beyond all legitimate expectations.

This second Zionade was not a mass movement. The Bible gives the number of true believers heeding Ezra's call as 1,760 souls. But what it lacked in numbers it made up in spirit. From Susa to Judah with his mini-host of volunteer redeemers marched Ezra, bent on reviving the Torah in Zion. But when they arrived in the Promised Land their eyes confirmed the tragic truth their ears had refused to believe in Susa. Judah was waste and Jerusalem barren, and Zion, their Zion, in shambles.

Nehemiah now enters the scene. The Bible tells us even less about him than about Ezra. It merely identifies him as an aristocrat who served as cupbearer to the king of Persia, once again indicating the high status of Jews in the Persian Empire. Nehemiah also petitions the king to permit him to go to Jerusalem, and off he goes, not at the head of a Zionade, but by himself, as the newly appointed governor of Jerusalem. The team of Ezra and

Nehemiah now begins to make its impact on Jewish history.

To Nehemiah's practical mind, "spirit" was fine, but if the Jews wished to survive they had better have a bastion in which to insure that survival. It was under his leadership that the wall around Jerusalem was rebuilt. The obstacles were great, including that of a surrounding, hostile, majority pagan population, a situation reminiscent of conditions of modern Israel today, where the Israelis are rebuilding their state in spite of a surrounding, hostile, majority Arab population. In the fifth century B.C., as in the twentieth century A.D., Jews with swords at their sides and trowels in their hands worked to fortify their country and gain a modicum of security.

Ezra and Nehemiah introduced three innovations to strengthen the Jewish identity of the returnees from Babylon: a ban on intermarriage with any Gentile, a stress on nationalism, and a further canonization of Scripture. These are destined to shape the character of the Jews and chart their course through the 2,000 years of the second act of our drama.

The ban on intermarriage between Jews and non-Jews was the first such prohibition in the history of man.[3] It inflamed the Jews, who recalled that the patriarch Abraham had sired a child with a pagan handmaid Hagar, that Moses had married the Midianite Zipporah, that King Solomon had a harem full of assorted *shiksas*. Nor did it sit well with other peoples. The gall of tiny Judah, just freed from captivity, in effect saying to their liberators and to the rest of the world that their sons and daughters were not good enough for the Jews. It was not the world which first rejected the Jews, but the Jews who did the original rejecting. Counter-rejections would come within a few centuries as the world reacted in self-defense against this unintended "snub."

[3]Some scholars have interpreted verse 3, chapter VII in Deuteronomy to be the first such ban on intermarriage. A careful reading of verses 1 and 2 in that chapter, however, will make it clear that this prohibition refers only to the sons and daughters of the Gentile people living in Palestine prior to its conquest by the Jews, and not to all Gentiles, as was decreed by Ezra and Nehemiah.

It must be stressed that this ban on intermarriage was strictly a defense against future religious dilution and not part of a philosophy of racial superiority. According to Ezra and Nehemiah, the Chosen People should stay chosen. Latter-day rabbis, however, were keenly aware that this ban could be construed as racism. They took pains to explain that "the bread of the heathens was prohibited on account of their wine, and their wine on account of their daughters, and their daughters on account of idolatry." Thus idolatry was made the villain—bread, wine, and flesh were merely the decoys that lined the road to hell. But no rabbi revoked the ban, for no Diaspora designer could prescribe a more effective survival pill. This ban on intermarriage would help the Jews to remain Jews when wave after wave of assimilation assailed them in their subsequent odyssey through alien civilizations.

The second innovation to preserve the Jews as Jews was Jewish nationalism. In the opinion of Ezra and Nehemiah, a people was not forged by kings or dynasties, nor was it held together with sword and chariot. They believed a people was unified by the intangible concepts of language and an ideological tie to its past. They set new boundaries for Judaism, and anything that did not fit their definition was rejected as un-Jewish. The religious ideas inspired by the Prophets and tested by the Jews in Babylon were jettisoned by Ezra and Nehemiah. Synagogues, rabbis, and prayers were for export only. For home consumption, all the pre-exilic symbols were revived and restored. Temple, priesthood, and sacrifice were trotted back to their former places of cultic eminence. The new Judaism was anchored in one God, one land, one Temple. The Ezrian creed was to have bitter repercussions for the Jews and the world in the Modern Age when nations turned nationalist and adopted variations of this slogan—France with its *un roi, une foi, une loi* (one king, one faith, one law), Russia with its "one creed, one Czar, one fatherland," and the Nazis with their "one Führer, one Reich, one blood."

It was the third Ezra-Nehemiah innovation, however—the canonization of the Torah—that was destined to make the greatest imprint on the Jewish spirit. Ezra and Nehemiah were not as concerned for the body of the contemporary Jew as they were for the "Jewish soul" in future generations. As a move toward forging an enduring spiritual character, they not only revised King Josiah's canonized Book of Deuteronomy but canonized the four other books of Moses as well. Under their direction, priest and scribe labored diligently to fuse the most important of the then-extant Mosaic documents into what is now known as the Torah, the Hebrew name for the Five Books of Moses, or the Pentateuch, the Greek name used by the English-speaking world.

Once canonized, these five books became divine. Thereafter, no changes, additions, or deletions were permitted, and the job of maintaining the text was entrusted to a class of scribes known as Masoretes. The twentieth-century discovery of the Dead Sea Scrolls, which yielded Old Testament manuscripts dating to 200 B.C., show what an excellent job these scribes did in preserving the original text.

The canonization of the Five Books of Moses cleared the way for the compilation of the Old Testament. The Jews in subsequent centuries began canonizing, one by one, all the books now constituting the Old Testament, completing the task in 90 A.D.

We must pause to note some curious omissions and admissions to the Old Testament canon. As if to prevent Jews from becoming too nationalistic, too forgetful that they also have a universal mission to fulfill, the Jews excluded the Books of the Maccabees, which preaches a brand of ultra-nationalism. But the Book of Ruth, with its tolerance for intermarriage (Ruth, the Moabitess, marries a Jew and becomes the progenitor of King David), is included, one is almost tempted to say as a rebuke to Ezra and Nehemiah, who forbade such intermarriage. Also included is the Book of Job, which upholds man's right to hold God accountable for His actions.

Their task of building a viable Judaism fulfilled, Ezra and Nehemiah fade out of the Bible as mysteriously as they entered. With their deaths in the fourth century B.C., our scene ends.

So far, in our drama, we have seen the first 1,500 years of Jewish history funneled either by Divine Providence or by the Jews themselves (or perhaps even by blind events) into an ever-narrowing channel toward a point of no return. In our first scene, the Jews were chosen; in the second, they received their constitution; in the third, they acquired a homeland; in the fourth, they were immunized with political shock therapy; in the fifth, they underwent universalist psychotherapy; and in the scene just ended, they received nationalist group therapy from a Torah-intoxicated team of reformers.

This sixth scene has, however, also served to introduce the Diaspora into Jewish history. Some historians date the Diaspora from the time of the destruction of the Kingdom of Judah in the sixth century B.C. and the subsequent captivity in Babylon. If that were so, there would be no difference between the word "exile" and "Diaspora." Actually, the true Diaspora began with the Edict of Cyrus permitting the Jews to return to their homeland. However, as we saw, most of the Jews chose to remain in Babylonia instead of going back to Jerusalem. Herein is the crux of the difference between the concepts of "exile" and "Diaspora." The Jewish sojourn in Babylonia before the Persian conquest had been involuntary and maintained by force. The Jewish stay in Babylonia after liberation by the Persians was voluntary. Before the Persian victory, the Jews had lived in actual exile; after the Persian victory, when the Jews voluntarily chose to stay in Babylonia, they lived in a Diaspora.[4]

Although the action in the next four centuries from Ezra to Jesus will be centered in Jerusalem, the Jews in Babylonia, though dormant, are waiting in the wings, ready to claim the symbolic scepter of Jewish history in the second act.

---

[4]There is no corresponding word in Hebrew for "Diaspora." The Hebrew word *galut* means "exile" and the Jews in Israel refer to the Jews outside Israel as being in *"galut,"* in "exile," and not in the Diaspora, thus missing a most essential distinction.

SCENE 7

At the Crossroads of Fate

THE HELLENIC SYNDROME

Technically speaking, the training program hammered out by God and history, by Prophets and zealots, in our first six scenes, should have forged an enduring team of Jews motivated by perpetual zeal. Technically speaking, after their successful "Little Diaspora" test in Babylonia, the Jews should now be prepared for their crucial expulsion into a universal Diaspora, where their mission is to begin. Technically speaking, at this point, after a proper intermission, the second act should begin. But instead of an intermission, the lights are about to go up on an unexpected seventh scene for which the Jews have no guiding script.

What is the function of this seventh scene? Has there been a shortcoming in the survival training program? Has God been so concerned with the purity of faith that He has forgotten the possibility of a danger to faith by reason? Thus far the world has not produced a civilization founded on reason. What if the Jews, after being catapulted into the Diaspora, were to march kin, kith, and Covenant into such a civilization, become bewitched by its philosophy, entranced by its science, and seduced out of existence by its intellectual brilliance? In this scene, then, the Jews must be prepared for such a contingency. They must be taught not to elevate reason above faith, but how to temper faith with reason.

In this seventh and last scene of our first act, the Jews are provided by history with a small, experimental laboratory in which they can test the efficacy of an assortment of responses to challenges they may encounter in the second act. In this scene, the Jews confront the Greeks, who provide them in miniature with precisely those challenges which they will encounter in giant form in the second act.

Whereas our first six scenes were acted out against a background of Semitic civilizations, this seventh scene will unfold within a new Aryan civilization ushered into the West by the Greeks. Here the Jews will meet head-on the three enemies of faith—education, coexistence, and philosophy. While we wait for the action to begin, let us examine the tapestry of Greek history for an understanding of the events that follow.

Never has one civilization been so fervently adored by another as ancient Greece by the modern West. As in all such love affairs, the lover has created an image of the loved one unblemished by facts. Sustained by blinding faith, this lover even yet sees the black-haired, dark-eyed Asiatic Greeks as flaxen-haired, blue-eyed European Nordics.

It was the German archaeologist Heinrich Schliemann (1822–1890), discoverer of Troy, who invented the legend of the blond, Aryan Greek. According to Schliemann, the first Greeks appeared from some mystic Nordic spawning ground, invaded Greece, and out of their own genius, effortlessly created a culture containing the seeds that gave birth to Western civilization. This hypothesis was so flattering that the West immediately accepted it as revealed truth. Endless repetition has hardened it into a dogma that is difficult to dissolve, even with contrary evidence.

Greek history did not begin with Aryans but with Semites, and Greek civilization did not begin in Greece but in Crete. The first Greeks, referred to as "Achaeans" by Homer and as "Mycenaeans"[1] by archaeologists, were

---

[1]Actually, there is no Mycenaean people, only a city given the name Mycenae by Perseus about 1350 B.C. The city was founded by a non-Greek people in the twentieth century B.C., but its original name is in doubt.

Asiatic nomads who invaded northern Greece around 2000 B.C., and then plundered their way down the peninsula, practicing their rites of secular pederasty, holy prostitution, and human sacrifice. Casually, cruelly, they eradicated the non-Greek-speaking native population under the delusion that their Asiatic barbarism was superior to the indigenous Helladic culture. Out of this dismal genesis grew classic Greek civilization. It was assisted by an accidental and fortuitous circumstance in 1600 B.C. when the illiterate Mycenaeans were baptized into civilization by the literate Cretans.

Recent archaeological discoveries have shown that the civilization of Crete was not Greek but Semitic. That island, first invaded by Egyptians and other Semitic peoples around 4000 B.C., was settled two millennia later by sea-faring northwest Semites—ancestors to the Jews—who sparked the civilization we know today as Minoan. "Cretans" would be a more correct designation, for there was no such people as "Minoans." The word was coined by the British archaeologist Sir Arthur Evans, who named the people of Crete after their first king, Minos.[2]

Most scholars hold that this Semitic Minoan (or Cretan) culture may reasonably be called the foundation for Western civilization because Greek cultural traditions were based on Minoan prototypes. As one scholar summarizes it,

> Once the start was made, progress in Crete was extraordinarily rapid; we have pointed out that around 2000 B.C., in the time of the first palaces, there already flourished in the island a brilliantly original civilization, representing what may be termed the "classical phase" of a pre-Hellenic style. Nothing like this art had ever been seen before in the Aegean world.[3]

[2]According to legend, it was King Minos who around 2000 B.C. founded the fabulous city of Knossos, famed for its castles of marble and gold, and for the labyrinth where Theseus slew the Minotaur.
[3]The Birth of Greek Art, by Pierre Demargne.

Minóan culture, though originated by Semites, differed from other Semitic cultures in that it sprang out of the world's first maritime society based on sea-lane commerce in artifacts rather than from an agricultural society based on land-route trade in natural products.

It was this Cretan civilization, transplanted by the restless Minoans to the southern tip of the Greek mainland in 1800 B.C., which greeted the Mycenaeans when their odyssey of plunder took them to Peloponnesus around 1500 B.C.

After making themselves the masters of Crete in the fourteenth century, the Mycenaeans sailed off in the twelfth century to destroy Troy at about the same time Joshua set out to capture Jericho. Again the parallel between biblical and Homeric accounts of the destruction of these two cities is striking. Troy fell after the Greeks had secreted spies who opened the city gates for Agamemnon's army. Jericho fell after the Jews had secreted spies who (though the Bible does not specifically state this) opened the city gates for Joshua's army.[4]

Just as a dark age fell on the Jews after Jericho, their history disintegrating into the squabbles of Judges before they emerged into their classical age of Scripture and prophecy, so too a dark age fell on the Greeks after Troy, their history also disintegrating into the squabbles of tyrants before they emerged into their classical age of literature and philosophy.

When the victorious Mycenaeans sailed home from Troy they met the same fate they had meted out to the Trojans. That same century, a new barbaric Greek tribe, the Dorians, invaded Greece from Asia, destroying the cities in its path and completing its conquest by 1150 B.C. with the annihilation of the Mycenaeans. The dark age that now fell over the Aegean world also resembles the dark age that fell over Europe after the invasion of the Roman Empire by the barbarians. Just as out of the Dark

---

[4] May it be suggested that the walls of Jericho did not come "a 'tumbling' down" because of the blast of trumpets, but that the trumpets were sounded in victory after the walls were successfully breached.

Ages in Europe the Renaissance gave birth to a new Western civilization, so out of the Greek dark age came the brilliant Hellenic civilization of classical Greece.

But the greatness that was classical Greece lasted but two centuries—500 to 300 B.C. In the fourth century, her genius was slowly strangled to death in the prolonged, suicidal Peloponnesian Wars, where Greek again exterminated Greek. A supreme irony now befell proud Hellas. History decreed that the dying Hellenic civilization should be resurrected by a "Slavic" conqueror, Alexander the Great, who would export it to the Semites of the Near East where it would assume a new life. With Alexander (336–323 B.C.), Hellas died and Hellenism was born.[5]

Alexander, presumably the son of Philip II of Macedonia,[6] a small kingdom north of Greece, was tormented all his life by the question of his own legitimacy. His mother, Olympias, a vestal strumpet given to orgiastic snake dances, was abandoned by her husband when he found out about her random lovers. After Philip remarried, Olympias conspired to have him assassinated, then slew his widow and infant son to pave the way for her own son Alexander to take the throne. It was this Macedonian Hamlet who within eleven years "conquered the world" with 32,000 infantry and 5,000 cavalry, two thirds of them non-Greek mercenaries who, like the *routiers* of the Crusades, joined Alexander's tour of conquest for pay and pillage privileges.

Alexander strove to establish not only a Grecian empire but to extend Hellenic culture the world over. His method of disseminating ideas was simple but effective. Instead of using sword and violence, he used sex and education. To implement his program, he ordered his officers and men to intermarry with the native populations and to beget

---

[5] The word "Hellenic" is the term applied to the classic civilization in Greece itself. The word "Hellenism" refers to the exportable phase of Hellenic civilization.

[6] Though the ruling class of Macedonia claimed an unproven direct Hellenic descent and spoke a Greek dialect, the people of Macedonia were mostly Thracians and Illyrians, non-Greek-speaking peoples of mixed racial stock, mostly Slavs.

many children. He, himself, set an ambitious example by marrying not one but two natives—Roxana, a Bactrian princess, and Statira, the daughter of the defeated Emperor Darius III. Within ten years, Alexander also founded twenty-five Greek cities in Asia Minor, all with a central gymnasium as an educational propaganda bureau to spread the gospel of Hellenism.

So effective was Alexander's method of acculturation by insemination and education that but for his untimely death at the age of thirty-two he probably would have succeeded in the manner he intended. As it was, he did succeed, but in an unanticipated way. The reverse happened. Instead of the Near-East Orientals becoming Westernized as he had hoped, the Greeks became Orientalized.

There was but one exception to this mass transubstantiation—the Jews. They took the route Alexander had envisioned for his entire empire—from east to west. When they enter the sphere of Hellenism at the beginning of our seventh scene (300 B.C.), they are Oriental, biblical Jews. At its conclusion (100 A.D.), they have been transformed into Westernized, Hellenized, Pharisee Jews. Hellenization acted like a drug on the Jews. It began as a kick and ended as a habit.

What was this Hellenistic world like that it made such an impact on the Jews? Why in the time of stress to come did Hellenism die and Judaism survive? What corroded the Greek cultural heritage but vitalized the Jewish idea? The fact is that whereas the glory that was Greece was born out of aesthetic ideals, the greatness that is Judaism rests on moral concepts. Whereas the Greeks saw permanence in nature, the Jews saw permanence in human life. The Jews held that it was man who was immortal, not nature.

Because the ancient Greeks have been overrated by Grecophiles as much as the ancient Semites have been underrated is no excuse to commit the reverse offense, though in attempting to rectify the present imbalance we may leave ourselves open to such a charge. Nevertheless, before assessing the impact of Hellenism on the Jews, we must look behind the Hellenic "Potemkin façade"[7] of its beautiful statues, majestic buildings, and impeccable prose to see what they really disguise.

The Grecophile holds up Greek art as the zenith of artistic achievement. Yet the art made so familiar by textbooks and museums shows but one side of this civilization. What is not shown is its preoccupation with bacchanalian orgies, lewd rituals, and phallic images. "Everything that is classical is comprehensible at one glance," declared Oswald Spengler, and this is certainly true of Greek sculpture and architecture. There is no strength, no emotion, no character in the beautiful faces of the Hellenic statues of gods and goddesses.[8] Greek architecture was primitive, based on lintel, post, and entablature because the Greeks had no concept of arch, dome, or flying buttress. Graceful at first glance, it holds little inducement for a return look. Inside, Greek structures are as empty and devoid of feeling as are the heads of the statues, and kind time has washed away the gaudy colors in which they were once painted.

How different Christian art is in both concept and content. Whether or not one is a Christian, one is awed and moved by the power and emotion of Christian art. The

[7]Grigori Aleksandrovitch Potemkin (1739–1791) was field marshall and favorite lover of Queen Catherine the Great of Russia. When a delegation of peasants complained of conditions to the Queen, she ordered Potemkin to arrange a trip for her up one of the nearby rivers so she could inspect conditions for herself. Potemkin ordered all houses along the river route to be repaired and painted (some historians claim the huts and homes were nothing but fake façades), and he arranged for happy peasants, dressed in their best Sunday finery, to show up to greet Her Majesty and entertain her with song, dance, and contentment. Impressed with the gaiety, finery, and well-being she saw along the banks, and incensed at having been so cruelly deceived by the peasant delegation, she had its members beheaded on her return. A scant 150 years later, the peasants behind the Potemkin façade rallied to the Russian Revolution and it was the turn of Russian royalty to stand before the execution squad.
[8]The statue of Aphrodite, known as Venus de Milo, which does have character as well as grace, is not a classic Greek statue but a piece of Hellenistic sculpture by an unknown second-century B.C. sculptor in the Island of Melos.

Cathedral of Chartres contains more beauty and humanity than all the temples of ancient Greece. Wherever one looks there is surprise and delight for eye and mind, because Christian artists substituted spiritual strength for Greek surface beauty. In the hands of Christian artists, stone, gold, and paint sprang into manifold expressions of life, whereas Greek artists produced one statue, one temple, one architecture, over and over again.[9]

Emperor Cyrus described the Greek market as a "place set apart for people to go and cheat each other under oath." As we read the literature of the Greeks, we find that most of their ideas are disguises for greed. The Greek concept of woman is well summed up in a much quoted aphorism of that age—"Courtesans for pleasure, concubines for daily needs, and wives for loyal housekeepers." The classical Greek man did not shudder in the face of violent death—he enjoyed it. Assassination and murder are as common in his history as adultery and pederasty. But he added elegance to bestiality; he did it with aplomb and grace.

The four pillars of ancient Greece—Sparta, Corinth, Thebes, and Athens—present a dismal picture of fact over fiction. All four cities were founded on slavery, exploitation, and questionable ethics which provided the

[9]It is regrettable that overzealous rabbis, who saw their duty and overdid it, interpreted the Second Commandment to include not merely a ban on making images of God but a ban on all pictorial art. It took several centuries for this narrow interpretation to take hold on the Jews. Archaeological finds have disproven the contention of the Orthodox that this interpretation has been accepted by the Jews ever since the days of Moses. For several centuries before and after Jesus, the Jews circumvented the rabbinic interpretations of the place of art in Jewish life, carrying their paintings, mosaics, and objets d'art not only into their homes but even into their synagogues and cemeteries. But after the destruction of the Temple, with the Diaspora, art as a medium of expression of the Jewish soul died. It was not resurrected until the nineteenth century A.D., when avant-garde intellectual Jews, rebelling against the tyranny of the Talmud, defied the rabbinic ban on art, and with Modigliani, Chagall, and Epstein in the vanguard led the Jews into the world of aesthetics where, after a 2,000-year absence, they began making noteworthy contributions to the world in this field.

wealth to adorn with colorful art the sordid framework of corruption. They were not the citadels of democracy and justice generally pictured in textbooks. Democracy was for the favored few; the vast majority of the people were helots or slaves, without rights. Sparta came close to being the very totalitarian slave state envisioned by Plato's *Republic*. Corinth was vulgar, famous for its export of commercialized vice, especially child-whores and pleasure boys. Thebes was a city of quislings, enriching itself by collaborating with the Persians at the expense of fellow Greeks. Athens was a businessman's paradise where *caveat emptor*—the philosophy of "Let the buyer beware"—was elevated into statesmanship.

Alexander the Great, perceiving the superiority of the science of the Near East over that of Greece, sent camel load after camel load of Babylonian, Assyrian, and Egyptian astronomical, mathematical, and other scientific material to Greece. But whereas Alexander's successors in Greece ushered in the decline of Greece, his successors in the Near East ushered in a new age of learning. Within a few decades after Alexander's death, the world's educational centers shifted from the mainland of Greece (Athens, Corinth, Sparta) to the Hellenistic centers outside the Greek mainland (Alexandria, Antioch, Rhodes). Hellas faded out and Hellenism took over. Whereas the men who sparked the classic age of Greek literature and philosophy—Sophocles, Euripides, Aeschylus, Socrates, Plato, Aristotle—were all born before 300 B.C. in Greece itself, the men who sparked the classic age of "Greek" science—Euclid, Archimedes, Aristarchus, Eratosthenes, Apollonius, Hipparchus—all flourished after 300 B.C. and outside Greece.

Though we have derogated some aspects of the Grecian civilization, we should not ignore the real greatness of the classical Greek achievement. The Greeks were a bold, imaginative people, not intimidated by taboos. With the mathematics and geometry they borrowed from the Semites, and with the logic they formulated, they transformed the knowledge of the Near East into science. They were the first people on earth to show that reason could help man understand nature. Where the Greeks went

wrong was that they relied on pure reason with few facts
to guide them. Nevertheless, though they were consistently
wrong in their conclusions, they were consistently right
in their generalizations. Though Anaxagoras, for instance,
categorically stated the sun was an incandescent stone
the size of Greece, he established the fact that the sun
was not a god and that eclipses were due to natural causes
and not the work of evil spirits. The Greeks had struck
a light that illuminated a new path for man to follow in
subsequent centuries. This is the enduring legacy of the
ancient Greeks to the world.

It was this transformation of knowledge by the Aryan
Greeks into science that caused the intellectual centers to
shift from East to West. For 5,000 years, from 5500 to
500 B.C., Semitic thinking had dominated the civilized
world, innovating its ideas, setting its standards, shaping
its destiny. Now the age of the Semites declined, and a
2,500-year era of Aryan thought, from 500 B.C. to the
present, began.

Such, then, is the miniature but formidable Greek laboratory in which the Jews encountered the prototypes of the
problems that will challenge them so vexingly in the second
act. This laboratory prepared them for ethnic and cultural
survival in the holocaust following the barbarian invasions
that were to sweep the Greeks and the Romans out of
history.

THE SYNOPTIC VIEW

As the curtain rises on our last scene in the first act, a
stage setting of Greek statues, temples, and gymnasia, re-
flecting the change in time, dazzles our eyes. Instead of
the clang of cymbals and tambourines, we hear the twang
of lyre and harp. Suddenly the stage fills with people—
Jews, Persians, Greeks, Parthians, Romans. The action,
which begins with a rattling of swords, will soon dissolve
into an embrace of cultures and culminate in an orgy of
destruction.

Contrary to general opinion, Alexander's conquest of the

THE INDESTRUCTIBLE JEWS

Near East did not mark the introduction of the Jews to the Greeks but heralded a marriage of convenience after a long engagement. Persian Jews and colonizing Greeks had been in business contact with each other ever since the sixth century B.C., when the Persians first unified all the nationals who lived in their expanding empire.

When the Persian military streak of luck ended in the late fifth century B.C. with the ill-fated plan to absorb Greece, it did not affect the status of the already conquered Aeolian, Ionian, and Dorian Greeks who inhabited the coastline of Asia Minor. Though the Persian Emperor Darius lost the battle of Marathon (490 B.C.), and Xerxes I saw his fleet sunk at Salamis (480 B.C.), the Greeks did not follow up their victories with an invasion of Persia. Greeks in Anatolia thus remained under Persian rule until liberated by Alexander the Great two centuries later. It was these expatriate and colonizing Greeks in the vast Persian Empire who first conveyed Greek ideas to Jewish Diaspora outposts.

We know little of Jewish life in Jerusalem in the two centuries between Cyrus and Alexander. But when Alexander and his Hellenizing shock troops arrived in the third century B.C., a vital schism split the Jews into two religious-political factions, one of Hellenizers and another of anti-Hellenizers. In a sense, the Hellenizers represented the "reform Jews" of their day. They accepted much in the Greek way of life without fear of losing their Jewishness, just as Reform Jews in America today accept much in the American way of life without feeling that they are compromising their Judaism. The anti-Hellenizers represented "orthodox Jews," who believed in keeping things much as they had been in "the old days."

After the death of Alexander, Judah was drawn into world politics. Alexander's empire had lasted a shorter time than all others but one, that of the "Nazi empire" of our time, which lasted but twelve years. Within eighteen years of his death, after an interim rule of a grotesque team—an infant (his posthumously born son) and an idiot (his half-brother)—Alexander's vast domain was ripped apart by three of his former generals. Antigonus grabbed Greece.

Seleucus founded the Seleucid Empire out of Asia Minor.
Ptolemy transformed Egypt into the Ptolemaic Empire.

Judah was first drawn into the Ptolemaic orbit for a century, then (in 198 B.C.) passed into the hands of the
Seleucids. Both gave the Jews full religious freedom and
great internal autonomy. But both gave political power to
the Hellenizers who, by introducing an ever greater number
of Greek ideas into Jewish society, succeeded in hardening
the opposition of the anti-Hellenizers into an implacable
hatred. It smoldered and finally erupted into the Revolt
of the Maccabees, or the Hasmonean War (166–143 B.C.).

Painful though it is, we must challenge the pious belief
that the Maccabees were liberal, tolerant Jews who led a
popular uprising against oppressive, intolerant Seleucid
Greeks. History does not support this romantic view.
Antiochus Epiphanes, the Seleucid king who warred against
the Maccabees, was one of the most enlightened and
tolerant kings of his age. But he has been so entrenched
in Jewish history as a villain that few Jews view the war
for what it was, not a revolt against tyrannical Greeks but
a religious war between Hellenizing and anti-Hellenizing
Jews, between "reform" and "orthodox" Jews, much as
the seventeenth-century Thirty Years' War was a showdown
between Catholic and Protestant Christians.

When Antiochus gave political power to the Hellenizers,
the anti-Hellenizers waited for a day of revenge. That
chance came in a most unexpected way. There was a
rumor that Antiochus had been slain in Egypt. The anti-
Hellenizing "orthodox" Jews began a systematic slaughter
of the Hellenizing "reform" Jews. As ruthlessly as French
Catholics murdered Huguenots in their beds on St. Bartholomew's Day, so anti-Hellenizers threw Hellenizer
officials off the hundred-foot Temple wall; as mercilessly
as the British slaughtered the Irish during the Ulster Massacre, so the "orthodox" Jews slew the "reform" Jews
throughout Jerusalem. Their task of purification accomplished, the anti-Hellenizers boldly declared their independence and took over the rule of the country (166 B.C.).

Alas, the rumor was false. Antiochus, full of righteous
indignation, marched against Jerusalem and slaughtered the
first 10,000 Jews encountered. This senseless revenge, and

the reprisals and counter-reprisals that followed, united the Hellenizers and anti-Hellenizers against a common enemy. The antireligious edicts which Antiochus promulgated to curb the rebellion were not the cause of the rebellion but its consequence. The ensuing fight between Jews and Greeks became the first religious war in history.

After an incredible twenty-five-year struggle against a foe a hundred times its size, tiny Judea achieved the impossible. The Jews won, and the Maccabees established the non-Davidic Hasmonean Dynasty on the throne of Judah. Independence, however, brought not peace but religious-political strife between two new parties called Pharisees and Sadducees. The Maccabean revolt, which had begun in a blaze of religious glory, was destined to drown in a cesspool of political ignominy.

After eighty years of rule under the Hasmoneans—mostly a succession of petty tyrants, vengeful fanatics, and sybaritic playboys—Jewish history inexorably collided with the expanding Roman Empire. In 63 B.C., the Kingdom of Judah succumbed to Rome, not so much through Roman perfidy and might as by internal Hasmonean treachery and strife. It is against this Greco-Roman background that the seventh scene of our drama unfolds in a trilogy of life, death, and transfiguration.

We have seen how a conglomeration of Persian, Greek, and Roman swords breached the walls of Jerusalem. But how did the Hellenistic pantheon of Greek ideas breach the walls of Judaism? Hellenism successfully assaulted the Jews with three simultaneous waves of ideas—a frontal attack by education, a flanking movement by ecumenism, and a fifth-column penetration of philosophy. Defeat of the Jews on all three fronts constituted a magnificent victory for Judaism. Though they lost every battle, the Jews won the war, and in the process added three essential tools to their Diaspora survival kit—universal education, ecumenical coexistence, and rational philosophy.

In every Greek city founded by Alexander, the central features were the gymnasia, temple, stadium, theater, agora (marketplace), and public building compound. Of these, the gymnasia, the schools in which the Greek way of life was disseminated much as the Catholic way of life is disseminated in parochial schools today, made the greatest impact on the Jews. In these gymnasia were taught the Greek equivalents of the three R's, writing, gymnastics, and music, courses subsequently enriched for the brighter kids with drawing and painting.

Mingling in school led to mingling in the business world, in the social whirl, and in lovers' lanes. But even more, embracing the Greeks also led to the embracing of Greek ideas. Jewish youth trotted from Ezra to Plato, from orthodox Judaism to devout paganism, on a road paved with sophistry.

The Greek gymnasia had an Achilles heel, however. They were for the rich and the free, not for paupers and helots. Jewish leaders, alarmed at the inroads of the gymnasia, trumped the threat with an innovation of their own—a Jewish public school system for everybody.

This system of universal, compulsory education, the first in the world, was the idea of one Simeon ben Shetah, the brother of Queen Salome Alexandra (78–69 B.C.). One of the few enlightened Hasmonean rulers, Queen Salome Alexandra had the good sense to appoint her brother not only head of the Sanhedrin but also to a post equivalent today to a superintendent of education. Ben Shetah decreed that there had to be at least one school in every town and hamlet with compulsory education for all, paid for by those who could afford to, but free to orphans and children of the poor. Realizing also that schools are only as good as their teaching staffs, he established in Jerusalem the world's first teachers' college. Within a century, the Romans adopted and augmented these two ideas.

Though the Jews in the subsequent twenty centuries have not always been able to provide universal education because of the intervention of war, hate, and chaos, they have always fostered this idea. If their educational institutions were smashed by outside political events, they rebuilt them as soon as new political conditions permitted.

The Jewish public school system had a profound effect on the future direction of Jewish destiny. It stopped Jewish youth from straying into paganism. Before they were graduated into the Hellenized world to make a living, they were already imbued with Jewish ideology.

The second inroad of Hellenism, the flanking movement of Grecian ecumenism in the form of an open society, undermined the social structure of the entire Near East. With the Alexandrian conquest, the Oriental parochial man discovered he had become a universal man, a citizen with rights and privileges that extended beyond the frontiers of his village and province, beyond his dreams. New loyalties replaced formed values. The Alexandrian Empire was a society in which race, color, creed, and geographic discrimination disappeared. Conquered peoples became members of a Hellenized brotherhood. They liked their new liberties and enlarged vistas. They adjusted themselves so thoroughly to this new ecumenism that they became assimilated and vanished as ethnic components when the Greco-Roman world fell.

The Jews likewise were profoundly affected by this spirit of Greek ecumenism. But how could they respond to the challenge of a Greek open society without becoming absorbed by it? Though they did not give their daughters to sacred prostitution, or encourage their sons to accept homosexuality as the noblest form of love, Hellenizing Jews did not protest too strongly when their children accepted the invitation to participate in the Greek social whirl. In the past, after the Ezra-Nehemiah reforms, the Jewish response to an opportunity to join the "enemy" in business and matrimony had been twofold—either total withdrawal from the threatening situation, resulting in the isolation of the Jews, or cutting offending members out of the community, resulting in the loss of Jews through intermarriage. The Hellenized Jews, on the other hand, wanted to eat their cake and have it too. And they did.

In the free society of the Greeks, the Hellenized Jews created a free society of their own, a world of coexistence rather than withdrawal or curettage. The result was something new, a Hellenic Jew who differed from the biblical Jew as much as the modern, American, suburban Jew differs from the eighteenth-century East European ghetto Jew.

In the days before Greek ecumenism, whenever Jews intermarried they disappeared among the pagans. Now it was no longer exclusively so. Instead of depleting Jewish ranks,

intermarriage increased their numbers, for rather than losing a son to the "enemy camp" via the bedroom, they
more often gained a daughter-in-law via conversion to
Judaism. Whereas during the Babylonian captivity the
Jews had numbered no more than 750,000, six centuries
later, the Jews in the Roman Empire numbered around
seven million. Not more than three or four million of this
total were Jews by birth. The rest had entered Judaism
through marriage or proselytization.

The Greek frontal attack via education changed the
pattern of Jewish intellectual life, and the flanking envelop-
ment of Greek ecumenism rearranged the pattern of Jewish
social life, but the fifth-column penetration of Greek
philosophy and assault of tolerance traumatized the old
pattern of the Jewish mind. Though the older generation
still wore the blinders of untrammeled faith to block out
the reality of the world around it, the younger generation
began asking why. Jewish faith had to justify its existence
to this younger generation with reason. Jewish leaders realized that their limited arsenal of secular works could not
withstand the massive intellectual works of the Greeks.
Though they inveighed against the Greeks publicly, as a
matter of practical politics, they began studying Greek
philosophy and science privately, as a matter of practical
survival. Enriched with Platonic thought, Aristotelian logic,
and Euclidean science, a new breed of Jewish scholars
approached the problems of contemporary life with new
intellectual tools.

Vast changes were taking place on the world political
front. Again a new conqueror was on the march—Rome—
and one by one the Alexandrian conquests fell prey to its
legions. Greece was reduced to a Roman province in 146
B.C. The Hasmonean Kingdom, established by the Maccabees in 143 B.C., succumbed to the Romans in 63 B.C.
The Seleucid Empire was annexed in 64 B.C., and in 30 B.C.
Ptolemaic Egypt came under the rule of Imperator Caesar
Octavianus, better known as Augustus the Great, founder
of the Roman Empire.

The Jews did not feel like strangers in the Roman
world. Having acquired education, a sense of world belonging, and a taste for science, the Jews felt they could

compete with both Greeks and Romans in the market-place of ideas. Proud of their heritage, they now looked at themselves as equal to if not better than their Greek intellectual mentors and Roman conquerors. They began rubbing cultural elbows with pagan bohemians, intellectuals, and aristocrats in the capitals of the Greco-Roman world.

With the influx of so much new blood and so many new ideas, Jewish life in the Greco-Roman world at the turn of the first century A.D. became as rich and diverse as Jewish life in Europe at the turn of the twentieth century. Just as the Jews in pre-Hitler Europe ranged all the way from black-caftaned religious fanatics and ear-locked ghetto dwellers to world-renowned bankers and Nobel Prize winners, so the Jews in the Greco-Roman world ranged all the way from poverty-stricken Judaic Baptists and celibate Essenes to aristocratic Sadducees and worldly Pharisees. The Jewish world at the time of Christ ran the gamut from rags to riches, from fanaticism to apostasy, from celibacy to promiscuity. Ordinary sins and transgressions did not vanish from Jewish life before, during, or after the times of Jesus. Jewish girls, like pagan and Christian maidens, drifted from the country to the cities to find a market for their favors, parents had trouble with their children, and rabbis were kept busy granting divorces. Like Paris, London, and New York today, Jerusalem and the Diaspora capitals had Jewish counterparts of Emma Bovary, Constance Chatterly, and Kitty Foyle caught between *lex* and sex.

The Jewish way of life, if one overlooked the peculiarities of some eating habits and the persistent rite of circumcision, made a great impression on the people in the Greco-Roman world. Judaism had become respectable. More and more pagans viewed the moral, invisible God of the Jews as superior to the immoral, visible gods of the Greeks. Many educated pagans liked the nonsexualized symbols of Judaism and respected the dignity of the Jewish God. They envied the devotion of the Jewish people for spiritual, family, and scholastic ideals.

The most important single reason for the great impact Jewish life and thought had on the Greco-Roman mind was a book called the *Septuagint*, a translation of the Old Testament into Greek, which gave the pagan world a new view of ethics, morals, and piety. The *Septuagint* confronted Greek reason with faith. Intellectual Greeks realized that they gave only bemused lip-service to their retinue of beautiful but borrowed gods, fashioned out of Cretan and Canaanite prototypes and given Greek names. Many Greeks believed no more in the mythical birth of Pallas Athene than many Christians today believe in the virgin birth of Jesus. As the Greeks lost faith in their gods, they became cynics and skeptics, questioning everything, attempting to find out through reason the values their gods did not inspire by faith. All too clearly they perceived that whereas God commanded the Jews, the Greeks commanded their gods. As the Greeks beheld the insensitivity of their society to human suffering, the adulation of beauty at the expense of spirituality, the barbarousness of infanticide in the name of aesthetics,[10] reason, to many of them, proved to be an illusory castle.

But though drawn to Judaism by its lofty humanism, the Greco-Roman man could not accept on faith the tenets of faith. He asked the Jews for proof of their assertions of a moral, invisible God, something his heart would be able to accept through the logic of his mind. It was inevitable that someone would arrive to fulfill that demand.

The man history selected for the role of mediator between Jewish faith and Greek reason was Philo of Alexandria, a millionaire Jewish businessman turned philosopher. His system of philosophy was destined to dominate Mohammedan and Christian religious and philosophic thought for seventeen centuries.

Jewish history ought to thank the Christians for rescuing Philo from oblivion. Because Philo's philosophy went counter to Pharisee Judaism, he was not only ignored but expunged from all contemporary Jewish records, and we know of him only through non-Jewish sources.

Philo was a contemporary of Jesus, who, like many other contemporaries of Jesus, apparently never heard of him.

---

[10]The Roman historian Tacitus contemptuously wrote of the Jews, "It is a crime among them to kill any newborn infant."

Philo was also a full-blown product of the Diaspora, born about 20 B.C. into the wealthiest Jewish family of his times, in the flourishing Jewish community of Alexandria. He was educated in the best schools, and fluent in Greek and Latin, though his knowledge of Hebrew is debatable. Until his death in 40 A.D., he was the embodiment of the Hellenized, cultured, emancipated Jew. A fun-loving cosmopolitan who enjoyed the Roman circus and the Greek drama, Philo was also entranced by the Greek philosophers, especially Plato. Yet he found no conflict in being both a world citizen and a Jew, believing that one was not a deterrent to the other. Convinced that Jewish Scripture was as divine as Platonic philosophy was perfect, Philo so brilliantly innovated the world's first synthesis of faith with reason that he anticipated and answered subsequent attacks on faith by such rationalists of the Modern Age as Spinoza, Hume, Locke, and others.

Philo was history's first "scholastic," that is, a marriage broker between religion and philosophy. He held that philosophy was but the handmaiden of religion, that it merely confirmed by reason what Scripture had already stated through revelation. In essence, Philo held that though God created the world from eternal preexistent matter, He did not directly influence the world or man, but did so indirectly, through *logos*—the divine "word" through which God communicates with man. Because the human soul is derived from God, Philo held that man can attain the concept of God in one of two ways—by the spirit of prophecy or through mystic meditation. Philo used allegory to explain Jewish theology, not so much to the Jews in the Diaspora as to impress the pagans of the world.

Philo's philosophy carried the Jews to a crossroads en route to their manifest destiny. One road led to Damascus and Christianity; the other led to Jabneh and the Diaspora. The leaders who took the Jews out of Judaism into Christianity used Philo's road to God via logos and mysticism; the leaders who took the Jews into the new Judaism of a universal Diaspora used Philo's road via revealed Scripture and prophecy. The Christians made the flesh of Jesus the logos whereby God gave man salvation; the Jews made the Torah the word whereby God communicated to man.

These two concepts of Philonic logos—as "Flesh" and as "Word"—are destined to clash in one of the greatest religious confrontations the world has ever beheld.

The first act of our predestination drama is drawing to a swift and chilling end. Roman oppression becomes progressively worse. The Jews clamor for a messiah to deliver them out of their misery, and lo, a Jew named Jesus appears, whose Jewish followers, to be known in history as Christians, proclaim him the messiah. The Christians then boldly declare that with the arrival of Jesus the Jewish mission is over, and that they will take over the task of leading mankind to salvation.

It seems as if the Christians might be right. In 66 A.D. the Jews stage one of their greatest uprisings against the Roman Empire. After a heroic, four-year stand, Jerusalem falls, the Temple is gutted, and the Jews are strewn to the four corners of the world. With this expulsion into a universal Diaspora, the way has been cleared for our second act, the antithesis heralding the interaction between Jewish and world history. The kablistic "vessel" has been broken, and the Jews have become the world's "exiled lights." Against this backdrop of a burning Jerusalem, the curtain ominously falls on the first act of our kabalistic drama.

ACT II

THE EXISTENTIALIST DILEMMA

Jews, God, and Divine Pragmatism

(TIME SPAN: FROM JESUS TO BEN-GURION)

FROM JESUS TO BEN-GURION

World History	*Jewish History*
	First Challenge: The Roman World
	100 B.C.–200 A.D.
100 B.C. to 200 A.D.	Roman republic overthrown and Octavianus Augustus becomes emperor of Rome. First century A.D. dominated by reigns of Augustus, Nero, Vespasian, and Titus; the second century by Trajan, Hadrian, and the Antonines. Persecution of Christians in full bloom. Parthians contain Roman expansion to the east.	First century B.C. opens with Hasmoneans as rulers of Judea and ends with the Romans as its conquerors. Hillel gives Mishna its scientific foundation. Jesus crucified. Jews revolt against Rome and are crushed. Sadducee Judaism dies in embers of gutted Jerusalem. Ben Zakkai founds his academy for Diaspora Judaism and Gamaliel becomes the St. Paul of the new doctrine. Revolt of Bar Kochba and beginning of flight of Jews to

Parthia. Judah Hanasi codifies the Mishna.

Second Challenge: The Parthian-Sassanid World

200–600

200 to 400	Reign of Semitic and "barrack room" emperors. Persians, reappearing as Sassanians, defeat the Parthians and establish Sassanid Empire. Constantine the Great ascends throne of Rome and converts to Christianity. Emperor Julian "repaganizes" the empire, dies in Sassania, and Rome is "re-Christianized." Barbarians start crossing Rome's frontiers.	Jewish destiny shifts from Rome to Parthia. Sassanid conquerors recognize the Parthian-instituted Exilarchate as an instrument for Jewish self-government in exile. Jewish scholars in Parthia-Sassania, known as Amoras, found School of Gemara. Age of Arrika and Samuel.
400 to 600	Rome divided into Eastern and Western empires. Huns ride into Europe, driving an assortment of barbaric hordes into Rome's backyard. Visigoths sack Rome, Attila is bought off from sacking Rome, Vandals resack her, and Christians claim the body. Western	Internal strife in Sassania disrupts Jewish life. The Gemara is closed, and Ashi begins work of compiling the Mishna and Gemara into the *Talmud*. Mar Jose completes the work at end of fifth century. Saboras become the caretakers of the *Talmud*.

half of Empire
disintegrates.
Chlodovetch (Clovis)
founds Frankish
Kingdom; converts
the Franks to
Christianity.
Visigothic and
Ostrogothic
kingdoms take root
in Spain and Italy.
Mohammed is born.

*Third Challenge: The
Islamic World*

a: Islam East:
   700–1000

| 600 to 800 | Arabs carve themselves an empire from the Indian Ocean to the Atlantic in one century; invade Spain in 711, cross the Pyrenees into France, but are stopped at Battle of Tours. Abbasid Caliphate rules "Islam East" and Umayyad Emirate holds sway in "Islam West" (Spain). Charlemagne crowned emperor in 800. | Conquering Arabs recognize Exilarchate as an instrument for Jewish self-government in exile. Saboras transformed into Gaons and become heads of the two leading academies. Gaons expand Talmudic influence with *Responsa*, making the Talmud the "common law" for Diaspora Jews residing on three continents. |
| 800 to 1000 | Charlemagne yanks Europe into civilization, but she | Karaism, greatest "heresy" in Judaism since Christianity, splits |

slips back into darkness upon his death. Capetian dynasty founded in France and Saxon in Germany. Vikings assault France and England, and penetrate deep into Russia. Papacy suffocating in morass of lechery and venality. Feudalism settles over Europe as the continent sinks to its cultural nadir and Islam rises to its intellectual zenith.

Jewish ranks. Saadia and Hai last of the great Gaons. Break-up of "Islam East" squeezes its Jews via North Africa into "Islam West" and feudal Europe.

b: Islam West: 1000–1300

1000 to 1200

Gregory VII, the "Jewish pope," humbles King Henry IV at Canossa in strife over Investiture. Schism between Western and Eastern Christianities. Western civilization introduced to England by William the Conqueror. First Crusades launched and first impact of Arab culture felt. Frederick Barbarossa founds Holy Roman Empire. Russia emerges into historical focus.

Fleeing Jews from "Islam East" spark an intellectual Golden Age in Spain, the best name-dropping period in Jewish history since the Prophets. Alfasi codifies the Talmud. Maimonides writes *The Second Torah*. Judah Halevi expresses the "Jewish soul" in romantic poetry.

*Fourth Challenge: The
Feudal World*

1000–1500

1200 to 1400	Christian reconquest of Spain gains momentum. British lords wrest a bill of privileges, the Magna Carta, from King John. Mongols conquer Russia; head west toward Islamic lands. Last Crusades peter out in ignominy. First Renaissance century begins in 1320 in Italy. Mamelukes stop Mongol drive west, but Ottoman Turks ride into Europe. The Black Plague sweeps the continent.	*Before 1000:* Jews in Europe survive barbaric invasions; become "fourth estate" in feudal system—the business and professional hierarchy. Ranks of European Jews augmented by Arabic Jews fleeing "Islam East." *After 1000:* Gershom ben Judah convokes Council of Mainz to formulate survival laws for Jews in feudal Europe. Rashi "Europeanizes" the Babylonian Talmud. Jews expelled from England. Jacob ben Asher publishes his *Four Rows.* The Black Plague, religious heresies, and economic dissension tear fabric of European society and shatter Jewish communal life. "Maharils" take over function of Talmudists and stultify Jewish intellectual life. Jews expelled from France.
1400 to 1600	Second Renaissance century. Turks capture Constantinople; write end to Byzantine Empire. Sixteenth century sets stage for the Reformation. Revolt of the Netherlands against Spain. Defeat of Spanish Armada. St. Bartholomew's Day Massacre in France. America discovered. Ivan the Great ends	

Tartar control over
Russia. England
expelled from
continent by France,
turns to colonialism
as a road to power.
The Elizabethan Age.

*Fifth Challenge: The
Ghetto World*

1500–1800

Christian conquest of
Spain spells doom of
Jewish Golden Age.
Inquisition established
in Spain by
Torquemada; Jews
expelled in 1492. Jews
of Europe funneled into
ghettos. Joseph Caro
codifies the Talmud into
a "Sephardic" *Prepared
Table* of laws for ghetto
Jews, and Jacob Isserles
throws an "Ashkenazi"
Tablecloth over it.
Jewish intellectual life
atrophies. Three
heresies—
Sabbateanism,
Frankism, and
Hasidism—rack Jewish
ranks.

1600 to 1800	Romanov czars come to power in Russia. Thirty Years' War erupts. Cromwell rules England. The Era of Enlightened	Age of enlightened despotism permits small segments of Jews to escape from ghettos as court Jews, salon Jews, and protected Jews.

Despotism: Louis XIII, XIV, and XV in France; Frederick the Great in Prussia; Empress Maria Theresa in Austria; Peter and Catherine the Great in Russia. Poland partitioned thrice. French *philosophes* sow seeds of rationalist revolt but beget the French Revolution. Napoleon enters history with a "whiff of grapeshot."

Moses Mendelssohn, the Luther of Jewish emancipation, forges a non-Talmudic Judaism for emancipated Jews.

Sixth Challenge: The Modern World

1800 to the Present Day

1800 to 1900	Europe surrenders to Napoleon, but Waterloo spells the end to his success saga. Congress of Vienna tries to reestablish pre-Napoleonic Europe but fails as revolutions reshape Europe's political and ideological frontiers. Greece declares her independence, Belgium frees herself from the Dutch, the Austrians send their reactionaries packing,	Walls of Europe's ghettos crumble in wake of Napoleon's victorious armies. Jews spill out into the nineteenth century to become statesmen, generals, and avant-garde intellectuals within one generation. Emancipation in West, generaled by Zunz, Frankel, and Geiger, identified with Western Enlightenment. Emancipation path in East illuminated by *Haskala,* an instrument of liberation forged

the French overthrow their monarchy, Italy is unified, and Bismarck forges a new Germany. Russia taken to the brink of disaster by three Romanov czars. Franco-Prussian War. Marx's *Communist Manifesto,* Gobineau's *The Inequality of Races,* and Houston Stewart Chamberlain's "scientific anti-Semitism" lay the foundations for twentieth-century totalitarianism.

by Jewish humanists. Anti-Semites, not rationalists, greet the nineteenth century's emancipated Jews. Hess, Pinsker, and Herzl lay foundations for modern Zionism. First Zionist World Congress convoked.

1900 to present

The twentieth century opens to sound of Boer and Russo-Japanese Wars, overtures to World War I. Europe becomes prisoner of dictators as Russia goes communist, Italy, Germany, and Spain fascist. Czechoslovakia betrayed by England and France. Nazi-Soviet invasion of Poland triggers World War II. United States launches the Atomic Age. United

Four Jewish leaders— Ussishkin, Weizmann, Jabotinsky, and Ben-Gurion lay foundations for a future Jewish state. Balfour Declaration unfurled. Seven million Christians and five million Jews murdered by Nazis. Jews march out of concentration camps to found Jewish state. United Nations votes for independent Jewish state. Arabs defeated thrice in attempts to overthrow Israel. Russia enters

Nations formed. Russia launches the Space Age. The Age of Anxiety settles over the world. conflict, threatening to undermine Western balance of powers.

RISE AND FALL OF THE TALMUD

200 B.C.–1800 A.D.

Challenge	Time	Response
First Challenge The Expanding Society of The Greco-Roman World	200 B.C.–200 A.D.	The Tannas and the Mishna
Second Challenge The Interim Society of the Parthian-Sassanid World	200–500	The Amoras and the Gemara

Fusion of Mishna and Gemara into Talmud

Challenge	Time	Response
Interregnum End of the Ancient World and Beginning of New World Order	500–700	The Saboras and the Talmud
Third Challenge The Open Society of the Islamic World	700–1000	The Gaons and the Talmud
Fourth Challenge The Closed Society of the Feudal World	1000–1350	The Poskim and the Talmud

Interregnum End of the Feudal Order and Beginning of Modern World	1350–1550	The "Maharils" and the Talmud
Fifth Challenge The Regression of the Ghetto Age	1550–1800	The Pilpulist and the Talmud
Sixth Challenge The Sick Society of the Scientific Age	1800–2000	Fall of the Tal- mud

PROGRAM NOTE

The Road to Mishna

Has everything in the first act actually taken place according to some divine plan, or have the Jews been the victims of a collective delusion? Do they have a blueprint showing them how to convert their accidental Babylonian exile to ethnic death into a deliberate Diaspora for ideological survival? If so, have they been properly prepared for their great but lonely odyssey in a world Diaspora? Is this "exile," or "Diaspora," a curse or a blessing? Have the Jews been doomed to extinction, or have they been exiled to freedom?

If there is a Jewish manifest destiny in which Act I was the training program for survival in exile, then Act II must transpire in an ever-expanding Diaspora where the Jews will be strewn among the dominant civilizations of the world to help achieve their mission. We saw their first-act training program provide them with the will to survive as Jews; we shall see the second-act Diaspora provide them with a setting for their indestructibility. We saw the first act proceed like an ancient Greek predestination drama, with God as the author; we shall see the second act proceed like a modern French existentialist drama, with the Jew himself as the author.

Jean-Paul Sartre, the French existentialist, conceives of each human being as eventually becoming the prisoner of the choices he is forced to make throughout life. Each time we make a choice, says Sartre, it shapes, limits, and

114

influences the number and direction of our future choices, until finally we checkmate ourselves into an inescapable cubicle of thought and action. We condemn ourselves to live in a world hewn by the pattern of our past choices.

The exiled Jews, standing in the lobby of history in the fateful first century A.D., waiting for the second-act curtain, are faced with just such an existentialist choice. They must either accept or reject the notion that they have a manifest destiny, a Covenant, to fulfill. They must either deny the meaning of their past or reaffirm it.

On the one hand, the Diaspora Jews can say that this talk of a predestination drama is a lot of nonsense. What has happened is only an interesting constellation of accidental, impersonal events, which some people have distorted out of all proportions to reality. We were defeated in war, they could say, we lost our land, we were exiled, and now it is our turn to disappear, just as under similar circumstances the Sumerians, the Hittites, the Babylonians, the Assyrians, the Persians—yes, even the Jews in the Kingdom of Israel—disappeared.

On the other hand, they can say that their ancestors could not have been pursuing a mere illusion for 2,000 years. They could say that if we are God's Chosen People as our forefathers affirmed, if we have been placed in an exile to accomplish a divine mission as our Prophets predicted, and since we did receive the Torah, then we must survive to fulfill our Covenant with God.

There is one more argument in favor of not rejecting the past but reaffirming it. Even if one were to assume that the idea of a special Jewish mission has been an illusion, have not the Jews nevertheless achieved enduring values in the pursuit of that "illusion"? Have they not given the world the concept of monotheism, an outline for a democratic governance of man, a prophetic view of justice?

What other people, what other nation, what other civilization could boast of such a string of accomplishments? The Jews had seen the hanging gardens of Babylon tumble, beheld the palaces of the Assyrians crumble, witnessed the pyramids of the Egyptians vanish in the sand. The mighty Greeks had been harnessed to the chariot of Rome, great empires had been tossed into the junkyard of past history, and pagan gods had been abandoned one by one. But the God of the Jews, the Prophets of the Jews, the ideas of the Jews had prevailed. Why exchange a winning team for a losing one?

The Jews have to make their existentialist choice. History tells us they chose not to deny their past but to reaffirm it. The Jewish Rubicon has now been crossed, the Jews became the prisoners of that choice. Whereas in the past, unconscious impulses may have motivated Jewish destiny, it is no longer so. In the second act it is conscious, deliberate, pragmatic actions that shape Jewish history. Not God but the Jew himself is at the helm of his destiny. Not God but the Jew himself writes his survival script.

Before we examine the nature of our second-act survival script, let us first ask why God did not continue to write it. Had He abandoned His Chosen People and handed the scepter of chosenness to the Christians, as that new sect claimed? Or was there another explanation for this seeming divine oversight?

Perhaps it was not God who had abandoned the Jews but the Jews who, unwittingly, had shut God out of their scheme of things. It was an unforeseen consequence of a necessary course of action. With the final canonization of the Old Testament, the Jews had stated in effect that God had said all there was to say. Thus, by closing Scripture, they had made further revelation impossible.

This decision to close Scripture had not been arbitrary but had been forced on them by the Christians. The Christian claim that their Gospels were divine postscripts that ought to be made part of the Jewish Testament alarmed the Jews. Other future sects might also give rise to messiahs whose followers might press for the inclusion of their gospels as supplementary chapters to the Holy Book. Closing the Torah to all further additions seemed to be the best solution against polluting it with false doctrine. Thus, by the end of the first act, the canonization of the Jewish Testament had become final and irrevocable.

This decision by the Jews to close Scripture placed the Christians in a quandary at first. But then they hit on a neat Jewish solution. They themselves went into the "revealed text" business, claiming that Jewish Holy Scripture was the "Old Testament" and that theirs was the "New Testament." But within a few centuries after the death of Jesus, the Christians themselves were confronted with the same problem the Jews had faced. Plagued with a rash of heretic Christian sects, which claimed that their new teachers of righteousness were messiahs with supplementary gospels, the Church gradually canonized its "New Testament" (completed by around 500) as the best solution against its being polluted with false doctrine. On pain of death, the Church banned all other gospels about Jesus then current except those it had chosen for canonization. Jesus, the Church claimed, had said all there was to say in its authorized works.

Having thus locked out further revelation from God, the Jews had maneuvered themselves into a corner.[1] How could God now communicate new ideas to His Chosen People? How could He write their second-act script if Scripture was no longer open for new ideas?

The Jews had three choices. They could unlock the Old Testament. They could abandon the idea of a manifest destiny. Or they could write the script themselves. They chose the third alternative.

But would a script written by man have the same validity as one written by God? Jewish leaders would not entertain, still less admit, the possibility of such a blasphemous idea as man writing a divine script. Yet, there was a path through the theological cul-de-sac. When the Torah was revealed to man, had it not become subject to human error? Once the Torah had been given to man, had not authority for interpreting it passed from heaven to earth? Surely, if God had destined the Jews to carry out His will, He had intended solutions to all problems to be contained in His already published guideline—the Torah. All they had

---

[1]This closing of the Jewish and Christian Testaments did not deter future prophets with divine messages, like Mohammed, the founder of Islam, and Joseph Smith, the founder of Mormonism, who found ways to write their own "gospels"—at the behest of God, of course. Mohammed asserted that he dictated the Koran at the command of God with the help of the archangel Gabriel. Joseph Smith claimed that he translated the Book of Mormon from Old Egyptic with the aid of the angel Moroni.

118　　　THE INDESTRUCTIBLE JEWS

to do was search the Torah for the right answers, and a way of writing a "divine script" with the implied consent of God would be found.

"Search the Torah and search it again, for everything is in it," says an old Jewish adage. The task of searching for God's intent in the already revealed text was taken over by a body of self-appointed Diaspora designers. To give their utterances the stamp of authenticity, they retroactively traced their authority as scriptwriters back to Moses, in much the same manner as the Gospel writers gave Jesus the stamp of authenticity as the messiah by tracing his ancestry back to King David.

The first Diaspora designers were "rabbis," that is "teachers of Judaism," who, after the destruction of the Temple in Jerusalem, broke the power of the priesthood and took over the task of interpreting Judaism for the people. They designed a new Jewish "science of divine jurisprudence," which became known as the "Oral Law," as distinct from the Torah, or the "Written Law."

In searching the Torah for new meanings, the rabbis, of course, insisted that they were merely affirming old truths. There is nothing new in this, for in trying to sell new ideas, leaders usually emphasize the affinity of the new with the old.

The new Oral Law did not spring from the brains of the Jewish Diaspora designers complete with footnotes. We have seen how in Jewish history the response persists in appearing prior to the challenge itself. "Before God sends a new illness to the Jews, He has already provided the cure," goes a Jewish saying. Just as the Torah constitution preceded the Jewish state, just as the Prophets preceded the exile to Babylon, just as Ezra and Nehemiah preceded the Diaspora, so the new Oral Law came as a response long before the first Diaspora challenge actually confronted the Jews. As a matter of fact, the concept of Oral Law was over 300 years old when the Diaspora designers seized it and shaped it as a tool useful for their own ends.

The seeds of Oral Law were sown in the fifth century B.C., in the early days of Persian domination, by two men, who had they lived to hear it, would have declared it blasphemous. They were none other than our Persian-Jewish zealots, Ezra and Nehemiah. In their zeal to preserve Mosaic Judaism as they saw it—and of course they saw it the same way God would see it—Ezra and Nehemiah decreed that the five canonized Books of Moses should be read aloud in every synagogue at special intervals every week. They also decreed that interpreters should be on hand to explain difficult Hebrew passages, because the man in the street no longer spoke Hebrew but Aramaic. Before the sixth century B.C., Aramaic was the language of the cultured and the aristocrats in the Semitic world in the same way that French was the language of the European courts during the Baroque Age. After the sixth century B.C., however, after the Babylonian exile, Aramaic became the lingua franca, the common speech of the plebeians, in the same way that English today has become a world language.

The task of explaining the Hebrew text of the Torah to the Aramaic-speaking Jews of Judah was entrusted to a group of men called *Sofers*,[2] literally "bookmen," but better known as "scribes," because the Gospels refer to them by that name. But, instead of dutifully inquiring the meaning of an obscure Hebrew word, practical-minded listeners rudely asked how obscure laws could be reconciled with current needs.

Determined not to show their ignorance or do themselves out of a job, the scribes transformed themselves from Torah explainers to Torah interpreters. They began to improvise answers. In the process they developed as a by-product a new "semantic science" that became known as *Midrash,* or "exposition." They contended that the Torah contained all the answers, and that it was only a matter of searching Scripture for the correct ones. The exposition used by these scribes in the early Midrash was naïve allegory and simple homiletics. Fortunately, as the audience

---

[2] The singular for a "scribe" in Hebrew is *sofer,* and the plural is *sofrim.* However, in order not to cause confusion with foreign plural endings, we shall take the liberty of anglicizing the plurals of most foreign words, be they Hebrew, Yiddish, Arabic, Latin, or Greek.

did not surpass the scribes in intellect, their banalities
passed for profundity.

The tranquil, nonintellectual life under Persian rule
came to an end in the third century B.C. with the Greek
conquest. A new generation of Jews, educated in the ways
of the skeptical Greeks, no longer accepted unquestioningly
the naïve biblical exegesis of the scribes, much as college-
educated Christian youths today no longer accept the naïve
Christology that was taught by the Church during the
Middle Ages. The educated Jewish youth wanted better
proof before accepting the Torah as a way of life.

Our unsophisticated scribes were unequal to the task, and
a new set of scholars known as *Tannas* (from the Aramaic
word "to repeat," hence "repeaters") took over. Instead of
using the allegory and homiletics of the scribes, the Tannas
used the reason and logic of the Greeks. This more refined method of drawing a new interpretation from an old
principle became known as *Mishna,* from the Hebrew word
"to teach."

A modern scholar succinctly states the origins of the
Mishna thus:

> . . . the development of commerce and trade under
> the Hasmonean rulers preemptorily called for the
> building up of a code of civil law. The few rules
> found in Scripture bearing on this branch of the law
> were not sufficient and could not be made so, not
> even by the most subtle reasoning or the cleverest
> interpretation. The time was certainly ripe for legis-
> lation. Every student of the history of jurisprudence
> knows that great as are the possibilities of interpreta-
> tion and commentation, an old code has limits beyond
> which it cannot be stretched. When the breaking point
> is reached, legislation comes to the rescue, abrogating
> obsolete laws and adding new ones which conform to
> the demands of the age. But how dare one tamper with
> sacred Scripture, in which the Divine Will is revealed?
> The sages and scholars of that time . . . had the neces-
> sary temerity. They took a very important step to-
> ward formulating what might be called, *de facto*

though not *de jure,* a new code—they created the *Mishna.*[3]

This new judicial science of Mishna, founded around 200 B.C., was a hit-and-miss proposition, however. It floundered between occasional brilliance and frequent mediocrity. It badly needed a methodology, a scientific approach that would give it a consistent professional touch. In His wondrous way, God provided the right man at the right time. His name was Hillel, the founder of scientific Mishna. With him the Tanna period proper begins.

Legend persists in depicting Hillel (born sometime after 100 B.C.; died sometime after 10 A.D.) as a yokel who drifted from Babylon to Jerusalem in search of a higher education. Having no financial means, he is said to have climbed the roof of an academy to eavesdrop on a class. One day the roof caved in, and Hillel fell into the classroom, thus becoming, presumably, history's first drop-in. Impressed with such a thirst for knowledge, the academy, so the story goes, granted him a scholarship, and in true Horatio Alger tradition he graduated magna cum laude and rose from the rags of a pauper to the silks of a president of the Sanhedrin.

Hillel may have come from Babylon[4] to Jerusalem, and he did become the president of the Sanhedrin, but his was no Horatio Alger story. His parents were rich merchants, and he was forty years old when he came to Jerusalem, where his vast erudition earned him attentive awe. It is more likely that he came to teach rather than to study. Legend attributes to him a knowledge of seventy languages, but seven seems more probable. Thoroughly familiar with Greek literature, thought, and science, he taught his rabbinic pupils to keep up with progress in science if they wished to be the keepers of a viable Judaism.

Hillel's greatest contribution was in laying a scientific foundation for the new Mishna. The demand of the intel-

[3] Louis Ginzberg, *On Jewish Law and Lore.*
[4] Many scholars today believe that Hillel was born in Alexandria and not in Babylonia, which would seem more likely in view of his knowledge of Greek.

lectuals to prove divine assertions by reason had to be met, and Hillel did this with his Seven *Middot,* his "Seven Rules" for properly deriving new concepts from old through the use of logic. His theory was that if a deduction could be shown to stem logically from a divine proposition, then the deduction had to be as divine as the source. In essence Hillel designed the intellectual apparatus for an orderly evolution of divine principles.

Until modern times, it was assumed that Hillel's Seven Rules were based solely on Aristotelian logic. But modern scholars have shown[5] that in reality Hillel's syllogisms went beyond those of his Greek masters, approximating the methods used in modern logic today. For instance, one of his rules, known as *Binyan Abh,* is almost identical to that of John Stuart Mill's "method of agreement." Hillel's *Binyan Abh* was used by rabbis to discover new laws of Scripture in much the same way that Mill's method of agreement was used by scientists eighteen centuries later to discover new laws of nature.

This new scientific method of tampering with the Torah was, of course, not accepted by all Jews with equanimity. The Mishna was rejected in the main by the Sadducees, the party that generally hewed to the pre-exilic Judaism of priest, Temple, and sacrifice. But it was accepted in the main by the Pharisees, the party that generally embraced the post-exilic Judaism of rabbi, synagogue, and prayer.

In Act II, we shall see how future Diaspora designers seized this living, pragmatic Mishna and turned it into a vehicle for new ideas to serve the Jews in coming centuries. Just as the Diaspora was the accidental but physically essential ingredient in Jewish survival, so we shall see the Oral Law becoming the purposive but spiritually essential ingredient in that survival.

Instead of the "Divine Director" of our first act, it will be rabbinic Diaspora designers, in the second act, who will sit in the director's chair and guide the fate of the Jews on the chessboard of world history. As the knights, bishops, and kings of the opposition converge upon the Jews, these

[5]Notably Louis Jacobs, in his *Studies in Talmudic Logic and Methodology.*

Diaspora designers will play mainly a defensive game, sacrificing a peripheral pawn here and there, but saving the main pieces for the crucial third act.

In order to survive in this second act, the Diaspora Jews will have to respond successfully to six successive challenges of history—namely, the impact of Rome, the rise of the Parthian-Sassanid Empire, the triumph of Islam, the paradox of feudalism, the regression of the ghetto, and the lure of rationalism. We shall see the Oral Law come to the rescue in response to the first five challenges, but fail in response to the sixth. After an 1,800-year rule, we will behold the Oral Law designers toppled from their pinnacle of power by a new breed of non-rabbinic Jewish laymen who will take over the task of Jewish survival in the nineteenth and twentieth centuries.

In this act, it will be the destiny of the Jews to live outside their homeland within the context of other civilizations. Because of this, Jewish history will no longer be a linear history, but a succession of six tangential circles representing the six societies within which it will evolve. During these twenty centuries, Judaism will not be molded by internal forces alone, but by external factors as well. Therefore, to understand this twofold evolution of Judaism, it will be as necessary to outline the external societies in which Jewish history evolves as it will be to clarify the internal structure of Jewish society itself.

Let us now return to our seats and await the beginning of the second act of our kabalistic drama, the 2,000-year span of *shevirat ha'keilim*, the antithesis. It will begin with the destruction of the Temple in the first century and end with the founding of the modern state of Israel two millennia later.

The First Challenge:
The Expanding Society
of the Roman World

"THE GRANDEUR THAT WAS ROME"

Caressed by the Mediterranean, Greece, Italy, and Iberia nourished Europe's first three civilizations, fathered by her respective Minoan, Etruscan, and Carthaginian rapist-lovers. One by one, subsequent Asiatic invaders—Aryans, Slavs, and Mongols—were infected with the germs of civilization spawning in these Semitic seminal cultures. The future Romans, one of the by-products of this social interaction on the Italian peninsula, were destined to have an even greater impact than Greece on the shaping of European history.

Who were these Romans who swaggered across the world for five centuries as if it were their private estate? What was the effect of their civilization on conquered cultures? And what was the nature of their obsessive hold on the diverse peoples who lived in their realm from the Jordan to the Thames?

As the first challenge to the Jews transpires in the cruel and enlightened world of Rome, let us scan the history of this paradoxical empire before we pursue the phenomena of a Jewish people, bereft of a country of their own, creating an invisible government of intellect to replace their former government of politics.

Roman history had as unpromising a start as Greek history. It began around 2000 B.C. with an Asiatic people, whom archaeologists call Villanovians, invading the Italian peninsula from the north and spreading down the "boot"

THE INDESTRUCTIBLE JEWS 125

like a slow fever. Through a series of wars, rapes, and marriages, the native Neolithics were "eliminated" from their land. By 1000 B.C. the descendants of this interaction between conquering Villanovians and vanishing Neolithics had given birth to several distinct tribes, the three most important being the Samnites, Sabines, and Latins—the future Romans.

About 900 B.C., another Asiatic people, known today as Etruscans, arrived via the sea on the western coast of central Italy in the vicinity of Rome. Etruscan origins and language, however, remain as irritatingly unknown today as do the Sumerian. But Roman legends, supported by Greek rumors, depict the Etruscans as descendants of the Hittites who had fled their disintegrating empire in the twelfth century B.C. in the aftermath of the fall of Troy.

Cruel, clever, and sexy, the Etruscans killed off the natives, invented gladiatorial games, drained the marshes, plied the seas with commerce, traversed the heartland of Europe with goods, and founded a religion built on fornication, death, and hellfire. The senior trinity of their gods consisted of a holy father, a virgin mother, and an immaculately begotten daughter. In Etruscan theology, the dead went first to purgatory for judgment, where, if found guilty, their souls were damned to various degrees of torment, the ultimate punishment being eternal hellfire. In the thirteenth century A.D., these concepts seeped into Christianity via the *Divina Commedia* of Dante, who was steeped in Etruscan mythology.

When the Greeks arrived in Italy to plunder, trade, and colonize, in that order, those Etruscans who survived the encounter acquired Greek culture. The Greeks, in return, received an education in sexual mores and table manners. It was not naked servant girls or uninhibited lovemaking in public that shocked the effete Greeks, but the barbaric Etruscan practice of permitting nice girls to sit down as equals with men at dinner.

The Roman Kingdom, founded by Romulus in the eighth century B.C., was conquered by the Etruscans in the sixth. Though their rule was brief, and though they did not invent the Roman civilization to come, the Etruscans did nevertheless influence Roman culture more profoundly than the Sumerians influenced the Babylonian.

The Roman Kingdom, begun with the rape of the Sabines (750 B.C.), ended with the rape of Lucrezia (509 B.C.), a rape that gave instant birth to a Roman republic, where plebeians voted, magistrates ruled, and the consuls held the power because they commanded the lictors who held the axes that chopped off the heads of opponents. These axes, or *faces,* hidden in bundles of straw, became, 2,500 years later, the symbol of Mussolini's fascism.

Before Rome began her march on the road to empire, however, she was almost erased from history in the fourth century B.C. by an amazing people known as Celts, or Gauls. The Gauls are harder to define than the Jews. They were not a race, nor a religion, nor a nationality, but a mixed lot of leftover nomadic tribes who had drifted from Asia to Europe around 1200 B.C. Through centuries of wanderings they had squatted on the continent from the Danube to the Atlantic. Time conferred upon them a common language and diverse customs, but no civilization.

The Gauls were a simple, murderous people who killed not out of ideology but out of necessity. What else could one do with captives? In 390 B.C., about 30,000 Gaul warriors with their womenfolk and cattle crossed the Apennines, leisurely plundering their way down to Rome. In attack, these Gauls, called "blond beasts" by Nietzsche, were a sight to behold. They rode to battle dressed in a mini-uniform of bangles around neck, wrists, and ankles, brandishing long, razor-sharp swords. When there was nothing left to eat, rape, or plunder, the Gauls agreed to leave the surviving Roman defenders upon the payment of one thousand pounds in gold. A millennium later, however, they returned as conquerors and as Christians.

Rome's slow and dreary rise to power was milestoned with unbelievable cruelty. Three Samnite Wars (343–290 B.C.) and three Punic Wars (264–146 B.C.) solidified her rule in Italy and made her master over the western Mediterranean. In the second century B.C., Greece was on Rome's timetable for conquest, and where Persia had failed Rome succeeded. Four Macedonian Wars (215–148

B.C.) and the crushing of the Achaean League (146 B.C.) brought Roman rule over all Macedonia and Greece.

While Roman legions staked out Rome's expanding frontiers, the Roman Republic degenerated into a farce of horror. A rash of social eruptions racked Rome's venal body for the six decades of three Servile Wars (135–71 B.C.). The third and most corrosive of these slave revolts, led by the Thracian gladiator Spartacus, broke out during the reign of the First Triumvirate of Crassus, Pompey, and Caesar. Each met a fitting death. Crassus, the usurer who defeated Spartacus and nailed captives to crosses along the Appian Way, was taken prisoner by the Parthians, who poured molten gold down his throat to quench his thirst for it. Pompey, the conqueror of twenty-two kings, who lost the crucial battle of Pharsala in a showdown with Caesar, was slain by the Egyptians in sight of his wife and son. Caesar, the uncrowned emperor of Rome, slyly referred to by intimates as the "Queen of Bythinia," was murdered by his friends on the steps of the Senate.

The Second Triumvirate of Lepidus, Antony, and Octavian was a sanguine affair in which 128 senators and 2,000 equites, the elite cavalrymen, were murdered to clear a path to power. While Antony courted favor with Cleopatra, Octavian courted favor with Rome. After thirteen years of callous murder and war, after his victory over Antony at the battle of Actium (31 B.C.), Octavian, the handsome hypochondriac and sophisticated lecher, graciously accepted the title of emperor, which he forced the Romans to bestow on him. At the age of thirty-two, Emperor Caesar Octavianus Augustus became the absolute master of the greatest empire the world had known.

Now followed a 500-year rule of caesars, a post so precarious that many who were offered the throne declined it, valuing life more than public service. In the five centuries from Octavianus Augustus to Romulus Augustulus (31 B.C. to 475 A.D.), a total of seventy-three emperors, with an average life expectancy as ruler of seven years, sat on the throne of Rome. Few died in bed. Most were murdered, their bodies dragged on a hook to the river Tiber, the Roman Westminster Abbey.

Until recently, it had been assumed that the first encounter between Jews and Romans took place in 142 B.C., when the Maccabees sent a delegation to Rome to ask for military assistance in their war against the Seleucids. We now know that Jews had settled in Rome in great numbers at least a century before that date. In 1961, workers widening the road to the international airport in Rome unearthed ruins of a synagogue built between 200 and 100 B.C. at Ostia, Rome's ancient seaport. The opulence and size of this synagogue, 1,250 square yards, indicate that it was the largest of all ancient religious buildings thus far unearthed in Europe and Asia, including the Parthenon, and served a big, prosperous, and long-established Jewish community.

The next Jews to arrive in Rome after the Maccabean delegation were not ambassadors but slaves—the ambulatory loot that fell to the Roman victors after the fall of Jerusalem. Eventually these captives were ransomed by fellow Jews and settled in Rome as beggars and peddlers. Within a century their descendants were financiers and bankers, scholars and professional men, as attested by the marble burial monuments that bear inscriptions of men of affluence. At the time of Augustus, Jews constituted 5 percent of Rome's population, and there were at least thirteen synagogues in the city.

Augustus, the first of the caesars, was a popular tyrant whose rule stood astride the confluence of the two fateful centuries that link the birth and death of Jesus. It was Augustus who instituted the rule of the procurators (6 A.D.) in Judea, with its tragic consequences. Nevertheless, the four decades of his reign constituted an age of peace and prosperity. History can unhesitatingly give the answer "Yes" to his question on his deathbed, "Have I played my part in this farce of life creditably?" But the subsequent emperors were mostly a sad and gruesome lot, a succession of tyrants, misers, madmen, lechers, and sadists, the likes of which the world has seldom seen.

Tiberius, the mentally deranged successor of Augustus, was a hypocrite who, under the pretence of righteousness, spread terror throughout the empire from his retreat at Capri. A brooding paranoid, he imposed the most frightful sentences on friend and foe, abolished free elections, and instituted the age of informers. It was he who appointed Pontius Pilate procurator of Judea, a sadistic, brutal soldier whom Christian mythology-makers love to portray as a compassionate humanitarian dedicated to justice and Jesus.

Tiberius' death was engineered by his successor, Caligula, a murderous monstrosity who chained senators to his chariot like bird dogs, abducted the brides of patricians in the middle of their wedding ceremonies, displayed his wife Caesonia naked to his friends, and had public intercourse with his sister Drusilla. Caligula demanded that he be adored like a god. The entire Roman Empire—its philosophers and priests, scientists and artists, plebeians and patricians—bowed supine to his statues. All except the Jews. They refused to comply even at the threat of death. This was the madman whom Philo, on his mission to Rome, had to face to ask that Jews be formally exempted from this worship. Philo's life was saved by Caligula's timely murder by trusted guards, who hacked him to pieces and bashed his daughter's brains against a wall. Thus the way to the throne was paved for Claudius.

To the amazement of the Romans, the driveling imbecile Claudius exempted the Jews from emperor statue-worship and added Britain to the empire. After the murder of his wife Messalina, Claudius married his niece Agrippina, who in turn poisoned him. He was succeeded by Nero, a homicidal maniac in royal purple, an artist who won all contests, including those he did not enter, a casual murderer who started his royal career by poisoning most members of his family, including his mother. A Kafkaesque figure with a squat body and bandy legs, his simpler pleasures consisted of raping vestal virgins, seducing boys, and forcing noble women into whorehouses.

Nero was the first Roman emperor to persecute the Christians, though it is not clear whether he regarded them as a sect of obstreperous Jews or as a nest of foreign subversives. It was during his reign that St. Paul traveled throughout the Roman Empire preaching Christian party doctrine, which most Romans regarded as subversive, just as today many regard the preaching of the communist doctrine as subversive. The beheading of Paul in 64 A.D.

at the command of Nero heralded the beginning of official persecution of Christians. Their deaths, in the words of the Roman historian Tacitus (55–117 A.D.), were "gruesome and farcical. . . . Dressed in wild animals' skins they were torn to pieces by dogs, or crucified, or made into torches to be ignited after dark as substitution for daylight." Thus began almost three centuries of relentless persecution.

Never in history has a people been as detested as the Christians were detested by the Romans. The paradox was that, whereas the worst of the Roman emperors generally tolerated the Christians the most, the best of the Roman emperors generally instituted the worst persecutions against them. Even that "philosophical Calvin Coolidge" of Roman emperors, Marcus Aurelius, viewed the Christians with contempt and persecuted them with a vigor totally variant to his philosophy of tolerance.

The fact was that the Christians got under the skin of the Romans. The Christian Eucharist especially filled them with disgust. To the Romans, this rite smacked of cannibalism, even if a wafer was substituted for the body and wine for the blood of the Christian son-god Jesus. Their preaching of an imminent Judgment Day also made the Christians unpopular with those Romans who wanted to live a little bit longer. Furthermore, Christians were viewed as bad citizens because they refused to bear arms. Death or recantation were the only alternatives given the Christians in a Roman persecution drive. Though there were wholesale recantations, many fanatic Christians welcomed their martyrdom, convinced that a martyr's death insured them redemption, a cheap price to pay for a box seat in heaven.

It was during the reign of Nero that the Jews staged the first of three momentous revolts against Rome. Nero sent Vespasian, his best general, to quell this uprising, which grew into a bitter four-year struggle. Halfway through the war (68 A.D.), Nero died when a slave thrust a dagger through his throat. Within the next twelve months, Rome had four emperors. Galba, the first, was murdered, his head presented to his successor, bowlegged, bald, pederast Otho, who lasted but ninety-five days. After his suicide, Otho was displaced by the glutton Vitellus, who, after ruling for eight months in a stupor of meals and murder, was dragged alive to the Tiber for hydrotherapy and death. In 70 A.D., Vespasian, busy besieging Jerusalem, was acclaimed emperor. Before leaving for Rome to assume the purple, he entrusted the conduct of the Jewish War to his son Titus. Though Vespasian scandalized the Romans by his virtue, he was one of the few Roman emperors to die in bed. He was succeeded by Titus.

The Talmud never mentions the name of Titus without appending the sobriquet "the evil one." Yet, contrary to this Jewish portrait, Titus was a charming, gentle, and generous emperor, on whose brow the crown of anti-Semitism can hardly be pressed. Jerusalem and the Jews fared no better or worse at his hands than did Carthage and the Carthaginians at the hands of Scipio. Titus had a love affair with a Jewish girl, Princess Berenice, sister of King Herod Marcus Julius Agrippa II, but jilted her when he was declared emperor. When Titus died of fever, only the Jews rejoiced; the rest of the Roman world mourned him as the great and benign emperor he was.

Titus was succeeded by his brother Domitian, a cruel, casual murderer, during whose reign Judaism became fashionable among Roman nobles. Especially popular was a Jewish group known as "Fearers of God," who attracted a large, aristocratic Roman membership with their advanced belief that Jewish monotheism could be safely blended with Roman hedonism.[1] To discourage further wholesale conversions to Judaism, Domitian instituted a heavy tax on Jews and even banished his wife for her secret practice of that religion. He was about to ban Jews from Rome when a dagger stab in the groin removed him from office and life.

Domitian's successor, Nerva, a colorless homosexual, left no important reminders of his regime except his choice of Trajan to succeed him. During Trajan's reign the Jews staged their second uprising (112–115), a war that so severely shook the empire that the emperor had to

[1]Orthodox Jews feel this is precisely the state of American Reform Judaism today—an unsafe and unholy blend of Jewish monotheism with American hedonism.

call off his campaign against the Parthians to concentrate on this new threat. The ferocity of the Jewish resistance and the tremendous cost to the Romans in suppressing it damaged for a second time the reputation of the Roman legions as invincible.

Though this Jewish rebellion was finally drowned in blood, restlessness nevertheless smoldered and spread along the empire's eastern frontier to flare up in new flames of revolt among the captive nations. With the ascension of Hadrian, the frontiers of the Empire began contracting for the first time since the days of Julius Caesar. The loss of Mesopotamia and Armenia marked the beginning of Rome's geographic atrophy.

The embers of this second revolt were fanned into a third Jewish War against Rome (132–135), under the leadership of a most astonishing Jewish sinner-saint team —a warrior messiah named Bar Kochba and a rebel rabbi named Akiba.

When Bar Kochba appears in history, he is a giant of a man with a hedonistic lust for life, a self-proclaimed messiah who placed more reliance on the sword than in God. He incurred the wrath of the rabbis by exclaiming, "Lord, you need not help us but don't spoil it for us either." Rabbi Akiba, the most famed and revered scholar of his day, was an illiterate sheepherder until age forty, when a rich man's daughter fell in love with the handsome ignoramus, promising to marry him provided he would acquire an education. Her father disinherited her, and in fairy-tale fashion, she sold her tresses as down payment for tuition at one of the academies after her husband was graduated from elementary school with their son.

It was Akiba who saved Bar Kochba from excommunication by endorsing Bar Kochba's appraisal of himself as a messiah and taking the post as one of his armor-bearers. The endorsement electrified the dispirited Jews, who took to arms in a fever of military revenge and messianic expectations. Jews of every political tint and religious sect joined in the rebellion, except the Christians, who, having a messiah in Jesus, could not fight under the banner of a rival messiah. The Jews viewed this refusal as betrayal, and it caused the final, irrevocable breach between Jews and Christians.

To the horror of the Romans, Bar Kochba's forces defeated their legions and recaptured Jerusalem. Julius Severus, Rome's ablest general, was recalled from Britain to prevent Palestine from disengaging herself from the empire. Severus arrived, some scholars say, at the head of as many as 50,000 legionnaires. A grinding three-year war ensued, in which the Jews showed no quarter and asked for none. Inevitably, Bar Kochba's political revolt against Rome failed as miserably as had that of Jesus' a century earlier. But whereas Jesus' messianic aspiration was successful after his death, Bar Kochba's was not. Killed at his final stand against the Romans at Betar (135 A.D.), his resurrection failed to materialize for lack of sufficient faith. Judah became a Roman province and was officially renamed Palestine.

Hadrian, too, has been depicted by many Jewish historians as an anti-Semite because of his ruthless suppression of this rebellion. Yet Hadrian's anti-Jewish measures were not based on prejudice against the Jewish religion or racial origins but on his conviction that the Jewish fighting spirit could not be broken unless their superstitious idolatry of an invisible God was also broken. Hadrian was a patriot who believed in the Roman melting-pot ideology of integration for everybody—white and black, pagan and Jew—all except Christians, whom he viewed with detestation. Even as Jewish soldiers massacred Roman soldiers in Palestine, Hadrian protected the rights of Jews in every other part of the empire, never restricting their political or civil rights. To the Jews, Hadrian was a mindless tyrant; to Hadrian, the Jews were a troublesome enigma.

The Roman Golden Age, ushered in by Vespasian in 70 A.D., began breaking up after the rule of the Antonines in 193. With the death of Marcus Aurelius (180), two centuries of Roman grandeur were entombed, and the "musical throne" game of murdering emperors began anew. Commodus, the misbegotten son of that great emperor, fancied himself a female Hercules. Dressed as a woman, he bravely clubbed to death chained prisoners or shot arrows at cripples dressed as snakes. He was eventually

134 THE INDESTRUCTIBLE JEWS

strangled by a wrestler hired to throw a match to the emperor. A few hours after his assassination, the dangerous purple was accepted with reluctance by Pertinax. Three months later his head was carried on a spear by the Praetorian Guard. His successor, Didius Julianus, bought the vacant throne for what turned out to be a two-year term that ended with his beheading in a bathroom, an exit that heralded the entry of a Semitic dynasty, the Severan.

The first in this Semitic gallery of Roman emperors was Septimus Severus (193–211), a Phoenician who spoke Latin with a Hamitic accent, had studied literature in Athens, and practiced law in Rome. He governed with cruelty and competence, and "did not allow philosophy to impede his wars or poetry to soften his character." Imprudently, Severus left his empire to his two sons, Caracalla and Geta. Caracalla slew Geta in his mother's arms, then embraced her in his. Alexandrians slyly referred to this son-mother team as Oedipus and Jocasta. Caracalla conferred citizenship on everybody in the Roman Empire except the Christians, whom he viewed as abominations.

In due time Caracalla was murdered by his soldiers, who, after proclaiming Macrinus emperor, slew him so quickly that he never had time to contribute his version of vice to Roman history. His successor Egalabalus, a curious mixture of obscene promiscuity and religious liberalism, tolerated Christianity, and had himself circumcised. Being an ardent devotee of the Baal cult, he schemed to introduce that mode of worship into the temples of Jupiter. Though Rome could tolerate his sadistic vices, it would not countenance his religious flamboyance. Emperor at the age of fourteen, he was slain at eighteen in a latrine and dragged on a hook to the Tiber.

The last of the Semitic emperors, Alexander Severus (222–235), also ascended to the purple at the age of fourteen, and also had a penchant for his mother. Wherever Severus went, his mother was sure to go. He managed to offend the Romans by having the audacity to respect senate members, to forgive opponents, and to see justice prevail without the aid of torture or bribes. His benevolent rule, drastic reforms, and indecent stand against vice understandably exasperated his soldiers who hacked him and his mother to death.

With the death of Alexander Severus, the pace of murdering emperors was stepped up. But, though Rome tenaciously survived her many absurd and vicious rulers, she could not take the continued pressure of the barbarians at her frontiers. For a while it seemed as if Constantine the Great (311–337), the first of the Christian emperors (though baptized only on his deathbed), would be able to nail together the tottering empire. But neither he nor subsequent emperors were successful.

The ascent of Constantine, a small-time boy who made good, marked the end of three centuries of almost unrelenting persecution of Christians. Though Christianity was the religion of but 15 to 20 percent of the population in the empire, Constantine made it the dominant religion. This tolerance, however, failed to survive his death. It took no more than a century for the formerly persecuted Christians to turn persecutors.

Although all Roman emperors from Constantine onward, with one exception, were barbarians, they were also Christian. The one exception was Emperor Julian, "the Apostate," a sobriquet bestowed on him by a worried Church that saw the powers it had so recently gained threatened by a fluke of faith. Julian, brought up as a Christian, found himself drawn to the paganism of his ancestors. He deposed the Christians from power, restored paganism to its former position, and assured the Jews he would permit them to rebuild their Temple. Fortunately for the Christians, Julian marched toward an ill-fated mission. With 68,000 men, he set out for the Sassanid capital, where, in the aftermath of an unsuccessful siege, he was struck by a javelin—some say a Christian one—that pierced his liver (363). As his life ebbed away in the sands of Sassania, his last whispered words were, *Vicisti Galilaee*—You have won, man of Galilee. Thus died the hopes of Jews and the fears of the Christians.

Though Rome barricaded herself behind her shrinking frontiers in the fourth century, her legions could neither hold out against the advancing barbarian hordes nor prevent the intrusion of chaotic economic conditions. Visigoths invaded Italy. Huns rode into Europe. Vandals sacked Rome. Moral decadence spread like cancer, further debilitating the patient, who outwardly still looked healthy. Toward the end of the fifth century, she died defeated. As her soul departed from her battered body, the Christians claimed the corpse.

Many Western historians have exaggerated the importance of Roman history to the extent of making it a fulcrum of world history. Actually, Roman history from Romulus to the Gracchi was as unimportant to world history as Hindu or Chinese history of that same period. Also, because these same historians present the 500-year rise and fall of the Roman Empire as though it were a unique phenomenon, we tend to forget that five centuries is the average life expectancy of a civilization. The names of people, countries, and cultures change, but the fundamental causes for the rise and fall of civilizations are the same. Economic, social, religious, and psychological factors all play major tunes in this recurrent symphony of birth, life, and death of civilizations.

First and last, Rome was an empire where brawn and wealth, not culture and brains, counted. The intellectual poverty of Rome is best demonstrated by the fact that in the half a millennium of her rule she gave birth to but a few second-rate philosophers and stylists, and no great men in mathematics, medicine, science, astronomy, or the humanities. Though the Roman Empire extended from Mesopotamia to Scotland, it produced not even a mediocre Herodotus. In the words of H. G. Wells, "The incuriousness of the Romans was more massive than their architecture."

Yet, though Rome's best thinkers contributed nothing original, though in the arts and sciences the Romans innovated nothing new, they did put an indelible stamp of civilization on the world Rome ruled. After first ravishing Europe, destroying her house, and smashing her furniture, the Romans did rebuild that house, did furnish it with a new decor, and did leave the fetus of a new, future Western civilization in Europe's formerly barren womb. And that in itself was a monumental achievement.

What was the nature of the culture that kept the spirit

of Rome alive in Europe after Rome itself had departed? Historian Will Durant sums up the Roman paradox this way: ". . . the essential accomplishment of Rome . . . was . . . that having won the Mediterranean world, she adopted its culture, gave it order, prosperity and peace for two hundred years, and held back the tide of barbarism for two centuries more, and transmitted the classic heritage to the West before she died."[2]

Here we have the key to Rome's claim to fame. Before Caesar, the Romans were barbarians on the march. With her conquest of the Mediterranean world, Rome entered its universalist phase in the first century B.C. After her contact with Greece, the Romans were metamorphosed from conquering barbarians to a conquering civilization. Rome's legionnaires spread among the people of Europe not only the old germ of venereal disease but also the new germ of culture.

In the final analysis, however, it was Hellenism that carried the Roman Empire from barbarism to civilization. Though we have used the word "Greek" throughout, it was not the indigenous Greek culture of classical *Hellenic* ideals that Rome spread in her advance through Europe, but *Hellenism*, the Semitic-tinted Greek cultural heritage of the Near East. Just as Alexander the Great transported the Hellenic ideal into the Near East and begot Hellenism, so the Roman emperors imported Hellenic thought but exported Hellenistic ideas. While the Romans themselves received a classical Greek education, the people in the western provinces of the Empire received an indoctrination of the Semitically tinted "Greek culture" we know as Hellenism. Rome did not "Aryanize" Europe; she "Semiticized" her.

But how was it possible for Rome to sell "Romanism" so easily to the barbarians of Europe, to people who had their own cults and cultures? Why did Romanism take root so quickly and so solidly in this alien soil?

The answer lies in two qualities of Romanism itself, in the nature of Roman law and in the nature of the

[2]Will Durant, *Caesar and Christ*, p. 670.

Roman people. These two assets outweigh all the senseless cruelties and persistent absurdities of her emperors.

The Jews had freed man's mind from magic by tying him with ethics to a moral God; the Greeks had freed man's mind from magic by tying him with reason to a relative truth. Thus Jewish law became tied to religious truths, and Greek law became tied to philosophical precepts. The Romans went a step beyond the Jews and the Greeks by totally separating their civil law from both religion and philosophy. By freeing their laws from pure divinity and from pure reason they also freed man's mind from dogmatic and logical straitjackets. It was not inherent superiority that facilitated the spreading of Roman law throughout Europe, for it had borrowed heavily from both Semitic and Greek concepts. What made Roman law so widely acceptable was that people could borrow its legal concepts without finding a Roman god or a doctrinaire trap tied to the end of a paragraph. Even the Jews could borrow from Roman law without fear of becoming beholden to its pagan deities.

The second reason for the swift acceptance of Romanism throughout Europe was the nature of the Roman people. Though they were cruel, they were free from prejudice, with the noted exception of their antipathy to Christians. They massacred people or gave them citizenship with equal impartiality, disregarding race, creed, color, or previous conditions of servitude. The Roman formula for tying a conquered nation to its victorious chariot was based on four basic principles—annex the land by the sword, connect it to Rome with roads, bind its people with citizenship, and govern them with secular laws.

Thus Europe was readied for the coming Western civilization through the injection of "Greco-Semitic Hellenism" into its barbaric arteries with Rome's legions as the carrying agents. In the words of the French historian Ernest Renan, "For a philosophic mind . . . there are not more than three histories of real interest in the past humanity, Greek history, the history of Israel, and Roman history. These three histories, combined, constitute what may be called the history of civilization, civilization being the result of the alternate collaboration of Greece, Judea, and Rome."[3]

From Plato, to Alexander the Great, to Caesar—thus the barbarians of Europe were Hellenized. Behind the Roman legions carrying their conquering Eagles marched the Jews carrying their conquering Torah, and behind the Jews marched the Christians carrying their conquering Cross. This trinity of Eagle, Torah, and Cross became the escutcheon of the new Europe, though only the Cross showed.

This then was the world in which the Jews faced their first challenge in the second act. They will enter it not as a cowed and martyred people but as the proud inheritors of a great tradition, firm in their conviction that their culture, their heritage, their mission are superior to the values of the dominant majority in the Roman-made world.

THE TYRANNY OF THE INTELLECTUALS

The expanding society of the Roman world tossed the Jews like flotsam and jetsam from the Jordan to the Atlantic. This first challenge to their survival during the first 200 years of our second act (1–200 A.D.) consisted of three simultaneous events—the destruction of the Temple, the elimination of Jerusalem as a home base for Judaism, and the dispersion of the Jews in the Diaspora. The challenge was met head-on by four intellectual tyrants who successively shaped the successful responses—ben Zakkai, a businessman turned scholar, who formulated the spiritual tools for survival; Gamaliel II, an aristocrat turned evangelist, who sold ben Zakkai's ideas to the Diaspora Jews; Akiba, the rabbi turned warrior, who strengthened them with social legislation; and Judah Hanasi, a prince of the House of David turned president of the Sanhedrin, who codified their achievements into a heritage.

When the curtain rises on the second act, it reveals an ordinary, most forgettable scene. History has a penchant

[3]Ernest Renan, *History of the People of Israel.*

for selecting obscure places in which to start momentous events. It was at Haran, an insignificant junction for the caravan trade, where Abraham had his first encounter with God. It was at Mount Horeb, tucked away in a remote corner of the Sinai wilderness, where God spoke to Moses from the burning bush. It was in Bethlehem, a small, unimportant, sunbaked town south of Jerusalem, where Jesus was born. And it is Jabneh, a drab village-town halfway between Jaffa and Askalan, that became the setting for this first challenge.

As in the opening scene of our first act, the spotlight focuses on one man—an eighty-year-old Jew named Johannan ben Zakkai. His function in Jewish history will be to take Sadducee Judaism, which had been tailored for Jews living in Palestine, and transform it into a Diaspora Judaism tailored for Jews who will be living outside Palestine.

Ben Zakkai's early life survives only in fragile legend. We do not know where or when he was born, but we do know he was buried in Tiberias around 80 A.D. We also know that at the age of forty he gave up a lucrative business career for the life of a scholar. Attending Hillel's academy in Jerusalem, where the early Mishna was being shaped, ben Zakkai became his brightest pupil, his intellectual heir, and the architect of a new Judaism.

When Jerusalem became embroiled with Rome in a life-and-death struggle, ben Zakkai was in his eightieth year. The city was torn between the opposite philosophies of two political parties—that of the War Party, which advocated a military showdown with Rome, and that of the Peace Party, which advocated a diplomatic solution to Judeo-Roman tensions. The War Party won, and a grinding, desperate, doomed, four-year struggle for freedom began (66 A.D.). Slowly, inevitably, with their numerically superior forces and inexhaustible supplies, the Romans gained ground. At last, in 68 A.D., they stood outside the gates of Jerusalem prepared to storm the city, though final victory was denied them for another two years.

Generally, the Sadducees favored the war and the Pharisees opposed it. Ben Zakkai, a Pharisee and Peace Party member, was trapped in besieged Jerusalem. He could foresee the final disaster. He knew what measures the Romans would take to teach the rebellious Jews a lesson. No matter how heroic the last stand of the Jews might be, Jerusalem would be put to the torch, prisoners would be massacred, and a large portion of the population would be sold as slaves and dispersed. Ben Zakkai feared not only the end of the defenders but the end of Judaism itself. If they were isolated too long from the mainspring of the religious centers in Palestine, the dispersed Jews might forsake their heritage in the vast reaches of the Roman Empire. They might be overwhelmed by other cultures. They might be lured into the tents of other religions offering more myth, cult, and fun. Or they might simply cease to believe in the importance of being Jews.

Granting that these dangers would confront the Jews in the coming Roman-made holocaust, what could ben Zakkai, an octogenarian suspected of being a traitor by the War Party zealots, do to avert them? What workable measures could he invent, devise, or enact to preserve the identity of the Jews under these circumstances? And even if he were successful, how could he enforce them without police, without an army, without a political organization? How much could he rely on the charismatic dynamo implanted in the Jews by canonized Scriptures? Would they heed the message inculcated in them by the Prophets? Would the nationalism preached by Ezra disintegrate or hold up in exile? What catalytic agent would be needed to fuse these ephemeral ideologies into a stable Jewish society in a chaotic Gentile world?

Brooding on the possible death and transfiguration of the Jews, ben Zakkai became convinced he was destined to be the savior of Judaism. The Jews would be exiled! Very well, a new framework for survival in the Diaspora must be structured. Jerusalem would be destroyed! Very well, Jerusalem must be transformed into a symbol, a link with the past. The Romans would be sure to destroy the Temple! Very well, the new Judaism must be made independent of Temple cult. The Mishna, the Oral Law, which was not tied to the soil of Palestine as was the Temple, must become the new "Temple" of Judaism; the Tannas, the teachers of the Oral Law, must become its spokesmen.

Ben Zakkai decided he had to plant the seeds of a new Judaism before history should decree him too late. He would open a school for training teachers of his new Judaism in some insignificant place—Jabneh, for instance —so as not to arouse the suspicions of the Romans. Who would suspect anything significant ever coming out of Jabneh? But somehow he had to escape besieged Jerusalem and reach the ear of General Vespasian, commander of the besieging legions.

History tells us that in 68 A.D. Johannan ben Zakkai did manage to escape besieged Jerusalem and reach Vespasian's ear. But whereas Johannan ben Zakkai was to achieve fame and veneration for his act of betrayal—deserting the besieged city and capitulating to the Romans—another Jew, General Flavius Josephus, was to go down in shame and ignominy for a similar act. Josephus, commander of the Jewish forces, convinced that the Jews could not win and that continued resistance would cause useless bloodshed in a lost cause, had capitulated earlier in the war to the Romans and was with Vespasian at the siege. Regrettably, neither history nor legend has left any record of whether the deserter Josephus was present in the tent of General Vespasian when deserter Johannan ben Zakkai appeared before him.

By predicting that Vespasian would soon become emperor (which he did that same year, after the murder of Vitellus), ben Zakkai received permission to found a small academy in Jabneh. What harm could come from an eighty-year-old Jew teaching a few other dying Jews some superstitions about an invisible God? It was the contempt of the sword for the idea.

At Jabneh in 70 A.D., ben Zakkai heard of the fall of Jerusalem, the sacking of the Temple, the looting of its vessels, the carnage and debauchery with which the Romans assuaged their vanity, bruised from having been denied victory for two years by a mere handful of defenders. But the end of Jerusalem did not spell the end of the Jewish resistance, which would continue for another two years until the fall of Masada, the last stronghold of the Jews.

Masada was a gray fortress on a brown rock, rising steeply

1,200 feet toward the sky, and separated from the west shore of the Dead Sea by a mile of desolate desert. Built as a fortress in the first century B.C. by the Maccabees, it was converted into a summer palace by Herod the Great. Reconverted into a fortress by the Romans, it was stormed by the Jews in 66 A.D. and its legionnaire defenders exterminated as a prelude to the war against Rome. To this fortress withdrew a remnant of the Jewish defenders of Jerusalem, a total of 906 men, women, and children, who for two years withstood the siege of a Roman legion. Finally, in 72 A.D., Flavius Silva succeeded in storming Masada and slaughtered the Jewish defenders (though Josephus maintains they committed suicide) just as, six years before, the Jews had slaughtered the Romans. Thus collapsed the last defense of the Jews in the first of their three great uprisings against Rome.

Masada and Jabneh have come to symbolize two antithetical aspects of Jewish history, the former that of resistance, the latter that of surrender. It is not a question, however, of which is the true spirit of Judaism. Both are expedients of history. The spirit of Masada permeated the first act. The Jew was a man of war who took on Caananites, Philistines, Assyrians, Egyptians, Babylonians, Greeks and Romans, scrapping his way through defeats and victories in a struggle for national survival. The spirit of Jabneh will permeate our second act, because it represents the kind of response the new world order will call for. The nations among whom the Jews sojourn in the first five challenges of Act II sought not the total annihilation of the Jews as an ethnic entity, but only their political defeat. There was no need for a do-or-die stand.

The lesson of Masada is as unmistakable as the lesson of Jabneh. At Masada died every Jewish defender and thus, symbolically, every Jew. But at Jabneh, because the new Jewish leaders correctly appraised the spirit of changing times, the Jews survived. In a sense, the zealots who defended Masada looked to the past, to a world that was vanishing; the men of Jabneh looked to the future, to the world that was to be. The secret of Jewish survival is summed up not in military triumphs alone but in Jewish ability to select the right weapon at the right time.

By the sheer force of his personality, by the tyranny of his will, ben Zakkai, within one decade, made Jabneh the center for the new rabbinic Judaism. Just as the philosophy of the nationalist Prophets had been the guide of Ezra, so the philosophy of the universalist Prophets became the guide of ben Zakkai. The cry of the universalist Prophet Hosea, "For I desire mercy and not sacrifice" (6:6), became the sword with which the Pharisee ben Zakkai eviscerated the power of the Sadducee priesthood.

The cult of sacrifice was anchored in the Temple of Jerusalem and entrenched in the hands of the priests who also dominated the Sanhedrin. With the Temple destroyed and Jerusalem sacked, ben Zakkai induced the Sanhedrin to move from Jerusalem to Jabneh, where he maneuvered his election to its presidency. Soon thereafter, the Sanhedrin was abolished and changed into the Great Assembly, the *Bet Din Hagadol*.

Ben Zakkai boldly took over the Mishna as a vehicle for his own ideas as to what Judaism ought to be and appointed the Tannas as his "legal staff." With the same hauteur that John Marshall, Chief Justice of the United States Supreme Court (1801–1835), handed drafts of his opinions to his legal staff with the admonition, "This is the law. You find the precedent," so ben Zakkai handed the Mishna to his staff of Tannas, giving them his ideas of what the law ought to be and charging them to find the precedents. In the same way that St. Paul tossed out Mosaic dietary laws and circumcision in order to sell his Pauline Christology to the pagans, so ben Zakkai tossed out the props of Sadducee Judaism to sell his rabbinic Judaism to the surviving Jews at home and abroad. But whereas Paul introduced the veneration of "God's son" through the worship of the "Flesh," ben Zakkai introduced the veneration of God's Oral Law through the worship of the "Word."

Within a decade, Judaism in Palestine and the Diaspora came to resemble the Judaism of the Babylonian exile, six centuries earlier. "Life can only be understood backward, but it must be lived forward," the Danish nineteenth-century theologian Søren Kierkegaard once observed. This is also true of Jewish history, which in review is much like a movie run first forward then backward. First, we see the Law given to Moses, the priesthood established, the Temple built and destroyed, the Jews exiled and innovating in exile the institutions of rabbi and synagogue to replace priest and Temple. Then the reel is reversed, and we see the Jews return from exile, rebuild the Temple, and re-institute the priesthood. The Temple is again destroyed, the Jews are again exiled, priests, sacrifice, and Temple are again abandoned, and rabbis and synagogues once again are ensconced in their old familiar places.

The transfer of power from priest to rabbi had to be legitimized, however, for the priesthood was an inherited function, whereas the rabbinate was not. The Tannas hit on a brilliant idea. They would ordain rabbis, and to give this ordination the patina of antiquity, they devised a "genealogy" that piously traced "ordination" all the way back to Moses. For proof they cited a passage in the Torah (Numbers 27:18) where God tells Moses to lay his hands upon Joshua as a means of transferring authority to him. According to this interpretation, Joshua in turn passed his "Mosaic ordination" to his successor, and so on, all the way to Ezra, to Hillel, to ben Zakkai, neatly skipping all Sadducees. The Christians, appreciating a good idea when they saw one, deftly applied it to legitimize the papacy, launched in the fourth century. They traced a similar retroactive ordination back to Jesus, who, according to this interpretation, laid his hands on Peter, who in turn laid his hands on his successor, and so on, all the way to the present pope.

Within a decade of the fall of Jerusalem, rabbinic Judaism was firmly entrenched in Jabneh. But in the Diaspora, where the need was greatest, it was almost totally unknown. The task of marketing Judaism in the Diaspora hinterland needed as dedicated a salesman as St. Paul had been in marketing Christianity in the Roman hinterland. The Jews were in luck. They found the right man a little bit ahead of the right time. He was Gamaliel II, a ruthless autocrat who preached humility while enjoying vast inherited wealth.

Gamaliel, as befitted a prince, lived on large estates in grand style, served by a retinue of slaves. After a hard

day's work preaching against Christian infidels and in-
veighing against pagan idolatry, Gamaliel II was wont to
repair to a Greek bathhouse, take a dip in a cool pool, and
view with aesthetic pleasure the naked statues of Aphrodite
that usually adorned such places.

We do not know whether ben Zakkai resigned or whether
he was forced out by Gamaliel, but about 80 A.D. Gamaliel
took over the reins of the academy at Jabneh and the
presidency of the Great Assembly. Whereas ben Zakkai
had been the unofficial spokesman for the Jews, Gamaliel
became their official ruler. Though a firm believer in the
efficacy of God's word, he was a realist who understood
that a little political power helps put a divine message
across. The Romans, realizing that the rule of the procurators had bordered on disaster, were willing to listen to the
question of new Jewish self-rule. Gamaliel proposed the
establishment of a patriarchate of Tannas who would be
willing to "render unto Caesar what was Caesar's," provided
the Jews were permitted to render unto God what was
God's. Quick to sense the advantage, the Romans recognized the new rabbinate as the voice of the Jews and conferred the title of *Nasi*,[4] "Prince" or Patriarch, on the head
of the Sanhedrin. Gamaliel was confirmed as the first
official Patriarch of Palestine.

Gamaliel saw his mission clearly. He had to unify the
Jews in the Diaspora and ruthlessly suppress all dissident
voices. He spoke softly but always carried the club of
excommunication for occasions when persuasion did not
work. Just as St. Paul journeyed through the Roman world,
speaking to the Galatians, Ephesians, Corinthians, Philippians, Thessalonians, so Gamaliel journeyed throughout the
Diaspora, speaking to the Jews huddled in the lands
around the Mediterranean. He took a dour view of the
Christian tenet that the destruction of the Jewish Law was
its fulfillment. When challenged with the Christian doctrine that God had given the leadership to Jesus, Gamaliel
nimbly quoted the Gospel of Matthew (5:17): "Think

---

[4] Actually the term *Nasi* was used by the Jews as early as the
second century B.C., but Gamaliel was the first one so recognized
by the Romans.

not that I am come to destroy the Law and the Prophets; I am not come to destroy but to fulfill." Gamaliel argued, expounded, and taught so effectively that wherever the new rabbinic Judaism was kept strong, Christianity made little inroads among the Jews.

In a sense, Gamaliel was the unwitting midwife in the birth of the Christian church. Noting that Christian preachers were using Diaspora synagogues as hunting grounds for new converts, Gamaliel inserted in the Jewish liturgy a curse on heretics to stop this practice. Upon hearing this excommunication, "Christian Jews" quit their synagogue membership and established their own meeting halls, which through the centuries grew into churches.

Meanwhile, the Mishna was growing up like a pampered child. The Tannas simply constitutionalized the reforms needed by finding a precedent in the Torah through the skillful application of Hillel's Seven Rules. By the second century, the Mishna had begun to dictate to its creators and, like any ideology, to take on a life of its own. It dashed off in a direction that threatened to destroy its function as a vehicle for saving Judaism.

Ben Zakkai, Gamaliel, and their immediate successors, known as the first two generations of Tannas, had been concerned with practical questions. The third-generation Tannas were intellectuals who scorned practical questions and used the Mishna as an intellectual whetstone on which to sharpen their wits. Like the Greeks, applying pure reason to science without regard to facts in order to see what new inferences could be derived, the Tannas now applied pure reason to faith, without regard to need, to see what new intentions of God could thus be discerned. A new pseudo-science, *pilpul*—hairsplitting—was born.

As there was no standard text for the Mishna, the Tannas used any teaching method or order they pleased. Consequently, contradictory opinions, all equally brilliantly deduced, soon led to uncertainty and doubt among the people. Different schools of Mishna began to flourish, fighting each other for supremacy. Each claimed it had arrived at the interpretation Moses had intended; all neglected the chaotic social conditions around them. By the second century, the situation bordered on anarchy.

Akiba, the warrior rabbi and armor-bearer of Bar Kochba, was among those who sensed the danger and did something about it. The devastating war with Rome had forced Judea over the edge of poverty into misery. A large, landless mass of peasants and unemployed workers had been created whom the intellectual elite contemptuously referred to as *am ha'aretz*—people of the earth, and looked down upon as scum. Of the "people of the earth" himself, and reputed to be the descendant of proselytes to Judaism, Akiba held that civil law should be used to rectify these social inequalities and that religious rituals should be of such a nature that the poor as well as the rich could participate. He insisted on the emancipation of women in social but not in sexual spheres, and limited the extent of slavery to protect the rights of free labor. He also tried to ban superstition, but failed ignominiously.

In the field of scholarship, Akiba attempted to stem the drift of the Mishna by adopting a systematized arrangement of subjects. But being a *pilpulist* at heart, he could not restrain the theorists, who began using his new system as a base for further theorizing and hairsplitting.

After the abortive Bar Kochba rebellion against Rome, Akiba was arrested, held prisoner at Caesaria for a while, and then executed on the orders of his friend Tineus Rufus, Roman governor of Syria. According to the traditional but unsupported account, he was flayed alive.

It was not until the intellectual tyranny of one man, Judah Hanasi (135–220), the great-grandson of Hillel, that the rambunctious Tannas were harnessed and the anarchic Mishna finally contained. Judah Hanasi not only saw the danger but overestimated it. He not only effectively codified the Mishna but ended it.

Judah Hanasi was born to rule. He took to the presidency of the Sanhedrin the way royalty takes to the throne. Endowed by God with a sharp mind, and by his family with great wealth, Hanasi consorted with scholars and emperors, and one of the Antonines, presumably Marcus Aurelius, was his personal friend. Hanasi was also an ascetic who, from the citadel of his wealth, piously spun the maxim that "He who accepts the pleasures of this world will be deprived of the pleasures of the world to come."

Hanasi was a great admirer of Roman law, and his idea of codifying the Mishna was greatly influenced by the standard textbook of Roman law, *The Institutes* by Gaius, published in 160.[5] Single-handedly, with the assurance of one born with intellectual arrogance, Judah Hanasi decided what the Law ought to be. Without consulting his colleagues or bothering with a majority vote, he legalized previously invalidated portions of the Mishna if he thought they served a purpose, or threw out huge chunks of previously "certified" Mishna if in his opinion they were neither needed nor valid. Then he began systematizing the Mishna, arranging his code according to subject matter, historical development, and relevance to Scripture.

So meritorious was Hanasi's codification that it rapidly gained total acceptance. All other Mishnas soon disappeared; today, only Hanasi's is extant. Hanasi's colleagues of the Sanhedrin viewed with horror this strewing of what they considered important parts of the Mishna along the path of codification like gear tossed out of a soldier's overstuffed duffel bag. So intimidated were they by Hanasi's deification by the masses, however, by his intellectual arrogance, and by his political power, that they dared not oppose him while he lived. But after his death they salvaged much that he had discarded and appended this to his codified Mishna as "footnotes" known as *Baraitas* and *Toseftas,* which are now part of the Oral Law legacy.

Hanasi not only codified the Mishna, he also "canonized" it almost as effectively as Scripture had been canonized a century previously. The Mishna, declared Hanasi, had said all there was to say, and henceforth no new material or interpretation could be added. Why, we cannot be sure, for neither he nor his contemporaries have left us any account of any possible motives. We do know, however, that many influential Jews, fearing that the Mishna

---

[5]Many scholars today see more than a coincidence in the publishing of the earliest Roman code of law, The Twelve Tablets, in 450 B.C., and Ezra's redrawing of the Mosaic Law into the Ezrian fundamental laws of Judaism shortly thereafter.

might one day rival the Torah as the source of final authority, wanted the growing influence of the Mishna curbed, lest the deduction eventually become more venerated than the source.

There may have been another reason. We know that Judah Hanasi viewed with alarm the growing number of Jews living to the east of the Roman Empire, in Parthia. Hanasi, like many of his predecessors, tried to curtail the influence of the Parthian Jews by refusing to ordain students from that country planning to return to their homeland.

Here, perhaps, may lie the real reason for Hanasi's closing of the Mishna. As yet there were no academies in Parthia, and the Tannas flourished only in Palestine. There was only the Palestinian Mishna, which all Jews, including the Parthian, had to use. However, there was nothing to prevent the Parthian Jews from starting their own academies, developing their own Tannas, and coming up with a new Mishna. If that were to happen, Judaism might become something other than what Judah Hanasi envisioned. By closing the Mishna, perhaps he felt that he could preserve Judaism in the shape he thought it ought to have. If Moses had done it, if Ezra had done it, why not he?

If those indeed were Judah Hanasi's fears, then history proved them justified. As long as he lived, Hanasi was able to enforce his dictates, but after his death his Parthian students abducted his Mishna, bent it to the needs of Parthian Jewry, and came up with a different mold of Judaism. Though Jewish intellectual life in the Roman Empire did not begin to decline until the fourth century, the center of intellectual gravity had already shifted in the third century to the Parthian Empire. Fortunately, Hanasi had not been able to bend history to his will.

For the two centuries of our first challenge, ben Zakkai and his successors succeeded in steering their stateless ship of Judaism through the uncharted waters of the Diaspora and avoiding the reefs ben Zakkai had sighted. To prevent the Jewish religion from breaking into sects, the Jewish liturgy was standardized. To make every Jewish community self-sustaining, it was decreed that any time ten Jewish males over the age of thirteen lived within commuting distance, they had to establish a community. To prevent the Jews from sinking in their own esteem, it was decreed that every Jewish community in the Diaspora was responsible for its own school system and was compelled to provide education for everyone, free to the needy. To prevent Jews from being reduced to beggary, a series of decrees, supported by Mishna interpretations that it was God's will, stipulated that charity had to be given to anyone demanding it. Jews were forbidden to seek help from outsiders, but were encouraged to extend help to all, regardless of race, creed, or color.

These Diaspora "survival laws," coupled with the ethics of the Torah, shaped the Jews into cohesive, proud, self-sustaining communities, where learning was esteemed, indolence abhorred, and charity elevated into a virtue. Though Rome left an indelible stamp on the Jews, the Jews also left an indelible stamp on Rome and through Rome on the world. Through their personal deportment, proselytization, and intermarriage, the Jews imprinted their ethical and moral values on the consciousness of the Roman people. By dignifying the work of freemen above slavery, by exalting the freedom of man above the rights of kings, and by elevating morality above sensuality, they undermined the Roman views of contempt for work, deification of emperor, and veneration of lust. This was no mean contribution when we remember that in the Greco-Roman world homosexuality, adultery, incest, and religious prostitution were popular institutions, and that in such a world the Jew, who considered these rites abominations, appeared as a ridiculous figure.

Perhaps the greatest internal threat to the Jews in this first challenge was the obscure religious sect later known as Christianity, which began as a Jewish heresy and ended as a world religion. In a metahistoric sense, Christianity was to serve Judaism as a steppingstone toward its ultimate goal of a brotherhood of man. The question thus presents itself as to whether Christianity is a parochial or a universalist aspect of the Jewish manifest destiny. We must leave this subject in abeyance, however, until our fourth challenge, when Jews and Christians will be united in a

historically meaningful though mutually abhorrent embrace of love and hate.

Within the terms of a Jewish manifest destiny, the
response of the Jews to this first challenge has succeeded
brilliantly. Riding their cultural surfboards on the crests
of the Babylonian, Persian, and Grecian civilizations, they
survived to emerge in the turbulent waters of the Roman
Empire. They continued their ride through history on the
crest of that civilization for four centuries of victories and
defeats.

But now with the Roman civilization disintegrating, the
Jews again find themselves sucked under by the whirl-
pool of a sinking empire. Can they free themselves from
this death grip, surface into the ocean of future history,
latch onto a new surfboard, and ride the crest of a new
civilization? Will they survive as a people the death of the
Roman Empire to face a second challenge, or are they
doomed to disappear from history along with the Romans
and their satellite nations?

But survive as what, for what? With their response to
the first challenge, have the Jews not forsaken the Judaism
of their forefathers—the Sadducee Judaism of priest,
sacrifice, and Temple, for another, "heretic" Judaism—
the Pharisee Judaism of rabbi, Mishna, and synagogue?
Are they still Jews, and are they still practicing Judaism?
With the insouciance of the victor, the rabbis retorted
that it was the Sadducees who had constituted the heretic
sect, and that they, the Pharisees, were the elect of God.

Whatever the speciousness of the argument, the rabbinate won the day. The central core of a Jewish manifest
destiny had to be preserved, even though the outer protective shell might have to be changed to withstand the
vicissitudes of history. The Jews had a mission to fulfill,
and fulfill it they would, even if they had to help God.
This program called for a dispersal throughout the world
to teach the Gentiles the Jewish concept of a brotherhood
of man. Very well! Whatever forms it might take for the
Jews to survive, to fulfill their vision of destiny, their
vehicle was Judaism. And history was still on the side of
the Jews.

Even while the dispersal of the Jews within the Roman

Empire is still being enacted on one level of our stage, a spotlight now illuminates a second level. Before our eyes we behold the strange world of Mongolian Parthians and Aryan Sassanids, the setting for the second challenge to the Jews.

The Second Challenge:
The Interim Society
of the Parthian-Sassanid World

"SODOM AND GEMARA"

Western historians have paid scant attention to the hybrid Kingdom of Parthia—a conglomerate of Mongolian rulers, Persian subjects, and Hellenistic culture—which flourished during the four centuries between 200 B.C. and 200 A.D. on former Seleucid soil. Jewish historians have paid it the dubious honor of enshrining it in their history under the wrong name, insisting on calling it "Babylonia."

When, around 250 B.C., the spotlight illuminates the stage for our second challenge, we see a nomadic Parthian prince named Arsaces riding with his skilled horsemen from the steppes of Turkestan into Iran. Here he carves himself a slice of real estate from the Seleucid Empire and founds the Parthian Kingdom.

Because the Romans were not able to destroy Parthia's cavalry, they could not decisively defeat the Parthians, who introduced the world's first armored cavalry by developing a super-strong horse that could carry its own protective armor and a completely armored soldier. While steppe barbarians showered it with arrows, the Parthian cavalry stood still; then, after the barrage, it advanced, to the consternation of the enemy. Parthian horsemen were also famed for their ability, while in seeming full retreat, to turn in the saddle and shoot an arrow with unerring accuracy into the heart of a pursuing foe, thus giving rise to the expression "a Parthian shot."

The Parthians, who had no roots in past cultures, left

neither literary nor intellectual shoots in subsequent civilizations. Their society was a patchwork of borrowed ideas—Persian manners, Zoroastrian religion, Seleucid art forms. They were referred to by their contemporaries as "Greek degenerates," because they squatted within the foundations of Hellenism, contributing nothing. On the other hand, they destroyed nothing.

In a curious sort of way, the Jews were right to persist in calling Parthia "Babylonia," for much of that terrain was former Babylonian country. Here Jews had dwelt ever since Nebuchadnezzer had carted their ancestors off into Babylonian captivity in the sixth century B.C. Though a few Jews had returned to Palestine, most had stayed in Babylonia during succeeding centuries, while history tossed that lush land into the successive arms of Persians, Greeks, Seleucids, and Parthians. No matter which conqueror succeeded in possessing Babylonia, the Jews multiplied without effort and prospered without intellect. In the first century A.D., by which time an estimated one to two million Jews lived there, "Babylonian" Jews reentered history, to shape not only their own destiny but that of the entire Jewish world.

We do not know how the Jews were governed in the first 200 years of Parthian rule, but by the middle of the first century A.D. Jewish self-government in Parthia received its start in that improbable fashion we have come to expect in Jewish history. Two brothers, Asineus and Anileus, starting in life as cattle rustlers, wrested a small chunk of land from Parthia and founded a tiny kingdom with themselves as co-rulers. Anileus fell in love with the beautiful wife of a Parthian general whom he sent to death in battle so he could marry his post-biblical "Bathsheeba." As queen, she poisoned her brother-in-law, Asineus, and goaded her husband into expanding his kingdom. As the invincibility of Anileus existed only in his wife's head, he was defeated in battle and slain.

The Parthians decided to forgive and forget, however, for there was no denying that the Jews were numerous, strong, and highly prized soldiers who, because of their hatred of Rome, could be relied upon as excellent allies. Toward the end of the first century A.D., therefore, they granted the Jews self-rule under a Jewish *Resh Galuta,* "Prince of the Exile," a title more commonly known today by its Greek equivalent, *Exilarch.*

Understandably, rabbinic sources on the Exilarchs are scant and untrustworthy. The Exilarch did not conform to that image of a pious, observant Jew so ridiculed by foes, abhorred by the Reformed, and revered by the Orthodox. Recognized by the Parthians as representative of a state within a state, the Exilarch arrogated unto himself royal powers and ruled with hauteur and grandeur. He held administrative powers, appointed judges, was supported by taxes, and lived on vast estates staffed by slaves. People had to bow before him as he passed, and when he attended the Parthian royal court, men of lesser rank had to pay obeisance to him. Like European feudal princes patronizing poor but talented artists, the Exilarchs patronized poor but brilliant scholars. The ultimate in social recognition was a badge allowing a scholar access to the Exilarch's sumptuous table, an honor that the more pious diplomatically declined because it was rumored that the kitchen of the Prince of Exile was not strictly kosher.

In the third century A.D., the Parthians disappeared as swiftly as they had appeared, removed from history in one decisive battle by the unexpected resurrection of the former Persians who, after their annihilation by Alexander the Great, were now restored to history as Sassanids.

According to legend, the Persian comeback began with an Aryan high priest named Sasan, who dreamed of a royal throne instead of a priestly altar. His son Papak realized his father's ambition by assassinating a petty Parthian governor and proclaiming himself king of the province. He was slain by his more ambitious brother, Ardasir, who, after a triumphant victory over the Parthians in 226, converted the Parthian kingdom into the Sassanid Empire.

Lord Acton's aphorism, "Power corrupts and absolute power corrupts absolutely," held as true two millennia ago as it does today. The subsequent rulers, holding the same absolute power as did the Roman emperors, abused it with equal facility but with less relentless sadism and greater humor. Usurpation and assassination, the order of the day in Rome, were rare in the Sassanid realm, where throne and altar were united in an effective alliance of royalty, nobility, priesthood, bourgeoisie, and peasantry.

The average educational curriculum in the Western world includes little about the Sassanid period outside acknowledging its existence. However, a brief review of the lives of a few of its more enlightened, erotic, and cruel emperors will illustrate the personalities, mores, and manners of an empire that sheltered the Jews for four centuries before passing them on to other hosts.

In addition to being known as the "father of his country," Ardasir is remembered in Sassanid history for making Zoroastrianism the state religion and—borrowing a leaf from the Jews—for canonizing its tenets. Legend records that Zoroastrianism was founded in the seventh century B.C. by Zoroaster, a Mede, who, after being torn out of his mother's womb by a monster, survived in the wilderness for thirty years by eating nothing but cheese. Zoroastrianism became the religion of the Persians in the sixth century B.C., when embraced by Cyrus the Great.

In the Zoroastrian view, the universe was held in balance by two opposite but attracting forces, that of the good god Ormuzd and that of the bad god Ahriman. As long as the Magians—the chief priests of Zoroastrianism—were around to stoke the temple fires of Ormuzd, the world was safe. The Magians frightened the masses into submission with threats of eternal hellfire; promises of bypassing purgatory for a direct passage to heaven on good behavior also assured a measure of cooperation.

Ardasir is remembered in Jewish history for recognizing the Exilarchate instituted by the Parthians. His successor, Shapur I (241–272), is remembered by the Jews for continuing that recognition. Shapur ushered in his reign not merely by recognizing the rights of Jews but by granting religious freedom to all, including the despised Christians. His hatred was concentrated on Rome. To show his contempt for the Romans, Shapur, who had captured Emperor Valerian at the battle of Edessa (260), used him first as a footstool, then had him flayed alive, his skin stuffed with dung, and hung in a temple.

After a brief breathing spell under six mediocrities, the

Sassanid Dynasty produced Hormuzd II (302–309), who inspired devotional hatred in the hearts of the nobles by improving the lot of the poor at the expense of the rich and by establishing courts with judges who could not be bribed. To prevent such radical ideas from taking root, the nobles deposed Hormuzd and elected his unborn child future king. They hung a crown over the queen's pudenda so that when Shapur II was born, he entered the world wearing it. Thus it was only natural that his career from womb to tomb should constitute one of the longest reigns (309–379) in the annals of royalty. Though cruel and ruthless in war, history recalls him as "great" because he was constantly victorious. Jews classify him as "benign" because he was their staunch friend.

Shapur's death ushered in a century of anarchy. In 490, a Zoroastrian priest named Mazdak proclaimed himself a messiah. As greed for gold and lust for sex were in Mazdak's views the root of all evil, he held that evil could be eradicated if gold and sex were more justly distributed. His solution went straight to the heart of the matter. Anyone possessing more gold and female partners than his fellow man should share these possessions with his less fortunate brethren.

The Mazdakites gleefully instituted an immediate program of social plunder and religious rape, pillaging the homes of the rich and carrying off the more desirable houris in their harems. One Jewish historian, however, has seen a ray of light in this darkness. "The one redeeming feature about it was that it affected Christians as well as Jews," he said.[1]

Chosru I (531–579), greatest of Sassanid rulers, codified Sassanid law, instituted just taxation, promoted commerce and industry, and set a commendable example for religious tolerance by including Christian, Jewish, and Zoroastrian women in his integrated harem of 3,000 wives and concubines. His grandson, Chosru II (592–628), prepared for the fall of the empire by a series of brilliant victories.

[1]History Notes: From Lectures Delivered by Dr. Jacob Mann, published by the Hebrew Union College, Cincinnati, Ohio, 1934, p. 65.

Chosru declared a holy war against all Christendom, and enlisted 26,000 Jewish volunteers, chafing to avenge the Byzantian slaughter of 10,000 Jews in Palestine. Chosru entered Jerusalem in 614, sacked the city, slaughtered 60,000 Christians, sold another 30,000 into slavery, burned most of the churches, including the Holy Sepulchre, and carried off the True Cross as a trophy. The Church of Nativity alone escaped his wrath, because a mural there portrayed the Three Wise Men costumed as Persians. By 619 Egypt and most of Byzantium were Sassanid provinces.

Hailed by his people as a conquering hero who had avenged their forefathers' defeats at Marathon and Salamis, Chosru retired to his numerous palaces to re-acquaint himself with his neglected stable of houris. But not for long, alas. Byzantium staged a stunning military comeback, and extracted gruesome revenge. Chosru was slain by a son, who, upon being proclaimed king, was forced to surrender to the Byzantines all his father had won, including the True Cross. It was an ill omen. Two decades later the Sassanid Empire was destined to be taken out of history in an ill-fated battle against a new religion on the march for land and converts.

Though the Sassanid emperors ushered in an age of splendor and learning, an age that saw art and architecture at its most sublime, no new thought, no new science, no new philosophy emerged during the 400 years of their rule. Neither the Sassanid language nor culture was Persian. They retained Pahlavi, the language of the conquered Parthians, and adopted the adopted Hellenistic culture of the Parthians. In matters of law, the Sassanids were on a par with the feudal Anglo-Saxons. The accused had to prove his innocence by walking through fire or stepping over glowing coals. But they did introduce courtly man-ners, and they laid the foundations for modern diplomacy by granting immunity to foreign diplomats.

Sassanid women were noted for their exquisite beauty, which encouraged excessive adultery. Like the Jews, how-ever, the Sassanids rebelled at the Greek custom of in-fanticide, punishing it by death. The Jewish view of the Sassanids has been preserved in a pithy aphorism by

Gamaliel III: "They are temperate in eating, modest in the privy, and courtly in their marital relations."

For the common man, the Sassanid Empire ushered in an era of unparalleled prosperity. It developed great industries and established trade routes to China, later taken over by Mohammedans and Christians. The Sassanid rule was also an era of unparalleled prosperity for the Jews. Preponderantly farmers and small landholders under the Parthians, they shifted in ever greater numbers from rural to urban life after the Sassanid takeover. Parents earned so much money that children could keep their own earnings. Whereas in past centuries, the son had to follow the father behind the plow, now, with savings in the "bank," father went into business and the son to "college." Time purchase came into vogue.

Women too enjoyed unheard-of freedoms. They dressed in silks, adorned themselves in jewelry, and anointed their bodies with perfumes to compete with the beautiful Sassanid women whom some Jews not only eyed appreciatively but also married. Though polygamy was not yet forbidden among the Jews, it was beginning to disappear because of the increasingly prohibitive costs of maintaining several wives in a social atmosphere that granted women ever greater rights and privileges.

As always, with freedom and prosperity came new occupations and new problems. There arose the question of wages, interest, profits, rights of labor, and remission of debts. New guidelines were needed to restrain Jewish life from ebbing into the pagan life surrounding it.

The second half of the second century became a turning point in Jewish history, for it is at this juncture that the first challenge begins to merge into the second. Palestine became a corridor for warring Byzantine, Parthian, and stray barbarian armies that ravaged the countryside and depopulated the villages, leaving desolation in their wake. The poor, who had no choice, stayed and got raped, enslaved, or killed. The rich, who had a choice, fled to the major cities of the Roman Empire, where their wealth could buy them comfort. The intellectuals fled to Parthia, where their thoughts could have freedom. Here these emigré Jewish intellectuals sparked the dormant cultural life of the "Babylonian" Jews in the same way that the Jewish intellectuals who fled Hitler's Europe in the twentieth century sparked the dormant Jewish cultural life in the United States.

To stem this drain on its dwindling pool of Palestinian intellectuals, the Patriarchs first tried intimidation by pronouncing that land outside Palestine was ritually unclean. When that failed, they resorted to excommunication. But to no avail. The Jews kept right on emigrating.

By the third century, the Babylonian Jews were so firmly entrenched in the Diaspora that they dared some counter-intimidation. They reversed the pronouncements of the Palestinian Patriarchs, asserting that whosoever emigrated from Babylonia to Palestine would break one of God's positive commandments—for was it not written in Scripture (Jeremiah 27:22): "They shall be carried to Babylon, and there they shall be until the day that I remember them, said the Lord." Even the Palestine Patriarchs felt the sting of this apt quotation and ceased their anathemas. When the Holy One, blessed be He, wants the Jews to stay in the Diaspora, who but an atheist would dare do otherwise?

Just as Judah Hanasi had feared, the intellectuals who fled Palestine for Parthia took the Mishna with them. But it proved of little value. The Jews in Parthia were confronted with an open society that posed problems the closed Palestinian Mishna did not answer.

Two historic factors further widened the gulf between Palestinian and Parthian Jews. First, Parthia represented a different civilization that demanded different social adjustments and economic outlooks. Second, because of Parthia's paranoid hatred of Rome, Parthian Jews dared not associate with Roman Jews for fear of being thought Roman fellow-travelers, much as Jews in communist Russia today dare not associate with Jews in the capitalist world lest they be thought capitalist fellow-travelers. As the Sassanids continued the Parthian policy of hatred for Rome, the Jews in the Parthian Diaspora had to innovate survival ideas independently of the Palestinian Jews still living under Roman rule

The breakthrough, simple as it was brilliant, came within a year of the Sassanid victory over the Parthians (226–

227). It was made by two of Hanasi's former star pupils, two Parthian Jews, Abba Arrika and Mar Samuel, who, after their education in Palestine, returned to "Babylonia" with Hanasi's codified Mishna. As neither could bring himself to defy Hanasi's ban on further Mishna, these intrepid Diaspora designers hit on a unique formula, bearing out Montaigne's epigram that "The more things change, the more they remain the same." They founded a new exegetical system, called it *Gemara* (meaning "completion" or "supplement"), which, under the pretense of clarifying the Mishna, actually amplified it.

This was the supreme irony in Jewish history. Here in former Babylonia, the "Sodom" where their ancestors in captivity had hung their harps and wept (Psalm 137), Arrika and Samuel led Judaism out of the cul-de-sac of a closed Mishna with their trailblazing Gemara. Fate decreed that this Gemara, the first cultural offspring of the Diaspora, would eclipse the intellectual pretensions of its Palestinian sibling, the Mishna.

BIRTH OF THE TALMUD

There is a popular belief that throughout their history persecution has held the Jews together and that therefore an occasional oppression is not so bad because it goes such a long way. There is scant historic evidence for this view. Freedom, not adversity, has been the creative crucible for Judaism. The great ages and ideas of the Jewish people were forged during periods of freedom, not during times of stress.

In our First Act, we saw the lively start of Jewish history under the management of the freedom-loving, patriarchal individualists Abraham, Isaac, and Jacob, and its stagnation during the subsequent 400-year period of captivity in Egypt. Though the Prophets flourished in an era of political upheaval, the Jews were not a persecuted people but respected scrappers. Under the oppressive rule of Assyrian exile, the Jews of the Kingdom of Israel disappeared, but under the tolerant atmosphere of the Babylonian exile the Jews of the Kingdom of Judah survived.

The Mishna, the response to the first challenge, developed within the freedom of the Greco-Roman world. Now we shall witness how the Gemara, the response to the second challenge, was conceived within the permissive womb of the Sassanid Empire, grew to maturity because of three centuries of tolerance, and came to an abrupt end only after winds of intolerance blew away the protective web of liberty.

Whereas the Tannas had regarded the Old Testament as the text and the Mishna as the commentary, Arrika and Samuel made Mishna the text and Gemara the commentary. The interplay between the two is like the counterpoint in a Mozart piano concerto—the Mishna, the orchestra, making the statements, and the Gemara, the piano, commenting upon them. Also, like the piano in the concerto, the Gemara never leads but always dominates. But no matter how performed, the Gemara was a replay of old Mishna tunes.

Because the Gemara used reason in the development of its interpretations, the teachers of the Gemara became known as *Amoras*—that is, "Reasoners." Like the Mishna, the new science of Gemara was taught in academies, especially at the two famed ones founded by Arrika and Samuel.

Abba Arrika (early third century) was a by-product of a technically incestuous marriage between a stepbrother and a stepsister. Born in Parthia, and known as "The Tall" because of his height of six-and-a-half feet, Arrika was one of the suspect foreign intellectuals who had studied at Judah Hanasi's academy in Palestine and been refused ordination by him. Arrika returned to Parthia, where for a while he held two jobs, as a liquor dealer and as a superintendent of markets. In the year 227, the first year of the Sassanid Empire, he founded his academy at Sura, a small town on the River Euphrates, where he attracted an unheard-of enrollment of 1,200 students.

It was here at Sura that Arrika set the framework for the Gemara. His method was to take the text of Hanasi's Mishna, add to it the interpretations of dissenting Tannas, and then subject all opinions to a test of reason. The answers, uncannily, always coincided with prevailing needs. As head of his academy, Arrika elevated Babylonian Jewry from obscurity to fame within twenty years.

Arrika moved in high social circles, including that of royalty. He was the first Oriental to attempt to abolish marriage arrangements made by parents without the consent of the child, and the first individual in history to excommunicate parents who would not send their children to school. Arrika also instituted the world's first free adult study courses, known as *Kallas,* consisting of a series of lectures given by renowned speakers. His death in 247 was mourned by Jews and pagans alike.

Mar Samuel (177–257), co-founder of the Gemara, was, like Arrika, born in Parthia. The son of a wealthy silk merchant, Samuel never thought of becoming an Amora, as he was already both a renowned physician and astronomer when he fell under the spell of Hanasi. Called upon to cure an eye infection of that famed Palestinian scholar, Samuel became entranced with the intellectual aspects of the Mishna, gave up his two professions to become a student in Hanasi's academy, and upon graduation stayed to help the great man edit the Mishna. After Hanasi's death, Samuel returned to Parthia. Here, seeing the social havoc caused by the closed Mishna, he joined forces with Arrika, took over an academy at Nehardea, and began to expand the new Gemara. Though chancellor of the academy, he was consulted as often on questions concerning eye ailments and astronomy as on questions of the Law.

Mar Samuel was not only a man of the Gemara but a man of the world who moved with aplomb in the palaces of nobility. He especially disdained Christian asceticism, declaring that anyone who mortified his flesh was a sinner. Among his notable contributions to the field of human relations was his decree that the courts should be made guardians of orphans, a totally new concept in the social history of man. Being a physician, Mar Samuel's medical views crept into his laws. He banned the widely held notion that an evil eye could cause illness, but fell prey to what his contemporaries regarded as an evil superstition. He rejected the accepted Greek view that illness was caused by an imbalance in bodily humors, holding instead that disease was caused by minuscule particles that entered the human body through air, water, and food. Out of deference to his position, people dared not laugh to his face.

Mar Samuel also formulated two of the most important early "Diaspora Laws." Realizing that the Diaspora was here to stay and that the Jews would be permanent guests in the world at large, he formulated the rule of the "Law of the Land." This law enunciated the then revolutionary principle that all laws of a country in which the Jews resided had to be obeyed as long as such laws did not forbid them to practice their religion or force them to worship idols, practice incest, or commit murder. His second "Diaspora Law" declared that Jews must fight in defense of the country in which they resided, even if it meant fighting against a fellow Jew in another country. So, for instance, when 10,000 Jews were slaughtered by the Sassanids in an uprising at Cappadoccia, Mar Samuel did not mourn their deaths but simply stated, "They met the death of rebels." This "Law of the Land," enunciated in the fourth century by a "Babylonian" Jew, remains the law of Diaspora Jews in the twentieth century and, incidentally, has become accepted by all nations that admit foreign-born nationals to citizenship.

The Amoras also enshrined the Diaspora in the Gemara as part of God's plan to spread Judaism throughout the world by stating "The Holy One, blessed be He, did not exile Israel among the nations save in order that proselytes might join them." (Pesachim 87 B.)[2] Jewish history had entered a new phase. The Diaspora was now openly asserting itself as the function of a divine manifest destiny.

For two centuries the Babylonian Amoras held the intellectual reins of the Diaspora, guiding and directing it with their accommodating Gemara. They knew what was needed and how to go about getting it. But they had the decency to deny this by constantly assuring the Jews that the Gemara was not a departure from former Judaism

---

[2] They also removed any stigma that might attach itself to the Diaspora by stating: "The Holy One . . . showed righteousness unto Israel by scattering them among the nations."

but merely a natural outgrowth of the Torah via the Mishna and in complete harmony with the wishes of Moses. As one scholar so aptly phrased it, "God's wishes invariably coincide with the wishes of Israel."

As history tends to repeat itself, the Gemara, after two centuries of success, began to recapitulate the follies of the Mishna. As the Gemara grew, it began to diverge from its source of authority. Not only could the Gemara grow into an independent discipline, it could develop into a heresy, perhaps even into a new religion. The time had come not only to harness the Gemara by codifying it, as had been done with the Mishna, but to fuse it with the Mishna and thus avert any possibility of either one taking an independent course.

History came to the rescue, in the guise of a minor calamity. The fifth-century Mazdakite socio-sexual revolution that swept so many Jews prematurely into the life hereafter also threatened to obliterate the Oral Law. The incredible fact was that the Oral Law had been preserved, not on parchment, but in the heads of the Amoras. And now these heads were in danger of being severed from their bodies by the scimitars of the revolutionaries.

A first century B.C. ban on preserving the Oral Law in writing was seemingly still in effect in the fifth century A.D. During the reign of the Maccabean Queen Salome Alexandra (76–67 B.C.), the Pharisee rabbinate had issued an interdict forbidding the writing down of Mishna on the theory that it would be difficult to change an interpretation at a later date if it was preserved in writing. The Mishna, decreed the rabbis, had to be committed to memory and taught from memory.

The teacher of the Mishna had not been called a Tanna, a Repeater, for naught. Conforming to the rabbinic injunction not to write down the Mishna, the Tanna first committed the text to memory, then recited it to his class. Thus most Tannas were selected not so much for their intellect as for their capacity to remember. The standard student joke was that "the more stupid the Tanna, the more reliable the Oral text."

Students attending Tanna colleges were taught sections of the Mishna; they in turn taught other students. Thus hundreds of living Mishna editions were produced and distributed to the academies like books in a circulating library. To make certain that a Tanna would not insert his own opinions in a recitation, he had to cite authority for each opinion quoted, a custom that gave rise to the procedure in Western courts of law of citing legal precedents when arguing a case before the bench.

Scholars agree, by and large, that the Mishna was not written down until its codification in the second century A.D. But they disagree as to whether or not Judah Hanasi's codified Mishna and the subsequent Gemara were written down. Each side cites impressive though inconclusive evidence. This schism in opinion developed from different interpretations of what constituted "being written."

The official way to publish a Jewish book in antiquity was to deposit the original, authenticated manuscript in a library, archive, or synagogue, so that its contents could be guarded against deliberate alterations. The unofficial way of publishing was to dictate the text to hundreds of copyists at one time from a nondeposited manuscript. Thus thousands of copies could be procured in a short time, but because they contained inaccuracies they were not regarded as official.

Until the fifth century, neither Mishna nor Gemara had been published officially—that is, an authenticated manuscript had not been deposited in an official archive. The reason was simple. The rabbis did not wish to give either the Mishna or the Gemara the sanctity of a canonized work. In this sense, scholars who maintain that the Mishna was not "written" are quite correct. On the other hand, evidence exists that both Tannas and Amoras kept cribbed notes as unofficial aides to faulty memories. Nor is there any doubt that Hanasi's codified Mishna existed in unofficial manuscripts.

With the Mazdakite revolution, the Jews faced a clear and present danger. The academies, the repositories for cribbed Mishna and Gemara notes, were being burned; the Amoras, the repositories for memorized Mishna and Gemara, were being killed. Thus portions of Mishna and Gemara were in danger of being lost forever. The public's concern for its heritage was running high. Now or never was the time to defy the first century B.C. ban, fuse Mishna and Gemara into one discipline, and publish an official text. It was the right time for history to send the right man to harness the deed to the need.

The task fell on the shoulders of a Babylonian boy wonder named Ashi (352–427), who at the age of nineteen became chancellor of the academy at Sura. Regrettably, history has left us nothing but two meager facts about his early life—that he was a friend of the Sassanid King Yezdegird I and that he was a successful businessman who, after inheriting his family's vast lumber enterprise, enlarged it by selling wood to Zoroastrian fire temples for their sacred fires.

The task undertaken by Ashi was monumental. It called for reconciling the texts of all Gemaras with Hanasi's Mishna. As the work progressed, the combination acquired a new name—*Talmud*—from the Hebrew word "learning."

Actually, it was not Ashi who originated this idea of fusing Mishna and Gemara into a "Talmud." Remarkably enough, this fusion was first conceived out of frustration by Palestinian scholars who, for a century and a half (200–350), had tried unsuccessfully to compete with their Babylonian peers.

At first, Palestinian Tannas tried to ignore the Babylonian Gemara and busied themselves with clarifying and reclarifying their own Mishna. But pressured by the increasing fame of the Babylonian Gemara, they reluctantly transformed themselves into Babylonian-style Amoras and started a Gemara of their own, fifty years late.[3]

Predictably, the Palestinian Gemara differed from the Babylonian in many respects, for the simple reason that the needs of the Jews in the Roman Empire differed from

---

[3] Orthodox Jews maintain that the Babylonian and Palestinian Gemaras originated simultaneously. This they prove by classifying the last generation of Palestinian Tannas (219–279) as the "first generation" of Palestinian Amoras. However, the Funk and Wagnall *Jewish Encyclopedia* lists them as "post-Tannas." Not until we come to the "second generation" (279–320) do we come across the first actual Palestinian Amoras—that is, scholars who developed Gemara as a commentary on the Mishna.

the needs of the Jews in the Sassanid Empire. The Palestinian Gemara, however, turned out to be a rather slipshod job. Lacking the dialectical skill of their Babylonian competitors, the Palestinian Amoras all too often resorted to mere assertions instead of logical developments of arguments.

In spite of the diverging needs of the Roman and Sassanid Diasporas, the more brilliant Babylonian Gemara gained continuous ground in the Palestinian sphere of influence. To prevent their Gemara from slipping from its pinnacle of mediocrity, the Palestinian scholars (around 350) began to peg it to Hanasi's brilliant Mishna, hoping to give their retarded brainchild a patina of scholarship. This task, taking about five decades, was completed in 395, and thus the Palestinian Talmud was born a century ahead of the Babylonian. But by the end of the fifth century, when Jewish life for all practical purposes came to an end in Palestine, the Palestinian Talmud also came to the end of its stunted growth and limited influence.

Ashi, perceiving the inadvertent greatness of the Palestinian idea, unabashedly adopted its method of fusion to his own ends. He set to work developing the Babylonian Talmud with such ingenuity and scholarship that the word "Talmud" became associated with his name.

Like a modern professor, Ashi used his students to carry the load of preliminary research projects. For thirty years he labored, often in the face of bitter opposition by orthodox Jews, who still felt, in spite of the urgency, that an official text of the Oral Law was against God's wishes. Death claimed him before his task was completed. Today, orthodox Jews venerate his Talmud as passionately as Jews once denounced it.

After half a century of neglect, Ashi's unfinished work was revived by a mother-oriented Talmudist named Rabina II, whose father, a famed scholar, had died while Rabina was a child. His mother orally transmitted to him his father's opinions, and with this learning as background, according to hoary tradition, Rabina undertook to bring order into the Talmud out of the chaos left by Ashi's death. He succeeded so well that the Talmud was published for the first time as one standard text during his lifetime.

Though there was no formal ratification, and though no copy was deposited as an official text, this Ashi-Rabina Talmud nevertheless gained quick acceptance. It was to have monumental consequences as it grew into a majestic network of law, ethics, and religion that would shape Jewish history until the nineteenth century, when the cult of science would finally overthrow the cult of the Talmud.

An enigmatic figure called Mar Jose now makes his entry. Though we know little of Mar Jose beyond his name, it is he who, in the year 500, according to tradition, declared the Talmud closed and "canonized" in the same offhand manner Judah Hanasi had "canonized" the Mishna. On the other hand, there is also evidence that this is a pious fiction created to gloss over the fact that the Talmud was not officially closed until the tenth century and therefore could have been tampered with for another five centuries.

The Babylonian Talmud was completed in the nick of time, for the sixth and seventh centuries presented the Jews an excellent chance for extinction. Not only was the Roman world collapsing, but the Sassanid Empire was also experiencing its first seizure of disintegration. No sooner had the Mazdakite rebellion been suppressed than the formerly tolerant Zoroastrian religion turned intolerant. Fanatic Magians were on the march, fanning flames of bigotry into conflagrations. Invading barbarians marched along with the Magians. Victory and defeat in new wars seesawed back and forth between Sassania and Byzantium. Each looted, maimed, and killed for its own reasons. All trampled paths of desolation across the troubled land.

True, the Talmud was by then preserved on parchment, though the danger of its being lost was still present. But in whose hands could it be entrusted? The three-century reign of the Amoras was over; with the unofficial closing of the Talmud, they had done themselves out of a job. The adaptable Amoras, however, saw a new function for themselves in these uncertain times. No longer "makers of the Talmud," they would become "keepers of the Talmud." This transformation is supposed to have been masterminded by Mar Jose, who changed himself over-night from the last Amora to the first *Sabora*, or "opinion-maker" (from the Hebrew word *sebara,* "opinion"). Even as he "closed" the Talmud one day, he began to deliver opinions about it the next, opening new vistas for the coming era of Saboras.

Though the Sabora operated behind the scenes of Jewish history, he played a far greater role in the final shaping of the Talmud than has hitherto been accorded him by Jewish theologians, who have done their best to shroud the 200-year Saboraic period in darkness. There is little doubt today that the Saboras were more than mere caretakers. They did indeed tamper with the Talmud, as editors, as exegetes, and as stylists.

As editors of the Talmud, the Saboras gave it a unanimity it had not previously had. There were many loose ends in the Ashi-Rabina Talmud. Many Gemara decisions were not tied to the Mishna; others did not enjoy the proper reasoning to justify the conclusions. Because they were not authorized to change the text, the Saboras practiced their editing covertly. To achieve the desired opinion, they attributed their own conclusions to a departed Amora, feeling that this deception was justified on the ground that even if the attribution was not authentic it was more apt. Many of these Saboraic interpolations can be detected by peculiarities of sentence structure.

As exegetes, the Saboras also undertook to excise portions dealing with the vanished Temple and priesthood cults. As they dared not omit any of the Mishna because it was too well-known, they restricted themselves to excising only those portions of the Gemara that dealt with these subjects. It was the final blow to the lingering remnant of the Sadducees and their hopes of ever restoring Temple and priesthood.

Fame as literary stylists did not catch up with the Saboras until the twentieth century, when their work was at last recognized. When handed to the Saboras in the sixth century, the Talmud was a rambling, verbatim report of discussions that had taken place in the Babylonian yeshivas. The Saboras took this raw material and shaped it into a literary product. They skillfully reorganized the discussions into dramatic presentations, closely examining each proposition according to merit and then neatly arranging each argument according to cogency, from the lesser to the larger element, to achieve a climax. Every unnecessary word was omitted. Point followed point in logical order. Like detective-story writers, the Saboras were careful not to reveal too much in the beginning in order to heighten the effect of the denouement.

In a sense, the Saboras were the forerunners of today's school of mathematical philosophers. Their Talmudic syllogisms follow a mathematically predictable pattern so exact and precise that each step can be punched out on a magnetic tape and processed by an electronic computer.[4]

For three centuries, adventurous Amoras expanded the Mishna with their trailblazing Gemara, and for two centuries, timid Saboras with a penchant for anonymity unobtrusively shaped the Talmud to the needs of the hour with their editorial, exegetical, and literary skills.

While Amoras and Saboras successfully met the external threats posed by political domination, they were not quite as successful in meeting the internal threats of religious schismatics. In the first challenge, the Christian heresy had been the internal schism that threatened Judaism, but the Jews had averted that danger by expunging the offending creed from their midst. In the second challenge, the threat came from a parade of pretender messiahs, beckoning the Jews to follow them down the apocalyptic road to the End of Days. As these messiahs operated within the framework of Judaism, they could not be expelled but had to be digested.

It was not the messiah who introduced the messianic age, or "millennium,"[5] as the Christians were to call it, but the other way around. The expectation of a messianic age called forth a rash of messiahs to fulfill that expectation. After the Book of Daniel (third century B.C.) had conjured up the messianic age, the Pharisee intellectuals concluded that the Jewish messiah would arrive 3,700 years

---

[4]For examples of Talmudic syllogisms represented symbolically, we refer the interested reader to *Studies in Talmudic Logic and Methodology*, by Louis Jacobs.

[5]The Christian millennium (from the Latin, "a thousand years") was expected momentarily with the second coming of Christ, but the first millennium came and went without Jesus showing up.

after Creation—corresponding to the first century A.D. And lo and behold, the expectation that the millennium would be ushered in at the turn of that century brought forth a plethora of messiahs, Jesus, of course, being the most prominent, though not the first or the last.

Several warrior messiahs had been executed by the Romans before the arrival of Jesus. And a bare ten years after the death of Jesus, a man named Theudas appeared, whose multitudinous followers proclaimed him the true messiah. The Roman Procurator Cuspius Fadus, mindful of the trouble a previous messiah had caused his predecessor Pontius Pilate, took no chances and ordered the immediate death of Theudas and all his adherents. Theudas was beheaded instead of crucified to insure immediate death, and his followers were annihilated.

With the abortive messiahship of Bar Kochba, messianic hopes faded for a while. The Jewish year 3700 (Christian calendar first century A.D.) arrived and departed without producing a lasting messiah for the Jews. But new messianic mathematics cropped up to rectify the situation. The Creation calendar was revised, and a new arrival date for the messiah was set for the fifth century A.D., although there was some disagreement about the exact year. The great Judah Hanasi categorically stated that the messiah would arrive in the year 435, exactly 365 years after the destruction of the Temple (70 plus 365). But the great Rab Hanina said no, the messiah would not arrive until 400 years after the destruction of the Temple, in the year 470.

What lent even greater credence than the mathematical conjectures of Hanasi and Hanina that the fifth century might herald the entry of the messiah was the end of the Roman Empire. The Jews saw the barbarians invade Rome and sack it. Was this not fulfilment of prophecy, the fall of the superstate as predicted by Isaiah? A collective messianic psychosis took hold of the Jews. Disappointment in one pretender messiah did not dampen their ardor, but merely readied them for a successor who might prove to be the right one. Deluded crackpots, undeluded fanatics, and sincere ascetics—all were regarded as equally valid by their respective true believers.

The most colorful of these pretender messiahs was

Moses of Crete. The atmosphere of the expectation of a messiah enabled him to convince the entire Jewish population of that island that he was the messiah who had come to lead them to the Promised Land. How to reach it was simplicity itself. He would smite the waters with his staff, which would part as the Red Sea had parted for Moses of Sinai, and they would walk across the Mediterranean to the Holy Land. On the appointed day, the Jews of Crete gathered on a promontory jutting into the Mediterranean and boldly leaped into the sea after their messiah. But the waters did not part. History records that those who could not swim drowned, but fails to record whether or not those who lost their lives saved their souls. Among those who perished was Moses of Crete. He could not swim either.

After a century of failures, the rabbis conceded that something was wrong with their calculations. On rechecking their figures they found that they had indeed erred, by a few centuries. Like the Christians, who continually had to postpone Judgment Day because Jesus failed to keep his appointment for a second coming, so the Jews, from century to century, had to postpone the arrival date of their messiah by new calculations.

Though this steady stream of messiahs constituted a minor deterrent to a stable Diaspora Judaism, it did not constitute a major political threat, for none of these messiahs advocated the overthrow of the Diaspora. They did, however, lay the foundation for a future heresy, an internal threat to the very existence of Diaspora Judaism in its next challenge.

With the closing of the Talmud in the sixth century, the second challenge is over. History now enters its modern phase, for the ancient world ended not with the death of Jesus in the first century but with the birth of a new prophet in the sixth.

A new religion is on the march, winning battle after battle in the name of its founder, Mohammed. With his entry, the thousand-year geographic unity of East and West is shattered into two spheres, Mohammedan and Christian. Peoples, nations, religions, cultures will disappear like fried chicken at a church supper. Only one people—the Jews—will survive ethnically, religiously, and culturally the indirectly genocidal effects of these two new galloping ideologies. The Mohammedan world will constitute the setting for the third challenge to Jewish survival, and the Christian world will become the setting for the three remaining challenges in our second act.

What are the origins of this incredible Arab world that arises like a mirage out of the desert in the seventh century to become in one century an empire larger than that of Rome? How do the Jews become embroiled in this civilization? What effect will their sojourn among the Arabs have in the development and furtherance of the Jewish manifest destiny? This challenge will take them into a totally new and original civilization that has no antecedents in the past. The Jews will need more than luck to survive.

The Third Challenge:
The Open Society
of the Islamic World

THE EMPIRE OF THE PROPHET

The seventh century was a barren season for civilizations. In China, the T'ang Dynasty, though it unified the country, ushered in no new cultural epoch and merely recapitulated the themes of the former Han Empire. The Indic civilization had desiccated in the sixth century, and until the rise of the new Hindu civilization, the subsequent history of India was a dreary interlude drenched in the blood of endemic warfare. The Sassanid Empire was tottering beneath the drifts of its cultural winter phase. The recently born Byzantine Empire, though strong militarily, was a congenital intellectual cretin. The Roman Empire had finally petered out, and feudal Europe, slowly recuperating from successive rapes by Vandals, Huns, and Goths, was 600 years away from her Renaissance. The prospects for the birth of a new civilization to brighten the hopes of man seemed dim indeed.

Yet, against all odds, a new civilization did make its debut in that dismal century. It was introduced not by a people touched by the genius of Greece or maimed by the sword of Rome but by a man inspired by the ethics of Jehovah. No historian, no dramatist, no cultural planning commission would have picked him or the Bedouins of Arabia—those nomadic dwellers of the dust from whom he sprang—as the harbingers of a new, incredibly brilliant civilization. And never in the history of man did a civilization mature so fast, exert such great influence, suffer so much neglect at the hands of historians, and disappear so swiftly as did the civilization known today as Islamic.

As with Judaism, this new civilization began with one man, Mohammed, with one God, Allah, and with a new religion, Islam. What took the Romans 500 years and would take the Christians 1,000 years, the followers of Mohammed accomplished in one century. In the words of historian Steven Runciman, "Unlike Christianity, which preached a peace that it never achieved, Islam unashamedly came with the sword."

Politically, Arabia before Mohammed existed "only in the careless nomenclature of the Greeks." Geographically, it is the world's largest peninsula, chained to Asia by what is now Iraq and separated from Africa by the Suez Canal.

In a few cities along its vast coastlines dwelled the Quaraish Arabs, living on handicrafts and trade. In its desert heartland dwelled the Bedouin Arabs, eking out a meager existence by tending sheep and raiding caravans. Spiritually, the Bedouin was akin to the frontiersman of the American West—both despised the city, both loved the freedom of wild, open spaces, both made their own laws. Avaricious, dishonest, and murderous in relation to strangers, the Bedouin was kind, generous, and faithful to his own kinsmen. The women were as beautiful as polished odes but did not last as long. Born as her father's chattel, married off at seven or eight to the highest bidder, a Bedouin girl's beauty soon faded in a life of drudgery.

The Quaraish and the Bedouins were united in their worship of celestial objects like the moon and stars and terrestrial objects like trees and stones. Both appeased their *jinns* (evil spirits) with human sacrifice. Through the centuries, their worship had become centralized in the adoration of the Black Stone, housed in the Kaaba in Mecca, an arid city in a valley of sanded waste along the west coast of Arabia. According to Arab legends, the Kaaba— a rectangular building 40 feet long, 35 feet wide, and 50 feet high—was erected by angels, and the Black Stone— oval in shape and seven inches in diameter—was sent from heaven, a not unlikely supposition, since it is a meteorite.

The Jews did not enter this Arabic world as late, uninvited guests but as charter members. Some scholars place

Jews in Arabia as early as the days of King Solomon (900 B.C.), when his ships sailed the seas in search of new markets. But archaeology establishes the date at about 200 B.C. The Arabs link their ancestry to the Jews through Abraham's son Ishmael, hence the term Ishmaelites for the Arabs. In the first century A.D., after the devastation of Jerusalem, the number of Jews in Arabia swelled with refugees from Palestine. They helped found the city of Medina, which, by the fifth century, had become the largest, most important city in Arabia, its 10,000 Jews constituting the majority of the population.

The Jews in Arabia, except for their religion, were much like the Arabs, organized in tribes and led by a sheik. They were fiery fighters, loved poetry, indulged in bloodfeuds, and sang about wine, women, and horses. They were also palm growers, skilled artisans, and tradesmen. As a group, they were the most wealthy and influential in Arabia, and exerted a great civilizing influence on their nomadic neighbors.

The biggest influence on the Arabs was Judaism, and the Jewish population grew as much through the conversion of Arabs as by immigration and procreation. In fact, one vigorous proselytization program in the sixth century led to the founding of a Jewish kingdom in Yemen. While besieging Medina in a minor war, the king of Yemen became interested in Judaism, and, instead of destroying the city, invited leading Jewish scholars to settle in his realm. His son Yusuf converted to Judaism, and upon becoming king (around 525) made it the official religion. The new Jewish kingdom died as casually as it was born. King Yusuf, hearing that the Jews in Byzantium were persecuted, massacred in reprisal Byzantine merchants en route to India. In retaliation, the black Christians in Abyssinia invaded Yemen. The Abyssinian king carried off Yusuf's beloved wife; Yusuf rode his horse into the sea, literally drowning his sorrows; and the Jewish Kingdom of Yemen was figuratively engulfed in the ensuing bloodbath. But the influence of Judaism did not die—it spread, serving as a foundation for the coming Mohammedanism in the same way that Diaspora Judaism in the Roman Empire had served as a foundation for early Christianity.

It was in this barren century devastated by wars, and into this turbulent land permeated by Judaism, that Mohammed, the founder of the Islamic religion and civilization, was born in 570, of poor but honest pagan parents. He never saw his father, who, after a three-day honeymoon, set out for a business trip to Medina from which he never returned. When Mohammed was six, his mother died, and the youngster's education was entrusted to an uncle, who neglected to teach him reading and writing. As with Moses and Jesus, we know little more of Mohammed's youth than that he was a shepherd, the favorite vocation for aspirants to the post of prophet.

Mohammed enters the memory of history at the age of twenty-five, when he became a rich and undistinguished businessman through his marriage to a wealthy widow named Khadija, who had employed him as a camel driver for her caravans. It is at this point, while traveling throughout Arabia, that Mohammed came in contact with Jews and Judaism and began to reflect on the differences between the naïve pagan pantheism of his people and the lofty religious concepts of the Jews.

History does not reveal at what point Mohammed began to conceive of himself as a prophet, for at this juncture of his life facts tend to blend with legend. He first identified himself with Abraham, like himself a heathen who discovered God and founded a new religion late in life. At the age of forty, Mohammed relates, he had his first interview with the archangel Gabriel, who informed him that he had been chosen by Allah to bring about a reformation in the religious, social, and economic life of his people. But no action followed.

We have in fact a curious parallel to the life of St. Paul. This Jew, who became a Christian saint, fell into a fourteen-year period of inactivity after his traumatic encounter with Jesus, springing into action only after he met Barnabas, a young apostle. Mohammed fell into a ten-year period of inactivity after his traumatic encounter with Gabriel, springing into action in his fiftieth year, when, after the death of Khadija he married Aisha, a seven-year-old girl. It is then, according to his stated word, that he had the ecstatic experience of ascending through seven heavens into the presence of Allah, who confirmed that he was indeed the chosen prophet.

The year 620 was not only a turning point in Mohammed's career as a prophet, it also sparked a sexual reawakening that netted him ten wives and two concubines, all fated to be barren. One of his wives was a seventeen-year-old Jewish girl, Safiya, and one of his concubines was a Negress. Most of his marriages, however, were either acts of kindness, like marrying destitute widows of departed disciples, or acts of diplomacy, like marrying an old-maid daughter of an enemy. Aisha alone remained his true love.

Proclaiming that he came not to destroy but to fulfill the laws of Moses and Jesus, Mohammed began a concerted drive for converts to his faith. Jews and Christians joined the general Arab public in its apathy to the self-proclaimed prophet. The Quaraish Arabs simply smiled at Mohammed's visions. But when he began attacking the idol worship in the Kaaba, a source of excellent revenue from pagan pilgrims, Arab tolerance turned to hostility, and in 622 Mohammed had to flee from his home town, Mecca.

Significantly, he fled to the Jewish city of Medina. Here he invited the Jews to join his cause. When they refused to do so, he and his followers looted their gold under the pretense of justified indignation. Equipping an army with that gold, Mohammed marched successfully against Mecca, which now prudently hailed him as the true prophet. Like Jesus riding into Jerusalem on an ass, headed for the Temple to drive out the money-changers, so Mohammed rode into Mecca on a camel, headed for the Kaaba to clear it of idolatrous clutter. Like a medieval cathedral housing a multitude of saints, the Kaaba housed an assortment of idols, the chief one being Allah, whom Mohammed, after smashing all others, elevated into the one and only God.

Mohammed's military ambitions expanded with his success. Within two years, the entire Arab peninsula fell under his dominion. But news of the grandiose growth of the Islamic Empire had to be transmitted to him in paradise, for in 632, at the age of sixty-two, he died of fever, his head on the breast of his beloved Aisha.

Like a desert whirlwind, the armies of the dead prophet swept east and west in a vast, unplanned pincer movement, which, if successful, would have encircled the Mediterranean and turned it into an Arab lake. In the eastern sweep, the pennants of Islam were planted in Mesopotamia in 641 and in Sassania in 644. After victories in Bokhara and Samarkand, the new conquerors stood at the Indus River where Alexander the Great had stood 900 years earlier. A second victorious tide of faith carried the Arabs over the Caucasus and across the frontiers of Khazaria, a strange Tartaric country between the Black and Caspian seas, where they inflicted a crushing defeat on the Khazars, a branch of the Hun people, which in the eighth century converted to Judaism. But the Khazars rallied, slowly drove the invaders out, and finally succeeded in making the Caucasus a permanent boundary between them and the Islamic Empire. Thus, with the Byzantine Empire also standing fast, Islam's eastern flanking movement into Europe was blocked.

In the western sweep, the successful rhythm of conquest continued as faith and scimitar paved the way for Islam's armies. Damascus fell in 635, the Star of Islam flew over Palestine in 638, and Egyptian treachery preceded Egypt's surrender in 655. By 705 all North Africa was vanquished, and the Arabs were masters of the southern half of the Mediterranean. In 711 a mixed force of Moors, Berbers, and Arabs, led by a freed slave named Tariq, crossed the Straits of Gibraltar and conquered Spain in a four-year campaign. The western pincer crawled across the Pyrenees and penetrated into the heartland of France, poised for a march across Europe to link up with the Islamic armies stalled in the east.

The crucial test came in 732. At the battle of Tours, the winning streak of the Arabs in the west was broken by Charles Martel, illegitimate son of Pepin I, the Mayor of the King's Palace, and grandfather of Charlemagne. Thus it came about that Europe was saved in the east by the Khazars, a residue of Huns recently converted to Judaism, and in the west by the Franks, a residue of barbarians recently converted to Christianity. The east and west were locked in a nutcracker grip around the Mediterranean —the southern jaw constituting the Mohammedan world, and the northern jaw the Christian domain. This new Islamic Empire, glued together from fragments of destroyed countries, became more than a mosaic of its component parts. It became a civilization that influenced and shaped the world around it.

The Islamic civilization received its impetus, its very life, from the Islamic religion, as embodied in the Koran (from the Arabic word "reading"), the bible of the Mohammedans. Mohammed rejected the concepts of Virgin Birth and Trinity, and insisted with the Jews that God was One, needing neither family nor companions. He was also repelled by the Christian worship of saints, which he viewed as idolatry, and like the Jews banned all statue worship. The predominant non-Arabic figure in the Koran is Moses, not Jesus.

Of the six basic tenets of Islam, four are derived from Judaism and two from Christianity. The four Jewish-inspired tenets are the belief in the immortality of the soul, the belief in one invisible God (Allah), the belief in a God-sent prophet (Mohammed), and the belief in the Book (Koran) as the revealed text, the last three corresponding to Jehovah, Moses, and the Torah of Judaism. The two ideas derived from Catholic Christianity are the concepts of Judgment Day and of the total surrender of the human will to God, a surrender known in Christianity as "God's grace" and in Mohammedanism as "Islam" (hence also the name for that religion).

Hell and heaven in the Koran surpass in threat and promise the hell and heaven of Christian belief. Dante's inferno is an air-conditioned sauna compared to the hell of the Koran, where seven levels of torture await the sinner. Here the drink of the day is offal dissolved in boiling water, and the damned are shod with shoes of fire. But in the Mohammedan paradise, seventy-two virgin houris—"beauties with swelling bosoms but modest gaze," as the Koran so deftly phrases it—dedicate themselves to each male's pleasures. For the more ascetically inclined, there is the intellectual pleasure of reading the Koran. And all who enter paradise will behold the face of Allah.

After a century of victories, the caliphs tempered initial tyranny with enlightened rule. The Islamic Empire became a tolerant haven for businessmen, intellectuals, and artists of all faiths. Not only did Europe get her peaches, apricots, rice, and lute players from the Mohammedans—she was also enriched with new ideas in the field of business, science, and art.

In the field of commerce and industry especially, opportunities were unlimited. Whereas the pre-capitalist mercantile revolution did not come to Europe until after the Renaissance, a mercantile revolution swept the Islamic Empire in the eighth century, for the new creed of Islam was not merely a religious affirmation but also a bourgeois revolution. By the ninth century, while Europe was wallowing in a stagnant agrarian economy, Islam rose to the status of the world's first mercantilist empire, establishing in many respects the framework for Europe's coming capitalist age.

The reason the Arabs became the world's first capitalists lies in the nature of the new society developed in the aftermath of conquest. As former Christian territories along the African north coast and Spain were subjugated, vast stores of gold, mostly church property, fell into the hands of the victors. Gold statues of saints were melted into ingots, and gold madonnas were sold to Hindu idolators as fertility goddesses. In a comradeship of profits, Christians and Jews followed the conquering armies, acting as middlemen, converting loot into gold. In a short time they became the new merchant class, in possession of a vast liquid wealth. Hand in hand with this accumulation of capital went the creation of a large, cheap, reserve labor force. As the Islamic wars progressed, dispossessed farmers flocked to the cities, where they competed with ruined merchants and artisans for jobs.

But something else also took place. The old caste systems crumbled, making upward movement possible for those on the bottom. Sword and gold became the stuff that greased the climb up the new social ladder. Victorious Arabs stepped into the vacated niches of aristocracy, and nouveau riche Christians and Jews stepped into the void of industry, building roads for the soldiers of the new elite, pioneering the growth of towns into cities to house the swelling populations, and instituting new commerce to feed, clothe, and amuse the people that thronged them.

In science, the Arabs outdistanced the Greeks. Greek civilization was, in essence, a lush garden full of beautiful flowers that bore little fruit. It was a civilization rich in philosophy and literature, but poor in techniques and technology. Thus it was the historic task of the Arabs and the Islamic Jews to break through this Greek scientific cul-de-sac, to stumble upon new paths of science—to invent the concepts of zero, the minus sign, irrational numbers, to lay the foundations for the new science of chemistry—ideas which paved the path to the modern scientific world via the minds of post-Renaissance European intellectuals.

Classicists have extolled to willing Western minds the view that Renaissance architecture was solely the heritage of Greek and Roman genius. Though Greece and Rome did influence European architecture, the scholar must also look to the Islamic Empire for new insights into the changing European architecture after the eleventh century. Admittedly, the Arabs at first came equipped with little architectural know-how. But in the conquered lands they found skilled architects who had inherited the strains of their former Christian, Sassanid, Greek, Persian, and Babylonian civilizations. The Arabs borrowed with skill from these diverse schools and came up with new, lofty concepts, creating a Moslem architectural style that surpassed its archetypes in beauty and technical engineering.

So, for instance, the Great Mosque of Damascus precedes by centuries the Pitti Palace of Florence. Many of the castles built by European knights after the Crusades remarkably resemble castles built by Arab nobles in the tenth century. The Bell Tower of Evesham (1533), styled after the Giralda Minaret in Seville (1195), is but another striking example of this extensive Moslem influence.

It was not vouchsafed for the prophet's immediate kin, but for his enemies, to rule the vast landmass conquered in his name. After Mohammed's death, the empire was ruled at first successively though disastrously for about three decades by two of his fathers-in-law (Abu Bekr and Omar), and two sons-in-law (Othman and Ali), of whom the last three were assassinated. Religious dissension broke out in the reign of Ali, and his brain was pierced by a poisoned sword. Muawiyah, a scion of the aristocratic Umayyad clan which had bitterly opposed Mohammed in the early days, seized power and proclaimed himself caliph, thus establishing the Umayyad Dynasty in 661.

For about a century (661–750) the Umayyad Dynasty ruled its vast realm from Baghdad to Cordoba with indulgent tolerance and adequate competence. But though successful in war and love, the Umayyads were hated by the faithful as former enemies of their beloved prophet. They prayed to Allah to send them a deliverer from the tolerant rule of the usurpers. Deliverance came in the person of Abu-al Abbas, a great-great-grandson of an uncle of Mohammed, who aligned himself with the Sassanids, fomented a revolt, and successfully established the Abbasid Dynasty. Styling himself "al-Saffah," "the Bloodthirsty," he ordered every prince carrying Umayyad blood in his veins slain to prevent a resurrection of that dynasty. His governor of Syria carried out the order with a dash of deceit and a touch of humor. Announcing an amnesty, the governor invited all leading Umayyads to a feast of friendship. While wine and concubines circulated, soldiers entered on cue and slew the guests of honor. Carpets were thrown over the bodies and the feast was resumed, the laughter and merriment above mingling dissonantly with the groans and agony below.

One Umayyad escaped the slaughter. "Armed only with his royal blood," he landed in Spain in 755, where he reestablished the Spanish branch of the Umayyad Dynasty that was to rule Spain for 300 years (756–1031) and form the heart of the western Islamic Empire.

Though eastern Islam's cultural decline did not begin until the twelfth century, her political unity began to crumble in the tenth. In Marxist language, the Islamic civilization contained the seeds of its own destruction; in Toynbeean language, the Arabs were resting on their oars, content that they had it made. Pederasty weakened the nobility, lechery diluted the royal blood, and both begot weaklings as successors who preferred the delights of the harem to the rigors of the council chambers.

Socio-economic factors also contributed their share to the downfall of Islam. Whereas in the first two centuries of their swift ascendance to power the Arabs had believed the life of a warrior the noblest form of life, they abandoned this notion when they achieved success, entrusting the soldiering profession to slaves and barbarians. The fiercest slave soldiers, eventually, were the Janissaries, former Christian boys, who had been taken forcibly from their parents, converted to Mohammedanism, and then trained as warrior servants.

With affluence, the Arabs forgot that the primary business of government is to govern. The administration of the realm was entrusted to non-Muslims, who were looked down upon for their government jobs, much as the nobles of feudal Europe looked down upon those engaged in commerce and the professions.

As internal control weakened, governors of provinces were emboldened to make their posts hereditary by declaring their independence. New caliphates, emirates, sultanates, and khanates sprouted all over the Islamic map. Slave soldiers exploited the countries they were entrusted to guard, fought one another, and created states of constant war. Old frontiers vanished as new conquerors appeared.

In the eleventh century, a tribe of Turks known as Seljuks, from their leader by that name, left their homeland in north central Asia. Overrunning the lands of Asiatic Islam, the petty dynasties acknowledged the overlordship of the Turks who, in turn, acknowledged the overlordship of the Islamic civilization. The Seljuks rapidly absorbed its culture, and infused the by now effete Arabs with a new vigor. They snatched eastern Islam from the brink of annihilation, and carried her to new grandeur under a succession of great Seljuk sultans.

One of the greatest of the Seljuk sultans, Saladin the Great (1174–1193), unwittingly almost upset the Diaspora. Just as King Cyrus the Great in the sixth century B.C. had strewn consternation among the Jews in Babylonia with his proclamation that they could return to their homeland, so Saladin startled the Jews in the Islamic Empire with his proclamation that they could return to Jerusalem. The Diaspora Jews in the days of Sultan Saladin did not choose to do so, any more than the Babylonian Jews had chosen to do so in the days of King Cyrus.

Eventually, Seljuk strength, too, ebbed out in the blood of new battlefields. The end was inevitable. It is a truism that civilized comfort attracts barbarian conquest. By the thirteenth century, the word was out that the remnants of the Islamic Empire were easy pickings. As with the Roman Empire seven centuries previously, the Islamic Empire was trampled under the boots of new Asiatic invaders.

The scourge of the Roman Empire in the fifth century had been the Hun Attila. The scourge of the Islamic Empire in the thirteenth century was the Mongol, Genghis Khan (1162–1227), Lord of the Earth. Born in the Lake Baikal region, he inherited from his father at the age of thirteen a motley horde of Mongols whom he welded into a disciplined army of cavalrymen. In 1206 he was chief of all Mongols, and in 1213 marched his "new Huns" east into China. In five years, the empire of Genghis Khan stretched from the Volga across China to the Pacific. Soon that empire was to reach west to embrace southern Russia, Iran, Iraq, and grab for Hungary and Poland.

Genghis Khan had never intended turning west. Only man's infinite capacity for expanding minor incidents into total devastation changed the course of history. The drive west began when Genghis Khan sent a delegation to the Shah of Khwarzim, the Asiatic remnant of the former Abbasid caliphate, to inquire why he had executed two Mongol merchants. With the insouciance of the ill-informed, the Shah had the spokesman beheaded and the delegates sent back to Genghis Khan with their beards shaved as a token of his contempt. Genghis headed west.

Genghis Khan was a most advanced military thinker, his philosophy of war being akin to that of the West today. He believed that only old-fashioned wars were fought to seek victory in the field against armies. Like modern Western military strategists, Khan believed that if the civilian population was prevented from supplying its fighting men, the armies in the field would capitulate. As he was not in possession of artillery and bombs to implement his strategy, he had to resort to more primitive weapons. So, for instance, the beautiful city of Bokhara was burned to the ground as thoroughly as if napalm had been used, and 30,000 of its inhabitants were eliminated through beheading and disembowelment as effectively as Nazi *Einsatztruppen* eliminated civilians with machine guns. City after city was devastated as neatly as if squadrons of bombers had passed overhead.

After Genghis Khan retired from the battlefield to his capital Karakorum to enjoy his 500 wives, a son carried the Mongol banners to Hungary and Poland. A grandson seized and sacked Baghdad in 1258, pacifying its 800,000 inhabitants by the sword as effectively, though not as effortlessly, as Nagasaki's civilians were by the atom bomb.

These tactics against civilians worked. The East was paralyzed. Europe shivered. The Mongol armies marched on into Syria, in a drive for Egypt and Africa. Here irrational fate dealt them a merited death blow. At the battle of Damascus they suffered an irreversible defeat by an incredible people known as Mamelukes—former Turkish slaves in Egypt, who in 1250 had rebelled against their masters and seized power. The Mamelukes not only sent the Mongols packing but kicked out the last remnants of the Crusaders, thus imprinting *finis* on the Latin Kingdom in the Near East.

The Mongols' streak of luck was over. Quietly, without losing further battles or announcing formal retreats, they headed back to the plains of central Asia whence they had originated, vanishing from glory as their vast empire atrophied through their sheer inability to govern.

There was a qualitative difference between the Hun invasions of the Roman Empire and the Mongol invasion of the Islamic world. Though the former had been a two-century affair, it was not fatal, as the invaders in the main tried both to preserve the fabric of the Roman civilization and to integrate themselves within it. The Mongol invasion, on the other hand, though lasting but forty years, had the opposite effect, because the Mongols came not to learn and preserve but to plunder and destroy. The populations

THE INDESTRUCTIBLE JEWS   189

of the Near East were decimated, the cities destroyed, the canals clogged, the libraries and cultural centers gutted.

The Islamic civilization provides an excellent example of the difference between survival as a culture and survival as a biological entity. Though there were vastly more Christians than Jews in the Islamic Empire, they contributed nothing intellectual to their host civilization. Living like parasites on the Islamic culture, isolated from the Christian world, and having no vision of their own, the Christians in the Mohammedan world stagnated intellectually, producing not a single name of renown in any scientific, literary, or humanistic field. The Jews, however, with their sense of a manifest destiny, not only accepted the challenge of the Islamic civilization but became part thereof, and developed an elite intellectual corps, whose works would become the heritage of Jews, Mohammedans, and Christians alike.

Let us now return to the Saboras whom we left sitting in the disintegrating Sassanid Empire, waiting for the third challenge to fall. In this challenge a new set of Diaspora designers will take a six-century ride on the swelling crest of Islam, tailoring the political, social, and cultural responses needed for survival in this remarkable civilization.

THE "EMPIRE" OF THE TALMUDISTS

When the Jews confront the open society of the Islamic world, they are 2,500 years old as a people. In defiance of every historic maxim they have survived seven centuries of exile, ethnically and culturally intact, while their previous hosts—the Greeks, the Romans, the Parthians, and the Sassanids—have passed out of history as cultural entities.

Nothing could have been more alien to the Jews than this fantastic Islamic civilization that rose out of the desert dust in the seventh century. Yet nothing could have been more the same. Though it represented a new civilization, a new religion, and a new social milieu built on new economic foundations, it resembled the packaged "intellectual pleasure principle" presented to the Jews a thousand years earlier when Alexander the Great opened the doors of Hellenistic society to them. Now Islamic society opened the doors of its mosques, its schools, and its bedrooms for conversion, education, and assimilation. The challenge for the Jews was how to swim in this scented civilization without drowning, or in the language of modern sociology, how to enjoy the somatic, intellectual, and spiritual comforts offered by the dominant majority without disappearing as a marginal minority.

The Jews did what came naturally. They fired the old scriptwriters and hired a new set of specialists. Instead of rejecting the Muslim civilization, they accepted it. Instead of keeping themselves apart, they integrated. Instead of becoming parochialized fossils, they joined the new swinging society as sustaining members. Arabic became their mother tongue; wine, women, and secular songs their part-time avocations; philosophy, mathematics, astronomy, diplomacy, medicine, and literature their full-time vocations. The Jews never had it so good.

There were dire predictions, of course, that Jews and Judaism would disappear in this permissive atmosphere. But though there was assimilation, conversion, and apostasy, neither the Jews nor Judaism disappeared. Instead of declining, the Jews multiplied. Instead of atrophying, the Talmud expanded. This unheard-of period of freedom took them not to the brink of extinction but to a Golden Age of intellectual creativity.

Islam East

After the death of Mohammed, the Muslims settled down to a policy of live-and-let-live vis-à-vis the religious minorities in their midst. Though there were special disabilities for minorities, they were seldom enforced as long as the unbelievers—pagans, Christians, and Jews—paid special taxes. Impressed with Jewish thrift, industry, and learning, and quick to assess the value of self-governing Jews who paid their taxes on time, the Muslims recognized the independence of the Exilarchate instituted by the Parthians. The Exilarch became a power in the courts of caliph and sultan.

The most colorful of the Exilarchs who strutted the Islamic stage was the first one, Bustanai (620–675), reputedly the son of the great Hananiel, a descendant of King David, and the last Exilarch under the Sassanids. Whenever one encounters a legend surrounding the birth of a hero, one must search for a sexual transgression. The legend surrounding Bustanai's birth is no exception. The story goes that the last Sassanid king, bent on destroying the House of David, was warned in a nightmare to cease and desist this evil practice and admonished to protect a Jewish lady who within her womb carried the last seed of the Jewish royal house. The king reformed, and the pregnant lady was brought to the palace, where in due time she divested herself of Bustanai. In all probability, this legend has the dual task of hiding the fact that the lady was the king's concubine and of legitimizing the birth of the future Exilarch.

Caliph Omar named Bustanai to the Exilarchate and to the Arab council of state. As a token of his esteem, the caliph also presented him with a slave-girl playmate, the beautiful Princess Dara, daughter of the deposed Sassanid King Chosru II. With her, Bustanai sired several children, including one son. Upon Bustanai's death, the drama moved from bedroom to court. The children of Bustanai's Jewish wife claimed that since Princess Dara was a slave, her children could not inherit nor her son succeed to the seat of the Exilarchate. To the dismay of the devout, the Jewish high court ruled against the plaintiffs, holding that Bustanai most assuredly had married Dara and set her free in order to ensure the legitimacy of their offspring. Thus it came about that the illegitimate son of a Sassanid princess and an Exilarch of the House of David came to rule the Jews of the Diaspora by a verdict of the Talmudists.

Within a century of their ascendance, the power of the Islamic Exilarchs was challenged from a totally unexpected and unlikely source—the timid Saboras. In the eighth century the Saboras shed their mantle of unctuous humility for

the purple of cultural arrogance. The Talmud was the instrument of this transformation. Faced with a closed Torah,
a closed Mishna, a closed Gemara, and orders to close the
Talmud, the Saboras devised an ingenious way of bypassing
that order. They worked diligently to fuse Mishna and
Gemara into the Talmud, but, by never announcing their
task finished they never closed it officially, so that as keepers of an unofficially open Talmud they could always render new insights into old outlooks. Thus judicial power
passed into their hands. By 700, the Saboras who headed
the two leading academies at Sura and Pumbaditha had
given themselves the new title of *Gaon*, "Your Eminence,"
and were soon recognized by the caliphs as the judicial arm
of the "Diaspora Empire" within the Islamic Empire. Thus
began the 350-year rule of the Gaons (689–1038).[1]

Strife between Gaon and Exilarch erupted early, often
leading to bitter fights of investiture, resembling similar
fights between medieval popes and kings. Just as such strife
between pope and prince over who had the right to install
whom often led to the election of pope and anti-pope, so
the investiture strife between Gaon and Exilarch often
led to the installation of Gaon and anti-Gaon, or Exilarch
and anti-Exilarch.

The Gaons, who held judicial power, were prudent
enough to pay yearly homage to the Exilarchs, who held
the administrative reins. Legislative power was held by
both, and all important laws and decrees had to have the
signature of both offices. This system of checks and bal-
ances between the judicial, administrative, and legislative
forces worked quite well. In the main it protected the
Jews, so that in the Islamic Empire of absolute autocracy
the Jews had a modicum of democracy.

The Gaons fathered no Mishna or Gemara. Their
great historic achievement lay in transforming the Talmud
into a symbolic substitute of a religious state for a nonexistent geographic state. In sessions similar to the Sanhe-

---

[1] The exact date of transition from Sabora to Gaon is in dispute
by as much as a century. We have accepted the view of Abraham
ibn Daud over that of Sherira Gaon, the two chief contenders in
this dispute.

drin of ancient days and to the United States Supreme
Court today, they took existing Talmudic law and by a
series of "constitutional" reinterpretations enlarged nar-
rower views into loftier concepts. These decisions, which
affected criminal, civil, and commercial law, were not
made part of the Talmud itself but became part of Talmudic "constitutional law." In the field of labor, Talmudic
law of the tenth century sounds remarkably like twentieth-
century democratic thinking. A working man's salary could
not be cut because of absence due to illness, nor could his
tools be taken as security against a loan. The Talmud also
set limits upon working hours and protected the rights of
guilds to set a wage scale. On the other hand, a worker
was liable for skills necessary for the job, and for damages
resulting from proven inefficiency, carelessness, or sab-
otage.

Talmudic law also claimed that ownership depended on
labor and moral right more than on occupancy and conquest. It held that occupancy had to be justified by rightful
claim. But ownership was never absolute. Though private
property was sacrosanct, it had to yield at times to moral
and human rights.

In the field of economics, the Talmudists generally
hewed to the principle that the more an article was needed
by the community the less profit should be made on it.
Profit should be in inverse proportion to its usefulness,
they ruled. Thus no ceiling was placed on profits for
luxuries or objects of art which could be set freely by
seller and buyer, whereas in times of stress the price on
grain was fixed.

As the fame of the Talmud and its interpreters spread,
"constitutional" questions began streaming in from Jews
in every part of the world. At first, the Gaons regarded
these questions as impositions, answering them with a curt
"Permitted" or "Not Permitted." But as questions continued to stream in from North Africa, Spain, France,
Germany, Italy, the Gaons realized that the Diaspora was
assuming international functions and that the Talmud was
the vehicle for an invisible government in exile. Aware
now that they were international jurists, the Gaons began
elaborating their answers and citing precedents with bril-

liant displays of scholarship that dazzled the as yet backward Jews of Europe.

The new "Oral Law" developed by the Gaons was disseminated throughout the Diaspora via a unique courier service that became known as the *Responsa*, which played as important a role in shaping world Judaism as the Epistles of Paul did in shaping world Christianity. Both Responsa and Epistles were letters of first principles, procedures and guidelines for survival. Within a century, Sura and Pumbaditha became "international headquarters" for a Talmudic "mail order" government for the governance of Jews in the Diaspora.

The man most responsible for the development of this Responsa was blind, seventy-year-old Yehudai ben Nahman, who, in spite of his disability, advanced age, and short term in office (760–764), set the future course for the Gaonate. In his *Decided Laws*, a first attempt at a systematic codification of Talmudic law, Yehudai dispensed with arguments and merely recited case histories and decisions. Correctly appraising the new age, he boldly expressed new views on travel, property, divorce, and inheritance laws. But most important, sensing the new international aspects of the Talmud, he used his Responsa for building an intellectual bridge from Baghdad to Cordoba, over which Jewish history raced a few centuries later, when world history destroyed the eastern caliphates.

By the tenth century, the Babylonian Talmud had become the "common law" of the Diaspora. But that century also ushered in the decline of the Abbasid caliphate, and with it the decline of the great yeshivas. Before their demise, however, both Sura and Pumbaditha each produced one last great Gaon whose careers epitomize the three centuries of Gaonic rule—Saadia, the intolerant liberal, and Hai, the tolerant conservative.

Latter-day rabbis depict Saadia, born in 882, as a saint, but ungracious history does not cooperate with this view. A product of a ninth-century small-town slum in Egypt, Saadia clawed his way to the top with calculated ruthlessness. Though in later life he gave himself a noble Jewish ancestry, it was rumored that his father, of low calling, was not a Jew. With his father-in-law's money and his own cunning, Saadia succeeded in having himself appointed Gaon of the academy at Sura, and promptly became embroiled in a conflict with the Exilarch. Like the pontiffs of Rome and Constantinople, Exilarch and Gaon placed each other under the ban. As the Exilarch was backed by the caliph, Saadia had to flee. After a seven-year banishment a truce was effected, and to heal the breach in Jewish ranks, the former enemies embraced each other with solemn insincerity.

The embodiment of the cosmopolitan Islamic Jew—Talmudist, scholar, grammarian, philosopher, poet—Saadia drastically influenced the future course of Judaism. At the age of twenty, he published a Hebrew lexicon and rhyming dictionary, then translated the Old Testament into Arabic. In his treatise, *Creed and Faith*, Saadia attempted to prove the superiority of faith over reason as a path to ethics. His greatest contribution to Judaism, however, was his rationalist interpretations of Talmudic law. Fearful that the stupidities of the orthodox might expand into all available space, he filled his Talmudic decisions with common sense. "It is inconceivable," he wrote in answer to a rabbinic attack on his views on science, "that honest investigation should be forbidden us."

The last of the great Gaons of Sura, Saadia died (942) of "melancholia"—a euphemistic term, perhaps, for schizophrenia. After him the academy declined, fading into oblivion in the eleventh century. Before joining Sura in decline, Pumbaditha flickered briefly into fame when an aged father appointed his son, the great Hai (939–1038), to succeed him to the Gaonate. Born in Baghdad, Hai attended the best schools, spoke Hebrew, Arabic, Greek, and Persian, and wrote with equal facility in both Hebrew and Arabic. Highly cultured, Hai was an orthodox Jew who did not permit his orthodoxy to impinge on his rationalism. Though he engaged in debates with Mohammedan and Christian scholars, he warned his fellow Jews against them, fearing that although he himself was tied securely to the mast of Judaism, those of lesser intellect needed the wax of ignorance in their ears so as not to be seduced by the siren song of the worldly philosophers.

Like Saadia, Hai was contemptuous of the orthodox

rabbinate, who, in revenge, denounced him to the caliph as a subversive plotting with Christians to overthrow the caliphate. Father and son were arrested, their property was confiscated, and both were thrown into a dungeon until exonerated several years later.

Hai's vast Responsa, modern and definitive, and his commentaries on the Bible and Mishna broadcast his fame throughout the Diaspora. More than any other Diaspora designer, he saw clearly how new world commerce and far-flung business enterprises scattered the Jews farther and farther into unexplored challenges. In his most famed book, *Buying and Selling*, he reexamined all previous questions on commerce, interest, contracts, and torts. His rulings were so cogent they are still relevant in international commercial law today.

Hai was well aware of the practical nature of his Talmudic decisions. He once observed, "We do not remember what we wrote, nor what our fathers wrote, but we say whatever pleases us and what we think should be done," an attitude that foreshadowed the remark of a twentieth-century United States Supreme Court justice, "The Constitution is what the Supreme Court says it is."

With Hai's death at the age of ninety-nine, the doors of Pumbaditha closed. The age of the great Babylonian yeshivas was over. Symbolically, the closing of the Babylonian academies signaled the end of Jewish intellectual life in the eastern half of the Mohammedan Empire, just as the closing of the schools in Athens in the sixth century signaled the end of Greco-Roman intellectual life.

The greatness of the Gaons lies in the fact that they cleared a path toward international coexistence through new concepts of constitutional law. They undoubtedly would have agreed with H. L. Mencken's aphorism that "Nine times out of ten there is actually no new truth to be discovered; there is only error to be exposed." Because the Gaons did not want to enshrine an opinion arrived at by majority vote as an eternal truth, they always left the door open for new interpretations by never formulating a universal principle. Whereas Western law begins with a universal principle and tries to find a particular application, Gaonic thinking was the reverse. In the Gaonic view the Jews already had their universal principles in the Torah. All that was needed were minor modifications of those principles to alleviate a temporary stress. They therefore reinterpreted only that part of a universal principle which seemed to contradict an existing reality. It was this willingness to amend nonessentials but hold on to the non-negotiable items in Judaism which gave the Talmudists their popularity and the Talmud its shock-absorbing qualities on a bumpy Diaspora road.

The Talmudic attitude toward the taking of interest from Jews, and the selling of wine to Christians, affords excellent examples of this pragmatic flexibility. The Torah forbids the taking of interest from anyone. The Mishna amended this general principle to forbid only the taking of interest by one Jew from another. But as Jewish enterprises grew, and it became imperative that Jews charge interest of other Jews if they wished to stay in business, the Talmudists came to the rescue. They ruled that the payment of interest on money lent in the further-ance of a Jewish enterprise was not interest—it was simply profit from an investment. This rethinking of the question of taking interest had profound repercussions in medieval Christian Europe. Christians, on beholding the lucrative money-lending business of the Jews, defied the Church, which had banned the taking of interest as "usury," and also went into the money-lending business. The Church, which had inherited the ban on interest from the Old Testament, now borrowed a leaf from the Talmud, and unofficially redefined "usury" as "banking." Thus the formerly abhorred Jewish practice of lending money for interest became a most respectable Christian enterprise.

The early Mishna forbade the drinking of wine touched by Gentile hands, or the selling of it to Gentiles because they were idolators. This was fine in Palestinian times when the Jews were a majority in their own country. But in eleventh-century France, it was impractical because the making and selling of wine was one of the chief means of livelihood for the Jews, and they were a decided minority. So the eleventh-century French-Jewish Talmudist known as Rashi simply exempted the Christians from the category of idolaters by grandly redefining Christianity as a religion. But though a Jew could now have Christians help him harvest his grapes, and could sell them his wine for general purposes, he could not sell wine directly to a church where it could be used for sacramental purposes. A Christian middleman could, of course, buy the wine for resale to the Church. But the spirit of the law had been kept even if the letter had been broken—in keeping perhaps with St. Paul's maxim, "for the letter killeth, but the spirit giveth life" (1 Corinthians 3:6).

This kind of thinking—that of retaining the universal principle by modifying only an interfering subclause, freed the Jews from the stranglehold of old definitions and helped them pave the way for rethinking old questions and new problems. It helped them author, among many survival laws, two more unique "Diaspora laws" which today have been adopted by most people living in alien lands. The first one stipulated that the Jews must recognize the validity of a non-Jewish document, and the second affirmed that all oaths are valid. In effect, the Gaons created the concepts for dual citizenship.

Thus far in our third challenge the spotlight has illuminated only the main characters. Now the spotlight shifts to focus on a gaggle of minor characters in our drama, the eternal dissenters—ignorant saints and learned heretics—who cling to Jewish history as tenaciously as bill collectors pursuing delinquent accounts. Regrettably, we can portray but a few of these messianic pretenders who now march across our stage, some with redemption in their hearts, others with larceny.

The march begins in the eighth century with an illiterate tailor from Isphahan. Pressing the messianic crown on his own brow, he modestly took the name Abu Isa, father of Jesus, declaring that whereas Moses, Jesus, and Mohammed were only prophets, he was the messiah chosen to reveal final revelation. By conferring prophethood on any rabbi joining his cause, he succeeded in raising an army of 10,000 Jews, which he marched against Caliph Abd al-Malik in a showdown to expel the Mohammedans from Palestine and restore that land to the Jews. His touching faith in his own invulnerability was cruelly shattered by his death on the battlefield.

Abu Isa's closest competitor for the messianic chair that century was a gentleman from Baghdad named Serene, who in 720 threw his credentials into the messianic ring. He is the only messianic coward on record. When captured and brought before Caliph Yazid II as a rebel, he faced death not like a martyr but prostrate in fear. Renouncing his messianic crown, he pleaded he had merely planned to mock the Jews. No crowd outside the caliph's palace shouted "Crucify him," but the caliph nevertheless turned him over to a Jewish court for punishment. There is no record of his resurrection.

The twelfth century is unique in having produced the world's only female messiah, whose name was buried with her body. So as not to sully the sacredness of marriage, she consummated her numerous love affairs without that sacrament. Understandably, in their purification of Jewish history, the rabbis have consigned the details of her messianic reign to oblivion. All that can be ascertained about her is that she faded out of the hearts of her male disciples around 1120. She was succeeded by a male messiah from Baghdad, who successfully combined larceny with revelation. He induced a great number of wealthy Jews to turn over their worldly goods to him and await his arrival on the rooftops of their homes for transportation to Jerusalem in a heavenly chariot. But neither he nor Judgment Day ever arrived.

Our favorite aspirant remains a God-intoxicated fanatic from Yemen who, upon announcing that the year 1172 was the year of the messiah, found himself proclaimed one. When brought in chains before the king of Yemen and asked for a miracle to prove his assertion that he was the son of God and not the father of an insurrection, our aspirant unhesitatingly stated, "Cut off my head and I will return to life again." The king agreed there could be no greater miracle than that. But alas, he lost his head for naught. The miracle failed to take place.

Colorful, sincere, and deluded, such false messiahs played a role in Jewish history far beyond enlivening it with their foibles. Whereas the messiahs in our second challenge had been harbingers of the apocalyptic, rebelling against no institutions, the messiahs in this third challenge

conveyed political overtones of ending the exile and returning to Palestine. Thus it was inevitable that eventually
one of them would rebel against Talmudism, the vessel of
Diaspora Judaism.

It is remarkable that in the first 3,000 years of Jewish
history there were but three major heresies. The first heresy
had been against the Judaism revealed by Moses himself.
The Bible tells us (Numbers 16) that Korah organized
250 nobles in a rebellion, challenged Moses, and that the
earth swallowed these schismatics in flames. We rather
suspect these flames were man-made, like the autos-da-fé
of the Christians. The second had been that of the
Prophets against the priesthood, which after smoldering
beneath the surface, erupted in the religious schism between Sadducees and Pharisees. The third had been
Christianity.

Now, in the eighth century, the fourth major heresy
rode in on Talmudism like a posse of avengers, uniting,
seemingly overnight, all the dissident elements in the
Diaspora into one massive rebellion. The name of the
heresy was Karaism, from the Hebrew word *Karah,* "to
read." It referred to "reading Scripture," and hence literally
meant "Scripturism," as opposed to "Talmudism." Like
many other heretic movements, it began with a blunder.

Seldom has a heresy had such distinguished sponsorship.
Founded by Anan ben David, the rightful heir to the
"throne" of the Exilarch, fate denied him that seat and
made him a heretic instead. In 740, the reigning Exilarch
died childless, and the Gaons elected one of two surviving
nephews, the younger brother Josiah, instead of the older,
more brilliant brother, Anan. A student of secular literature, educated in Persia, Anan was suspected of doubting
the infallibility of the Talmudists. Rejected from a post he
rightfully felt was his, Anan united protesters against Talmudism into the religious movement of Karaism, which
he hoped would take them back to "real Judaism," back
to the Torah. But he was an unsuccessful Jewish Luther.
The Church, a few centuries later, noting the parallel,
hurled the epithet "Karaites" at the early Protestants. Yet
the Karaites were as far from being heretic Jews as the
Protestants were from being heretic Christians. They were

pious Jews who viewed Talmudism as so much rabbinic trickery that separated the people from the Torah, just as the Lutherans were pious Christians who viewed Catholicism as so much papal trickery that separated the people from Jesus.

To repudiate Talmudism, the Karaites began a scientific study of the Bible, an examination of the Hebrew language, and an investigation of the very foundation of Judaism in order to give their new judgments a firm basis in Scripture and history. They attracted the imagination of intellectuals to their cause, and within a century of its founding Karaism embraced the loyalty of almost a third of the Jews. The rabbinic world was stunned at the repressed antagonism against the Talmud implied in this wholesale disaffection.

The Karaites rejected the doctrine that the Diaspora was an essential ingredient in Jewish destiny. They championed an immediate return to Palestine, not under the leadership of a messiah but through their own volition; not by conquest but through resettlement. Thus the Karaites, in spirit, were the forerunners of the twentieth-century Zionists. Anan himself set the example. Repeatedly throwing off the messianic crown conferred upon him by the overly devout, he led his followers to Palestine, where he and his successors styled themselves Patriarchs. Under the Karaite impetus, Jerusalem for two centuries again became a Jewish intellectual stronghold.

As a force in Judaism, Karaism lasted four centuries. Then, though stubbornly clinging to life for another four centuries, it began to wane. Three successive blows—schismatic, physical, and intellectual—combined to bring about its demise.

Karaism's worst enemy was its own inconsistency. When faced with the realities of everyday life, the Karaites could think of nothing better than their own version of Oral Law. In searching for justification, they adopted too many Islamic and Christian rationalizations. Never striking a path uniquely its own, Karaism wandered off on schismatic byways that diluted their original doctrines and led them to oblivion.

The second blow to Karaism was its physical extinction

in Palestine. In 1060 Seljuk Turks captured Jerusalem; thirty years later the Fatimids reconquered Jerusalem; and in 1099, in the ferocious onslaught of the First Crusade, Jerusalem fell. The Karaite movement in Palestine collapsed in a pool of blood and a pyre of fire.

The intellectual onslaught on Karaism was led by Saadia, the first Gaon to perceive that it could not be drowned with invective or buried with excommunication. As a counteroffensive, he opened the gates of Talmudism to the intellectual currents sweeping the Islamic world. Jewish intellectuals deserted the banners of Karaism in droves to settle in Saadia's renovated house of Talmudism. His policy was a stunning blow to the Karaites who had not expected such a flanking movement.

In his fight against Karaism, however, Saadia had unwittingly opened the door to science, hitherto absent in Jewish life. Titillated by the fascinating world of secular thought now open to them, the new intellectuals relegated Talmudism to an avocation and took to science as a vocation. But instead of a Jewish renaissance taking place in "Babylon," as one might expect, it took place in Moorish Spain.

Islam West

Before the curtain can be lowered on the third challenge, there is one more scene to be played out—the greatest, so far, perhaps. It is the Jewish humanistic renaissance in Moslem Spain, which is more in the nature of a prologue to the fourth challenge than it is an epilogue to the third. Though the age of the Gaons is over, the age of the Islamic Jew is not; though the Jews in Spain move in a Moslem milieu, their thought has a Western orientation.

As in nature so in history there is a causative agent from a state of rest to a state of motion. As an assortment of Asiatic invaders advanced into Islam East during the tenth to twelfth centuries, the Jews fled across North Africa to Islam West, to Moorish Spain. It is here that the intellectual heirs of Saadia's liberal Talmudism took root and flourished.

The Arab conquest of Spain in 711 had put an end to the forcible conversion of Jews to Christianity begun by King Reccared in the sixth century. Under the subsequent 500-year rule of the Moslems emerged the Spain of three religions and "one bedroom." Mohammedans, Christians, and Jews shared the same brilliant civilization, an intermingling that affected "bloodlines" even more than religious affiliations.

For some inexplicable reason, the Moorish aristocrats of Spain had a penchant for blond Christian women, whom they preferred not as wives but only as mothers for their children. Legitimacy, in their view, did not depend on whose womb an issue matured in, but rather whose seed was gestated. As blond Christian maidens fetched fancy prices in the slave markets, raids in Christian lands by Muslim private entrepreneurs became big business. Female captives were pedigreed like dogs. Their Christian antecedents, their genuine blondness, their virginity, and their ability to bear children were all ascertained and notarized before they were marketed.

As there was also constant intermarriage between Arabs and Christians on lower social levels, less and less "Aryan blood" flowed in the veins of Spanish Christians. The notion that the war of reconquest was fought between Latino-Goths in North Spain and Andalusian Arabs in South Spain is a popular myth. As a matter of fact, there was no such thing as racial purity in the Islamic world. To term the inhabitants of that peninsula "Moors" or "Arabs" is a misnomer, for their ancestors might be Greeks, Egyptians, Cretans, Libyans, Moors, Romans. The Arabs in Spain were united not by race but by the Islamic creed. The same held true for the Jews, for they intermarried almost as much as the Arabs. What kept them apart was not the purity of their blood but the exclusiveness of their creed.

Under the Umayyad caliphate, Spain had become the most civilized country in the world. From the inception of Islam's conquest, Spanish Jews had soared to the highest government posts. A series of brilliant Jewish viziers—

viceroys—enriched the caliphate's coffers and helped usher in an age of splendor and learning. Cordoba, the gay capital of Europe, became known as the city of 60,000 palaces and the home of a library of 400,000 volumes. Though the Jews in Spain became influential in court circles and wealthy in the marketplaces, their intellectual life languished for three centuries, until the influx of these "Babylonian refugees" from Islam East in the tenth century.

The remarkable aspect of the 600-year Jewish experience in the Islamic world is that it can be split into two equal, sharply defined periods. From 700 to 1000, the Jews in the eastern caliphate produced a plethora of great Talmudists, but few secular scholars. From 1000 to 1300, the Jews in the western caliphate produced an abundance of great poets, philosophers, and scientists, but few great Talmudists. Collectively, they sparked the Jewish Golden Age in Spain.

Worldliness and a sense of tragedy brands the Jewish poet-philosophers of this Golden Age. Moses ibn Ezra, grammarian, philosopher, and a poet of sorrow, hit the roads of the world to escape his love for his niece whose red lips made him forget his gray hair but not the commandment against incest. Abraham ibn Ezra, grammarian, exegete, and poet, penned poems of love to God and women with equal fervor, and opened a path to modern biblical criticism by intimating that Isaiah was the work of two writers and Job a translation from the Greek. Dunash ibn Labrat, in his dual role of poet and grammarian, reintroduced sex in Jewish literature (absent since the Song of Songs) and set the framework for modern grammar by developing the theory of the three-letter root for Semitic languages. Solomon ibn Gabirol, orphaned in childhood, reared on philanthropy, and depressed by poverty, became the author of philosophical works that made him "the first philosopher of the Middle Ages." Abraham ibn Latif, physician and philosopher, created an epochal work by combining Greek philosophy and natural science into a unified system of thought that laid a new foundation for modern scientific methodology.

In science, Spanish Jews were especially prominent in

astronomy, geography, and mathematics. Abraham bar Hiyyah, encyclopedist, philosopher, and scientist, laid the groundwork for a Hebrew scientific terminology, authored works on geography and astronomy, and predicted the arrival of the messiah in 1358. Abraham Zacuto, astronomer at the court of King John II of Portugal, was famed both for his astronomical tables used by Columbus and Vasco da Gama, and for his scientific works which influenced the coming European sciences. Levi ben Gerson, inventor of the quadrant known as "Jacob's Ladder," was the first to criticize the faulty methodology of medieval science. He also authored famed works on trigonometry, later boldly taken over by Johann Muller of Nuremberg, now credited with being the "father" of modern trigonometry. Immanuel Bonfils (born in France) invented the decimal system a century before it was absorbed into European mathematics as an Arab innovation.

The Talmudists, too, were noted for their versatility. Moses ben Nahman interjected mysticism in his Talmudic tractates, rationalism in his biblical comments, and wit in his disputations on Judaism versus Christianity. Solomon ibn Adret, known as the Rabbi of Spain and noted for his Responsa that influenced later codifiers, opposed messiahs and mystics as well as the study of science and philosophy for Jews under thirty. David Kimhi, grammarian and philologist, who fused Babylonian, Spanish, and French Talmudic currents into a unified philosophy, wrote Bible commentaries of such cogency that Christian scholars used them as source material in their translations of the Bible into European languages.

Three men in particular, however, epitomize the Golden Age in Spain—Judah Halevi, the poet of the Diaspora, who unified all emotional currents of his time into one psychological identification with Jerusalem; Moses Maimonides, the pro-Aristotelian Talmudist, who erected a philosophical bridge between Jews and Christians; and Hasdai Crescas, the anti-Aristotelian rabbi, who paved a path to Western science.

Born in Toledo to wealth and success, Judah Halevi (1071–1141) attained early renown as a physician. But success was not his goal. Torn by yearnings he could

neither understand nor control, he abandoned his family
and set out for Cordoba, there to alleviate his anxieties
with promiscuity and his passions with poetry. He introduced Arab poetic forms into Hebrew literature and
scandalized the fundamentalists by daring to express in
the sacred tongue of Hebrew the joy of kissing a woman's
breast. But the pleasures of the senses soon waned. He
gave up his life of revelry to become a wandering trouba-
dour of God, summing up the mission of his people in
sublime poetry. In his greatest work, *Ha'kuzari,* Halevi
became the first philosopher to speculate on the meaning
of the Diaspora in Jewish destiny. In his view, the successful conclusion of the Diaspora and the restitution of
Palestine would herald the redemption of not only the
Jews but all mankind. His idea of the Diaspora as a
function of the Jewish manifest destiny took hold of the
Jewish imagination with an obsessive fervor.

Moses Maimonides (1194–1270) was a link between the
dying East and awakening West, a transmitter of Hellenic
thought in Arab garb. Born in Cordoba when it was in
the hands of fierce Almohades tribes engaged in relentless
persecution of Christians and Jews, his family fled Spain,
eventually settling in Egypt. Though a physician by profession, Maimonides was at first associated with his brother
in a lucrative jewel trade with India. But after his brother
and fortune were lost at sea, he returned to the practice of
medicine, becoming Egypt's most renowned physician.

Maimonides was the first Jewish writer to perceive of
Christianity and Mohammedanism as historical extensions
of Judaism. He also clearly saw the new pattern of Jewish
dispersal and its attendant dangers to the Jews. With few
islands of tolerance left in the Islamic world, with Jews
fleeing the East to the land of the Franks, with no authoritative yeshivas left to give definitive legal decisions,
Maimonides' lofty aim was to codify the entire Talmud to
ensure its authority and survival. With the insouciance
of an intellectual snob, he unabashedly states in his pref-
ace: "This work will assemble the entire Oral Law from
the days of Moses to the completion of the Talmud. . . .
For this reason I have called it the *Second Torah.* One

needs only to read the Torah first, then study my book to learn the entire Oral Law."

Written with elegance, in terse lucid Hebrew, the *Second Torah* is a tour de force of Jewish law and literature. Its systematic arrangement proved unsurpassed. "Custom precedes law, and custom annuls law," Maimonides declared loftily, as he selected "the right law" for the Jews in the Diaspora whenever he disagreed with previous Talmudists.

The publication of the *Second Torah* stunned the Jewish world with its pioneering and *chuzpah*. A shower of denunciation fell on this self-styled Moses who presumed to hand down a second Torah as though he had received it personally from God at Sinai. But with time, as the brilliance of his work highlighted the ignorance of its critics, denunciation gave way to cautious praise and from praise to unbridled adulation.

The invective hurled at the *Second Torah* was but watered vinegar compared to the undiluted vitriol heaped on his subsequent philosophical work, *A Guide to the Perplexed,* which introduced the "heretical" thought that Judaism was a rational religion, a notion that would have bewildered the first Moses. The book was promptly banned to anyone under twenty-five, but as this did not deter those over that age, the Jews of France denounced the work to the Church. An obliging cardinal burned all available copies in Paris (1238), an act which prefaced a subsequent three-century wave of public burnings of the Talmud by the Church.

These two works by Maimonides heralded a coming cleavage in Jewish ranks. The *Second Torah* became the heritage of the zealots who used it to stultify Jewish thought; *A Guide to the Perplexed* became the heritage of the intellectuals, who used it to clear a path to rationalism.

Few would expect a medieval rabbi to become an anti-Aristotelian crusader with such objectivity that for three centuries he would be thought of as an Arab philosopher. Yet such was the fate of Barcelona-born Hasdai Crescas (1340–1410) who, in his youth, was sentenced to death for alleged participation in the assassination of a Jewish friend of King Enrico of Castile. Like Dostoyevsky,

Crescas was pardoned just before execution. After a prolonged prison sentence, he settled in Saragossa, eventually becoming the crown rabbi of the province of Aragon.

Ironically, the work that brought Crescas three centuries of obscurity before it brought him fame was an attempt to undermine Maimonides by attacking Aristotelian thought. Crescas, unwittingly, however, undermined the entire medieval philosophical structure, paving the way for the scientific methodology of Descartes, Galileo, and Newton. In rejecting the arguments of Aristotle, and thus laying the groundwork for modern philosophy, Crescas applied the deductive method of Talmudic reasoning, which in reality applied scientific procedure to textual study. Though Crescas disproved the Aristotelian theories of naturally light objects and natural motion upward, it did not occur to him to do what Galileo did—climb up a tower and drop two objects of unequal weight, observe their simultaneous landing, and thus frame the universal laws of falling bodies.

The Jewish renaissance in Islam West, however, was based on Greek ideas, not Arab. It was, in fact, the successful conclusion of an intellectual revolution that should have taken place a thousand years earlier in the Hellenistic phase of Jewish history, but did not. Why did not the Jews produce poets, philosophers, and scientists in the Hellenistic Age? Why did Jewish history have to wait a millennium before Hellenism could flower in the Jewish mind?

The answer is that the Jews back in the days of Greece had feared that a dose of the original, undiluted, superior Hellenic culture might wipe out the Jewish idea in a direct intellectual confrontation. Now the infusion of the thousand-year-old dormant germ of Hellenism through the needle of the Islamic civilization was like an inoculation with a dead virus that guaranteed immunity. No longer afraid of becoming spiritually involved with Hellenism, the Jews for the first time dared examine its intellectual contents. Instead of being "Arabized," the Jews "Hellenized" themselves. Thus the Jews in Islam West were intellectually closer to Western civilization than to the Jews in

Islam East. This also facilitated their transition to the Christian world in the coming fourth challenge.

The demise of the Jewish Golden Age in Spain coincided with the political events reshaping Europe's balance of power in the thirteenth century. Though the Mongol curse that devastated the eastern half of the Islamic caliphates was lifted at the battle of Damascus, the western half was not saved from devastation. Galloping disintegration played havoc with the western remnant of the Islamic world. Moors and Berbers bent on plunder probed weak borders, seized the land fringing Africa's northern shore, and set up petty states that strangled each other in senseless warfare. The tide of the *reconquista*—as the five-century (1000–1500) Christian reconquest of Spain from the Pyrenees to the Gibraltar has been dubbed—could not be stopped. Slowly the Moors were forced back into Africa. By 1300, the northern half of Spain was back in the bosom of the Church. As the Islamic Empire slowly sank into a sea of cultural oblivion, feudal Europe slowly rose from its Dark Age into the light of its Renaissance.

For seven centuries the magnificent Islamic civilization had illuminated the cultural scene of the world with its beauty and grandeur, its wit and valor, its reverence for learning and penchant for business—a busy civilization, though never too busy to pause and pay tribute to a stanza of poetry. Neglected by most Western scholars because of their narcissistic preoccupation with Greek and Roman classicism, perhaps future writers with broader concepts of history will restore this vanished civilization to its rightful place in the museum of past civilizations.

One cannot help wonder if the subsequent subjugation of the Arab world by the West, which crushed its spirit, was not more devastating than the Mongol depredations which destroyed only its physical assets. Today, we once again see the Arab world striving to rise out of the dust to make a place for its people in the modern world. One day, perhaps, the Arab nations will establish another, equally magnificent Semitic civilization to illuminate the hopes of man, and Arabs and Jews will once again live side by side with respect for each others' genius.

The hostilities that divide Jews and Arabs in the twentieth century are not deep-seated psychological animosities but shallow political differences. A turn of history or better diplomacy could solve them without bloodshed. The destruction of Israel would merely gain the Arabs a sliver of land; the destruction of the Arabs would only isolate the Jews from the Semitic world that gave them birth. The real enemies of the Arab people have been Western and Russian imperialists who, under the pretense of friendship, and with slogans and bribes, have striven to maintain the inferior position of the Arabs, the former to exploit Arab oil, the latter to gain a military foothold in the Near East. Together, Arabs and Jews could spark a new humanistic civilization that would be a beacon of light to the underdeveloped third of the world.

As this Jewish adventure in the Islamic civilization draws to a close, let us pause to assess the special role of the Diaspora in Jewish survival thus far. If the first act served as a training program for survival in a world exile in the second act, then it has thus far succeeded beyond all reasonable expectations. No matter how much Tannas, Amoras, Saboras, and Gaons changed the prevailing modes of Jewish common law, they did not change the monotheistic concept of God or tamper with the Mosaic commandments. They did not relinquish the idea of a national homeland in Zion nor deviate from the guidance of canonized Torah. They did not abandon the universalist philosophy of the Prophets, and steadfastly clung to the uniqueness of Jewish nationalism.

If there is a Jewish manifest destiny, wherein the Diaspora plays a predetermined role of saving the Jews in order to preserve them for the successful accomplishment of a mission in the third act, then it has so far delivered all that was required of it by God, man, or fate. But can the Diaspora continue to serve this function in the challenges of the Christ-oriented civilization into which history is about to hurl the Jews?

The first and second challenges unfolded on two coexistent levels simultaneously. One, the Roman, led to a phase-out of Western Judaism; the other, the Sassanid, led to the ascendance of Eastern Judaism. The response to the third challenge unified the Western and Eastern currents of Judaism with the Talmud. Throughout this challenge, Western Judaism remained the recessive strain and Eastern Judaism the dominant. In the fourth challenge, however, as the Jews flee the Islamic world for the Christian, these roles of recessiveness and dominance will be reversed.

When the curtain rises on this fourth challenge, we will be confronted with a completely new stage setting, that of the Western world. When feudal Europe awakens out of its Dark Age in the tenth century, we will see Jews and Christians commingle in their first meaningful embrace, an ambivalent love-hate relationship that will proceed passionately in three distinct movements—a theological shotgun marriage in the fourth challenge, a social divorce in the fifth, and a semantic cohabitation in the sixth.

As a clinical psychiatrist must probe into the childhood of a patient to discover the etiology of his hostility toward society, so a clinical historian must probe into the childhood of Christianity to discover the etiology of its hostility toward Judaism. As we remove accumulated layers of myth, fraud, and rationalization, we will discover that the nexus of this Christian neurosis was a Jew named Jesus.

As a knowledge of Jesus and the origins of Christianity are essential for an understanding of the metahistoric ramifications that will transpire in a Christian world, let us avail ourselves of a brief intermission to walk on the low road of everyday life, from Bethlehem to Golgotha, to reconstruct the life of the historical Jesus from birth to death. Subsequently we shall walk on the high road of faith, from Golgotha to Rome, to trace the evolution of the theological Christ from a minor Jewish creed to a major world religion.

PROGRAM NOTE

A Cross-Examination of the Crucifixion

For 2,000 years, Christians and Jews have claimed that their religions had nothing in common except the Jewish origin of Jesus. Christians have extolled the uniqueness of Christianity and denigrated Judaism as an empty, arid religion bogged down with laws lacking spiritual comfort. Jews have extolled the moral grandeur of their own faith, and derogated the self-proclaimed uniqueness of Christianity as superstitious nonsense.

But in the spring of 1947, on the eve of the birth of the state of Israel, the prophetic discovery of the Dead Sea Scrolls shattered the myth of the uniqueness of Christianity and confirmed the idea of its evolution from Judaism. To the horror of devout Christians and the dismay of orthodox Jews, the Dead Sea Scrolls revealed a prototype for Jesus a century before his birth. They unveiled the fact that most of the rites derided by the Jews as "pagan claptrap" and lauded by the Church as uniquely Christian had been conceived and practiced by Jews two centuries before Christianity existed.

The Dead Sea Scrolls were discovered accidently by an illiterate Bedouin teen-age shepherd named Muhammed the Wolf, when one of the goats he was driving through the dreadful, desolate Judean Wilderness along the northwest shore of the Dead Sea strayed into a long-forgotten cave. It was one of the caves where, 2,000 years before, the members of a Jewish sect known as Essenes had carved out one of their communities. Here Muhammed found parchment scrolls dating back to the second century B.C. that contained scriptural writings of the Essenes, the first "Christians" in history.[1]

Subsequent expeditions to the Qumran area, pockmarked with weird rocks and serrated by naked cliffs, led to the discovery of other caves, yielding more scrolls and over 600 fragments of diverse Essene writings. Six of these scrolls, now known by the names of *Manual of Discipline, Habakkuk Commentary, Book of Jubilees, The War of the Sons of Light with the Sons of Darkness, Zadokite Fragments,* and a collection of *Hymns,* contain the heart of the Essene creed and present us with a sketch of the future Christianity.

In their remote cave retreats, the Essenes developed a new, curiously Judaic creed that diverged from both Sadducee and Pharisee Judaism, yet resembled both. Though rejecting the Sadducee cult of sacrifice, they accepted its idea of a priesthood; though rejecting the Pharisee Oral Law, the Mishna, they supplemented the Written Law, the Torah, with their own interpretations, the Scrolls. The celibate Essene priesthood refrained from marriage. New members, including children, were generally initiated into the sect through the rite of baptism. At the head of each community was an overseer, or bishop. One of their rituals, administered by the priests, is almost an outline of the Christian communion, and prescribes a protocol for seating foreshadowing the Last Supper. The Essenes referred to themselves as the "Elect of God" and to their religion as "the New Covenant."

A remarkable figure known only as the Teacher of Righteousness is the central figure in Essenism. His disciples viewed him as the suffering servant of God, "called from the womb" to restore the "True Covenant." All who

[1]Many theologians, both Jewish and Christian, pained by the thought of the Jewish paternity of Christianity, have tried to prove that the Dead Sea Scrolls were written several centuries after and not before Jesus. We need not refute them for, in espousing their respective alternate sects and dates, they have brilliantly refuted each other.

believed in him as the messiah would be healed, for as stated in Isaiah, "By his bruises we are healed." The Teacher of Righteousness was also a "man of sorrow," foredoomed to death, destined to be slain at the hand of a "Wicked Priest." But the Teacher of Righteousness was chosen by God as the instrument of salvation for mankind. He was the "Nazarene"—the *nezer*, the "shoot" of the House of David, the rock on which the future "Church" would be built.

The name of this Teacher of Righteousness is not known, for his followers never pronounced it nor wrote it down. His ministry began about 104 B.C. and lasted to about 65–53 B.C., when he was slain by the Wicked Priest, whose name is also unknown. Convinced that their slain Teacher of Righteousness would reappear amongst them, resurrected from the dead, his disciples settled in the area around Qumran. Here they awaited the return of their messiah while preparing themselves for Judgment Day.

The resemblance between the Teacher of Righteousness and Jesus Christ a century later is incredible. In many respects Jesus appears to be an astonishing reincarnation of the Teacher of Righteousness. Like him, Jesus preached chastity, penitence, humility, poverty, and was viewed as the messiah of God, the redeemer of the world. Like him, Jesus was hated by the priests, and also put to death. Like him, Jesus was thought of as the "Nazarene"—the "shoot" of the House of David. And, as in the case of the Teacher of Righteousness, a church was also founded in the name of Jesus, whose adherents also fervently awaited a miraculous return.

The Essenes disappear from history in the first century A.D., although we hear of their creed again in the Gospels, but not by that name. We find it espoused by John the Baptist, preaching in the Judean Wilderness near the main Essene monastery. In Essene fashion, John calls for the people to repent, to confess their sins, to be saved through baptism. His real mission, however, according to the Gospels, is to wait for the messiah and to baptize him into the faith, in fulfillment of prophecy. The man who appears is not the resurrected Essene Teacher of Righteousness but Jesus, destined to concentrate upon himself through his subsquent crucifixion the adoration of men denied the Teacher of Righteousness.

Though the crucifixion of Jesus took place nearly 2,000 years ago, the drama is not yet over. Though his accusers are dead, the witnesses vanished, and the judges dust, the trial of Jesus nevertheless goes on. Though crucified, dead, and buried, he continues to rise in the hearts of his followers. To them, his resurrection is a living reality. The death of Christ, not the life of Jesus, is so central to Christianity that without the crucifixion theme there would be no Christianity.

From a historic viewpoint it makes no difference whether a physical or a spiritual resurrection took place, for as we have persistently pointed out, it is ideas, not blind facts, that shape history. We must, therefore, examine the crucifixion as an event founded in fact, and view the resurrection as a drama shaped to fit an idea.

Who was this Jew Jesus who failed to make an impression on history until a century after his death, but whose one-year ministry on earth shaped the foundations of Western civilization? There is not enough historical material about him "to write a decent obituary." There are but three facts known about his birth and early life. He was born the eldest son of a Jewish mother who kept a kosher house, he was circumcised on the eighth day, and he had two or more sisters and four brothers named James, Joseph, Simon, and Judas.[2] All else concerning his birth—the visitation of the Holy Ghost, the Virgin Birth, the three wise men, the genealogy traced to King David, the flight to Egypt and back—is pious theological license designed to prove that in Jesus the Old Testament prophecies were fulfilled.

The phenomenon of a virgin birth is older than recorded

[2] Catholic dogma today denies that Jesus had any brothers or sisters. It was not always thus. After the Church had made Mary, the mother of Jesus, officially immaculate in 1854, it was also deemed advisable to deny that the newly "divine" Mary should have had carnal intercourse with her husband Joseph, even after the birth of Jesus. This is denied by Protestants, who point to the plain text in Matthew 14:55–56, which explicitly names the brothers of Jesus.

history. Among the more familiar heroes and gods of royal virgin birth are Hercules, Perseus, Theseus, and Romulus. The Hindu princess Kunti holds the record for multiple virgin births. In Hindu mythology, the sun-god Surya seduced Kunti, who bore, as a virgin, the boy Karna. Thereafter she had three more sons, all through divine contact and virginal deliveries.[3]

The stories of the Holy Ghost visiting Mary and the three wise men visiting the child Jesus have their prototypes in an Egyptian legend dating back to 1400 B.C. in connection with the birth of King Amenhotep III. A divine spirit (a holy ghost) appears before the virgin queen, advising her she will conceive a boy fathered by a heavenly fire. The newborn child is nursed by divine cows in a manger. Three kings from far away come to adore and pay homage to the newborn child, which has been proclaimed god by the ghost that impregnated the virgin mother.

Jesus had to be born in Bethlehem to fulfill the prophecy of the Prophet Micah that the messiah would come from Bethlehem, the home of King David, and Matthew and Luke link Jesus to him through two differing genealogies. What puzzles three billion non-Christians is why the ancestry of Jesus should be traced back to King David since, according to these two saints, the Holy Ghost and not Joseph was the father of Jesus.

There is no physical description of Jesus in the entire New Testament. Each age, therefore, has had to interpret his looks according to its own image. In Byzantine art he was a swarthy Semite, badly in need of a haircut and shave. In Renaissance paintings he was a dark-complected Latin, with a neatly trimmed beard. In Protestant paintings he became a blond, clean-shaven Nordic. And in modern times, as exemplified in the paintings of Rouault, he has again become a swarthy, cadaverous Semite, badly in need of a haircut and shave.

---

[3]Readers interested in the recurrent theme of men, gods, and ghosts siring illegitimate children by virgin mothers are referred to Otto Rank's *The Myth of the Birth of the Hero* for a psychoanalytic explanation, and to Lord Raglan's *The Hero* for an empiric view.

The New Testament is as maddeningly silent about the childhood and adolescence of Jesus as the Old Testament is about Moses. Was Jesus a Sadducee who went to Temple to sacrifice to God under the supervision of priests? Was he a Pharisee who went to synagogue to offer prayers to God under the leadership of rabbis? Or was he an Essene who had rejected Temple and synagogue for the monastic life of that sect? The forcible conversion of the pagan Galileans to Judaism in 135 B.C. by the Hasmonean King John Hyracanus raises yet another interesting question. Were Joseph and Mary, the Galilean parents of Jesus, the descendants of generations of Jews, or were they the offspring of a recently converted pagan family?

The messianic history of Jesus begins when at the age of thirty he has his fateful meeting with John the Baptist, whose theological function is to "baptize" (symbolically to "anoint")[4] Jesus according to prophecy. At this point Jesus becomes "the Christ," "the anointed," for the word "Christ" is the Greek equivalent for the Hebrew word *mashiah*, meaning "one who is anointed." "Jesus Christ" is simply the Greek translation for the Hebrew "Joshua the anointed."

With this act of anointment, the die is cast. Jesus, "the Christ," now heads for Jerusalem to act out his predestined or self-chosen role. From a political viewpoint, he has chosen the worst possible time; from a messianic viewpoint, the best possible time. One rebellion after another was sweeping the turbulent land of Judea as political zealots and warrior messiahs stirred the population into successive uprisings against Rome. Chief instigators behind this unrest were the Zealots, among whom the most notorious were the *Sicarii,* the "daggermen," who murdered Roman officials with special daggers.

When Jesus entered Jerusalem, hatred of the Romans was at its peak. A new rebellion in Galilee had but recently been quelled with blood and crucifixions. People were talking about a new rebel leader whose followers had proclaimed him "the messiah, the son of David." To the

---

[4]The Jews in ancient times did not crown their kings but anointed them with oil.

Romans, who had executed dozens of such warrior messiahs, such talk spelled trouble. It would take little to
ignite this explosive mixture of hatred, zealotry, and
messianic fervor into another costly revolt. The new
procurator of Judea, Pontius Pilate, decided to play it safe.
At the head of a legion, he left his administrative capital
at Caesarea and went to Jerusalem to take personal command.

The events that followed the decisions of Pontius Pilate
and Jesus Christ to go to Jerusalem are shrouded in obscurity, wrapped in acrimony, and smothered with tons
of conflicting scholarship. Yet if we look beneath the
learned verbosity of most theologians, we find that they
all have but one basic source for their opinions, namely
the four Gospels (and to a lesser extent the Apocrypha).
It is therefore imperative that we keep in mind a few
facts about the Gospels and their authors.

The word "gospel," derived from the Anglo-Saxon "good
spell," means "good news," and the story of the messiahship
of Jesus was the good news the Gospel writers gave
Christian converts. Of the four Gospel writers—Mark,
Matthew, Luke, and John—only Mark and Matthew were
Jews. Mark's Gospel, written sometime between the
years 70 and 85 A.D., though the second in the New Testament is the first chronologically. Matthew, an unidentified
teacher, wrote his Gospel between 85 and 95, primarily to
attract new pagan converts. Luke was a pagan physician
who, like Matthew, used the manuscript of Mark as a
basis for his Gospel and finished his work after the year
75. John, an enigmatic figure whose pagan antecedents
are still unknown, completed his Gospel sometime between
95 and 105. As John did not base his text on the manuscript of Mark, his Gospel differs from those of Mark,
Matthew, and Luke, which are known as the "synoptic
Gospels" because they espouse one viewpoint. All four
Gospel writers were later canonized by a grateful Church
for writing the "good news" about Jesus, but this does
not make their words divine. They did not pretend to
write history; they wrote theology.

Historians have never accepted the Gospel accounts
of the trial of Jesus, because, though the theology may

be impeccable, the facts are questionable. In essence, the Gospel writers state that those Jews who did not believe that Jesus was the messiah, conspired to arrest him at night, hauled him to a kangaroo court presided over by the High Priest, went out in the night in search of false witnesses, convicted him on false evidence, and dragged him the following morning to Pontius Pilate. There they begged and threatened the procurator to crucify Jesus for them. The Gospels further state that Pilate, after pleading with the Jews not to force him to crucify Jesus because he could find "no fault" with the man, finally acceded to their wishes out of fear, and reluctantly sentenced Jesus to the cross.

The Gospel accounts of the trial and its aftermath abound with contradictions, improbabilities, and impossibilities. In fact, in these four Gospel writers we have the unseemly sight of four saints fighting for the gospel truth. What Mark says is contradicted by Matthew and Luke. What Luke says is contradicted by Mark and Matthew. What Matthew says is contradicted by Luke and Mark. The fourth Gospel, that of John, presents an even greater problem to biblical scholars, for John contradicts Mark, Matthew, and Luke even where these three agree.

Yet, in spite of contradictions, inconsistencies, and pious frauds in the Gospel accounts, the arrest, the trial, and the crucifixion of Jesus are not the invention of the Gospel writers. Though they may have been blind to history, though they may have been motivated by theology, though they may have rearranged details to match faith, the Gospel writers nevertheless dealt with basic, historic facts. Jesus did live, he was arrested, he was tried, and he was crucified. But by whom and why?

If we scrape off the theological frosting, if we eliminate all contradictions, if we concentrate upon the few points the Gospels agree on, then we have the following schema: the three synoptic Gospels agree that Jesus was brought before Jewish authorities for questioning, but they do not spell out exactly what crime Jesus might have committed to merit a death sentence. On the other hand, all four Gospels agree that Jesus was tried by the Romans for a political crime, and that they crucified him for aspiring to the throne of Judea.

Viewed this way, a new Gospel drama in two scenes emerges. In the first, Jesus is arrested and convicted by the Jews on an unspecified charge of blasphemy, but is not executed for that crime. In the second, Jesus is tried by the Romans for the explicitly stated crime of treason, and is executed for that crime.

Why this sudden switch from the crime of blasphemy against the Jews to the crime of treason against the Romans? If Jesus had committed a religious crime, then he was innocent in the eyes of the Romans but guilty in the eyes of the Jews, who would not have hesitated to stone him to death, the Jewish punishment for blasphemy. On the other hand, if Jesus had committed a political crime, then he was innocent in the eyes of the Jews but guilty in the eyes of the Romans, who would not hesitate to crucify him, the Roman punishment for sedition.

For eighteen centuries, scholars shied away from cross-examining the Gospel witnesses simply because it was dangerous. One was burned alive by a vigilant Church for looking too closely into these matters. Not until the eighteenth-century Age of Rationalism did scholars dare contradict the dogmatic pronouncements of the Church. Though there are today hundreds of explanations for the crucifixion enigma, essentially they all fall into four main theories—the preordained destiny, the deicide drama, the political conspiracy, and the "Passover plot."

The preordained destiny theory, twenty centuries old and still in vogue with sophisticated theologians, casts the crucifixion drama as a prophetic fulfillment. Even before creating heaven and earth, this theory goes, God had planned for the birth, death, and resurrection of Jesus to occur in the year 30 A.D. as a means of redeeming man through the blood of the slain Christ. There are no heroes or villains in this view. Everybody—Mary, the Holy Ghost, Jesus, the High Priest, Judas, Pilate—all do the bidding of God, and play out their divinely assigned roles. The Holy Ghost is as much the instrument of the Lord's will as Judas is. And the Jews, if they did kill

Jesus, did so only on the bidding of God, the theory goes, in order to bring forth Christianity.

The preordained destiny dogma placed the Church in an agonizing dilemma. If the Jews did God's bidding, they were God's chosen instrument in giving life to the very religion the Jews rejected as false. Therefore the Church came up with an alternate theory, the deicide drama, in which the Jews were portrayed as slayers of Jesus instead of midwives of Christianity. The Church trusted that the masses would never catch on to its casuistry, a correct appraisal of the human mind which can entertain two opposite views without too much intellectual strain. Everybody is evil in this Church-inspired explanation of the crucifixion—Pharisees, Sadducees, priests, scribes, Jews—except Jesus, Pilate, and those who blindly follow Jesus. Jews who do not believe in the messiahship of Jesus are depicted as despicable quislings and satanic conspirators—in short, Christ-killers. This is still the most popular view among the Christian masses, as it has the merit of instant understanding.

The proponents of the political conspiracy view, born of modern biblical exegesis, see Jesus as a warrior messiah leading an unsuccessful rebellion against Rome, suffering the fate of a rebel. Jesus, these scholars claim, was not only thought of as the savior by his disciples but was looked upon as their leader in a revolt against Rome.

In further support of this political conspiracy theory, its advocates point out that the Temple with its palaces and courts was a huge place, 600 feet wide and 1,500 feet long, with thick fortified walls, attended by a staff of 20,000 functionaries, and protected by a Roman cohort of 500 men. Jesus could hardly have dropped in at the Temple, driven out the money-changers, and then walked off without being arrested by Roman soldiers, any more than it would be possible today for a modern reformer to drop in at Vatican Square in Rome, beat up the numerous vendors of postcards, crucifixes, commemorative stamps, candles, Bibles, and beads, and walk off without being arrested by Vatican gendarmes. Perhaps Jesus did not merely drive the money-changers out of the Temple, the theory goes, but actually seized it, as so many passages in the Gospels seem to indicate. Then, after a Roman counterattack, he was forced to flee into hiding.

If Jesus was one of the many warrior messiahs who took up arms against the Romans in that fateful first century A.D., then subsequent events can be reconstructed historically within the framework of the Gospel narratives. In the year 33 (or 30) A.D., on the fifteenth day of Nisan, rumors abounded about a plot to take over the city. There had been a disturbance, or revolt, at the Temple, and the Romans were looking for a man whose followers had openly declared him King of the Jews.

Could it be, speculate the political conspiracy theorists, that Jesus, who had entered Jerusalem as a self-proclaimed messiah, was arrested by the Jews to be held in protective custody until the trouble blew over and Pilate departed with his legionnaires? But the Romans, on a tip by Judas perhaps, found out about the suspect being held by the Jews and demanded that he be handed over to them for trial, which was their prerogative as conquerors. This would explain why Jesus would be taken to Pilate to be tried, sentenced, and crucified as a rebel by the Romans. The tag hung on Jesus, according to Roman law, unmistakably spells out his crime—"King of the Jews."

But if this was the actual sequence of events, why did the Gospel writers blame the Jews? We must recall that by 75 A.D., when the first Gospel was written, the Romans already despised the Christians for their idolatrous religion, and abhorred them as subversives. The Gospel writers realized it would be dangerous to make the Romans the villains in their drama. On the other hand, the Jews at this time were at the height of their unpopularity with the Romans, having so recently engaged the empire in a devastating four-year war. The expedient thing was to portray the Jews as villains, by simply showing that the trial held by Pilate was forced on him by the Jews. Having rapacious Pilate defend Jesus was a stroke of sheer genius. It would show the Romans that their own procurator thought well of the Christians because their leader Jesus had cooperated with the Romans by "rendering unto Caesar what was Caesar's."

The proponents of the fourth theory, the Passover plot,

pose the startling hypothesis that perhaps it was not Jesus who was the victim of the Romans and Jews, but vice versa. The big problem facing any aspiring messiah, they point out, is how to convince people that he is truly the messiah. Could it be true, then, as the Passover plot theorists contend, that it was not Jesus who was the victim of Jews and Romans, but Jews and Romans who were the "victims" of Jesus? Could it be that Jesus manipulated both Jews and Romans into doing what he wanted them to do as part of a plan to win the messianic crown via an engineered death and resurrection?

If Jesus was convinced that he was the messiah, how could he convince other Jews? This is not an idle question. What would happen, for instance, if a bearded gentleman were to arrive tomorrow in a Fiat at Piazza San Pietro in Rome and start beating the vendors of crucifixes and rosaries on the steps of St. Peter's, saying he was Jesus come to cleanse the churches dedicated to him? Would he be arrested as a disturber of the peace? Would he be given a psychiatric examination and thrown into a psychiatric ward? How would a returning Jesus convince the world he was a savior come back according to prophecy? What credentials would he have to show? What wonders would he have to perform before Catholics and Protestants would believe him?

Fortunately, Jesus did not have as difficult a task in Jerusalem 2,000 years ago as he would have in Rome today. Fortunately for Jesus, the Prophets had dropped many hints about the circumstances under which the messiah would arrive, what conditions would have to be met, and what fate would befall him. The Jews were familiar with these prescriptions for messiahship. If someone arrived who fulfilled them, he would automatically be proclaimed messiah.

What were some of these conditions? In addition to being a descendant of King David and anointed by a Prophet, an aspiring messiah would have to enter Jerusalem on the colt of an ass, be denounced by the High Priest, stand silent before his accusers, be betrayed by one of his disciples, be mocked with gall and vinegar, die between two outcasts, and be resurrected within three days. The Gospel writers claim that these and all other conditions outlined in the Old Testament were met and fulfilled in Jesus and therefore prove his messiahship.

How did it happen that all events in the life of Jesus as portrayed in the Gospels correspond so accurately to every hint dropped by the Prophets 500 to 700 years before his birth? Was it all due to fortuitous accident? Did God manipulate events on earth in such a manner as to fulfill each prophecy? Or did Jesus, in a sincere belief that he was the messiah, help arrange events in such a way that these prophecies would be fulfilled in him? And did the Gospel writers later fill in those prophecies Jesus could not have arranged for? The Gospel writers constantly remind us that Jesus was fully aware he had to fulfill these prophecies to attain his messiahship. Not only was he aware of the events to come, he even briefed his disciples as to who he was and outlined for them the forthcoming proof, as in this passage in Mark (8:27–33):

> And Jesus went out with his disciples, to the villages of Caesarea Philippi; and on the way he asked his disciples, "Who do men say that I am?" And they told him, "John the Baptist; and others say, Elijah, and others one of the Prophets." And he asked them, "But who do you say that I am?" Peter answered him, "You are the Christ." And he charged them to tell no one about him.

> And he began to teach them that the Son of man must suffer many things, and be rejected by the elders and the chief priests and the scribes, and be killed, and after three days rise again. And he said this plainly.

Either Jesus knew that God would make these events happen, or else he was unfolding his own plan. He continually predicted events before they took place, as if charting a course laid out by the Prophets. Before entering Jerusalem, for instance, Jesus made sure that a colt would be waiting for him so people could say he arrived in the manner prescribed by the Prophet Zechariah. As Matthew so explicitly explains it: "This took place to fulfill what was spoken by the prophets saying, Tell the daughter of Zion, Behold, your king is coming to you, humble, mounted on an ass, and on a colt, the foal of an ass." The disciples went and did as Jesus had directed them. It had its effect. On beholding Jesus arriving in the prescribed manner, the people shouted, "Hosanna to the Son of David. Blessed is he who comes in the name of the Lord."

But assuming that Jesus did arrange these events so as to fulfill prophecy, how could he mastermind his own resurrection? Passover plot theorists contend it all hinged on the simple fact that it took at least twenty-four to forty-eight hours to die on the cross. The plan therefore called for Jesus to commit a crime that would insure his death by crucifixion and then be betrayed by one of his disciples to fulfill prophecy. Once sentenced to the cross, one of his disciples could drug him so he would appear dead, seek permission to take down his body, then hide him in a secret cave to recover from his ordeal. After the prophetic prescription of a three-day wait, Jesus would reappear to his followers—"resurrected." Thus, say the Passover plot theorists, Jesus could have masterminded his conviction, punishment, and escape from the cross in such a manner that all prophecies surrounding the coming of a messiah would be fulfilled.

At his last Passover meal, Jesus "predicts" that one of his disciples present will betray him, whereupon he dips a morsel and gives it to Judas, saying, "What you are going to do, do quickly" (John 13–21:30). As if on a prearranged signal, Judas leaves to betray him. Jesus is arrested and brought before Pilate who asks him if he claimed he was King of the Jews. Jesus answers, "You have said it," in effect a pleading that is known in legal terminology today as *nolo contendere*, a "no contest" admission of guilt. This reply permits Jesus to stand silent before his accusers as prescribed by prophecy and at the same time insure himself a death sentence by crucifixion for the crime of sedition.

This is also the course outlined in the Gospel narratives. After six hours on the cross, Jesus states he is thirsty. In fulfillment of prophecy, he is handed a vinegar-soaked rag on a stave. But instead of being revived by this stimulant he sinks into a coma and seemingly expires. A friend rushes to Pilate to ask permission to take down the body. Pilate, suspicious that Jesus should have died so soon, sends a centurion to investigate.

To prevent anyone from dying too soon on the cross, the Romans usually placed a supportive pedulum under the feet of the condemned, but they now and then broke the legs of a crucified person to allow him a quicker, "merciful" death.[5] As the two rebels crucified with Jesus were still alive on their crosses, the centurion breaks their legs so he will not have to make a second trip to Golgotha, but the legs of Jesus he does not break, says Mark, in fulfillment of prophecy, or perhaps, seeing Jesus lifeless, he does not deem it necessary. Suspicious, nevertheless, the centurion sticks Jesus with a spear. According to John, blood and water spurt from the wound, which would indicate Jesus was alive, for blood does not spurt out of a corpse, as there is no heartbeat to pump it. Nevertheless, as Jesus gives no sign of life, permission is granted to take down his body, and the disciples remove Jesus to their secret cave. But the unanticipated wound inflicted by the Roman soldier proves fatal. Though the body is moved from the cave to a burial place, several people have, however, seen Jesus before his death.

Such a sequence accounts for all events in the Gospel narratives without having to resort to the supernatural. People who swore that the stone had been moved from the entrance of the cave where Jesus was supposedly buried, and people who testified to seeing Jesus walking on earth after have seen his body on the cross, would be telling the truth. And thus, according to the Passover plot theorists, in death Jesus realized the resurrection he had hoped to gain in life. This might be the historical Jesus Albert Schweitzer had in mind when he said, "We must be prepared to find that the knowledge of the personality and life

---

[5] By breaking the legs, the crucified victim was deprived of the support of the pedulum, and the weight of the body, now dangling from the arms, choked off the blood supply from the head, causing a quick death by suffocation.

of Jesus will not be a help but perhaps even an offense to religion."

Which of these four theories of the life and death of Jesus is correct? We may never know. We do, however, concur with Ernest Renan, who stated: "For those who believe in the Messiah, he [Jesus] is the Messiah. For those who think most of the Son of Man, he is the Son of Man. For those who prefer the Logos, the Son of God, he is the Logos, the Son of God, the Spirit." We would add only that, whichever view the reader prefers, one must not forget that Jesus was never a Christian. According to the New Testament (Acts 11:26), the word "Christian" was used for the first time in Antioch in 50 A.D., some twenty years after the death of Jesus. Jesus was born a Jew, was looked upon as a Jew by his fellow Jews and contemporary Romans, and died a Jew with a Jewish prayer on his lips.[6] The Gospel writers subsequently combined in this Jewish Jesus the two currents of Jewish messianism—the spiritual and suffering messiah (the servant of the Lord) as outlined in Isaiah, and the material and political messiah (son of man) as outlined in the Book of Daniel.

This cross-examination of the crucifixion would be pointless unless it also provided us with a new insight into the future pattern of Jewish and Christian eschatology— that is, the final outcome of things. If the concept of a messiah is to be lifted from the narrow confines of a Christian resurrection drama with redemption for individual sinners, into a larger scope of a Jewish manifest destiny with redemption for all, the Christians will have to demythologize the life of Jesus, and the Jews will have to re-evaluate his philosophy.

Having familiarized ourselves with the Jewish origins of Christianity, let us now return to our seats and await the rise of the curtain on the strange continent of Europe,

---

[6] Just as the Christian view of the Jews runs the ambiguous gamut from the spawn of the devil to God's Chosen People, so the Jewish view of Jesus runs that same ambiguous gamut from the belief that he was the illegitimate son of a Jewish slut and a Roman soldier named Pander to the present view of him as a Pharisee reformer.

as it emerges out of limbo to become the complacent concubine of Asiatic invaders, the surprised mother of the world's grandest civilization, and the reluctant midwife of a crucial millennium in the development of the Jewish manifest destiny.

The Fourth Challenge:
The Closed Society
of the Feudal World

THE INCREDIBLE CONTINENT

In Greek legend, Europa was the beautiful, dark-haired, light-skinned daughter of the Phoenician king of Tyre for whom Zeus lusted. Disguising himself as a white bull, this Aryan god offered the trusting Semitic princess a ride, after which he duly ravished her. Ever since then, Europe's history has been a series of miscegenous love affairs; to her willing loins were attracted the riffraff of Asia. But such was Europe's allure that all her ravishers fell in love with her and stayed, except the Huns, who came, raped, and vanished. By the sixth century A.D., Europe had not only lost her chastity several times over but also the purity of her blood.

For all her beauty, however, Europe was culturally a late bloomer, 3,000 to 4,000 years behind her Semitic sibling. While Mesopotamia basked in her Bronze Age, Europe lay in the cradle of her Stone Age. While the Semites of Asia lived in cities, the aborigines of Europe lived in caves. While the Prophets in Palestine thundered their deathless prose, exhorting mankind to walk humbly with their moral God, the Gauls of Germany drank human blood as a toast to their lecherous deities.

The notion that the white-skinned aborigines of Europe might someday become the culture-bearers of the world seemed as ludicrous to the bronze-tinted Semites in the third millennium B.C. as the notion that the black-skinned aborigines of Africa might someday become the culture-

bearers of the world seems to white men today. But ignorant of these prejudices, history casually fused improbable
events into incredible consequences and gave birth to a new
civilization in Europe so brilliant in intellectual grandeur
that it surpassed the ·achievements of all previous ones.

Three features distinguish the history of Europe from
that of the other continents. Though no one discovered
Europe, she discovered all other continents; though Europe
has dominated other parts of the world, no foreign power
has ever dominated her; though Europe never had an indigenous population, she is the only continent to have
produced a civilization adopted by the entire world. Yet
the curious fact is that the people who laid the foundations for the history of Europe all came from Asia in four
huge migratory waves.

The first wave of migrants was homo sapiens, man himself, who drifted into Europe from Asia around 30,000 B.C.
These hairless creatures, advancing across the continent as
the Ice Age receded, exterminated the remnants of Nean-
derthal pre-man, the only "native" Europe ever produced,
and ushered in Europe's Paleolithic Age.

The Mesolithic Age was introduced to Europe with the
second Asiatic migration, around 8000 B.C. These new-
comers brought with them bows and arrows, skis and
sleds, fish nets and domesticated dogs. The "Mesolithics"
displaced the "Paleolithics" either through integration or
with their bows and arrows.

It was in the third migration, spanning the twenty centuries between 3000 and 1000 B.C., that the revolutionary
Neolithic innovations of the Near East were introduced
into southern Europe by Asiatics filtering into Greece, Italy,
and Spain. It was at this point in her history, as we have
already noted, that the offspring of the cultural embrace
on European soil between Asian Aryans and Near East
Semites matured into that continent's first civilization, the
Hellenic. We saw Rome acquire it by conquest, implant
it in her empire, and beget the first historic Europe.

The Romans envisioned Europe not as a cluster of nations but as one continental community. During the
height of the Antonine power and prestige in the third
century A.D., this Roman dream of European unity seemed

within realization. It was shattered in the fifth century when a giant peristaltic movement, caused by a military spasm in China, squeezed the fourth, most consequential, Asiatic migration into Europe.

Between Lake Baikal and the Gobi Desert in Central Asia roamed Mongolian nomads known as Huns (from *H'siung Nu*, savage slaves, as the Chinese called them)— short men with slit eyes, intensely hardy, and unbridled in their cruelty—skulking like jackals in search of prey along the Chinese frontier. The third-century Chinese Hahn Dynasty, taking the offensive, hurled this roving, marauding *patrask* toward the Caspian Sea. When the Huns, in their retreat, crossed the Volga, their advance units ran into the rear settlements of the Ostrogoths—the Asiatic forefathers of the Germans—squatting between the Don and Dnestr. A seething mass of humanity was now set in motion with disastrous consequences for Rome.

The fleeing Ostrogoths crossed the Dnestr and ran into a north-south line-up of barbarian Saxons, Lombards, Vandals, and Visigoths. They, in turn, pushed these squatters west, right into a second belt of barbarians strewn along Rome's eastern frontier—Franks, Burgundians, Alemanni, and some more Visigoths, killing cousins of the Ostrogoths. In wave after wave, these barbarians crossed the Roman frontier, turning Europe into one vast smelting pot as invader and settler locked in a two-century-long loot and rape struggle.

The invaders, with the exception of the Huns and Vandals, were not savages but merely barbarians (from the Greek *barbaroi*), that is, "foreigners." In their leisurely conquest-trek across the continent, most became Christianized, albeit with the wrong Christianity.

A serious schism had developed in the Church in the fourth century over the question of the nature of Jesus. Arius, churchman of Alexandria (d. 336), maintained that Jesus, though of the same substance as God, was not coequal to Him. Athanasius, patriarch of Alexandria (d. 373), averred that not only was Jesus cosubstantial with God but also coequal to Him. At the Council of Nicea (325), Emperor Constantine, a *mavin* on Christianity by virtue of his recent conversion, declared the Arian view of

Jesus a heresy and the Athanasian, or Catholic view, the only true Christian perspective. To the consternation of the Church, the invaders generally accepted the Arian concept of Jesus. In the subsequent three-century fight between Arians and Athanasians, more Christians exterminated each other over the question of the coequality of Jesus with God than were killed by the Romans in three centuries of persecutions.

Out of the chaos of the barbarian invasions rose the framework of a new Europe. Out of the Visigothic, Ostrogothic, and Frankish kingdoms founded by these Asiatic invaders emerged roughly the countries we know today as Spain, Italy, France, and Germany, which, by and large, forged the framework for Western civilization.

Rome was the main target of the invading barbarians. The first to sack the city were the Visigoths. Not since the Gauls, 800 years earlier, had a foreign army been able to force its way into the womb of Rome, not even Hannibal. "They have captured the city which once took the whole world captive," wailed St. Jerome in his monastic cell in Bethlehem.

The sack lasted three days. As good though Arian Christians, the Visigoths, singing hymns as they worked, first carried the city's holy vessels to safety. Then they began their program of rape and rapine at an unhampered, joy-filled pace.

Waiting in the wings for his turn to sack Rome was Attila, king of the Huns, slant-eyed and flat-nosed, a shrewd brain housed in a large head, precariously perched on a too small body. It had taken the Huns about a century to murder their way from the Volga to the Danube, driving the Ostrogoths before them like a herd of pigs. In 411, Attila crossed the Danube into "Germany" with half a million men. Domination of Europe by the Huns seemed inevitable. Only an ironic twist of fate saved her from Asiatic vassalage. As all Europe trembled, the former "scourge of God," the Visigothic King Theodoric I, in league with the Roman general Aëtius, met Attila, the new "scourge of God," in battle at Chalôns near Troyes (451), defeating him. Leaving a trail of burned cities as milestones in his retreat, Attila marched on Rome. Emperor

Valentinian III fled, but Pope Leo I, a man of "harmless simplicity," armed with God and gold, met Attila across a bargaining table and bought him off.

Attila did not live long enough to carry out his promise to return to Rome for another payoff. Heedless of advancing age, he imprudently added one too many a young bride to his considerable harem. On the morning after the wedding night he was found dead of a broken blood vessel. His empire, reaching from the Caspian to the Rhine, was divided among his numerous but collectively incompetent sons, who were more interested in wenching and gluttony than in ruling. Within a few decades, the Hun empire fell apart and vanished from the map of Europe, as Slavs, Avars, Bulgars, and Magyars from the steppes of Asia wrested Europe's eastern hinterland from the dwindling Huns, thus changing one set of Asiatic invaders for another.

The third, most devastating blow to Rome was a low punch by the Vandals, also converts to Arian Christianity. The Vandals had butchered their way through Germany, France, and Spain into north Africa, where they established the Vandal Kingdom (439) with its capital at the ancient site of Carthage. In 455, lame, cruel Gaiseric, king of the Vandals, set sail from Carthage to sack bypassed Rome. The ensuing merciless plunder gave birth to the word "vandalize" as an enduring legacy of their dark deeds.

With the dawn of the sixth century, the force of the successive invasions was spent, and the spawn of barbarians covered the continent. But for Rome the respite came too late. She could take just so much sacking. The city of Caesar and Christ, which before the invasions had boasted over a million people, now numbered barely 50,000. The lingering farce of a Roman Empire died (476) when Romulus Augustulus, its boy ruler, was pensioned off by the barbarian general Odoacer. After forwarding Rome's royal raiments to the emperor of Constantinople with the explanatory note they were no longer needed, Odoacer styled himself king and founded the Kingdom of Italy.

It had a glorious, but short life. Odoacer was murdered by the Ostrogothic general Theodoric, next on Rome's long list of new conquerors. Remembered in history as Theodoric the Great, he founded the Ostrogothic Kingdom of Italy and instituted a reign of peace, stability, and enlightenment. But with his death the new Italy fell apart, becoming the successive prey of Byzantians, Mohammedans, Lombards, Franks, Normans, and Germans, who, for over a millennia, fragmentized her into miniature kingdoms, principalities, duchies, republics, and papal states that resisted unification until the arrival of the Modern Age.

First of the barbarians to hit the Iberian Peninsula were the Vandals. Though St. James himself, according to legend, had first preached the Gospel in Spain and founded its first shrine there at the command of the Virgin Mother, Catholicism nevertheless crumbled in its first encounter with heretic thought. The Vandals succeeded in aborting the Catholic creed with their Arian heresy. Next, the Arian Visigoths, noted for their tyrannous and vengeful rule, arrived on the heels of the departing Vandals. Brief succor came to the Church when King Reccared was converted to Catholic Christianity (587). With the fierce zeal of a convert he mercilessly force-fed his newfound Athanasian concept of Jesus into the minds of his unwilling Arian subjects. He encountered even greater resistance from the Jews, who were as reluctant to accept the new Athanasian view of Christ as they had been in accepting the old Arian view of him.

The Visigoths were taken out of history in 711 by the invading Mohammedans, who were greeted as liberators by forcibly converted Arians and Jews. While the rest of Europe was dragged into a morass of ignorance and squalor by her Christian liberators, Spain was hoisted into a world of learning and splendor by her Mohammendan conquerors.

The history of France begins in the fifth century, with Chlodovetch, now known as Clovis, pagan chieftain of the barbaric Franks, who founded the Merovingian Dynasty and the Frankish Kingdom (481). A king of crafty mind, who enlarged his domain by assassination and trickery, Clovis became the protector of a terrified but unified people. A pitiless cynic, he converted to Catholic Christianity to receive the religious blessing of pope and Church in his political deals with prince and state.

The subsequent three-century rule of the Merovingians was distinguished for its monstrous crimes perpetrated by lusty royal murderers. Their court became known as a house of prostitution where mothers of kings were servant girls forced into royal beds. Because of their lazy incompetence, power passed in the seventh century from the hands of the kings into the hands of their chief servants, the Mayors of the Palace. Merovingian rule came to an end in the eighth century, when the last Mayor of the Palace, Pepin III, known as The Short, seized power and was elected king of France. He married a duchess with the inelegant sobriquet Big-foot Bertha, and they begat a son, Charlemagne, who became the greatest emperor in Europe since Julius Caesar.

Six feet tall, mustached, but beardless in spite of legend, emperor for forty-two years (771–814) of the Frankish Empire he wrought, Charlemagne presided like a patriarch over a household of five successive legitimate wives, four supplementary spouses, a stable of mistresses, and a retinue of lovers for his daughters. But though indiscriminate in love, he planned his wars carefully and won them consistently.

To extend his empire from the Atlantic to the Vistula, encompassing what is today approximately France, Germany, and Italy, Charlemagne used the pretext of converting pagans as an excuse for invading their territory. Being an enlightened ruler, he always gave the pagans a democratic choice—conversion or death. As most of the first conversions did not take, he had to return several times to make the pagan converts reaffirm their vows to Christ. Most troublesome were his Saxon cousins to whom the worship of the skull of a horse nailed to a tree seemed more attractive than the worship of the body of a Jew nailed to a cross.

Espousing the cause of Catholicism, Charlemagne ruthlessly stamped out Arian Christianity, making the world safe for the Athanasian dogma. On Christmas day, in the year 800, a grateful pope crowned him emperor. Hope for a unified, civilized, and Christian Europe again flickered in the hearts of men. But in vain. The frail giant collapsed. Charlemagne's empire, a pastiche of Latins, Teutons, and Slavs, was a short-lived phenomenon that barely survived its founder. Soon after his death, it was portioned among his weak Carolingian successors into Italy, France, and Germany. Under their stewardship, Italy galloped into immediate oblivion; France fell into a two-century political disintegration until a new dynasty, the Capets, revived it in the twelfth century; and Germany, seemingly the least likely country to succeed, emerged as a superstate in the tenth century, after it shrugged off its Carolingian rulers.

Poor Germany! Chief pretender of "Aryan purity." Raped by Huns and Slavs for centuries, she had become the most mongrelized of the mongrel nations of Europe. Because of her many Asiatic inseminations, Germany also became most resistant to Christianity. Even the half dozen successive turns of Charlemagne's conversion screw could not make it stick. After his death, the Germans relapsed into their former heathen ways. Not until the arrival of the tenth century did a semblance of Christianity at last take hold among them. Prussia did not find its way to Christ until the thirteenth century, and then only by the light of a flashing sword.

In the tenth century, under a new dynasty of Saxon rulers, Germany began testing her conquest reflexes. Otto I transformed the Kingdom of Germany into an empire by annexing the northern half of Italy. Frederick I Barbarossa (1152–1190), in anticipation of conquering the world, named his realm the Holy Roman Empire. But his ambition remained a dream, and his kingdom, though dominant in Europe, was, in Voltaire's phrase, "neither holy, nor Roman, nor an empire."

It remained for Frederick II (1194–1250), *Stupor Mundi,* the Great, to realize his grandfather's dream of grandeur. His entry in history was dramatic. For some unfathomable reason, his mother, Princess Constance of Sicily, had insisted on a public delivery. Nineteen cardinals and bishops squeezed into an improvised delivery chamber in the marketplace at Jesi, one hundred miles north of Rome, to witness Frederick's birth. All that the prelates could vouch for, however, was that the child was a male and that Princess Constance undeniably was the mother. Later, however, the Church established his paternity as that of the devil.

Pitiless and arrogant, enlightened and unprejudiced, half Norman by birth, Sicilian by inclination, and with little if any German blood in him, Frederick II became the greatest of German emperors. Crowned king of the Romans in 1212, king of the Germans in 1220, and king of Jerusalem after purchasing that city from the Saracens in the Sixth Crusade, Frederick was twice excommunicated by a Church suspicious of this "baptized sultan of Sicily" who surrounded himself with Jewish and Arabic scholars and ruled Germany from a Mohammedanized court with a well-stocked harem guarded by eunuchs. The Church viewed him as an atheist and an infidel. The memory of his once asking a pope what angels did all day did not help to endear him to the vicars of Christ.

In spite of all bans, Frederick built his empire so solidly that most of it held together for three centuries after his death, until the Reformation, after which it fell apart into more than 300 principalities, duchies, palatinates, and kingdoms. Yet the fiction of a Holy Roman Empire prevailed until put to an end by Napoleon.

All too many Jewish historians portray the Jews during these invasion centuries as suffering lambs prey to anti-Semitic wolves. What such injustice-seeking historians forget in their concentrated search for Jewish calamities is that this was an age of plenty of injustice and calamity for all. If any Jew expected the invading barbarian to ask him "You Jewish?" and set him free if the answer was affirmative, then he expected too much.

Because the Jews had arrived in Rome as early as the second century B.C., they were an integral part of the casualty statistics in the successive sackings of that city. Having arrived in southern France and Germany as early as the first century B.C., they were there in ample time to be decimated by Vandals and Visigoths. As they were already established in Spain by the second century A.D., the Jews had the privilege of being part of the catch in King Reccared's conversion roundup. As the invading gentlemen from the East slaughtered Jews, Christians, and fellow pagans with equal glee, the blood of the Jews commingled with Italian, French, and Spanish blood on battlefields and city streets. Jewish communal organization became as disrupted, diffused, and chaotic as that of the Gentiles.

No one should imagine that Jewish maidens escaped their turn at being ravished; when it came to sex, the barbarians never practiced social, racial, or religious discrimination. They yielded to temptation with questionable haste but with commendable impartiality. As in the Talmudic view Jewishness was reckoned through the mother, on the theory that whereas paternity is based on hope maternity is a matter of certitude, the offspring of these brief encounters were declared full-fledged Jews by dint of birth. Historically speaking, the Jews were infused with a sturdy strain of barbaric vigor at a time when world conditions might otherwise have dangerously depleted their ranks.

By the ninth century the Jews were settled in northern France, in ample time to feel the impact of another invasion that was to rack the continent. It also placed them in a position to be among the first new settlers of a fifth country to join the West European quadrumvirate of Italy, Spain, France, and Germany in the eleventh century. The invaders were the Vikings, and the new nation was England.

The Scandinavian countries, which had bequeathed the itinerant Visigoths to the European continent in the fourth century B.C., presented her with the marauding Vikings in the ninth century A.D. The Vikings, fearless men of the sea, conquered Iceland and Greenland, invaded England and France, penetrated Spain and Sicily, raided Tunis and Alexandria, made their way through White Russia to Constantinople, plundering, trading, and colonizing as resistance, prudence, and opportunity dictated, leaving a trail of blue-eyed, blond-haired progeny as mementos of their visits.

By the end of the tenth century, Danish Vikings overran England and only odd irony prevented her from being annexed by Denmark. She was conquered instead by the Normans, descendants of Vikings who a century earlier had raided, raped, and settled along the northern shore of France and given that province the name of Normandy, Land of the Norsemen.

From the time of the prehistoric Celts to the Norman invasion, English history is as unimportant to world history as is the history of Rome from the Villanovians to the Gracchi. Skillful English writers, however, who do not distinguish between sociology and history, have enshrined the dreary tale of early brutish British kings with limited intellect into the pleasing fiction of a free and glorious people that invented democracy, constitutional government, freedom of speech, and all other rights of men.

About 5000 B.C. the marshlands between England and France sank, separating England from the continent. For three millennia, the natives of the British Isles lived like animals, their civilization never attaining a higher plateau than the Mesolithic. Then a venturesome Mediterranean people in the course of their travels (east all the way to India and north all the way to Norway) invaded England, erected the fascinating stone structures we know as Stonehenge as a benchmark of their journey, and managed to lift the British to a higher level of civilization. When this brilliant people left, the British lapsed into a cultural stupor from which they were not rescued until the Roman occupation (57 B.C.–450 A.D.). But no sooner had the Romans withdrawn than the British again regressed into their ancestral torpor. Until the eleventh century, her subsequent history was a dreary tale of invasions by Angles, Jutes, and Vikings.

It was William the Conqueror, bastard son of Duke Robert of Normandy and the daughter of a tanner, who brought England into the mainstream of European history. Greedy and mendacious, cold and brutal, he was also a great soldier and organizer. As he viewed his new Anglo-Saxon subjects as swilling swine crawling with lice, incapable of developing an economy, William brought over a contingent of French Jews to establish commerce and banking for that country. Though Christianized in the sixth century with no less a godfather than Pope Gregory the Great, England also had the distinction of generating the most ignorant, corrupt, and greedy clergy. Into this motley Anglo-Saxon mass, the Normans infused a new spirit, which, after a three-century gestation in French and Romanesque culture, matured into the grandeur of the

English Renaissance. The marvel is that out of such in-
auspicious beginnings should rise the genius of Chaucer,
the greatness of Shakespeare, the grace and beauty of the
King James Bible, the glory of the Elizabethan Age.

Thus were the political, economic, and religious boundaries set for the coming western European civilization.
The new order settled over Europe slowly, imperceptibly,
until by the ninth century, the central features of what is
known today as feudalism emerged. Western historians
usually depict this feudal society as consisting of but
three estates—the nobles who did the fighting, the serfs
who did the tilling, and the priests who did the praying.
But there was a fourth estate, consisting of the Jews, who
were the business and professional men for whom no
formal provisions had been made.

The feudal system was not designed by a planning commission for a new civilization, but grew haphazardly as a
response to the challenge facing a disintegrating Roman
Empire. It was an interim government, which by default
inherited the burdens of state because no national government emerged. A Chinese historian might view the
period between 500 and 1000 as the "Age of the War-
lords," which would not be too wrong. The lords and their
knights of the medieval world were nothing but glorified
gangsters selling protection.

A series of accidental factors had brought about this un-
happy circumstance. During the waning years of the
Roman Empire, the peasants, to escape the rapacity of tax
collectors and the looting by roaming soldiers, had placed
themselves under the protection of their nearest largest
landowner. In return for part title to their lands, these
large landowners protected the helpless peasants from
rapacious taxation and pillage. Alas, within a few centuries,
the protectors were exacting more in rent than the Roman
tax collectors had in revenue. The formerly free peasant
found he had sold himself into semi-slavery. Though he
was free to will his land to his children, he was not free
to sell it, or move away. He had chained himself to his plot
of ground, which he had to till day and night to satisfy his
payments in goods and labor.

As time went by, these "gangster" landowners conferred

titles upon themselves. The bigger ones became lords, and these chose an overlord, or king. Each lord surrounded himself with an elite group of warriors known as knights. To make sure their children would inherit and perpetuate what they had bought, wrought, and fought for, the lords made laws which said that only those born lords could be lords, and those who were born peasants should stay peasants. Thus developed the closed society of the feudal world where everybody stayed in the social station he was born in, a society tied to its crib. The emerging Church supported the new feudal state, preaching that it was the best of all possible systems, ordained by God, and that tampering with it was tampering with God's will.

Though there was constant struggle between the state, which had arisen out of the disintegrating Roman Empire, and the Church, which had sprouted out of the mind of Paul, neither wished to do away with the other. Medieval strife never constituted a revolution, merely a succession of revolts. The feudal order was never in question, merely who ought to control it, the prince or the Church.

The road for the Church to this summit of power had been long and sanguine. After the death of Jesus, the leadership of the Christian sect gravitated toward two men. One was James, the brother of Jesus, who tried to keep Christianity within the fold of Judaism but failed. The other was Paul, the reformed persecutor of Christians, who set out to sell Christianity to the pagans and succeeded. James, like Jesus, was not a Christian. He was a Jew who admitted pagans to the new Christian sect only after their conversion to Judaism. Paul stood for the direct admission of pagans into Christianity without a prior induction into Judaism. It is doubtful if James ever understood the significance of Paul's views, which transubstantiated his brother Jesus from a Jewish preacher to a Christian redeemer.

A blend of his times—a Jew by birth, a Roman by citizenship, and a product of Greek culture—Paul was the perfect sales manager for marketing the new Jewish sect. Whereas Jesus was a messiah-intoxicated Jew who died a Jew, Paul was a Christ-intoxicated Jew who died a Christian. The first thing he did when he "received the message" of Christ on the road to Damascus was to sacrifice the historical Jesus for his creation of the theological Christ. Whereas Jesus the Jew, like the Jews, had taught that man could earn God's grace through repentance and righteousness, Paul the Christian taught that salvation could only be obtained through the dead Christ. Shrewdly, he aimed his Epistles (letters) at the Diaspora Jews, just as a few decades later the Pharisees, equally shrewdly, were to aim their Oral Law at them. Paul's letters to the Corinthians, Galatians, Ephesians, Philippians, Colossians, and Thessalonians were written to instruct these Diaspora Jews who thought they were getting a new variation of Judaism. Imagine their surprise when instead of finding themselves in the tabernacle of Judaism they found themselves in the fold of Christianity.

For two decades, the Christianities of James and Paul competed as the true creed of Jesus. The destruction of Jerusalem selected the victor. Just as Sadducee Judaism perished in that holocaust, so did Jamesian Christianity. And just as Pharisee Judaism rose out of the rubble, so did Pauline Christianity. Both were universalist religions in outlook, tailored for a "Diaspora"—the former for Jews in exile, the latter for pagans at large.

Within a century, Christianity became a force in history through the rise of a new institution. In the famed epigram of Alfred Loisy, "What Jesus proclaimed was the Kingdom of God, and what arrived was the Church." In the name of Jesus, this new Church reversed many of his policies to gain larger membership. To achieve this, it ingested many of the ideas of Essenism, which had also perished with the fall of Jerusalem.

Though Jesus may have been an Essene, as many scholars presume, he rejected much of the Essene dogma. The Teacher of Righteousness had been a priest, but Jesus, like the Pharisee rabbis, was a layman who rejected a priesthood. Jesus founded no church, sought no institutionalized hierarchy. The Church, however, realizing it needed a devoted hierarchy for future growth, dragged in through the back door the priesthood Jesus had thrown out the front. The Church institutionalized its creed and established an elaborate organization of judges and tribunals. Where Jesus had de-Essenized his creed, the Church re-Essenized it. In effect, therefore, the historical Jesus stands closer to ben Zakkai's Judaism, which also rejected Essenism, than to Pauline Christology, which absorbed it. In the words of Ernest Renan, "Christianity is an Essenism which has largely succeeded."

The perils to the new Church were many, however. After successfully surviving the contempt, hatred, and persecutions of the Romans, and after surviving internal fights over what constituted the true faith, Christianity was almost eclipsed in the third and fourth centuries by two competing Persian resurrection religions, which threatened to paganize it with their mythology.

The first of these, Mithraism, was founded by Mithras (fifth century B.C.), who was born in a cave where shepherds came to adore him on hearing that a son of god had been given unto them. His chief contribution in life was the slaying of a white bull to fertilize the earth. His chief legacy in death was his annual reincarnation in early spring as a white bull or lamb which was slain over a grating so that naked neophytes below could be baptized with the blood of the lamb. Bread and wine were taken by adherents in a mass communion meal.

Mani (216?–276?), a Sassanid priest, was the founder of Manichaeism, the second of the Persian resurrection cults that threatened the future of Christianity. He was flayed alive by an outraged priesthood after he had declared himself a messiah. Undeterred, his disciples declared that Mani had been resurrected and spread his teachings on the evils of sex, birth, and material things throughout the Near East.

Greek and Roman soldiers carried Mithraism and Manichaeism to Europe where these creeds infected the Christian body as disastrously as venereal disease infected Napoleon's army in Spain. By the fourth century, the Church abandoned its losing policy of free competition in the marketplace of religions and resorted to the systematic slaughter of Mithraists and Manichaeans as a more effective program.

But these two Persian cults were so all-pervasive that even after their proclaimed deaths they so diluted original

Christian dogma with their mythology that at times Christianity came to resemble the former creeds of its new pagan converts. December 25, for instance, the birthday of Mithras, was so popular that the Church was forced to make that date the official birthdate of Jesus in order to stop a mass regression into paganism. Though the Church eventually recovered from these pagan inroads, the process of demythologizing their contributions to Christianity still continues today.

Also, to prevent its becoming engulfed by the multitude of pagan creeds, the Church maintained as many Jewish institutions as she could, though careful to give them Christian names. The Temple of Jerusalem became the Vatican of Rome; the synagogue became the church; the rabbis became the priests; the *tzitzes,* the fringed garment worn by Jews and Jesus, became the scapular of the priests; Jewish liturgical music became the Gregorian chant. Through generations of denials by the Church that these institutions were Jewish in origin, the Christians became convinced that they had invented them all.

But what in the long run saved Christianity from degenerating into paganism was not sword and fire but the Beatitudes of Jesus and the Decalogue of Moses. Rome had no spiritual message to give its people, only grinding poverty and unsatisfying luxuries. The Church held out hope for the downtrodden. Like early communism, the teachings of Jesus placed no intrinsic value on culture or race; all souls had equal status. The early Church was able to offer the Gospel of Jesus to all barbarians, in contradistinction to the later evangelism of Western Christianity which gave only its religion, not its status, to non-white converts.

Though Christian theologians portray Judaism as the withering trunk of the healthy branch of Christianity, we must not allow Christianity's success to obscure the unwitting role it played in the furtherance of Judaic ideas. It was the Christians who with sword in hand converted the pagans of Europe, thus bringing them their first knowledge of the Old Testament and its concept of a manifest destiny. While Christianity's mythological trappings held immediate attraction for pagans, it was the moral and ethical values of Judaism that gave Christianity its long-range appeal. In a theological sense, Christianity was a steppingstone by which pagans crossed over into Judaic concepts.

As there was no such thing as nationality, the people did not live within a national state but within the Church. Public officials in feudal society were not governors, senators, and congressmen, but cardinals, bishops, and priests. A public building was not a courthouse or a senate but a church or cathedral. Though all lived, loved, and worked on earth, everyone was busy preparing his soul for the hereafter. The head man in this "universal kingdom of God" was the pope, who held the keys to paradise. Everyone stood outside the door, wondering if he would make it, hoping for God's grace or the pope's good will.

Once Catholic Christianity was safely seated in the ecclesiastical saddle, the Church took the offensive with Gospel and sword. The Poles submitted to the Cross in 966. The Asiatic Magyars, who had invaded and terrified eastern Europe in the ninth century, were tamed with Christ and transubstantiated into Christian Hungarians in the tenth. Monks followed the Vikings to their Scandian lairs, converting the Danes, Swedes, and Norwegians in the twelfth century. In a crusade that almost wiped out the Finns, the Swedes converted the remaining Finns to the true faith in 1155. The last holdouts in Europe were the Prussians and Lithuanians. The former were baptized in their own blood by Teutonic Knights. The latter were ingested into Christianity in the fourteenth century through the holy rite of matrimony when Jagiello, the pagan grand duke of Lithuania, embraced the body and faith of Jadwiga, the Christian queen of Poland.

But in spite of its victories at the baptismal font, the Church suffered a series of defeats along its moral front. From lowly priest to princely cardinal, the Church hierarchy was encrusted with corruption and depravity. Men of the cloth lived with concubines; others married and passed on to their children their soft-cushioned jobs. Simony, the buying of priestly office, was the order of the day. Equally corrosive was the system of lay investiture, kings appointing lay persons to high church posts to do their bidding.

The papacy too had degenerated. Only one seat in the history of the West has been more precarious than the throne of the Caesars, and that was the chair of St. Peter. In the 500-year period that followed the fall of Rome—from Symmachus to Gregory VI (498 to 1045)—a total of ninety-eight popes, with an average tenure of less than five years, sat on the throne of St. Peter. During these five feudal centuries, one pope was martyred, two were blinded, five abdicated, nine were deposed, eleven were murdered, and two simply fled the honor with its attendant dangers.

In the tenth century, the See of Rome reached a floodtide of treachery, lechery, murder, and rape. A chain reaction of pontifical murders was sparked by a macabre event. The exhumed body of excommunicated Pope Formosus was tried by a papal court, sentenced to perfidy, and the corpse thrown into the Tiber after its three benediction fingers had been hacked off. A year later, the pope who had ordered the trial was strangled. The Roman matron, Theodora, noted for her beauty and feared for her power, had her son, John IX, crowned pope at the remarkable age of eighteen. At twenty he was found dead in the arms of his teen-age mistress, a martyr of "amorous excess," as the scandalmongering Bishop Liutprand of Cremona so decorously phrased it. Undaunted, Theodora became the mistress of Pope John X, who was strangled on the orders of her equally beautiful but more powerful daughter Marozia. Married to the duke of Spoleto, Marozia bedded with Pope Sergius III, with whom she had an illegitimate son who was crowned Pope John XI at the age of twenty-five. When Marozia remarried, the Vatican witnessed the touching scene of her bastard son performing the wedding ceremony as pontiff. John XII, grandson of Marozia and pope at the age of sixteen, was a playboy at whose feet the German Emperor Otto I knelt in homage to receive his crown. No decent woman dared set her foot in the Vatican for fear of being seduced. At age twenty-four, John's career was over, through assassination. Pope Benedict IV was deposed and killed; Benedict VI strangled; Boniface VII murdered; John XVI blinded and murdered. Benedict IX, youngest pope in history, elected to the Chair of St. Peter at the age of fifteen (some sources say twelve), fled the post after announcing his intention to marry his beautiful cousin.

A revulsion swept Christendom. The time for change was at hand. Though the impulse for reform came from many directions, the man who channeled all currents of disapproval into one tide of reformation was a pope who, had he lived in the twentieth century, would have been exterminated by the Nazis. To the horror of prince and priest, Gregory VII (1073–1083), the pope destined to restore decency to the papacy, was of Jewish descent. Though it was all right for Jesus Christ, St. Paul, St. Peter, and the first fifteen bishops of the Jerusalem Church to have been Jewish, it somehow did not seem proper for a pope.

Gregory VII was the son of the granddaughter of Baruch, a Jewish banker in Rome, founder of the House of Pierlone, often compared in wealth and influence to the later House of Rothschild. In 1030, at the age of seventy, Baruch was baptized into Christianity under the name of Benedictus Christianus—Baruch the Christian. Within one century the House of Pierlone gave Christendom three popes—the first, Baruch's son, John Gratian, who became Pope Gregory VI (1045–1046); the second, Gregory VII, destined to be one of the three greatest popes in the history of Christianity;[1] and the third, a great-grandson, Peter, who became anti-pope Anacletus II (1130–1138). These three "popes from the ghetto" were all reform popes who "Judaized" the overpaganized Christianity with their reforms and helped pave the way for Luther, called the greatest of "Judaizers" by the Roman Church.[2]

Gregory VII was as ugly as St. Paul was reputed to have been—squat, dark, ungainly—"more like a Saracen

[1]The other two are Gregory I (590–604), who transformed the patriarchate of Rome into the papal system of the Middle Ages, and Innocent III (1198–1216), who continued the reform policies instituted by Gregory VII. It was he who placed England under the interdict of 1208, and deposed John of England and Otto IV of Germany.

[2]For a scholarly but absorbing account of this incredible interlude in papal history, see Popes From the Ghetto, by Joachim Prinz.

than a Christian," as one chronicler so circumspectly expressed it. Known as "Holy Satan" by his friends and a "damn Jew" by his enemies, Gregory VII was a man of prodigious ability and fantastic energy, detested by nobles, feared by prelates, and sainted after his death by a grateful Church.

Gregory envisioned the papacy as God's kingdom on earth with the pope as supreme authority. None could be a true Christian unless he also agreed with the pope. Toward this end—and perhaps even borrowing a page from the Talmudists—Gregory ordered the leading scholars to organize Christian canon law into channels favorable to his views. When the codification was complete, it showed papal absolutism as God's idea, and proved that the Church was founded, not by Jesus the son, as one might expect from a Christian, but by God the Father, as one might expect from a Jew. With the authority of this new canon law, Gregory decreed that all married clergy had to set aside their wives and families, much as Ezra 1,500 years earlier had decreed that all Jews had to set aside their pagan wives and families. Seducing parishioners by prelates was prohibited. Simony was abolished. An interdict was placed on lay investiture.

Challenge on lay investiture came from Emperor Henry IV of the Holy Roman Empire, who felt more secure than prudence dictated. Gregory acted swiftly by excommunicating the emperor. But Gregory, who had expected the haughty emperor to defy the ban and thus cause his own downfall, was outmaneuvered. Instead, barefoot and in sackcloth, Henry made his way as a penitent through Alpine snows to the castle of Canossa to beg the pope's forgiveness.

Gregory kept the emperor waiting for an audience for three days, but fearing the world would think him cruel and heartless, he had to capitulate before Henry's brilliantly calculated maneuver and grant him absolution. The ban removed, Henry adroitly repaired his political fences, successfully defied a second ban, installed an anti-pope, and finally, not daring to have Gregory murdered, forced his banishment.

Though the comedy at Canossa ended in a draw on the

question of lay investiture, the other Gregorian reforms took hold. The new caesars of Europe had to be anointed by the heirs of St. Peter. Though the coming schism of the Avignon popes was to divide the ranks of Christendom, though the Borgia popes were once again to degrade the Vatican with scandal, the papacy never again fell to the depth of depravity of the pre-Gregorian centuries. After Gregory VII, not a single pope was blinded, martyred, or murdered, nor did a teen-ager ever again sit on the throne of St. Peter—not inconsiderable benefits to the Church from the tenure of a Jewish pope.

Thus was the closed society of the feudal world constituted. The odds were against the Jews surviving this holy alliance of crusading Christianity and marauding feudalism. Yet, incredibly, they not only survived it, they changed it radically—economically by ushering in Islamic capitalism, intellectually by reintroducing Greek thought, and religiously by Judaizing Christianity. The Jews in turn were also to be changed radically—economically, intellectually, and religiously. But whereas the Christians, after sinking to the bottom of their feudal civilization, were destined to progress, the Jews, after simmering to the top of that culture, were destined to regress. This is the dramatic action of our next scene.

THE INCREDIBLE JEWS

When we return to the world theater where our drama of Jewish history is being enacted, the curtain is raised and the action is about to begin. The setting is western Europe. Popes have replaced caesars, cathedrals have replaced mosques, monks not *imams* dart across the stage, and serfs not fellahin till the soil. In the midst of these new surroundings stands the Jew. He is incredulous at what has happened to the mighty empire of Rome. He is perplexed by what has taken its place. Will he be able to survive in this strange land where the lively pantheon of Roman gods has been replaced by a dead Jew?

In the first thousand years of this second act, the Jew

has lived in the universalist worlds of the Roman, Sassanid, and Islamic empires. Now, in feudal Europe, he is confined to petty principalities. Before, he lived in a world of scholars, where literacy was a qualification and learning was viewed with respect. Now, he lives in a world of knights, where preparation for tournaments and concern for the hereafter are all-consuming activities. Previously, the Jew could mingle with the humanities and flirt with the sciences in search for new formulas to enlarge his social, economic, and intellectual horizons. Now, his religion is derided, his rights are questioned, and his livelihood threatened.

How will the Jew meet this incredible challenge? Will the Talmud once again come to his rescue, or has he gone as far as he can in stretching it into yet another protective tent against new gathering storms? Can a Babylonian Talmud, fashioned for other times, other threats, help the Jews of Europe? Before any Talmud can help him, he realizes he will first have to break out of the deadlock of the closed Christian feudal society—a serfdom which threatens to embrace him, a priesthood to which he does not aspire, and a nobility which rejects him. As he has no armies, force is no solution. What he needs is a bit of blind luck to break the impasse. Then, perhaps, he will be able to help himself, with or without a Talmud. Incredibly, history providentially provides him with not one but two lucky breaks.

Two stereotypes about the Jews during the Middle Ages still prevail—that they suffered unremitting persecution by the Church, and that they were condemned to a life of degradation by the state. Though they will suffer such disabilities in the coming fifth challenge, the available facts do not support such myths in the fourth. On the contrary, while Christians were gripped in a vice of theocracy and servitude, Jews found a way to live in a world of democracy and freedom.

We saw it take about ten centuries of armed conversion drives—from about 300 to 1300—to securely establish Christianity on European soil. When the carnage was over, everyone on that continent was either Christian or dead, except the Jews. They were alive and non-Christian. How did they, the most vulnerable people in Europe, a people with no state, police, or army, survive these dangerous, fateful centuries? Why were the Jews not exterminated along with non-Jews when they refused conversion to Christianity? In this paradox lay their first bit of luck.

The simple answer is that, ironically, the worst enemy of the Jews, the Church itself, was their witting though reluctant protector. The Church had maneuvered itself into this situation via a theological dilemma. It could not exterminate the Jews because it needed them as living witnesses to the divinity of Jesus. Should they disappear, who would testify to the pagans that the rightful heir to the Old Testament was the new Christian Church? By leaving them alone, the Church hoped the Jews would in time perceive the error of their ways and convert to Christianity. This attitude is best summed up in a prayer of the fifth-century Pope Gelasius: "We pray for the unbelieving Jews that our God and Lord should remove the veil from their hearts, and they should themselves recognize our Lord Jesus Christ."

Alas, the prayer had little effect. To explain the embarrassing continued existence of the Jews as Jews, the Church ingeniously suggested that their exile was God's punishment for their not having acknowledged the divinity of Jesus. This explanation was too good to be wasted on Jews alone. When the barbarians invaded and denuded the Danubian basin, home of the heretic Arian Christians, Saint Ambrose, an Athanesian, interpreted their defeat as a punishment for their having accepted the wrong Christianity. When Alaric sacked Rome, the pagans explained it as a punishment for Rome's having accepted atheistic Christianity instead of adhering to the ancestral theistic paganism which had protected the Romans since the days of Romulus.

Though the Church at first was willing to take the long view and patiently await the voluntary conversion of the Jews, events were not so patient. Too many Christians were attending synagogue services that did not demand image worship. Too many Christians were seeking justice in Jewish courts which did not demand trial by combat to prove innocence. Too many Christians were marrying Jews, because they deemed them better spouses and parents. To prevent such shakings of its foundations, the Church first passed laws against sexual intercourse between Christians and Jews and then against intermarriage itself, much as Ezra and Nehemiah had passed such laws against intermarriage between Jews and pagans. But these edicts were observed more in the breach than in performance. Through the centuries, the Church felt obliged to take more and more drastic steps as countermeasures. It tried to exclude the Jews from communal events, issued decrees against Jews holding public office, and forbade Christians to convert to Judaism. When these measures failed, the Church gave new turns of the screw to hasten that elusive conversion day. But the Jews learned to brace themselves for each successive turn. By and large, until the end of the thirteenth century, by which time this ambiguous relationship had hardened into a stalemate of mutual contempt, Jews and Christians lived quite peaceably together.

The second bit of luck unexpectedly freed the Jews from the shackles of feudal society. While the Church was maneuvering itself into an ambiguous position regarding the Jews, the Jews were unwittingly maneuvered into an equally ambiguous position regarding the state. There is no doubt that the Jews were excluded from the corporate structure of feudal society. But it was not the state which originally excluded the Jews; the Jews excluded themselves with fortunate consequences.

To exact obedience, the feudal prince demanded an oath of loyalty from his knights and yeomen that in the name of Christ bound them to state and Church. The Jews were also asked to take this oath, but because it contained the name of Christ they refused. No prince was willing to kill or expel them for such a refusal, because Jews were too valuable to the state. Instead, they hit upon a clever legal fiction that enabled the Jews to reside in, yet not be part of, feudal society. Instead of asking them to take an oath to the state in the name of Christ, they were requested to take an oath to the prince in the name of the state. Thus European Jews became *servi camera*, or "servants of the king," instead of subjects of Christ.

For five centuries, from the rule of the Carolingians to the end of the Crusades (800–1300), being "servants of the king" freed the Jews from feudal restrictions and bestowed upon them special privileges. Few dared attack them, for this was tantamount to an attack on the king's property. Like nobles, Jews were privileged to bear arms and defend themselves. Socially, throughout the Middle Ages until the Crusades, Jews stood far above serfs and a little below knights. Thus came about the paradoxical situation of the Christians unwittingly locking themselves in a feudal prison and throwing away the keys, while permitting the Jews to move in freedom outside it. It took the Christians six long centuries to perceive the short-sightedness of their planning board. When at last they did break down the walls of their feudal prison, there was hell to pay for the Jews. But until this appointment with regression, the Jews of Europe made the most of the luck history had handed them.

The sixth-century correspondence of Pope Gregory the Great confirms that the Jews survived the barbarian invasions and were fairly numerous in the territories that were to become Italy, France, and Germany. Theodoric the Great invited an ever-greater number of Jews to resettle in Italian cities, where they became scholars and bankers, merchants and farmers, artisans and professional men. In France, they formed a wealthy merchant class, with great estates and vast business enterprises. Charlemagne, too, invited more Jews to his realm, offering them high government posts, including the ambassadorship to the court of the fabled Harun al Rashid. In ninth-century Germany, 95 percent of the Christian German population consisted of lowly serfs, whereas 50 percent of the German Jews were professional and business men, and the rest independent artisans and farmers. In England, beautiful stone mansions built in the eleventh and twelfth centuries are still known as "Jew houses," after their original occupants. But above all else, wherever the Jews settled, they demanded and received special grants of land in which to establish their own communities, and city charters granting them the right to elect their own officials and chart their own destiny.[3]

Though they achieved wealth and status, these native European Jews lived unhistorically during the first four centuries after the fall of Rome (500–900), while their co-religionists in the Islamic Empire were shaping the Talmud and giving birth to great scholars. With the tenth century, however, a new intellectual dawn beckoned for the Jews of Europe.

When the curtain closed on our third challenge, the Jews had arrived at a point in their journey through time when history was slowly squeezing Islamic Jews into feudal Europe. As they filtered into western Europe they infused the European Jews, as they had the Spanish Jews, with a new intellectual awareness. Within a century of their arrival, a coalition between the cultures of the Sephardic (Oriental and Spanish Jews) and the Ashkenazi (European Jews) would revolutionize European Jewish life and propel it into the mainstream of Judaism. History was handing the Jews of Europe the scepter of Jewish destiny.

The Sephardic influx into Europe was not a mass migration but flights of individual families over several centuries. In a sense, these emigrés fled from a highly sophisticated, mature society into the unsophisticated, adolescent phase of an emerging Western civilization. At first, they looked down on the native Jewish inhabitants as yokels, but they soon learned to appreciate the nimbleness with which these European Jews trod the treacherous ground between knight and bishop. They also learned that far from being yokels, the Jews of Europe constituted a unique elite.

True to the Darwinian maxim of the survival of the fittest in time of stress, only the most nimble, versatile

[3]Readers brought up on a contrary view of the Jew as a down-trodden lout, wearily treading a path of derision through feudal centuries while pushing a peddler's cart, should acquaint themselves with such works as *The English Jewry under Angevin Kings*, by H. G. Richardson; *Urban Civilization in Pre-Crusade Europe*, by Irving A. Agus; *The Jews in Medieval Germany*, by Guido Kisch; and *The World History of the Jewish People: The Dark Ages*, edited by Cecil Roth.

Jews had survived the centuries of invasions. They had done so without the aid of the Talmud. Not until the ninth century did they become aware of it, second-hand, mainly through the Responsa of the Gaons. Now, in the tenth century, they got their first good look at this Babylonian opus through the refugees from the crumbling caliphates who brought the Talmud with them. It was not a reassuring look. They despaired at its well-nigh incomprehensible, esoteric Hebrew and archaic Aramaic. Those who got beyond the language barrier despaired at the chasm revealed between life as reflected in the Babylonian Talmud and life as lived in Europe.

Whereas our first act proceeded like a Greek predestination drama, with God as the author, the second act should be proceeding like a French existentialist drama, with the Jew himself as the author. The fourth challenge will present clear evidence that history supports this thesis. It will show that the Jews deliberately chose to write their own script and that they did chart their own course, though retroactively attributing their actions to divine inspiration.

In the tenth century, the Jews of Europe stand at a crossroad in their history, faced with a momentous decision. Should they dump the Talmud and seek another road to survival, or can they induce this thousand-year-old common-law code of Jewish experience to yield more survival mileage? Their decision to choose the Talmud is clear and deliberate. The Jews themselves realized that this was a calculated risk, for as one popular Jewish saying exults about one of the new European Diaspora designers, "Were it not for Rashi, the Talmud would be forgotten in all Israel."

As the new Diaspora designers, the European Talmudists had to perform a new function. Jewish history has unerringly chosen the right name for them—the *Poskim,* the "Decision Makers." With the scalpel of "codification," these skilled dialectical surgeons deftly removed those parts of the Talmud no longer needed, and with the clamps of "commentaries" they transplanted into the Talmud the new ideas needed for survival.

Though both codification and commentaries were the

modes most extensively used by European rabbis to make the Talmud say what needed to be said, those two innovations were originally by-products of Gaonic genius. It was blind Yehudai ben Nahman, back in the eighth century, who penned the first codification of pertinent Talmudic decisions. And it was Hai, in the tenth century, who cautiously added a few commentaries in the margin of the Talmud as a preparatory step for the acceptance of some Responsa. But it was the European rabbis who seized these two undeveloped ideas and refined them into effective idea-expanding vehicles for survival.

The new "hospitals" in which the *Poskim* performed their surgical feats were modeled after the old academies in Babylon. Their transition from the Islamic world to the rapidly growing Diaspora centers in Europe was swift, transpiring within one century (950–1050). In the way the unknown "Stonehenge" people erected altars in their path of conquest across North Africa to England in the tenth century B.C., so the Jews founded academies in the path of their flight across North Africa to Europe in the tenth century A.D.

A legend tells how the academies of eastern Islam were transplanted into southern Europe via North Africa. A Spanish captain, having captured a ship bound for Italy, lusted for the beautiful wife of one of four Talmudists aboard, and invited her to spend the night in his cabin. After dutifully inquiring from her learned husband if it would be lawful to commit suicide rather than yield to evil, and upon being informed that under the circumstances it would be a virtue, the lady leaped overboard and drowned. Furious at having been foiled, the pirate sold the four Talmudists into slavery in ports from Tunis to Fez. Ransomed by fellow Jews, each in turn founded a famed yeshiva.

In reality, our four rabbis had been sent into the world by the academy at Sura to raise money for the Babylonian Gaonate, which had come upon hard times. But the rabbis, sensing the drift of the times, stayed where the action was and opened their own academies.

The action in the tenth century was in North Africa. Under the enlightened rule of the Fatimid Dynasty, North

Africa had risen to a high peak of splendor. For a century, Kairouan, south of Tunis, became a center of Jewish learning. Here, two native Talmudists, Hananel ben Hushiel and Nissim ben Jacob, performed a most unique Talmudic transplant.

Hananel and Nissim were an odd pair of Talmudists. The former, rich as a corrupt vizier, was blessed with nine daughters whose dowries ate up a goodly portion of his fortune, and the latter, poor as a yeshiva mouse, was forced to marry the ugly elderly daughter of a rich Spanish scholar in order to keep body and study together. In corresponding with the Gaons of Babylon and the rabbis of Europe, Hananel and Nissim came to realize the disparity between Jewish life in these two civilizations. Working as a team, they resorted to the expedient of "commentaries" to bridge the gap. Together they also hit upon the fortuitous idea of grafting a twig of the neglected Palestinian Talmud onto the trunk of the Babylonian. Though fashioned under Roman rule in the fourth century, the Palestinian Talmud in many ways mirrored life in tenth-century Europe more accurately than did the revised and edited Babylonian Talmud.

It was a Moroccan rabbi named Alfasi, however, who actually first transplanted the Babylonian Talmud to European soil. Alfasi (1013–1103), born in Fez, was denounced at the age of seventy-five as a subversive, and with his life at stake he fled to Lucena, Spain. Here, to reconcile life as it had been in Babylon to life as it was in Spain, he undertook the momentous first major codification of the Talmud. The results were to reverberate throughout European Jewish history. Defying the orthodox, he omitted laws that had no practical application; he deftly and concisely summarized pertinent laws, citing no authorities. Where Tannas differed, he unabashedly presented his own opinions or plagiarized the Palestinian Talmud for needed views. Until the appearance of Maimonides' *Second Torah*, Alfasi's was the most definitive Jewish legal code.

It was the realization of the function of the Talmud that induced the European Jews to try to modify the "impossible" Babylonian Talmud to serve their needs. Because it had to serve European institutions, it was not the more experienced Sephardic Jews who laid the foundations for European Judaism, but three Ashkenazi Jews. They were Gershom ben Judah, who went outside the Talmud to structure new foundations for Judaism; Rashi, who almost single-handedly fashioned the Babylonian Talmud into a European instrument for survival; and Jacob ben Asher, who fused three centuries of European Talmudic thought into one great code.[4]

Jewish history has callously preserved little of Gershom's personal life (960–1040) beyond the facts that he was born in Metz, France, and that he opened an academy in Mainz, Germany. We also know that his wife and son were forcibly converted to Christianity as a punitive measure for the successful conversion of Christians to Judaism by an overzealous former priest turned Jew.

With the vision of a prophet, Gershom appraised his age and the position of the Jews in it. Whereas the Jews in the Islamic Empire lived under one law in one state, the Jews of Europe lived in small communities separated from each other on a politically fragmented continent. In the Islamic world, Jewish leadership came from a narrow base of the rich and powerful. In Europe, because of the isolation of each Jewish community, such a hereditary Jewish elite could not readily develop. Instead of viewing this as a handicap, however, Gershom saw it as an opportunity. Local ordinances could be used to develop an independent democratic society within each isolated community, and Talmudic law could be used to knit the Jews in these communities into an "international" brotherhood. Instead of depending on leaders developing from a small elite, the base of future Jewish leadership could be broadened and cultivated from the grassroots of all communities by letting natural talent float to the top.

[4]There were, of course, European Talmudists before Gershom ben Judah. The first known European scholars who penned rabbinic literature were Kalonymus of Lucca (*circa* 880–960), his son Meshullam, and Judah ben Meir haKohen, the principal teacher of Gershom. Primarily shapers of the early European Responsa, they had, however, little influence (with the possible exception of Judah ben Meir) on the shaping of the Talmud itself.

Gershom grandly enters Jewish history in the year 1000 when, to implement his ideas of a European Jewish community, he borrowed a leaf from the popes and convoked the Council of Mainz, composed of Europe's leading rabbis. Here, in essence, Gershom outlined the principles that governed the old Greek city-states—each state an independent entity, yet all bound in a community of common interest, fused together with one ethic. Here Gershom laid the foundations for an organized, democratic community of Jews in feudal Europe. His contribution to the coming constitutional history of the West must not be minimized. His bold insistence that a community can establish its own ordinances in a democratic fashion for its own economic, social, and moral guidance foreshadowed the principles of self-government which were to sweep Europe several centuries later. Incredibly, at a time when Christian man was being tied into semi-slavery to Church and state, the Jews at the Council of Mainz were creating democratic enclaves within this same feudal society.

At the Council of Mainz, Gershom rammed through a series of far-reaching *takkanas,* or decrees, that defied both Torah and Talmud. Polygamy, sanctioned by both Torah and Talmud, was abolished. Gershom's decree that no man could divorce his wife without her consent, except in cases of insanity and immoral behavior, completely nullified Talmudic law. Furthermore, seven centuries before being embodied in Western law, the Council at Mainz forbade searches without a warrant and banned the opening of private mail by anyone except the person to whom it was addressed. The Council also rejected the Roman idea of *caveat emptor,* "let the buyer beware," for *caveat vendor,* "let the seller beware." This *takkana* forbade describing goods in a deceptive manner, or packaging goods in deceptive containers—a moral concept that has only recently seeped into Western commercial law.

On the threat of excommunication, the Council also banned the cutting of pages from manuscripts belonging to institutions. From this ban, Talmudists a century later promulgated the world's first copyright laws. Based on a commandment in the Torah forbidding the removal of a neighbor's landmark (Deuteronomy 19:14), they deduced that the product of an author's mind was his property, and forbade the unauthorized publication of any original work for a specified period of time so that the author and publisher could realize a just profit from their effort and risk. This Talmudic precept was embodied in the first Western copyright law passed in England in 1709.

In subsequent centuries, other rabbis convoked other councils at which other decrees were hammered out to form a body of new common law that would harmonize with existing reality. Gershom's concept of the value of councils in Jewish life and the efficacy of takkanas independent of Talmud became a first principle with the Feudal Age Diaspora designers.

Whereas Gershom structured the secular house of European Judaism, Rashi (an acronym for his full name, *RA*bbi *SH*lomo *I*tzhaki, 1040–1105) furnished its religious decor. Born in Troyes, in northern France, he was undistinguished as a student, perhaps because having married while still at school, the distracting demands of a young wife competed with the rigors of study. Returning to Troyes to run his father's vineyard, Rashi opened a small yeshiva to augment his income. Here, as an aid to teaching, he undertook, almost parenthetically at first, to "commentate" some sense into the Babylonian Talmud his students could hardly comprehend. In the process he "Europeanized" it.

The "reinterpretation" was no easy task, for as a passage in the Talmud warns, "He who translates a biblical verse literally is a liar, while he who elaborates is a blasphemer." But Rashi managed to trample a path to greatness between this Talmudic Scylla and Charybdis. His commentary was written with such warmth and humanity, in such clear Hebrew, so artfully interspersed with French expressions where Hebrew lacked the precise words, that it became loved as literature as much as it was revered as Scripture. Rashi's commentary on the Talmud influenced Jewish destiny; his subsequent commentary on the Bible influenced Christian history.

Two centuries after his death, the Franciscan monk Nicholas de Lyra studied Rashi's biblical commentaries in order to refute Judaism. Alas, Rashi's mind was no match for De Lyra's incisive logic. De Lyra either pointed out the flaws in Rashi's arguments or showed how they actually supported the Christian view. Although De Lyra won most of the polemic battles, Rashi eventually won the war through the exposure De Lyra gave him. The German scholar Johannes Reuchlin, after studying the works of De Lyra, took up the cause of Jewish humanism, and popularized the Jewish concept of the "city of God." In his monastic cell, young Martin Luther came in contact with Jewish thought by reading both De Lyra and Reuchlin, and the fury of the coming Reformation took shape in his mind.

For two centuries, in a constant effort to harmonize text with life, a series of brilliant French and German Talmudists shaped and guided Jewish destiny through the reefs of feudal life with their decrees, commentaries, and codifications. Most prominent among these scholars were two of Rashi's grandsons who founded a new school, that of the *Tosafists,* from the Hebrew, "to add." In essence, these Tosafists devised yet another method of adding new commentaries that explained the old commentaries which elucidated the Gemara which augmented the Mishna which elaborated on the Torah. The two-century work (1100–1300) of these Franco-German Talmudists was so brilliant that it caused a Spanish scholar to exult, "From France will come the Torah, and the word of God from Germany."[5]

In the thirteenth century, the French Tosafists clashed with the Spanish rationalists. Whereas the Spanish were clear and logical, often giving definitive rulings without stating the source, the French were critical and profound, always appending previous authorities as proof of their assertions. The former school culminated in the *Second Torah* of Maimonides; the latter, a century later, culminated in the *Four Rows* of Jacob ben Asher.

Born in Germany, Jacob ben Asher (1270–1343) was forced to flee to Toledo, Spain because of local persecution

[5]From the Responsa of Ribash (an acronym for Isaac ben Sheshet) No. 376.

of Jews. The family fortune vanished, and Jacob lived in poverty and sickness. A failure in all he undertook because of his all-consuming interest in the Talmud, he became famed throughout Europe for his writings but shunned in Toledo for his poverty. Through his father, a great Talmudist in his own right, Jacob ben Asher became acquainted with the works of the Franco-German scholars; in Spain he became familiar with the writings of the Spanish Talmudists, and his subsequent wanderings through western Europe familiarized him with the customs of its varied communities.

Jacob ben Asher's code became an immediate success. His lucid writing, his logical arrangement of subject matter, his encyclopedic knowledge of the entire range of Talmudic development over three centuries, and his clever way of presenting dissenting opinion while pointing a way out of the jungle of dissent, made his *Four Rows* the most popular and definitive code. It cogently answered the need of the times because it combined the rich strands of French, German, and Spanish learning into one magnificent tapestry of European Talmudism.

The Torah-Talmud not only performed a decisive role in Jewish life, it played a direct and vital part in the creation of the legal systems of Western civilization. The Talmud bears the same relationship to the Torah as English common law does to her statutory laws, or American constitutional law to the Constitution. We can most clearly see the influence of the Talmud in the development of English common law, because of the late arrival of the Jews in that island (1000–1100) and its isolation from the rest of the continent.

When the Jews arrived in England, they viewed the barbaric, illiterate Anglo-Saxons with as much contempt as did the conquering Normans. Especially repugnant to the Jews was the English method of settling legal disputes through trial by combat. Accustomed as they were to judicial procedure based on evidence, examination of witnesses, and impartial judges, the Jews did not view the prospect of having to fight a knight trained for killing as a sound foundation for either justice or business. As "servants of the king" and the business elite of the feudal order, they demanded and were granted the right to use Talmudic guidelines in disputes with Christians.

As early as the second century A.D., Talmudic law had specified that in property disputes the verdict of three men agreed upon by the litigants would be legally binding on both parties. In cases of litigation with Christians, a compromise was worked out. Disputes among them were settled by twelve impartial hearers—six Jews and six Christians—whose verdict was to be binding upon both parties. After a century, even the Anglo-Saxons found the Jewish method of settling disputes better than trial by combat. By the thirteenth century this "jury" method found its way into British common law. Trial by combat fell into disuse, though it remained legal until 1817, when a prisoner accused of murder challenged his accuser to trial by combat. As the "appellant" declined this opportunity to be killed, the murderer was discharged, but the trial by combat statute was hastily repealed.

The famed due process of law concept, so firmly embedded in the Fifth and Fourteenth Amendments of the American Constitution, and derived from the Magna Carta,[6] stems from a tenth-century interpretation of the Talmud. This Talmudic concept of due process of law was stated most succinctly by Maimonides several decades before the signing of the Magna Carta. "Every law which the king enacts for all, and which is not intended against one person alone, is not robbery. But when the king takes away from one person alone, not in accordance with the law known to all . . . it is robbery." The same Talmudic decree that men had to live by the law of the land and not by bills of attainder also held that no crime could exist unless there was a law forbidding it to all.

Such familiar terms in British and American law as the lien, recognizance (confession of debt), the general release, and the common law warranty, all dealing with the conveyance of property, are also of Jewish origin.

---

[6]"No freeman shall be taken or imprisoned, or disseised or exiled or in any way destroyed, nor will we go upon him nor send upon him, except by lawful judgment of his peers or by the law of the land." Point 39, Magna Carta.

Throughout the centuries, the Jewish experience with Christians was not an inspiring one. Huge sums were involved in banking transactions between Jews and Christians, and noblemen conceived of the most ingenious ways of cheating their Jewish creditors. As many baronial manors and cathedrals in Norman and Angevin England were financed with Jewish capital, the Jews were granted the right to attach the debt to the land. This attachment, or lien, was known as the "Jewish gage," which held that the debt went with the property no matter to whom sold. To prevent expensive, time-consuming lawsuits because of debtors simply denying their debts, the Jews devised a formula known as the *Odaita*, which became the English recognizance, or "confession of debt." It was a formal declaration in court, in front of witnesses, by the debtor at the time of the loan, in which he "confessed" the debt he was about to make was just. This recognizance served as a court order to foreclose, in case of default, without a trial. The phraseology of many sentences in today's common law warranty, the common law mortgage, and the general release almost parallels the Hebrew text of the Talmudic laws they were modeled from. A fundamental law of property, succinctly stated by Maimonides, "By mere words, no rights of property can be transferred," is so firmly entrenched in Western law that its Jewish origin has long since been forgotten.

There is a difference, however, in the philosophy underlying common law and Talmudic law. Whereas the former is based on individual rights, the latter is based on individual duty, for the Talmudist viewed equity and rights not as matters of law but as matters of morality. Law is for the citizen, an external force to ensure order in government; morality is for man, an internal force to ensure peace of mind. The former asks for the payment of a debt, the latter for the fulfillment of an obligation. Herein lies the uniqueness of the Talmud.

Because of these differences, common law courts tended to become remedy-oriented, whereas Talmudic courts became duty-oriented. Common law tended to formulate general standards, whereas Talmudic law formulated precise rules. In common law, the judge is an umpire between litigants, and merely advises them of the rules; in Talmudic law the judge is an interpreter of the law, and determines who committed a sin.

There was a practical reason for the revolutionary road the Talmud had to take. It was not only a code of law; it was also a defense guard. Whereas the Torah grew on native Palestinian soil, the Talmud grew on foreign soil. Whereas the Torah, as it was formulated from the twelfth to the first centuries B.C., had a state behind it to enforce its decrees, the Talmud did not. Because the Talmud had to serve a Diaspora which had no state apparatus to enforce its decrees, it had to develop laws as duties of the heart instead of fears of the state. What has amazed Western jurists is that the Talmud did succeed in its quest for self-enforcement, and that Jews as a group have been the most law-abiding citizens of the world with one of the lowest crime rates of any people.

As European history reaches the 1500s, watershed years that divide the Feudal from the Modern Age, the five-century-long fourth challenge to the Jews approaches its end. In this challenge we have seen history hand the scepter of Jewish destiny to the Jews of Europe. We have seen them entrench their leadership with the brilliant performance of the Poskim who, with their commentaries, eclipsed the achievements of the Goans with their Responsa. But if history needs extra confirmation that Jewish destiny has indeed shifted from East to West, the host of false messiahs, those ubiquitous friends of Jewish history who now appear, supply it. It is no longer the East which produces them, as in the past, but the West. They are no longer illiterate tailors concerned merely with Jewish salvation but sophisticated scholars concerned with the redemption of Christians too.

The first of this new breed of scholarly, European-born, Christian-oriented pretender messiahs was Abraham Abulafia (1240–1291), scion of a prominent Spanish Jewish family. Having declared himself a prophet, he headed for Rome to convert Pope Nicholas II to Judaism. Miraculously escaping being burned at the stake, he next declared himself a messiah. The rabbis excommunicated him, worried lest he try to convert another pope, and

Abulafia disappeared from history. A century later the Spanish Jew, Moses Botarel, appeared, whose messiahship was authenticated by no less a scholar than Hasdai Crescas. To convince the king of Spain that he was a Judeo-Christian messiah, Botarel asked to be cast into a burning furnace from which he would reappear among the living. The king complied with his modest request. As with Abulafia, there is no record of his fate.

The first recorded Ashkenazi aspirant for messiahship is Asher Lemlin, who appeared in Venice in 1502, modestly announcing that he was the Prophet Elijah. Because of this modesty he was exalted by the Jewish populace as a messiah. Lemlin asked the Jews to purify themselves in preparation for being whisked to the Holy Land in a heavenly chariot. But when no chariot appeared on the appointed day, many Jews, who had undergone severe fasting in preparation for the event, felt cheated and had themselves baptized into Christianity on the rebound.

The fourth challenge also unveiled the most remarkable diplomat-messiah team in history, a Jewish gnome named David Reuveni (1490–1535) and an apostate messiah named Diego Pires (1500–1532). Claiming to be the diplomatic envoy of his brother, the king of Khaibar, commander of 10,000 fierce Jewish warriors mobilized behind the lines of the Turks, Reuveni implored Pope Clement VII for an alliance with the West to defeat the common enemy. The pope sent him to see King John III of Portugal, an expert on Khaibar, who promised him eight ships and 4,000 cannon.

The deal, alas, fell through when Christians in Portugal joined the Jews in hailing Reuveni as a messiah, arousing the suspicions of the king. The gnome quickly headed back for Rome where he teamed up with Pires, a Portuguese Christian convert who reconverted to Judaism and declared himself a messiah. Under the name of Solomon Molko he joined Reuveni in a campaign to enlist the aid of Emperor Charles V in a combined crusade against the Turks. Charles clapped them in irons and turned them over to the Inquisition. When asked if he was the messiah, in much the same manner as Jesus was asked by Pilate if he was "King of the Jews," Molko's answer, "God forbid," proved to the Inquisition that he was a blasphemer. Molko was burned. Reuveni escaped from prison and vanished from history.

Whereas the messianic pretenders in our second challenge were religious fanatics, and those in the third were political visionaries, the pretenders who stalk the stage in this fourth challenge were intellectual mystics, tainted with a new metareligion called kabalism, from the Hebrew *kabeil*, "to receive." Though of late origin in Jewish history, the kabalists maintained that God had handed both the Torah and Kabala to Moses at Sinai, with the admonition that whereas the words of the Torah were for everyone, the words of the Kabala were for a select, intellectual elite only.

Be it so. For 1,200 years, from Moses to Jesus, kabalism was an underground movement, spoken of only in whispers, its contents not much more than a blend of Jewish superstition, Babylonian astrology, and Alexandrian spiritualism. Not until the second century, after its merger with a Jewish heresy known as Gnosticism, did kabalism surface as a distinct Jewish mystic philosophy.

The first Gnostics (from the Greek *gnosis*, "knowledge") were beatnik Jewish intellectuals who combined Mosaic monotheism with Greek philosophy into a Zoroastrian theosophy of good and evil. The world was not created by God, contended the Gnostics, but by his viceroy, Satan, on orders by God. Thus evil was a manifestation of God's will, and therefore divine. This veneration of evil, with the serpent of the Garden of Eden as the supreme symbol of adoration, attracted an ever-greater number of Christian adherents. The Church joined the Jews in excommunicating the Gnostics as heretics. But before gnosticism expired under the impact of Judeo-Christian bans, it entered Jewish mysticism, where it was seized by the kabalists. Instead of venerating evil, the new kabalists viewed evil as the cocoon out of which man had to emerge in his reach for God.

Kabalism, which until then had coursed like a subterranean stream underneath the Torah, was now seized by the Talmudists as an aid to bridge the gulf between man and God. Slowly they Judaized all foreign currents in kabalism, utilizing the best Greek reason, logic, and "scientific evidence" to prove its assertions. But though many of the most prominent Talmudists toyed with kabalism, it had little influence in Jewish life until the tenth century, when a Babylonian scholar synthesized ten centuries of kabalistic thought into one work, *The Book of Formation*. Published in Italy in 870, the book became a sensation in Spain, espoused by its leading Talmudists.

The publication of another sensational kabalistic work in the thirteenth century, the *Zohar*, "The Book of Splendor," a brilliant, original "forgery," blasted kabalism loose from Talmudism. The author, Moses de Leon (1250–1305), was a poet, scholar, and charlatan who charmed drawing-room audiences with his polished epigrams and learned dissertations. For years he labored at enlarging the vistas of kabalism by fusing his own ideas with those of past scholars. To gain his work immediate recognition, he attributed its authorship to a famed second-century Palestinian Tanna. What gave De Leon away was not deficiency in scholarship—the work was written in flawless Aramaic, the language spoken at the time of the Tannas—but the fact that he could not resist ascribing passages from his own previously published works to a scholar who had preceded him by a thousand years.

De Leon need not have been apprehensive. The Zohar brought a new breath and insight into kabalism, gaining immediate fame and becoming synonymous with kabalism itself. Though his work also made kabalism independent of the Talmud, it did not become a threat to Talmudism until after the sixteenth century, at which time it branched off in two directions. One current coursed into the Western Christian world, where as a metaphilosophy, it aided in the birth of theoretical science. The other current flowed into eastern European Jewry, where it petered out into superstition and congealed in a massive heresy.

With the dawn of the fourteenth century, the Age of the *Poskim*, the Decision Makers, came to an end. Though the Jews in 1300 thought they stood at a summit of achievement, they actually stood on the brink of a new disaster. The brilliance of ben Asher's *Four Rows* was but the flush of false health on the face of a doomed patient.

As the latent genius of western Europe pushed against the bars of feudal confinement, as the resentment of serfs swelled into thoughts of rebellion, as knights blithely performed their doomed arabesques of frivolous fighting, new storms were gathering on the European horizon. Pope and prince confronted peasants and burghers in a showdown for power. Heresies and revolutions were to wrack Christian ranks; persecutions and expulsions were to play havoc with Jewish life. But the Jews had been so accustomed to the continuous turns of the screw that at first they did not feel the hurt of the new turns that would shatter the life they had known.

Within the blueprint of our Jewish manifest destiny, this fourth challenge has been an unmitigated success. The first three challenges, though strengthening Judaic ideals among pagans and Mohammedans, did not appreciably expand the physical arena of Jewish operations. In the fourth challenge, however, the Jews broke out of the Mediterranean world into the heartland of Europe, poised at the right time in the right place for a probing penetration into the new world to the west and Russia to the east.

The fourth challenge did not end abruptly, but subtly melded into a fifth challenge within a time span of two centuries, during which both Christian and Jewish life was shattered into totally new constellations. The Christians broke out of their feudal prisons into a mercantile world shaped by the Jews, and the Jews were herded into the feudal prison abandoned by the emancipated Christians.

On this ironic note, the curtain quietly descends.

The Fifth Challenge:
The Regression of the Ghetto Age

The overture of our fifth challenge opens to the joyful rhythm of pounding horseshoes as gallant knights, sword at side, shield at arm, banners unfurled, ride east to Jerusalem in a Crusade to wrest the Holy Grail from the Saracen. The coda is ushered in with the mighty crescendo of a savage conflict between the soldiers of Christ and the minions of Mohammed. Two centuries and eight Crusades later, the Crusades have petered out, and the knight, that proud symbol of feudalism, is Europe's Don Quixote, an anachronistic figure soon to be mercifully taken out of history.

In these two centuries, as history merges the Renaissance into the Reformation (1300–1500), we see the Jews slowly funneled from free cities into ghettos where they will be preserved as fossilized specimens for 300 years (1500–1800). That they were not swept into oblivion by the social, economic, and religious currents of the two turbulent Renaissance centuries, or did not stagnate into a meaningless existence during the subsequent three centuries of ghetto imprisonment, bespeaks their unyielding stubbornness and a blind faith that anesthetized their misery.

This ghetto phase was accidentally brought about by three clusters of events—a clash between the economic ideologies of feudalism and capitalism, a schism between the contending religions of Catholicism and Protestantism, and a surge of expulsions of the Jews from west to east. We must therefore go back to the eleventh century, and examine the forces that gave impetus to the Crusades which shattered the feudal face of Europe, imposed a new capitalist profile on her, and clamped the Jews in dank ghetto quarters.

We saw the eleventh century deal the cards that shaped medieval Europe—France to the Capets, Germany to the Saxons, England to the Normans, Italy to an assortment of invaders, and the Jews to the kings. From the Elbe to the Atlantic, cathedrals rose to ring this rising feudal civilization with fortresses of faith, Romanesque architecture gave it a visual unity, great artists endowed it with the silent language of stone and paint, and *Chanson de Roland* was heard in the land. But this was only the outer shell of faith, art, and song. The inner core of Europe festered with ignorance, poverty, and sudden death.

In the eleventh century these social iniquities threatened to erupt into a revolution of discontent. The immediate cause was land, most of which had already been parceled out, leaving little to bequeath to the innumerable legitimate and illegitimate sons of the new nobility cropping up in the bedrooms of Europe. The continent had become a vast battlefield for bickering nobles who slew each other out of rivalry, chivalry, or boredom. The serfs were dissatisfied with their servitude. The already creaky feudal machinery of government was on the verge of a complete standstill.

At this point Palestine reenters Christian history. Though Palestine had passed into the hands of the Arabs in 638, it had occurred to no one in all Christendom to reunite Rome and Jerusalem into one spiritual domain until, four centuries later, it occurred to the "Jewish mind" of Pope Gregory VII. Beset with other problems, however, Gregory implanted the idea in the mind of his protégé, the future Pope Urban II, first French pontiff to sit on the throne of St. Peter. It was Pope Urban who was to transform this Gregorian cant into political faith.

Toward the end of the eleventh century, the internal threat of nobles in strife was eclipsed by the external threat of Turks on the march. After having vanquished the Abbasids, the Seljuk Turks pressed on Constantinople. Byzantium's Emperor Alexius appealed to Western Christendom for help. That cry was heeded by Pope Urban.

Where others saw danger, he saw opportunity. With his famed speech at the Council at Clermont, in 1095, he launched the first of eight Crusades—the euphemistic name given these bloodbaths in the name of Christ. On an ideological level, it was meant to extend the Kingdom of God to include the city of Jerusalem, a sort of Freudian pilgrimage back to the womb of Judaism. On a practical level, it amounted to ecclesiastical imperialism, planned to divert the nobles from fighting among themselves to fighting the Saracen, to gain land in Palestine for land-hungry Christian progeny, and to leave the papacy free to extend its temporal powers in Europe.

Alas, Pope Urban was to find that "something desirable and something possible are not always the same." Nothing went as planned. Though Urban had envisioned but one Crusade, his speech at Clermont set in motion eight, ushered in the Renaissance, and gave impetus to the Reformation. The Crusades ripped the economic fabric of the feudal world, the Renaissance illuminated its intellectual darkness, and the Reformation severed the unholy alliance between Church and state. Each event affected Jewish history.

Christians stress the romantic aspects of the Crusades —gallant knights out to wrest the Holy City of Jerusalem from the Saracens (from *Sarakenoi*, the Greek name for the Arabs). Jewish history books portray the Crusaders as despised barbarians who combined holiness with horror. Jews who had the bad luck to reside in the paths of Crusaders en route to the Holy Land were the first to feel the lethal effects of their mobilized zeal. Their stores were ransacked, their women violated, their communities burned. But though they suffered grievously, the devastation which befell the Jews does not compare in total horror to what befell Christians also in those same paths.

The First Crusade, launched in 1096 from French soil, set the pattern for future pillage and devastation. In March of that year, a People's Crusade, a rabble in arms led by one Peter the Hermit of Amiens, headed for Palestine. Peter, a small, thin man with a long, gray beard, and a hypnotic appeal that went beyond religion into the realm of hysteria, was of such commanding presence that his charisma rubbed off even unto the ass he rode, for people plucked hairs from its tail to preserve as relics. This ascetic hermit always waved to his wildly cheering audiences a letter from Christ commissioning him to lead the crusade. Promising indulgences for all sins, including those not yet committed, Peter recruited a motley army of 300,000, and then, without provisions, headed across the European continent for Constantinople as a jumping-off place for a march on Jerusalem.

Peter's route took him through the Rhine Valley, whose Jewish inhabitants became the first victims of his food-starved and sex-hungry band of Crusaders. After pitched battles, the small Jewish communities were usually overrun, most of the men and children slain, and the women ravaged. Long before this ragged army reached Hungary, it ran out of Jews to plunder, and left instead a trail of smoldering Christian villages and raped Christian women. The Hungarians, loath to extend the courtesy of being plundered, murdered, or raped by Western Christians, took to arms. In a passionate orgy of fear, hate, and revenge known to history as the War of the Peasants, they massacred 200,000 of Peter the Hermit's followers.

When the motley remnants of this People's Crusade reached Constantinople, the Byzantine emperor slyly suggested that they cross into Turkish territory for some easy loot. He neglected to mentioned that a Turkish army awaited them there. Peter's Crusaders walked into the trap. Of his remaining 100,000 men, a third were slain in battle, a third sold into slavery, and a third used as targets for archery practice.

Four months after the People's Crusade had started its march to doom, a Crusade of Princes, an army of 600,000, was launched. Led by Godfrey of Bouillon, a "man of blind but sincere piety," Count Raymond of Toulouse, a knight "whose piety was not exempt from avarice," and Bohemond of Otranto, who owned as many castles "as there are days in the year," this royal rear-echelon of the First Crusade had a little better success. After a three-year trek of plunder and butchery, about 25,000 reached the Holy Land in 1099. The rest had perished of disease and hunger, or had died gruesome deaths in revengeful up-risings by the Christian populace whose lands the rapacious Crusaders had traversed.[1]

After a forty-day siege of Jerusalem, the 25,000 Crusaders overcame its 1,000 defenders and showed the quality of their mercy. After duly ravishing the women, crushing the heads of infants, massacring 70,000 civilian Moslems, and herding the remnants of the Jewish population into a synagogue to be burned alive, the Crusaders repaired themselves to the Holy Sepulchre to proffer thanks to Christ for having vouchsafed them a righteous victory. As a chronicler who was there noted in his diary, "The horses waded in blood up to their knees, nay up to their bridle. It was a just and wonderful judgment of God." The Crusaders wept for joy, for with the annihilation of Jerusalem's pagans, Mohammedans, and Jews they believed they had solved their social, economic, and religious problems, just as the twentieth-century Nazis would believe they could achieve a solution to all their problems by exterminating Europe's Jews and Slavs.

The eight Crusades today stand as an uninspiring monument to human folly and faith.. In the First Crusade Jerusalem was won and after the Second it was lost. In the Third Crusade the best of the Moslem and the worst in the Christian worlds clashed when Saladin the Great of the Seljuk Sultanate matched wits and valor in battle against homosexual Richard the Lionhearted of England, crafty Philip II Augustus of France, and dead Frederick I Barbarossa of Germany. Frederick, who had drowned crossing the Saleph River in Asia Minor, had been pickled in vinegar and carried as a charm into battle to ensure victory. Alas, the sun proved too strong for vinegar to serve as an adequate preservative and the magic too weak to hex the Saracens; the sacred battle of Acre was lost and the cadaver of Frederick was buried. Brave King Richard, in order to gain by barter what he could not win by war, proposed that his sister Joanna marry Saladin's brother who

---

[1] Statistics about the Crusades are contradictory. We have relied in the main on those used by Henry Treece in his most readable work, *The Crusades*.

was to be made ruler of Jerusalem. Politics made strange bedmates even in feudal days.

The Fourth Crusade shocked all Europe with unparalleled horrors perpetrated by the Crusaders who slaughtered a million Greek Catholics when Constantinople fell into their hands. The people at home began to realize that the goal was not the Grail but gold, that whereas nobles were ransomed, soldiers were left behind in slavery, and that taxes far exceeded the loot.

Perhaps the most reprehensible Crusades were the two sideshows known as the Albigensian (1208) and Children's (1212) Crusades, both launched by Pope Innocent III. In the former, one million French Catholics suspected of heresy—99 percent of a sect known as Albigensian—were exterminated. Only a few thousand survived, a holocaust more devastating to the Albigensians than the Nazi holocaust to the Jews. In the Children's Crusade, 50,000 boys and girls were enticed into slavery and death. Bishops preached that God would deliver lost Jerusalem into Christian hands if innocent children took up the holiness of the Crusades. God, they promised, would give them dry passage through the Mediterranean, just as he had given Moses dry passage through the Red Sea. Christians kidnapped most of the children en route to Jerusalem, auctioning them off in Algiers and Cairo as girl whores and pleasure boys to the Saracens. Few survived.

Though the glamour had gradually rubbed off, Pope Innocent III, unwilling to let go of the grand illusion painted by Pope Urban II, preached a Fifth Crusade that ended in gruesome failure. In the Sixth, Jerusalem was bought in 1229 from the Saracen at a bargaining table and lost in 1244 on the battlefield. The army of the Seventh Crusade was massacred. The Eighth and last Crusade, launched by Louis IX of France and Prince Edward of England, petered out in ignominy when the former "fell sick of flux in the stomach" and the latter deserted the standard of the Cross to grab the crown of England. Acre, the last Christian stronghold in Palestine, fell in 1291 to Sultan Khalil, its 60,000 prisoners massacred or enslaved. Thus the Crusades, launched in faith and piety, were strangulated in blood and cruelty.

This brief excursion into the follies of the Crusades is not intended to minimize Jewish suffering at the expense of Christian, but to emphasize that Jews have no monopoly on martyrdom. The grandeur of Jewish history does not rest on suffering but on its transcendence of suffering. It is not the Crusades or their calamities that are important to either Christian or Jewish history, but the aftermath, when Christians, Mohammedans, and Jews mingled in the West European marketplaces of ideas. The resulting clash of minds gave birth to a new humanism that altered both Christian and Jewish fortunes.

The consequences of the Crusades to the Christians were an intellectual reawakening known as the Renaissance that led to new social values, an economic protest that toppled feudalism and opened a path for capitalism, and a religious revolt that convulsed the Church and paved the way for the Reformation. For the Jews, the consequences were catastrophic. The Renaissance toppled them from their intellectual pinnacle, the economic revolution severed them from their business enterprises, and the religious revolution alienated them from their social milieu.

The term "Renaissance," applied to the intellectual reawakening of Europe between 1300 and 1500, was not coined until the nineteenth century by the Swiss historian Jacob Burkhardt, who was the first to note that a rebirth of learning began to stir the mind of Europe right after the Crusades. What Burkhardt never asked, however, was why it took place precisely where and when it did, and who the father might be. Subsequent Christian scholars ascribe this intellectual pregnancy to an infusion of Greek learning by Petrarch and Dante into the body of Italy.

If an insemination of Greek culture did give birth to the Renaissance, then the Jews must be considered as possible contributory fathers. Several centuries before Petrarch and Dante, Jews helped reintroduce Greek learning into Europe. In fact, as early as the fifth century, Theodoric the Great, realizing the superiority of the learned Jews over the ignorant barbarians, had asked Jews, scattered by the invasions, to resettle in Ravenna and Milan, where he wanted them to stimulate arts and crafts, humanities and business. Several centuries later, Frederick II invited Jews to Naples to translate Greek, Arab, and Hebrew learning into Latin, and to teach Hebrew to Christian scholars.

Jewish intellectual activity preceded the Renaissance by 700 years precisely in those areas where it was to take root and flower. During those centuries the Jews were an intellectual elite—philosophers, mathematicians, astronomers, physicians, diplomats, bankers, and international businessmen. Would the Renaissance have flowered where it did, as it did, when it did, if the intellectual soil had not previously been seeded by the Jews?

Jewish history needs a Jewish Burkhardt to assess the role of the Jews in ushering in the Renaissance. But no Burkhardt is needed to assess what happened to the Jews after the arrival of the Renaissance. There were no Jews around to compete with the genius of Petrarch or Dante. The Jews possessed no Donatellos or Verrocchios. They had no Botticellis nor Leonardo da Vincis. Maimonides was no match for Francis Bacon. The latent Christian genius, bursting from the thousand-year confinement of its feudal ghetto, overwhelmed the manifest achievements of the Jews. Thus the first consequence of the Renaissance was to loft the Christians to new intellectual heights and to relegate the Jews to the feet of their new intellectual peers.

Almost simultaneously with these changes in intellectual climate came the economic consequences of the Crusades. For the Marxist, the Renaissance heralded the fall of the three great "impostors"—Moses, Jesus, and Mohammed. When artists dared to paint a smile on the face of the Madonna, say the Marxists, writers dared to attack the foundations of Church and state. In the Marxist view, the eight Crusades were not religious pilgrimages in quest of the Holy Grail but trade excursions in search of gold that paved the way for the rising bourgeoisie. In this sense, the Marxist is right. The two centuries of the Crusades saw the rise of the Christian gentleman businessman who displaced the feudal knight as a ruling elite and ushered in the new capitalism.

Capitalism, so revered today as a mode of production

handed down by God, was not graciously accepted by either Church or state in the waning Middle Ages. Both viewed it as a Jewish disease, much as today's capitalist views communism as a Jewish disease. The new capitalism was feared by the Church, which saw it challenge its supremacy as an arbiter in the marketplace, and was hated by the prince, who saw it shatter his feudal system of barter. Both Church and prince lost in the showdown that loomed around the corner of the sixteenth century, when capitalism rode in on the back of the Reformation. Ironically, the Jews, who had originally introduced capitalism into medieval society, were not to be part of what they had wrought. How then did they rise to the commercial preeminence they held in the High Middle Ages (1000 to 1350)?

The barbarian invasions of Europe left devastated cities in their wake. By 700, with the exception of such cities as Athens and Rome, no great population centers existed in Europe. Commerce and industry had ceased. Then suddenly, after the year 1000, towns again began to dot the devastated landscape. Cities, which had disappeared in the sixth century, reappeared in the eleventh, and the commerce which had died with the demise of the cities was resurrected with the revived urban growth.

Scholars assessing the impact of the Jews on the early medieval economy point out that trade was reestablished in seventh-century Venice by barbarians and Jews. Trading posts arose along the northern arc of the Mediterranean between Spain and Italy. Gold flowed again. By the ninth century, the Jews, whom we saw following the conquering scimitar as they once had followed Rome's conquering Eagles, were already famed international merchants whose ships plied the seas with goods. Thus the Jews, as the economic go-betweens of the Mohammedan and Christian civilizations, helped introduce Islamic capitalism into the mainstream of Europe's feudal arteries.

Known as Radanites (the origin of the word is unknown), these ninth- and tenth-century Jewish merchants established routes of commerce from Spain to China by land and sea, routes followed three centuries later by Marco Polo. Speaking Arabic, Persian, Greek, and the languages of the Franks (the Arab collective term for the French, Italians, Spaniards, and Germans), European Jews embarked from seaports in France, Italy, and Spain, heading east via three routes—one by sea to Syria, by land across Iraq to the Persian Gulf, and thence by sea to India and China; another across Gibraltar, along the North African coast to Egypt, and thence to the Far East; and a third through the center of the European heartland to the Kingdom of Khazar, and then across the Asiatic mainland to China. From the Mediterranean coast cities, commerce slowly spread north into France and Germany.

For three centuries, intrepid Jews monopolized Europe's glass, silk, and wool trades, controlled the dying industry, and dominated the import of spices, not because they were intrinsically more brilliant but because in the Talmud they had an international law that provided them with the advantage of being able to risk capital in long-range investments.

Seeing the Jews dispersed on three continents, entrenched in commerce and industry from Baghdad to Cordoba, the Talmudists, who at first had viewed business as "un-Jewish," fit only for pagans, at last yielded to the inevitable. To facilitate the new way of life, the Talmudists, often in business themselves, introduced new methods of doing business based on credit and negotiable securities instead of gold on the barrelhead. Whereas Roman law had held that indebtedness was personal and that creditors could not sell a note of indebtedness to someone else, Talmudic law recognized impersonal credit arrangements. Talmudic law held that a debt had to be paid to whoever had honestly acquired a debtor's note.

There is clear evidence that these new easy-credit arrangements, and the Talmudic laws enforcing the honoring of notes and debentures, led to the coming of international capitalism. The business voyages of the Hanseatic League (1200–1600) resembled armed incursions, because the gold they carried to transact business had to be heavily protected, whereas the Jews merely carried small pieces of paper—promissory notes. If robbed, the robbers got nothing but a worthless scrap of paper, since a demand note illegally acquired had no value. On the other hand, no merchant—whether Jew, Christian, or Mohammedan—in any part of the world hesitated to accept a note from a Jew, because each knew that the "international Jewish Talmudic court" would enforce payment of that note wherever presented.

To facilitate the exchange of goods and clearing of negotiable securities, the Jews established resident representatives in cities studded along the main routes of business. Such a representative was the "banker" whose office served as an informal clearing house. Money was deposited with him and he made payments as bills were presented to him. Merchandise was stored here, prices fixed, discounts arranged, and latest market quotations exchanged. In essence, these tenth- and eleventh-century Jewish representatives served as prototypes for the commercial consulates that arose during the Renaissance in Italian cities.

This Jewish preeminence in trade and industry began to shrink in the post-Crusade centuries. Those Crusaders who escaped an appointment with death at the Holy Sepulchre, returned disillusioned and disgruntled. The splendor of the Saracen world had spotlighted the squalor of their own state. Instead of going back to the feudal farm, they settled in towns. Here they discovered Jews ensconced as bankers, merchants, and businessmen, posts Christians had formerly derided as un-Christian, fit merely for Jews. The new Christian bourgeoisie did what seemed to them the only sensible thing to do. They kicked out the Jews and went into business for themselves.

The Church denounced Christian businessmen as "slaves of vice" and "lovers of money." Christian merchants struck back by contemptuously referring to clergy as stupid, seedy, and hypocritical. Not only did Christians take over the business institutions of the Jews but also their modes of doing business, their communal organizational principles, and their city charters. Within a century, these former serfs turned burghers had industry humming, commerce thriving, and trade flourishing on a grand scale. Nouveau riche Christian merchants now vied with the nobility for power and prestige. Though the Jews did not like it, they had to admit that their former Christian underlings were most apt pupils who now even surpassed their teachers. The state no longer needed the Jews to fill the posts the feudal order had forgotten to provide for.

Thus did the second phase of the disastrous consequences stemming from the ill-fated Crusades take place. The Jews were being alienated from the mainstream of the new economic activity. Within another century, these former international businessmen and financiers would be reduced to petty money-lending and peddling.

The third horseman of the medieval apocalypse, the religious revolt, rode in side by side with the other two calamities. Popes fared no better than nobles. Just as knights had proudly ridden off to the Holy Land, little suspecting they would return to a homeland swept by revolt, so the popes little suspected that the slogans they used to urge those knights into battle would turn into winds of heresy that would sweep them out of power. The Renaissance had not only awakened the Christians intellectually, but had also stimulated new scientific thought that clashed with religious dogma. As economic revolutionaries joined religious dissenters in a search for a new religion that would sanction their capitalist method of doing business, the stage was set for the coming Reformation.

In the twelfth century, the first serious flames of heresy appeared on the Catholic horizon. The Church unerringly recognized the Jews with their satanic ideas of freedom of thought and religion as the source of its troubles. And the Church was right. Jews and Judaic ideas were at the nexus of the three earliest and most dangerous heresies— the Waldensian, Albigensian, and Passaghian—which cropped up precisely in those areas where the Jews were the most numerous and influential.

The Waldensians, remote harbingers of the Reformation, had their origin in Lyons, where for centuries Jews had been ensconced in business and finance. The Albigensians, a curious reincarnation of the early Gnostics, were entrenched in southern France, where Jews exercised a great influence through their many academies. The Passaghian heresy festered in the Pope's own backyard, in Lombardy, where Jews had attained positions of wealth and prominence.

Though these three heretic sects differed from each other in many external observances, they had many Jewish-inspired features in common. Whereas the heresies in the early history of Christendom had concerned themselves mainly with differences about the nature of Christ, in these new heresies the center of gravity shifted from the Gospels to the Old Testament. The Waldensians opposed image worship, detested the deification of the Cross, refused to invoke the Virgin Mary, and identified themselves as the elect of Israel. The Albigensians rejected the sacerdotal system of the Church, protested against image worship, and though they were anti-Mosaic, the Kabala fascinated them. Claiming themselves heirs to Jamesian Christianity, the Passaghians contended that the fundamental Mosaic laws had to be observed, insisted on the literal observance of the Sabbath, and most remarkable of all, practiced the rite of circumcision. These heresies were Christianity's first attempts to divest itself of the paganization it had undergone during its formative years.

But though these first heresies were mercifully drowned in blood, new voices of dissent were reverberating in England, Bohemia, and Italy. One of the first to be heard above the murmur of general discontent was that of John Wycliff (1320–1384), famed as the first translator of the New Testament into English, who challenged Vatican power. Though Wycliff managed to die a natural death, a papal court posthumously condemned him to death by burning. His body was disinterred, burned at the stake, and thrown into a river. In Bohemia, John Huss (1369–1415), who revived the ideas of Wycliff, was consigned alive to the flames. But his death, instead of stilling the masses, inspired the bloody Hussite Wars, precursors of further religious conflicts to come. In Italy, Girolamo Savonarola, picking up the relay stick of protest from Huss, fulminated against pope and pomp, and the Florentinians helped the friars carry out his triple sentence —torture, hanging, and burning.

Burning no longer proved a cure for dissent, however. Above the roars of the flames were heard renewed protests that hardened into a counter-intolerance. There was but one lone voice of moderation, that of Desiderius Erasmus (1466–1536), a bystander, not a marcher. "Let others affect a martyr's crown," he wrote. "I do not think myself worthy of this dignity." Had the Vatican heeded him, there might have been a Universal Christian Church instead of a divided Catholic and Protestant Christendom. But it did not. Perhaps it was too late. The tolerance of Erasmus could no longer exert a force on men whose loyalties were caught between the opposing intolerances of Church and anti-Church. Instead of abolishing the sale of indulgences, the center of so much controversy, the Church started a drive for the sale of improved indulgences. Like the absolutions of Peter the Hermit, the new indulgences promised forgiveness for sins not yet committed. The thunder of the three giants of the Reformation —the German monk Martin Luther, the French theologian John Calvin, and the Swiss pastor Ulrich Zwingli—muffled the voice of Erasmus.

An Augustinian monk and ordained priest, Martin Luther (1483–1546) challenged the Church in 1517, was excommunicated in 1521, and married a nun in 1525. Upon beholding his son suckle at her breast, he exclaimed, "Child, your enemies are the pope, the bishops, and the devil. Suck and take no heed." This advice encapsulates his own life. In a tide of verbal invective that equated pope and priest with devil and anti-Christ, Luther swept half of Germany's Roman Catholic Christendom with him into Lutheranism.

John Calvin (1509–1564) was the antithesis of Luther. Whereas Luther, a shrewd German peasant of round jolly face, was loquacious and given to ribald humor, Calvin, a stoic French aristocrat of hard-chiseled features, was laconic and a man of subtle wit. Calvin, too, threw his gauntlet in the face of the pope and became the French religious dictator of Geneva, making it the "Protestant Rome." Whereas Luther put his faith in the secular ruler, Calvin placed his trust in man, provided man thought as he did. Like the pope, Calvin was convinced of his own infallibility.

The third of this triumvirate of Protestant faithmakers,

Ulrich Zwingli (1584–1631), destined since boyhood for the priesthood, proclaimed the Reformation in Switzerland in 1521, entrenching himself as firmly in Zurich as Calvin did in Geneva. Zwingli held that God was a rational creature, and that only the Kabala could prove the divinity of Jesus. Faithful to the Second Commandment, he ordered all images and relics in Swiss churches to be removed.

The Church accused these leaders of the Reformation of being Judaizers, an epithet that fitted them as if measured to size. The main practices of the Waldensian, Albigensian, and Passaghian heresies had become the dominant features of Protestantism. Huss, Luther, Calvin, Zwingli were all Hebraists, familiar with the Old Testament, who believed their teachings representd a return to a Judaism enriched with Jesus. Before burning Huss, the Church accused him of being a Judas who had consulted with Jews. Calvin, who burned Michael Servetus, founder of the Unitarian movement, for being a Judaizer, was himself branded one by the Church. Luther was dubbed a "half-Jew" by the Vatican tenants, and he accepted that designation in his characteristic trenchant prose:

> They [the Jews] are blood-relations of our Lord; if it were proper to boast of flesh and blood, the Jews belong to Christ more than we. I beg, therefore, my dear Papists, if you become tired of abusing me as a heretic, that you begin to revile me as a Jew.[2]

Convinced that under his leadership Christianity represented a new Judaism, Luther invited the Jews to join his cleansed "Jewish Christianity." When they refused his kind invitation, his love for the Jews was transformed into blind hate, for he viewed their refusal as an act of betrayal.

After a century of resistance unto death, the Church capitulated to the Protestant "Judaizers." At the Peace of Augsburg (1555) Protestantism was recognized as a

[2] As quoted in *Jewish Influence on Christian Reform Movements*, p. 618.

legitimate branch of Christianity. The Protestant countries became in the main the new capitalistic nations, and the Catholic countries in the main retained their feudal social structure. Europe had entered its Modern Age.

But the Church did not believe the Treaty of Augsburg would contain the Protestant heresy. It was especially fearful that the Jews within its domain would further "Judaize" Catholic minds with their notions of freedom. The Church was now prepared to join the Christian merchants who, fearful of Jewish competition, were demanding that the Jews be legislated out of the mainstream of business. This would solve the Church's problem too. It would isolate the Jews from the Christians and thus help the Church in her fight to keep the purity of the faith in uncontaminated minds.

The Church was aided in its decision to isolate the Jews from Christian society by a series of unrelated expulsions of the Jews that began in England in 1290 and culminated with their exodus from Spain in 1492. Historically, this served to shift the Jewish population from west to east. Demographically, it brought about a large, rootless population of nonindigenous Jews among indigenous Christians.

Christians have nurtured the notion that the Jews were expelled from these various countries because they were usurious money-lenders, which puts the onus on the Jews themselves. Jews have propagated the myth that anti-Semitism was the propulsive force, thus placing the onus on the Christians. In reality, a simpler cause than either was behind these events. At their root was greed, which makes it a human folly.

The first expulsion, in England, occurred right after the last Crusade. The pious version of English monks, that the Jews were banned by a benign monarch because of their extortionate usury, has been rejected by scholars, who attribute the expulsion to the mendacity and greed of Edward I. His talents for chicanery became apparent early in his life when he raided the deposits entrusted to the Templars of London and stole a sum amounting to 10,000 pounds sterling. After having imposed such a heavy tax on the Jews of England that it deprived them of all liquid wealth, he expelled them in order to appropriate their property. This was an exact repetition of the formula he had used in exiling the Jews from Gascony a few years earlier. The English people at first rejoiced to see the Jews leave, for they had the ecstatic vision of all their debts to the Jews being remitted. Alas, their joy was short-lived, for Edward's tax collectors squeezed out every shilling owed to the Jews by the Christians, taking their land if they did not have ready cash. Rapacious Lombards, replacing the Jews as bankers, went into partnership with English clergy and noblemen and raised the interest rates to such usurious heights that the population mourned the departure of the Jews.

King Philip of France set the example for a series of expulsions from France with a unique double ploy. After confiscating their property, he banished all Jews, then permitted them to return provided they pay a heavy fine for having been so presumptuous as to leave *La Belle France.* Between 1300 and 1400, avaricious French kings used this ploy several more times until the Jews learned the name of the game and stayed away for good. When there were no more Jews to swindle, the French kings turned to fleecing the Templars, an order of monks who had grown wealthy as international bankers during the Crusades. Never at a loss how to cheat an honest subject, the French kings first accused the Templars of heresy and then burned them as heretics so they could confiscate their gold and property for just cause.

This game of expulsion and recall of Jews was refined by German dukes, margraves, and assorted princelings. As the Jews were banished from one of the hundreds of duchies, palatinates, or principalities that comprised the Holy Roman Empire, they were admitted to others, after confiscation of their property at one end and the payment of a fine at the other.

The exception to this game of greed was Spain, from which the Jews were expelled in 1492 under complex and chilling circumstances which laid the foundations for modern racism by blood.

Brilliant though the Jewish culture in Spain was during the Moorish occupations, it was not original. It did not shape Moslem civilization; it only contributed to it. But when the Christians wrestled Spain from the Moors, the Jews did make an original contribution to Catholic Spain, for they represented a superior civilization to that of the conquering Spanish. In the process of bringing the splendor of the Islamic civilization to Christian Spain, they left an imprint of Jewish humanism on that country. By virtue of their learning and sophistication, they rose to great positions of power, many attaining high ranks of nobility. The Jew in fourteenth-century Spain was not an outsider, as he was in the rest of feudal Europe. He was part of the ruling class.

Resentment against these Jewish "outsiders" as "insiders" smoldered for a century, then erupted into an anti-Jewish movement popularly known as the "Second Reconquest," a movement to force the Jews to "give" Spain back to the Christians. It climaxed in the great conversion drives of 1391, when thousands upon thousands of Jews were forcibly baptized into Christianity so that "Christians," not Jews, would rule Spain. Instead of solving the Jewish problem, however, Spain begot the Marrano syndrome.

There is a myth deeply ingrained in Jewish history that the Marranos were pious Jews who were not only forcibly converted to Christianity but also forcibly held in the Christian fold. Their love for Judaism was so great, the myth contends, that at the risk of their lives they continued to practice Judaism in secret while professing Christianity in public.

This version runs into some contradictory facts, the most puzzling being the word *Marrano*. The Spaniards called converted Jews and Moors *Conversos,* that is, the converted ones. It was the unconverted Jews who called converted Jews "Marranos," the Spanish word for "swine."

Though Jews had risen to high government posts and married into nobility during the fourteenth century, they had not risen into royal and Church ranks, the highest posts the country had to offer. But now, after the flower of Jewish aristocracy and intelligentsia had been converted to Christianity, they were entitled, as full-fledged Christians, to all the rights, ranks, and privileges of state and Church. Though some of these Jewish Conversos did practice Judaism in secret, many did not. Some married into royalty. Others entered the service of the Church, becoming bishops, archbishops, cardinals. These converted Jews became known as "New Christians," and began to dominate Spanish intellectual life. It was this "Jew in Christian clothes" who became the villain, with disastrous results for Jews and for Spain. The cry was raised by the "Old Christians" that the "New Christians" were not loyal to the Church. They held that *limpieza de sangre,* purity of blood, undiluted by Jewish ancestry, should determine one's fitness for Church office, not mere ability. *Limpieza de sangre* introduced the concept of racism by blood.

The concept of *limpieza* was not a Church doctrine. The Church fought against it, arguing that Jesus had been crucified to redeem all men. The adherents of the *limpieza* cult conceded that Jesus was for everybody, but maintained that high Church posts were for Old Christians only. So persistent was the feeling that the Inquisition was introduced in 1480 at the insistence of many New Christians to distinguish the disloyal from loyal. The stage was set for Torquemada and the *auto-da-fé,* "the act of faith"—the rite of purification by being burned alive.

Tomas de Torquemada (1420–1498), Inquisitor General of Spain, a devout Dominican and a true son of Rome, was noted for excessive piety and excessive modesty, and was suspected of being a descendant of Marranos. Universally hated, he was in constant dread of being poisoned or assassinated, and always traveled with a bodyguard of 250 men. The Inquisition procedure he instituted was calculated to achieve the greatest degree of horror with the least amount of publicity. Yet in spite of its reputation, the Spanish Inquisition was not as merciless as the French Revolutionary Tribune, and far less inhuman than the Communist GPU or German Gestapo.

Torquemada viewed with alarm the heresies sweeping Europe. To him the dread of heresy diluting True Faith was far worse than Jewish blood diluting royal lineage. He felt that to save the purity of Spanish Catholicism, the threat of incipient heresy posed by worldly Marranos, relapsed Moslems, and cynical Christians would have to be stamped out before it was too late. To Torquemada's credit, it must be stated that he did not link religious infidelity to *limpieza*. But what the Inquisition did find out was that more New Christians were prone to "error" than Old Christians.

Torquemada elevated the *auto-da-fé* into a masterpiece of showmanship, deliberately planned to resemble the popular concept of the Last Judgment. The *autos-da-fé* were frightening yet exhilarating spectacles that drove home a lesson. In the same spirit as Robespierre, who guillotined aristocrats while quoting Rousseau, Torquemada burned heretics while quoting Jesus.

If we want a rational view of history, we must fit events into proper perspective. The Inquisition cannot be equated with the modern police state, nor can the Spaniards be accused of being anti-Semitic. The Inquisition did not kill by formula, as totalitarians do for "final solutions." The Spanish Inquisition generally preferred not to burn, and sought for "penitence"; more were burned in effigy than in the flesh. More Jews were killed by criminal folly in other European countries than by the *autos-da-fé* in Spain. If the Spaniards had been anti-Semitic, they could easily have murdered all the Jews in Spain, as Hitler did in Germany. But they did not. Torquemada did not ask for the death of unconverted Jews, nor were they brought before the Inquisition. He asked for their expulsion. No charge was brought against them other than that they were not Catholic. Unconverted Mohammedans were expelled in the same manner. The remarkable fact is that even as the Spaniards expelled the Jews in 1492, any Jew who wished to convert to Catholicism could stay in Spain. Some 50,000 Jews, almost a third of the Jewish population in Spain, did convert rather than leave a land which had been their home for 1,500 years.

Here, perhaps, we have an explanation why Jewish chroniclers do not condemn the expulsion of the Jews from England, France, or Italy with the same concentrated invective they do the expulsion from Spain. The banishment from those other countries, unlike the events in

Spain, did not constitute a threat to Judaism because few British or French Jews converted to Christianity. The actual threat may not have been the Judaization of Christian Spain, but the Christianization of the Spanish Jews. Perhaps that is why Jewish Conversos were called Marranos—swine—by the unconverted Jews.

The 50,000 Jews who chose to stay in Spain by converting to Christianity became the new Marranos. But because of the all-pervading effects of *limpieza,* they did not soar to high posts and intellectual eminence as had the Jews and Marranos of the two preceding centuries. Within a century after the Jewish expulsion, the intellectual lights in Spain went out.

Where did the expelled Jews go? English, French, and German Jews went mostly to Austria, Prussia, Poland, and Lithuania, at the invitation of enlightened kings who, like Theodosius, Charlemagne, and Frederick II in previous centuries, wanted Jews to settle in their emerging domains to foster trade and industry, to stimulate the arts and crafts. The Spanish Jews scattered over half the globe, finding sanctuaries in northern Italy, in the Ottoman Empire, in Palestine, and eventually in Holland. More importantly, they also extended the frontiers of the Diaspora to the New World, being among the earliest settlers in Brazil, the West Indies, and thence to North America.

Thus, by 1500, the center of Jewish gravity had shifted from west of the Rhine, where the fourth challenge had transpired, to east of the Rhine, where the fifth challenge will unfold. With the expulsions of the Jews from the West, all parts of mind, time, and events fall into place. All the dissident elements from Crusades to Reformation are now brought together into a pattern of tragedy for the Jews. The Church, fearful that the continued presence of Jews among Christians would accelerate the spread of heresy, began to see eye to eye with Christian merchants who were clamoring for the complete elimination of Jews as competitors in business. The refusal of the Jews to support the Church in its fight against godless Protestants had not endeared them to the Church either. As for the Protestants, their love for the Jews had ebbed when the Jews refused to join them as comrades in arms against the godless papists. The sixteenth century seemed to be a good time to solve the Jewish question.

To the credit of both Catholics and Protestants, it did not occur to either to exterminate the Jews, even though they did their level best to wipe out each other in a century of religious wars. The Jews were not to be killed, but merely expelled from the mainstream of Christianity. Out of sight, out of mind, out of influence, they would not compete with honest Christian businessmen and not contaminate with heresy the minds of God-fearing, Jesus-loving Christians. Placing the Jews into *cordons sanitaires,* "antiseptic enclaves" or ghettos, seemed an excellent solution.

Haphazardly, without a master plan, the isolation of the Jews in ghettos was achieved within a century. The Jew, who for a millennium had been an integral part of the economic, social, and intellectual history of Europe, was now relieved of all his rights and privileges. He was now neither essential for Christian salvation nor necessary for national economic survival. The Jew had become the superfluous man in Europe.

THE FALL OF THE TALMUD

We have thus far traversed 3,500 years of Jewish history and beheld a bewildering succession of incredible and dazzling scenes—a burning bush in the wilderness of Sinai, true believers marching from Susa to Judah to revive the Torah in Zion, Rome staking its conquering Eagles around Palestine, Sassanids ushering in an age of splendor in art and architecture, Crusaders riding off to the Holy Land to wrest the Grail from the Saracens. But now, in the fifth challenge, our stage setting reveals one of the most bizarre scenes of all. It is a street that begins nowhere and ends nowhere.

There is a surrealistic quality about this street enclosed by a wall with locked gates at both ends. Lining this street, so narrow a wagon can hardly turn, are slender, three- and four-story buildings that give an illusion of touching roofs, conspiring to keep out the rays of the sun. The architecture too has an elusive quality. Though the buildings are unmistakably medieval, the structures take on regional characteristics—now Rome, now Prague, now Frankfort, now Warsaw.

Something familiar about this scene haunts our memory. Suddenly we penetrate its mystery. We have seen this street before, caught with paint on canvas by Marc Chagall. It is the main street that runs through the medieval ghetto, the artery that for three centuries sustained Jewish life as it languished in this macabre prison.

The ghetto was not an arbitrary creation by the Church, but a totally unanticipated end result of Jewish policy. We have seen how, throughout the centuries, the Jews demanded land of the local prince on which to develop their own communities. But as towns and cities grew, these Jewish quarters were encompassed by swelling Christian settlements. Most Jewish neighborhoods became choice locations, and within the shadow of synagogue and *mikveh* (ritual bathhouse) sprouted church and palace.

Considering an entire continent and a time span of ten centuries (500–1500), and allowing for national wars, regional faiths, and local hates, for the most part Jews and Christians lived amicably side by side. But in the sixteenth century, with the decision to isolate the Jews, the Church demanded that Christians evacuate Jewish neighborhoods. Slowly, under threats of ban and ostracism, the Christians reluctantly abandoned their homes in Jewish quarters.

Walls were built around these now all-Jewish sectors. At sundown, the gates were locked and none could enter or leave until sunup. By the end of the century, these formerly gay, cosmopolitan neighborhoods where Jews could once come and go as they pleased had become squalid ghettos where they had to slink in and out with heads hung in humiliation under the taunts of foul-mouthed gatekeepers.

Capricious history has reversed the former roles of Christians and Jews. The Christians, who for seven centuries had been locked in a feudal prison, have entered a new age of enlightenment, while the Jews, who during those same centuries had lived in freedom, have regressed into an age of ghetto darkness.

In this fifth challenge, we shall see the Jews trying to escape in diverse ways from their horrifying ghettos—via apostasy into Christianity, via Sabbatean messianism, via the sensuality of Frankism, via the religious ecstasy of Hasidism. But we shall see them fail in all these attempts until freed, *en passant*, by the French Revolution, which did not even have the Jew in mind.

Can the Talmudist, who until now has been called upon to respond to challenges of expanding vistas, respond to this challenge of regression? With the Jews locked away in ghettos, the riders of the Responsa are no longer free to gallop from community to community with their latest "supreme court" decisions, as in the Islamic times of the Gaons, or as in the feudal times of the Poskim. Whereas in past challenges the problem of the Jew has been to universalize the contents of the Talmud, the main job of the Talmudists in the ghetto age is the opposite. The task of the Talmud is no longer to extend the frontiers of the mind, but to help the Jews preserve their sanity and identity. We shall see the Talmudists come once more, a final time, to the rescue. But almost too late.

In previous challenges, the cure arrived before the illness, but this time only a nostrum was available. The two centuries preceding the ghetto age had been a period of interregnum for the Jews. Between 1300 and 1500, as their old political and business institutions crumbled under the impact of the Renaissance, the Talmudists, seeing no new social patterns emerge for the Jews, hesitated about what to do next and lost the initiative. Into the vacuum of their hesitation stepped a new set of specialists, a succession of mediocrities with rabbinic titles, who paved the first of two sections of the ghetto survival road. They did so by freezing accidental custom into paralyzing tradition. With them, ghetto Judaism was born before the ghetto itself had been created. Their success eventually stultified Jewish life into a stubbornly lingering caricature of Jews and Judaism.

Among the first of these early shapers of ghetto Judaism

was Jacob Molin (1360–1427), a dull, undistinguished rabbi from Mainz, Germany, also known as the Maharil (an acronym based on his Hebrew name). We could substitute a dozen other equally mediocre rabbis who performed essentially the same service for ghetto survival as he did. But this Maharil suits our purposes because a book written in his name by his disciples sums up the spirit of the times of all the "maharils" between 1300 and 1500 who formalized the infinite variety of Jewish life into one conforming standard.

Jacob Molin was everyman's busybody. He reduced Jewish life into a ritual of trivia, from how to tie a shoe lace or slaughter a chicken, to how to have sexual intercourse or love God. He never let anything happen the first time. Everything—marriage, birth, divorce, death— was standardized into a common law of tradition. Most of the rituals so revered as eternal forms of Judaism by the orthodox today—like wearing a hat and keeping the sexes segregated while attending synagogue service—are not Mosaic law. They are simply stratified customs.

The second section of the survival road through the ghetto was laid 200 years after the Maharil, toward the end of the sixteenth century, at the very portals of the ghetto, by two Talmudists who suddenly awakened to the real problem. They constituted an odd set of Diaspora designers—one a brilliant, paranoid Palestinian scholar named Joseph Caro, who designed a "Spanish table" for self-service law, and the other a rich, enlightened Polish rabbi named Moses Isserles, who covered it with a "German tablecloth."

It is difficult for the historian to give life to Jewish scholars, because through the ages Jewish myth-makers have manufactured only two models of biographical hoods —the halo of saintliness for heroes and the horns of satan for villains. With the advent of Joseph Caro, however, the Jewish historian gets a break. It is not that the myth-makers did not try to suffocate Caro the man with their "halo" model. They did, but Caro did not cooperate. To their chagrin, Caro kept a diary in which he recorded his conversations with a messenger from God, a *maggid*, who styled himself "the son of Mishna." When this diary was discovered after Caro's death, the orthodox hailed it as proof that he was divinely inspired. When twentieth-century Freudian psychoanalytic insights suggested that Caro might have been a paranoid with possible homosexual tendencies, the orthodox denounced the diary as a fraud.

Caro's maggid was a Jewish version of the Christian incubi—lewd demons who came disguised either as handsome clerics to make love to virtuous nuns or as beautiful virgins to pollute the dreams of monks.[8] Caro's maggid, however, was a sublimated Jewish incubus who only talked and never performed. But just as the dreams of nuns and monks seduced by incubi reveal repressed sexuality, so the visitations of the maggid reveal much about Caro's repressions. The maggid speaks to Caro in such frankly sexual terms as "Lo, I am the Mishna speaking in your mouth, kissing you with kisses of love," or "I embrace you, and cleave unto you with kisses of love," or "Let him kiss me with kisses of his mouth, for I am the Mishna that speaketh in your mouth." In one night session, the maggid reveals "the secret" of Caro's third wife. "You must know," he confides, "that in her past transmigration she was a male, a virtuous rabbinic scholar."[4]

The diary also reveals Caro's ambition to become a martyr. Though the maggid assured Caro that he would burn at the stake for the greater glory of God, Caro evaded the fulfillment of this ambition by prudently staying in Ottoman territory instead of setting foot on Christian land.

Whatever psychoanalytic insights one can draw from Caro's relationship to his maggid—whether a latent homosexual or a sublimated martyr—we find nothing of this

---

[8]The Church charged Luther was the son of an incubus who had seduced his mother.

[4]Caro's nightly maggidic visitations can be inserted into a wider framework of mystical piety as practiced by many rabbinic lawyers, according to *Joseph Karo—Lawyer and Mystic* (Oxford University Press), by R. J. Zwi Werblowsky of the Hebrew University of Jerusalem, a work we have relied on heavily for the above views.

personality split in his Talmudic writings, which reveal a brilliant, logical mind touched with genius.

Joseph Caro (1488–1575) was born in Toledo, Spain, just four years before the expulsion of the Jews from that country. His parents, choosing expulsion rather than conversion, settled in Constantinople. Caro eventually settled in Palestine in 1525, and in 1537 founded an academy in Safed, where he died. He was married five times, but being a Sephardic Jew, not subject to Gershom's ban on polygamy, it is possible that he may have had more than one wife at a time. Consummating his fifth marriage at the age of seventy-nine, Caro prayed to the Lord that he might beget another son who would study the Law. His prayers were answered two years later, thus confirming both his piety and potency.

Caro correctly appraised the need of the times. He saw the Jews of Europe isolated in their ghettos, all their great academies in Spain, France, Germany, Italy closed. He realized that the Jews needed an instant law so lucid it would not require a body of learned judges to decide the issues. Viewing himself perhaps as another Maimonides, he decided to write a code of instant decisions where each ghetto could look up the right or wrong of questions in dispute.

Caro's first work, the *House of Joseph,* a commentary on Jacob ben Asher's *Four Rows,* caused a sensation in the rabbinic world, for it was the first step to an "everyman's Blackstone." But it was his later classic, *The Prepared Table,* that conferred on him the distinction of being the greatest Talmudist Judaism has produced. In this magnum opus, Caro compressed the zeal, faith, and wisdom of over 1,500 years of Talmudic evolution so brilliantly that he achieved the ultimate in codification— a code that permitted any Jew in the remotest ghetto instantly to avail himself of the appropriate law. No Responsa needed, no academy necessary.

However, the paean of praise for Caro's work was accompanied by a pizzicato of rabbinic cries of foul. The rabbis who accused Caro of basing most of his decisions on the Spanish Talmudists and relegating German scholars to second-class status were correct. After their expulsion from Spain, the Spanish Jews had lost their former intellectual preeminence. The centers of Talmudic learning had shifted to eastern Europe with the shift of the Jewish population. The new dominant majority was the German "Ashkenazi Jew," not the Spanish "Sephardic Jew." Caro's work should have reflected the needs of the new dominant majority, not the thoughts of the vanishing minority.

Foremost among the critics of Caro's work was Moses Isserles (1525–1572), the first and greatest of the Polish Talmudists. A man of great wealth, he founded a private academy, providing scholarship funds out of his own means for bright but poor students. Though an orthodox rabbi, he had a penchant for the philosophy of Aristotle and for the sciences of the West, claiming it was permissible to read the "pagans" on the Sabbath provided one spent the rest of the week studying the Talmud. Convinced that the Zohar was revealed to Moses at Sinai, he defended the kabalists when their views coincided with his, but condemned them as heretics when they did not.

It was Isserles who transformed Caro's Sephardic-oriented code into an acceptable Ashkenazi-oriented one. No sooner had Caro's *House of Joseph* appeared, than Isserles wrote *Roads of Moses,* a critique of that work showing the Ashkenazi bypaths to God. No sooner did Caro's *The Prepared Table* appear than Isserles threw an "Ashkenazi" *Tablecloth* on it to hide its Spanish design. Jewish scholars, aware of Caro's genius and Isserles' cogency, quickly combined Caro's main text with Isserles' footnotes. This combined work became the authoritative code, recognized as such even today by orthodox Jews throughout the world.

Great as they were, however, Caro and Isserles arrived too late. The "maharils," for all their mediocrity, had been the leaders, whereas these two Talmudists, for all their brilliance, were the followers. They could only formalize *de jure* what their predecessors had achieved *de facto.* To overcome the paralyzing effects of "maharil" nostrums, they had overreacted and injected Judaism with an overdose of Talmudism. The tragic irony was that the perfection of *The Prepared Table* spelled the doom of

Talmudism. Subsequent Talmudists, instead of adjusting Caro's code to new conditions, forced Jewish life to conform to its sixteenth-century mold. Within a century, Caro's code became to the Torah what Jesus became to God. Just as Christians venerated Jesus, though they know that behind him there is God, so ghetto Jews began venerating *The Prepared Table*, though they knew that behind it was the Torah. What Judah Hanasi back in the second century A.D. had feared when he forbade all further Mishna became a reality in the seventeenth. The commentaries were consulted more than the Torah. Or, to paraphrase Loisy, what Moses proclaimed was the Torah, and what arrived was the Talmud.

Little can be said for Jewish intellectual life during the three centuries of ghetto existence. Estranged from the mainstreams of learning, the vast mass of Jews became parochial "fossils" eking out a miserable existence on the periphery of life. The ghetto Talmudists lost themselves in the hairsplitting of *pilpul*, an intricate maze of subtle absurdities about minutiae. In the stagnant ghettos, divorced from life, the Talmud not only stopped growing, it atrophied, and strangulated the spirit of Judaism. The codification road ornamented by the stately works of Alfasi, Maimonides, Jacob ben Asher, and Caro had come to a dead end. From the darkness of the first ghetto century to the dawn of the Atomic Age, little new significant Talmudic commentary has appeared.[5]

Had the Talmudists gone too far in their compact with the "maharils" to restrict Jewish life within an artificial tradition? Some rabbis began to doubt the system. A most skillful attack on Talmudism was an anonymous work later revealed to have been authored by Leon de Modena (1571–1648), a colorful, Venice-born Talmudist, whose grandfather had been made Knight of the Golden Fleece by Emperor Charles V. At the age of twelve, De Modena translated Latin poetry into Hebrew, and at fifteen he wrote a famed treatise against gambling. It was revealed later that he was an inveterate gambler who had lost

[5]The greatest Talmudist during this period, the Gaon of Vilna (1720–1797), enjoys a reputation in excess of his Talmudic works.

fortune after fortune. But because he moved in the highest circles of Christian nobility, because his famed sermons were attended by priests, scholars, and noblemen, the rabbis dared not defrock him.

De Modena is famed for two works. One published in his own name, presented a spirited defense of all Talmudic laws and the right of rabbis to freeze custom into law. The other, published anonymously, even more brilliantly attacked his own previous work, showing the invalidity of ghetto Talmudic laws, holding the Talmudists up to scorn, and accusing them of charlatanism. In this anonymous work, De Modena advocated that Judaism slough off many of its dietary restrictions and abolish such rites as the use of phylacteries, imposed on the Jews by the Talmud but not required by the Torah. Though he escaped excommunication and death for his views, De Modena was nevertheless a "Jewish Huss" who arrived two centuries before the "Jewish Luther."

Where religion fails to serve life, can heresy be far behind? Within less than half a century after Caro's death, the stereotyped ritualistic life prescribed by the new Talmudists transformed the ghettos into turbulent breeding grounds for heretic movements. The dynamic force was kabalism, which in the sixteenth century had broken loose from Talmudism. Just as the grandeur of the Talmud was degraded in the search for a sustaining faith in the ghetto, so the grandeur of the Kabala was degraded in the search for a miraculous escape from it. Demagogues of mysticism reduced the Kabala to its least common denominator, and fashioned it into a new, popular, pseudo-messianism. Opportunists embraced it as a weapon against Talmudism. The offspring of this union constituted three new heretic theologies—Sabbateanism, Frankism, and Hasidism.

Christian theologians had set aside the year 1648 as the definitive date for the second coming of their messiah. But instead of the ascetic Palestinian Jew named Jesus Christ arrived an impotent Turkish Jew named Sabbatai Zvi, who chose that year to reveal that a heavenly voice had proclaimed him the redeemer.

Sabbatai Zvi is an anachronism of history, a man who never should have been born in the same century that saw the works of Galileo, Kepler, and Descartes. Born in Smyrna in 1626, Sabbatai was an incredibly handsome man with black, piercing eyes, a magnetic voice, and a commanding personality. A mystic by choice, he was an ascetic by necessity. Married twice within two years, he was divorced by both wives after three days for not consummating his marriages. His third marriage was symbolic, and lasted a little longer. After revealing himself as the messiah in a Salonika synagogue, he had himself solemnly wedded to the Torah. Horror-struck, the rabbis excommunicated him. Sabbatai then headed for Egypt where, in fulfillment of the prophecy that the messiah would marry an unchaste woman,[6] he took as his fourth wife a whore named Sarah.

Sarah's life imitates fiction. Born in Poland, she was raped at the age of eight by Cossacks who had slain her father and violated her mother. She was found hiding in a cemetery by some nuns, who took her to a convent and after converting her to Catholicism brought her up as a nun. At the age of fifteen Sarah ran away, settling as a teenage prostitute in Amsterdam. Here she awaited the arrival of Jesus, certain she would become his bride. When she heard of the messiahship of Sabbatai, she jilted Jesus and announced she would marry Sabbatai instead. And thus it came about that a former Polish-born Jewish nun living in Amsterdam as a whore became the bride of a Turkish-born Jewish pseudo-messiah living in Egypt.

There is nothing in Jewish history to compare with the psychological impact of the Sabbatean heresy. A collective messiah mania swept the Diaspora. Reason took a holiday. Within a few short years, Sabbatai's adherents from India to England numbered a third of the Jews in the world. His chief followers were not the poor and downtrodden, but the rich and the prominent, the scholars and the intellectuals. Just as Jesus demanded no observance of law, merely

[6]In fulfillment of this prophecy, the whore in the life of Jesus was Mary Magdalene, whom he redeemed but did not marry.

belief in salvation through faith, so Sabbatai demanded of his followers nothing more concrete than faith. Like Christianity, Sabbateanism came to liberate mankind from all institutional religious restrictions on the human condition.

In 1656, Sabbatai headed for Constantinople to depose Sultan Mohammed IV, who threw the madman in jail. Thousands of his followers flocked to his prison to pay him messianic honors. Exasperated, the sultan gave Sabbatai the choice of conversion to Islam or death. The redeemer chose conversion. But even this act of apostasy did not shake the faith of all his followers. Some believed their messiah had to plummet to the nethermost depths in order to redeem the lowliest sinners.

Sabbatai died a prisoner of the sultan. But the Sabbatean psychosis lived on to mature into a new heresy called Frankism, whose lusty founder, Jacob Frank (1726–1791), more than made up for Sabbatai's impotency. Born in the Ukraine, Frank became a traveling salesman in Turkey. A contemporary pen portrait of him shows an aquiline John Barrymore profile, a small rakish moustache, and a fez perched atop a high forehead.

Frank's entry into the messianic world resembled that of Jesus. Just as John the Baptist, a self-proclaimed prophet in Palestine, had announced he awaited Jesus to baptize him a messiah, so one Leib Krysa, a self-proclaimed prophet in Poland, announced he awaited the coming of Frank to anoint him the messiah. Frank came, was anointed, and accepted his messiahship with aplomb. Grandly, he abolished the Talmud, proclaimed the Zohar the new Bible, and added another dimension to Judaism—vice. A frenzy of obscene orgies that included adultery and incest became the central liturgy in this swinging heresy. The rabbinate promptly excommunicated him.

When a series of new revelations by Frank called for him and his followers to convert to Christianity, the Frankists loudly proclaimed a belief in the Trinity. The Polish Church welcomed them with open arms, and the Jews rejoiced at being rid of this fornicating riffraff.

Alas, the Frankists had not informed the Church that they had expunged Jesus from their Trinity and substituted

Frank as the son of God. Enraged at this blasphemy, the Roman Catholic Poles clapped Frank in irons, but the Greek Orthodox Russians, on invading Poland, set him free. Supported like a prince by his numerous followers, Frank lived out his days in extravagance, but after his death the Frankists gradually disappeared through inter-marriage into Polish society and nobility. Thus these rejects of Jewish ghettos became Polish aristocrats.

In spite of the deep disaffection with Talmudism implied by the Sabbatean and Frankist heresies, the Talmudists went right on squeezing the joy out of Judaism and reaped a merited third religious revolt. This heresy, called Hasidism, from the Hebrew *hesed,* piousness, swiftly swept a third of East Europe's Jewry into its fold.

Just as Jesus was the founder and center of early Christianity, so Israel ben Eliezer, known to his disciples as Bal Shem, Master of the Name, was the founder and center of early Hasidism. There is a remarkable parallel between the lives of Jesus and Bal Shem. Just as an angel appeared unto Joseph to inform him that his espoused Mary would have a son whom he was to call Jesus, in fulfillment of prophecy,[7] so an angel appeared before Eliezer to inform him that his wife would have a son whom he was to call Israel, also in fulfillment of prophecy.[8] Like Jesus, Bal Shem performed miracles. When he wanted to cross a stream, he spread his mantle on the water, stepped on it, and floated to the other side. Like Jesus, he was an expert at exorcising evil spirits. He had but to touch the sick and they were healed. Just as Jesus saved a whore, so Bal Shem saved a fallen woman. His messages, like those of Jesus, came wrapped in parables. Unlike Jesus, he was twice married.

Bal Shem (1700–1760) was born in Podolia, at the foot of the Carpathian mountains, of poor but ignorant, one-hundred-year-old parents, who promptly orphaned him up-

[7]According to Matthew, 1:20–23. In the Gospel according to Luke, however, the angel did not come to Joseph but to Mary.
[8]"Isaiah XLIX. "Thou art my servant Israel in whom I will be glorified."

on his birth. To the world, Bal Shem presented a lazy student and an inveterate truant. But in the dead of night, his disciples aver, he studied kabalistic literature. He grew up to become a sexton in a small synagogue, married at eighteen, and after his wife's death remarried, this time to a rich man's daughter whose family disinherited the bride. The couple settled down to a life of desperate poverty, until finally he became the proprietor of a small village tavern. In his fortieth year, Bal Shem threw off his cloak of boorishness and revealed himself in the splendor of a messenger of God. Henceforth, he led a life of saintliness and piety, and word of his wonderworks spread far and wide.

In essence, Hasidism was a Jewish revivalist movement in which, as in Christianity, personality took the place of doctrine. Unencumbered by higher learning, Bal Shem stripped kabalism of its metaphysics, which he did not understand. He neutralized the messianic content of Sabbateanism and substituted frenzied religion for the sexual frenzy of Frankism. In Bal Shem's view, all men were equal before God, the ignorant a little more equal than the learned. Instead of venerating the 613 basic Mosaic commandments, he urged his followers to sing and dance their way into God's grace. Evil could be overcome by joy, melody was exalted above prayer. The Hasid became a hymn-singing, dancing, Jewish dervish.

The Talmudists placed Bal Shem and his followers under the ban, but to no avail. Though excommunicated time and again, new followers swelled Hasidic ranks. Hasidism became more Jewish than Talmudism. It became orthodoxy. It could not be excommunicated.

After Bal Shem's death, the unity of Hasidism was shattered into sects, headed by *Zaddiks*, or saints, noted for their sensuous lust for power and regarded as nonmessianic messiahs by their followers. Of all the major "heresies" in Jewish history, Hasidism was the only one that did not identify itself with a return to Israel. In a sense, it was the only totally Diaspora-oriented Jewish ideology. Leadership soon bypassed the capable, and was handed down from saint to son. By mid-eighteenth century, Hasi-

THE INDESTRUCTIBLE JEWS

dism was in decline. It fell because the Hasids were ignora-
muses, incapable of thought beyond an aphorism.[9]

Paradoxically, however, though the Sabbatean, Frankist, and Hasidic heresies represented regressions in Jewish
life, they also represented liberating influences. Their successive failures produced a healthy skepticism, a distrust
of messianism, mysticism, and Talmudism that created an
atmosphere for the acceptance of nineteenth-century reform movements.

Have the heretics been a disruptive or a liberating force
in Judaism? Throughout the ages, zealots have always
guarded the status quo as passionately as the frigid guard
their virginity, even though that which they so jealously
preserve was once a heresy. In the first act, we saw Judaism enriched by a succession of heresies that became ortho-
doxies. It was a heretic Abraham, who, by shattering the
entrenched idols of his forefathers, founded Judaism. It
was a heretic Moses who imposed the Torah on recalcitrant
orthodox Jews who worshipped the Golden Calf. It was
heretic Prophets who hammered away at the enshrined
priesthood, the essence of traditional Judaism in their day.

In the second act, too, we saw a succession of iconoclasts, the trailblazing Talmudists in the first four challenges, hammer away at established orthodoxy. Each new
set of Talmudic exegetes were revolutionaries who dared
change old forms for new, even while proclaiming they
were merely reverting to first principles.

In the sixth challenge, we shall see the Talmudists fail
because with the fifth challenge they ceased being innovators. They no longer dared to lead, but strove to fit life
into the straitjacket of the past. This failure must not be
allowed to obscure the past grandeur of the Talmud, however. Instead of intoning *kaddish* (the prayer for the dead),
let us pay tribute to its great past achievements, and return
to the Jews standing at the threshold of their emancipation and assess the traumatic impact of the ghetto period.

[9]This does not mean that Hasidism cannot be regenerated into a
new revivalist movement as was done by Paul with Jamesian
Christianity. Already powerful influences are at work, notably the
writings of Martin Buber, to infuse Hasidism with intellectual and
theological ideas it did not possess in the past.

Three stereotyped notions survived the fall of the ghetto and persist to this day. One is that the Jews have always been paragons of tolerance, with nary a wicked thought in their collective mind. Another is that the Church has been eternally anti-Semitic. The third is that the Jew and Judaism which emerged from the ghetto are the true prototypes of the Jew and of Judaism.

Let us not deceive ourselves. The image of a meek Jew with an arsenal of clichés about tolerance is a projection of the ghetto age, cultivated by modern, public relations-minded historians. In the Feudal Age the Jew was a scrapper. He exchanged not only physical blows but verbal. The invective he heaped on the Christians to counteract that heaped on him was a daring exercise in villification. Far from being tolerant and supine, the medieval Jew had the guts to fling abuse at the dominant Christian world in equal measure to the abuse flung at him. What the emancipated modern Jew in a democracy would not dare do, the medieval Jew did. Called the "spawn of Satan," and a "people forsaken by God," by the Christians, the Jews in turn called the Virgin Mary a whore and Jesus a bastard. They compared the Gospel account of the Virgin Birth—of God visiting Mary in the guise of a Holy Ghost and then sending an angel to inform her she was with child—to the Greek legend of Zeus visiting Leda in the guise of a swan and then sending Hera to inform her who her seducer had been.

Paradoxically, it was this very intolerance of the Jews which eventually forced tolerance upon them. The Church, at first, did not catch on to the abuse heaped on its dogmas, until Jewish apostates, who knew what was going on, whispered in the ears of the mighty about this Jewish perfidy. In a series of public disputations, the Jews were called upon to explain and defend themselves. As the evidence was clear and damning, the Jews were in a tenuous position. The plea that this invective was the work of hotheads and not an official view was unacceptable to the Church, which felt it had a monopoly on slander, on the theory that to the victor belongs the right of calumny. To escape the wrath of the Church, the Jews had to seek safety in tolerance. In self-defense, they began to write nice things about the Christians, conceding, by the twelfth century, that perhaps Christianity was even a religion. Though at first these writings were exercises in insincerity, in time the Jews became the victims of their own apologetics. The new tolerance, which began as a reformation of former intolerance, ended up as a tenet of modern Judaism.

The portrait by many Jewish historians of the Church as implacably anti-Semitic is an equally erroneous concept. Though Judaism was feared as a competing religion by the Church, though Jews were persecuted for their religious beliefs, though the Church from Constantine to Luther was guilty of many crimes, it never demanded the extermination of the Jews as a people. Though every other possible pressure was applied to the Jews to lead them to the baptismal font, forcible conversion, though it did occur, was frowned upon. Anti-Semitism, as a calculated policy to eliminate the Jews from society through murder, was totally alien to the Church.

Peering into the mirror of Christian medieval art, one can detect little that can be construed as anti-Semitic. The Jew, as a historic individual, is treated with respect. Is there anywhere a more magnificent interpretation of the Jewish spirit than Michaelangelo's Moses? Or a more reverent depiction of the Old Testament than that in the panels of the Ghiberti doors in the Baptistery of San Giovanni in Florence? As we study the intensely religious windows or murals in the early cathedrals, as we scrutinize the centuries of Gothic paintings from Giotto to Pietro, as we behold fifteenth-century masterpieces from Van Eyck to Botticelli, we do not see the Jew portrayed as a villain. Michaelangelo's ceiling in the Sistine Chapel in the Vatican is a hymn to Judaism. Tintoretto's *The Crucifixion*, though it portrays the gruesomeness of Roman cruelty, hints of no Jewish perfidy. Though Raphael's *Disputà* shows a heated argument between Christians and Jews, no Jew is caricatured. Even in El Greco's scene of Christ driving the money-changers from the Temple, the Jew is not symbolized as evil.

It is not until after the Reformation, after the Jew has been stuck in the ghetto, after he has lost his image as a universal man, that we see him evolve into a symbol of evil. Not until after the Jew lost his meaning as a religious symbol for the West, after he became a competitive integer in the marketplace of gold, do we see a changed attitude toward the Jew in Western art corresponding to the changed attitudes toward him in Western life. When the Jew emerges in the seventeenth century as a maligned stereotype, it is not a result of ecclesiastic evil but of secular propaganda.

The corruscating effect of three centuries of ghetto life on the Jew was that he emerged looking like a caricature of his former self. The stultification of the Talmud by narrow-minded *pilpulists*, the absurdities of the "maharils," the farce of Sabbateanism, the vulgarity of Frankism, the deification of ignorance by Hasids, all contributed to shaping and begetting the queer-looking, black-hatted, caftaned, earlocked Jew that reduced the Jewish manifest destiny to a joke of history. How could one seriously view this grotesque, archaic fossil as one of God's Chosen People, as the man entrusted by God with the message of salvation?

The third stereotyped notion surviving the fall of the ghetto is even more tragic than the creation of this grotesque figure. Instead of the Jews disavowing this caricature forced upon them by Church, state, and *"maharil,"* they have accepted it as a true portrait. There is an assumption by too many Jews and Christians that the ghetto Jew represents the true Jew, and that the well-dressed, worldly-minded Jew is a deviation. Nothing could be further from the truth. The Jews in Hellenic times dressed like the Greeks; the Jews in the Islamic Empire were undistinguishable from their Arab contemporaries; the Jews in the Renaissance dressed in the silks and finery of that age. The ghetto Jew in his ridiculous clothes, with his bigoted, narrow views, is the ill-begotten product of his three-century imprisonment, a travesty of the Jew and of Judaism. Yet the ghetto Jew, though he represents but a brief segment of Jewish history, even now is made to exemplify the Jew throughout the ages. But such a Jew would be unrecognizable by Moses, David, or Isaiah, who never wore phylacteries or the garb of Hasids. Aristocratic Judah Hanasi would have looked upon the ghetto Jew with disdain, and fastidious Maimonides would have shuddered at the sight.

Thus the ghetto challenge to the Jews was not merely a yoke imposed on them by Christians, but also a tragedy of their own making. The only reason the Jews survived that dark degrading period was that their ideas were bigger than they were. The indestructibility of the Jews resided not in the people but in their ideas that survived for three centuries in the hostile soil of the ghettos.

In the next challenge, it is not the ghetto Jew who will be the hero, but the emancipated Jew, now waiting off-stage for the curtain call, ready to accept the responsibility for furthering the Jewish manifest destiny. And the zealots, even while they mourn the past and curse the iconoclasts, will readily clamber aboard the new Jewish survival chariot driven by these new secular Diaspora designers for a free ride to the next rendezvous with history.

The Sixth Challenge:
The Sick Society of the Scientific Age

The Modern Age for Western civilization began in 1500 with the era of the great explorers and ended July 16, 1945, with the explosion of the first nuclear bomb that ushered in the present Space Age. The Modern Age for the Jews began in 1800 with the French Revolution and ended May 14, 1948, with the establishment of the state of Israel that heralded the third act of their manifest destiny. For both, the Modern Age began with the fall of "Faith" and the enthronement of "Reason." Hailed by both as the panacea for the state, it ended as a sickness of the soul.

For the Christian world of Europe, the four centuries between 1500 and 1900 constituted an era of splendor. Everything it touched turned to victory or gold. It conquered the continents on the planet Earth as effortlessly as Rome had conquered the lands around the Mediterranean. But whereas Rome had depended on Greek thought to sustain herself intellectually, Europe forged its own arsenal of ideas so brilliant that the minds it breached were Europeanized as easily as the minds seduced by the Greeks had been Hellenized.

For the Jewish world of Europe, the century and a half between 1800 and 1950 constituted a fantastic episode. Beginning with French rationalism promising liberty, fraternity, and equality, it ended in a collision with communism, fascism, and anti-Semitism that nullified these promises.

Beginning with secular Judaism embracing secular enlightenment, it ended in a clash of messianism with totalitarianism. It unfolded as a political *danse macabre* that proceeded as compulsively as a totemistic ritual: Christians worked themselves into a frenzy of anti-Semitic fervor, slew the Jews, proclaimed God dead, and then sat down in the United Nations to vote for the state of Israel.

During the previous challenge, we saw the highly cultured medieval Jews marched into ghettos where they degenerated into the "sad sacks" of Europe. In this challenge we shall see the fossilized Jews flee those ghettos —in the West via an Isaiahn route of universalism identified with Western values, and in the East via a Hosean route of humanism identified with Jewish values—to once again become avant-garde intellectuals. We shall see both paths merge into one road traversed by a new Zionade, generaled by secular messiahs who will lead a new breed of true believers back to the Promised Land.

While the Jews stagnated in their ghettos, the Christians viewed the plays of Shakespeare, Molière, and Racine, read the works of Cervantes, Montaigne, and Schiller, and listened to the music of Bach, Haydn, and Mozart. They eyed the worldliness of Rembrandt, the dream world of Watteau, and the romanticism of Goya. They beheld Bacon, Descartes, and Spinoza revive the intellect of Europe, and witnessed Galileo, Kepler, and Newton reduce the earth to the size of a pebble. Gutenberg converted a wine press into a letter press, exploding new paths to wisdom and folly, and superadventurers conquered the Americas, stealing Inca gold while quoting the Gospels.

The Jews had to await the nineteenth century for full emancipation from their ghettos, though there was a partial liberation in the seventeenth century as an accidental by-product of Christian religious wars, and a larger exodus in the eighteenth century as a peripheral benefit of enlightened despotism. But, as it was the blood spilled during the religious wars of the Reformation that tinted Europe's new political complexion and shaded subsequent Jewish destiny, we must review Western history from

Luther to Napoleon to establish our framework for these events.

The sixteenth century, which Voltaire likened to "a silken robe smeared with blood," was a fortuitous blend of religious bigotry and secular refinement that permitted Christians to savor the delights of massacring one another in the name of Christ while sincerely expecting divine grace for their deeds. This century of religious wars, during which the Church tried to force its religious system on a people who wished to convert to Protestanism, resembled the Cold War of the twentieth century with the capitalist establishment trying to impose its economic system on people who wished to embrace communism. Just as many today feel that communism must be fought to death lest it spell the doom of man's liberties, many in the sixteenth century felt that Protestantism had to be fought to death lest it spell the damnation of man's soul. But then, as now, men used their creeds as cloaks for greed, resulting in a frightful slaughter that denuded the continent of joy and peace. Perhaps it was not a total calamity that history had chosen this nightmare century in which to funnel the Jews into ghettos, out of the mainstream of unstinted bloodshed.

Thus it came about that in the sixteenth century, Europe was headed for the same total disintegration it had faced in the sixth century following the barbarian invasions. Though she lacked the good fortune to inherit a second Charlemagne to unite dissenting factions, she did have the luck to escape the disaster of having a Spanish profile impressed on her by a Hapsburg monarch named Charles V.

In three centuries the Hapsburgs had fornicated their way from humble beginnings to become rulers of the largest empire on the continent. The first Hapsburg, Rudolf, born in 1218, was an insignificant feudal lord, master of a few hundred acres of Swiss and Austrian scenery. He was offered the crown of the Holy Roman Empire on the theory that he was the least likely person to usurp its hollow title. Hapsburg fortunes fluctuated until Emperor Frederick III bequeathed his heirs a new success formula—"Let others wage war, but you, happy Austria, marry." This motto enabled the Hapsburgs to acquire an empire before they were able to forge a nation. Henceforth, the Hapsburgs sought brides not for their beauty or intellect but for the size of their dowries, because the map of medieval Europe was shaped as much in sumptuous bedrooms as on bloody battlefields.

By the time Emperor Charles V appeared on the scene, he had acquired the Netherlands from his father, Spain from his mother, Austria from his grandfather, and the Holy Roman Empire with a liberal bribe. But Charles unwisely abandoned his great-grandfather's sage motto and set out to acquire the rest of Europe through deceitful diplomacy and calculated aggression. Though he was a great warrior, he had the misfortune to encounter shrewder ones. He finally abdicated his throne, his dream of a united Europe under Hapsburg rule unrealized. His son, Philip II (1556–1593), the personification of divine rights of kings, took up his father's dream, but in his overzealous hands even his inheritance shrank. Entering history in a blaze of glory with a sea victory over the Turks at the battle of Lepanto, he lost the Netherlands in a cruel, senseless war, and his influence in Europe waned with the destruction of his invincible Spanish Armada by the despised British.

These world events had a microscopic repercussion in Jewish history. The defeat of Philip's Catholic forces by the Protestant Dutch opened the springboard for the settlement of Jews in the Netherlands.

The real nemesis of Hapsburg expansionism, however, was not the Dutch or the British but Francis I (1515–1547), the young, handsome, chivalrous, cunning king of France, who outmaneuvered Charles V on the checkerboard of continental power diplomacy. To break the Hapsburg power, Catholic Francis did not hesitate to align himself with Turkish infidels and German Protestants. Builder of the Louvre and Fountainbleau, founder of the Royal College, it was Francis who welcomed the Renaissance into his realm, coddling it with luxury and elegance. Dissolute living prepared this promising king for early decay, and new religious wars waited only for his death to break out anew.

After the death of Francis I and the abdication of Charles V, the regnant powers tried to repair the disorganized frontiers of Europe with the peace formula *cujus regio, ejus religio*—to every man the religion of his prince. But the formula broke down with the threat of a new period of religious anarchy that in France culminated in the St. Bartholomew's Day massacre (1572), with Catholics slaughtering Calvinists known as Huguenots.

France was faced with civil war. The hero who averted this disaster was a Huguenot apostate to Catholicism named Henry of Navarre. "Paris is worth a Mass," he said, as he pressed the Catholic crown of France on his former Protestant brow in the coronation that made him King Henry IV, founder of the Bourbon Dynasty which was to lead France to revolution and its nobility to the guillotine. Though stained by corruption and coarsened by the brutality of his age, Henry IV, under the influence of the gentle skepticism of Montaigne, was a wise king. With his Edict of Nantes that granted toleration to the Huguenots, France became the first nation in Europe to know religious freedom. Adroit at seducing men's minds, Henry calmed passions; cunning at winning wars, he cleared the land of foreign invaders. His "Great Design" was to turn Europe into a Christian Society of Nations, governed by sixty elected members. But his life was prematurely snuffed out one evening in 1610 when a fanatic named Ravaillac calmly stepped into his carriage and stabbed him to death.

No sooner had the flames of religious revolt been extinguished in France than they broke out in Bohemia, where they were fanned into thirty years of strife. Like World War I, this Thirty Years' War (1618–1648) started in a haphazard manner—nobody wished it, everyone welcomed it, all thought it would be of short duration. Like World War I, it began with a minor incident, exploited by incompetence into a major disaster. Instead of an assassination like that at Sarajevo, however, it was a "defenestration" in Prague. Czech Calvinist nobles, fearing curtailment of their religious freedom, hurled some Catholic representatives out of a Prague castle window into a manure pile sixty feet below, and the fight was on. Spain, Germany, and Denmark became embroiled. Protestantism was in danger of being wiped out in Germany; Europe was threatened with total devastation.

Again we have a parallel with modern history. Just as today many believe that capitalism and communism cannot coexist but that one must exterminate the other to make the world safe for its own brand of economics, so three centuries ago Catholics and Protestants believed that they could not coexist, but that one had to exterminate the other to make the world safe for its own brand of religion. After a century of exhausting hate and slaughter, both sides at last perceived that they had to coexist or perish. The Treaty of Westphalia (1648)—in essence establishing an invisible east-west line through the middle of the continent —permitted them that coexistence. The treaty recognized the religious status quo. Everything north of that invisible east-west line was to remain Protestant and capitalist, and everything south of it to remain Catholic and feudal. This arrangement lasted until after World War II, when the impact of another ideology shattered that line. Today, an invisible north-south line, recognizing a new status quo, runs through the center of Germany, dividing the European continent into two new ideological camps, depending not on how one worships God but on how people produce their goods. Everything west of the north-south line today is essentially Christian and capitalist, while most of the terrain east of that line is essentially communist and totalitarian.

Three seventeenth-century men, who saw the latent economic revolution in the manifest religious revolt, reshaped the map of Europe by giving it the religious and economic outline it was to retain until after World War II. They were Gustav Adolph II, the Snow King of Sweden, who through military intervention in the Thirty Years' War saved Protestantism in Europe; Cardinal Richelieu, his Red Eminence of France, who through diplomacy laid the political foundations of a new Europe with the Treaty of Westphalia (1648)[1] that ended that war; and Oliver Cromwell, the Lord Protector of England, who though he

---

[1]Though Cardinal Richelieu died one year before the Treaty of Westphalia, he was, nevertheless, the chief architect of its provisions.

did not intervene militarily in the war was the first statesman to channel Protestanism into the service of capitalism.

The end of the Thirty Years' War also had repercussions in Jewish history. By the Treaty of Westphalia, France acquired the Rhineland where dwelt a sizable segment of German Jews who thus now came under French jurisdiction. Sensing the enterprising spirit of the Jews in the Netherlands, Cromwell invited them back, to speed England's transition from a feudal to a capitalist economy. But though now there were Jews back in Holland, France, and England, they played but a minor role in Jewish history. The major roles were to be enacted by Jews in Russia, Prussia, and Austria.

Russia unobtrusively entered European history in the ninth century A.D., with 150,000 square miles and half a million people. Ten centuries later, she brazenly entered world history with 9,000,000 square miles and 200 million people. The impetus for each debut was the ideology of a Jew—Jesus Christ and Karl Marx, respectively. With her Christianization in the tenth century, Russia's course as a European nation was set; with her communization in the twentieth century, Russia's role as a world power was cast.

Racially, the Slavic Russians are the most European people on that continent, for the Slavs are not only the direct descendants of the same Asiatic Aryans who fathered the Greeks, Italians, French, and Germans, but are less intermingled with Mongols than most European people. Though Russia was dominated by Mongols for more centuries than the rest of continental Europe, little Mongol blood was infused in her veins because there was little social intercourse, beyond the payment of an annual tribute, between victors and vanquished.

Russian history begins in the ninth century when Swedish Vikings known as Varangians, or Rus (the rowers), oared their boats of prey down the rivers from the Baltic to the Black Sea, and founded the Principality of Kiev. A century later, Kiev's pagan Grand Duke Sviatoslav embraced the Greek Orthodox faith, which he in turn forced upon his people.

When the Vikings arrived in Kiev, they had also been

greeted by Jews. Legend persists in attributing the founding of that city to Jews who claimed descent from the lost Ten Tribes of Israel. History does trace the first arrival of Jews in southern Russia to the eighth century B.C., to a segment of Jews banished by the Assyrians after the fall of the Kingdom of Israel. The next contingent of Jews arrived in Russia in the sixth century B.C., in the aftermath of the destruction of the Kingdom of Judah by Nebuchadnezzar. A third Jewish migration wave in the wake of a calamity took place six centuries later, when the Romans sacked Jerusalem. From then on a steady trickle of Jews settled between the Black and Caspian seas.

Most of these Caucasian Jews were skilled horsemen or small farmers who dressed like the native Circassians, always armed with dagger and sword, even while attending synagogue. Ignorant of the latest Responsa, they enriched whatever Talmud lore they possessed with native demonology. Their contributions were never enshrined in the Talmud.

With the twelfth century, the glory of Kiev faded in direct proportion to the rise of the Principality of Moscow, as colonizers slowly "won the North" in the same way American colonizers "won the West," by clearing the wilderness and exterminating the natives. Though the histories of Russia and the United States are similar in that both countries cried out for colonization and both were able to expand their territories phenomenally within a relatively short space of time, they differ in that the United States was built by men dedicated to the idea of freedom, while Russia was built by men possessed by the spirit of tyranny.

Russia's colorful hero-king, Alexander Nevsky (1220–1263), cleared a political path by breaking the backs of the Swedes at the River Neva, and routing the Teutonic knights at Lake Peipus. But the Mongols who had invaded Russia in the thirteenth century, establishing the Khanate of the Golden Horde, continued to rule Russia loosely though cruelly until driven out in the fifteenth century by Prince Ivan III the Great, who established the first monarchy with centralized government. His grandson, Ivan IV, remembered in history as "the Terrible" for excesses of cruelty noteworthy even in Russia, became the first to use the title of czar, or caesar. With the accession of Michael, the first Romanov czar, Russia turned her conquest interests toward Europe. She was now ready for the entry of Peter the Great (1689–1725), who dragged his reluctant country into the Western orbit of politics and culture.

An ungainly six-foot-seven-inch syphilitic giant who liked dwarfs and had a hysterical fear of black beetles, Peter was a compulsive drinker and lover, with an obsession for humiliating people by forcing them to eat offal and bite corpses. An avowed sadist, he exulted in the screams of the tortured, and enjoyed a sexual ecstasy by touching his victims as they died in agony. He even watched while his son Alexis was tortured to death for the crime of having tried to escape his father's tyranny.

Yet this disgusting creature had an inquiring mind, a high intelligence, a dedication for serving his people, and a passionate love for his country. Upon returning from an extensive trip to western Europe, mostly in Holland, where he had worked incognito as a laborer to master Western industrial techniques, he lined up his boyars, shaved off their beards, and cut their floor-trailing skirts to the knees. He freed women from their harems, trained a modern army, and built his new capital, St. Petersburg, facing the Baltic. In a war with Turkey he strengthened his hold on the Sea of Azov. From the Swedes he wrested the Baltic coast down to Riga. Russia had another window to the West.

From the death of Peter I to the accession of Catherine II, a fascinating succession of incompetents ruled Russia. There was Peter's second wife, Catherine I, a Livonian army whore who founded the Russian Academy of Sciences . . . Peter II, czar at twelve, murdered at fifteen . . . Empress Anna, a dissolute slut dominated by her German lovers . . . Ivan IV, who reigned less than two years, deposed by a military revolt to make way for Elizabeth, youngest daughter of Peter the Great, an engaging bitch who set up a brilliant though uncouth court . . . and finally, Peter III, an impotent nitwit who lasted six months, long enough to be married off to a minor German princess, Sophia of Anhalt-Zerbst, who, after having her husband assassinated, became empress of Russia under the name of Catherine II, later known as the Great, the undisputed ruler of Russia for thirty-four years (1762–1796).

Sex and glory were Catherine's passions. Accused by her favorite, Prince Potemkin, of having entertained fifteen lovers more or less simultaneously, she indignantly defended herself by stating it was only five. Fearful of venereal disease, she had all candidates for her bed medically examined and tested with a lady-in-waiting. Though lustful, she was intelligent, warmhearted, generous, and unpredictable. Intellectually French, she suppressed her German origins and cultivated a Russian outlook. She corresponded with Voltaire, yet remained a reactionary. Though the works of the French rationalists were but vehicles for polished conversations in the Russian salons of her time, their ideas did generate new, liberalizing forces in nineteenth-century Russia.

It was Catherine who undertook the incorporation of another chunk of Europe into Russian territory. Poland, which had annexed more territory than she could hold, was ripe for rape. With the aid of the other two "Greats" of Europe, Maria Theresa of Austria and Frederick II of Prussia, Catherine invaded Poland and carved that country out of existence.

Technically the Romanov bloodline ended with Catherine, for her son Paul I was fathered not by her short-lived husband Peter II but by a random lover, named Saltikov. Weak-minded, unbalanced, and tyrannical, Paul was nevertheless the first czar to limit the spread of serfdom and to grant the peasants basic rights. His assassination in 1801 with the connivance of his son, Alexander I, ushered in a schizophrenic period in Russia's history. Four "Romanov" czars divided the ninteenth century amongst themselves, tossing Russia back and forth from the arms of reactionaries to the folds of liberals, finally plunging her, through ineptitude, into the bed of communism.

Surprisingly, considering the fate of the indigenous pagan populations in the path of the colonizing Russians, and the hazards of native Christian citizens under their sadistic rulers, the Jews in Russia did not fare too badly in the three centuries from Ivan III to Catherine II. Generally, it was a farce with overtones of tragedy. After the Mongols had been driven out, a xenophobia swept Russia. This distrust of foreigners was all-encompassing, embracing pagans, Mohammedans, Roman Catholics, and Jews. To speak of Russian anti-Jewishness at this time is a misnomer, for the Russians burned mosques and banished Roman Catholics faster than they burned synagogues or banished Jews. But whereas Russia was successful in stamping out other dissident religious beliefs and driving foreign elements from her soil, she was not equally successful with the Jews. For some inexplicable reason Judaism held a fascination for the Russians.

Until 1500, Jews were permitted to reside wherever they wished in Russia. Then a strange Judaizing heresy that swept Novgorod mobilized the fears of the Russian Church. The archbishop and a host of lesser priests became converted to a new Judaic creed which held that it was not Christ who had arrived but only his image, and that until the real Christ came, imagery should be abolished and Mosaic Law rule the land. This creed spread to Moscow where it infected high Church and court dignitaries, including Princess Helena, daughter-in-law of Ivan the Great. The heresy burst into the open when a covey of drunken priests, secret members of the Judaizing sect, blasphemed publicly against the Church. The bells of alarm were pealed, and impenitent heretics were burned in cages. The Jews were banned.

Soon, however, Jews trickled back into Russia via Lithuanian trade routes. But Ivan the Terrible, fearful that these returned Jews might foster degenerate ideas of personal freedom, ordered all Jews who would not accept Greek Orthodoxy to be drowned in the River Duna. The Jews hastily betook themselves back to Lithuania, only to be reacquired by Peter the Great with his conquest of the Baltic States. Banished again by his sister, Empress Elizabeth, history a few decades later placed 900,000 Jews in the lap of Empress Catherine II with the successive partitions of Poland.

This time Russia gave up the struggle, not merely out of exhaustion but out of necessity, for Jews were needed for the economy of the conquered territories. But to prevent the ideas of Jews from muddying the purity of her peasants' ignorance, Catherine hit upon an eastern adaptation of the western ghetto. She instituted the so-called *Pale of Settlement*, a strip of land roughly encompassing all Russian territory west of a line from Riga on the Baltic to Rostov on the Sea of Azov. West of that line the Jews could move at will, but east of that line, with a few exceptions, they could not. Here, in towns and villages known as *shtetls*, the greatest part of Russia's Jews vegetated until the arrival of the Jewish Enlightenment in the nineteenth century.

The partitions of Poland not only settled 900,000 Jews in Catherine's lap, it also placed hundreds of thousands of additional Jews in Maria Theresa's Austria and Frederick the Great's Prussia. Like Empress Catherine, Maria Theresa and Frederick the Great were regarded by history as "enlightened" because they, too, had read Voltaire. Under the impact of the French Encyclopedists, these absolute monarchs did crack the door of tolerance enough for a few novel ideas of freedom to slip through. Protestant Prussia began to grant Catholics a modicum of human rights, and Catholic Austria conceded human attributes to Protestants. This tolerance also rubbed off on the Jews, who were thus presented with new avenues of escape from the ghetto.

A number of Jews had already managed to slip into Western civilization in the seventeenth century via four painfully hewn-out routes, each of which had created its own distinct prototype—the Court Jew, the Salon Jew, the Protected Jew, and the Apostate Jew.

Court Jews were men of financial genius who could guide a king in his emancipation struggle from the nobles. They served as financial advisors and masters of the mint, negotiated loans, and devised new taxes. They were, in fact, the equivalent of today's Chancellor of the Exchequer or Secretary of the Treasury. Salon Jews were intellectuals, who by their wits managed to gain a secular education, and after amassing wealth became social leaders in glittering salons where they entertained a select elite of European society. They were men of letters, patrons of art, founders of academies, editors of publications, and in the case of beautiful Jewesses, often the mistresses of important Christian personages. Protected Jews constituted a mixed bag of talents. Usually they were Jews with business dexterity who by sheer ability propelled their way to the top against currents of prejudice, and establishing vast business enterprises in most of Europe. Apostate Jews were, of course, those who took the easy way out by converting to Christianity, an act which opened all doors of opportunity to them.

However, these seventeenth-century escapees from the ghetto represented but a trickle. Until the dawn of the eighteenth century, the bulk of the Jews remained ignorant prisoners of the ghetto, more victims of the "maharils" than of the Christians. But with the eighteenth-century era of Enlightened Despotism, the crack in the ghetto gate was widened. This trickle grew into a rivulet as ever greater numbers of young Jews stepped out of the squalor of ghetto confinement into the brilliance of Western civilization. Here they were confronted with the absurdity of their sixteenth-century ghetto values in an eighteenth-century world.

On the one hand was the ghetto world they had been born in, an anachronistic way of life regulated by a maze of piccayunish laws that had lost their raison d'être. It was a world that resembled a ward in a madhouse, where, like schizophrenics, Jews were absorbed in a compulsive recital of prayers an an obsessive ritual of phylacteries.[2] On the other hand was the exciting world of Western civilization, with its philosophers and scientists, its artists and musicians, its universities and museums, a world of elegance and beauty that winked a flirtatious come-on to the culture-starved youth of the ghetto.

No anti-Jewish crusade, no medieval papal bull, no conversion drive wrought as much havoc among Jewish youth

---

[2]The wearing of phylacteries during prayer—small cubicles containing quotes from Scripture—is the invention of the Talmudists, not a Mosaic injunction. The Torah commands the Jews to wear *totaphot*, a word of unknown meaning, a *zichoron*, or "remembrance," and an *oth*, a "sign," but does not give any descriptions. Orthodox Jews have only the say-so of Talmudists that the *tephillim* they describe and the *totaphot*, *zichoron*, and *oth* mentioned in the Bible are the same things.

as did the massive intellectual assault of the Enlightenment that greeted them at the ghetto gates. In the marketplace of ideas, ghetto *pilpulism* was a patently inferior product to Western humanism. In ever-greater numbers, Jewish youth abandoned the ghetto and lined up at the baptismal fonts to enter Western civilization via Christianity, the "passport to civilization."

The danger to Judaism was as grave as in past challenges, but this time the Talmudists were no longer innovators of new ideas but caretakers of old customs. They did nothing except excommunicate apostates and mumble curses at Christians. It was clear that someone other than a Talmudist would have to rise to the challenge or Jews and Judaism would fade out of history as a cultural force.

Whom would Jewish history choose for its first non-Talmudic Diaspora designer? Would it be a majestic Moses come to reveal a new law? A fiery prophet thundering in immortal Hebrew a new ethos for the Jews? Or a giant Bar Kochba come to preach the gospel of force? Capricious history rejected these precedents. It chose an ugly hunchback Jew from the ghetto of Dessau, Germany, who threw off the sackcloth of the ghetto for the lace of Western civilization. It chose Moses Mendelssohn, a Jewish Luther arriving 300 years late to reveal Reform Judaism in flawless German prose to the Yiddish-speaking orthodox ghetto-dwellers.

If not for a fortuitous accident, Moses Mendelssohn (1729–1786) would have ended up another ignorance-stricken ghetto tenant like his father, a poor Torah scribe. As a boy, Mendelssohn stumbled upon a treasure of forbidden literature, a copy of Maimonides' *Guide to the Perplexed* in Hebrew, and a volume of Locke's essay *On Human Understanding* in Latin. With time stolen from Talmud studies he absorbed the philosophy of Maimonides and with a Latin-German dictionary he unlocked the mysteries of Locke's essay. The ghetto could no longer contain him. He had to know the world beyond, and at the age of fourteen he hitchhiked to Berlin for a secular education in mathematics, philosophy, and languages. He married a plain, lowly girl from Hamburg, and on his honeymoon he wrote an essay on metaphysics for a contest in which he won first prize and Immanuel Kant second. He gradually became recognized as a German stylist and famed for his critical essays in philosophy. After having amassed a small fortune in a business partnership, he was transformed into a Salon Jew, the showcase Jew of the Western world.

Mendelssohn had a difficult time reconciling ghetto Judaism with Western civilization. From his own experience, he perceived the coming predicament of young intellectual Jews and the inherent danger to Judaism. The situation was analogous to that of the American Indian today. Facing but two choices—life on a reservation that perpetuates their anachronistic ways, or life in a society where they could soon disappear—most Indians are choosing to stay on the reservation to retain their identity, because they have no program to insure their ethnic survival in the world at large. If there had been but two choices for eighteenth-century Jews—ghetto Judaism or Christian Enlightenment—most would have chosen Christianity. Only a pitiful remnant would have doomed themselves to remain *pilpul*-bound fossils. This dilemma was agonizingly dramatized in Mendelssohn's own family. One of his daughters eloped with a Protestant nobleman, another became a bigoted Catholic, and a grandson, Felix Mendelssohn, the famed composer, was brought up as a Christian by his converted father. Thanks to Moses Mendelssohn, however, the Jews had a third choice.

Like ben Zakkai, who released the Jews from the constriction of Temple Sadduceeism to meet the challenge of the Roman world, Mendelssohn liberated the Jews from the shackles of ghetto Talmudism to meet the challenge of the modern world. Like Luther thundering to the Christians to free Christ from pope and imagery, Mendelssohn implored the Jews to free the Torah from Talmud and "maharil." Religion, he averred, should be concerned with eternal truths, not with current minutiae. The Torah should be taught along with philosophy and science to inspire mankind, rather than be buried in Talmudic footnotes to confuse Jews. Like the framers of the American Constitution in that same century, Mendelssohn argued for the separation of Church and state. Religion, he claimed, was an individual affair. Neither state nor Church should have the power to punish man for his religious convictions.

Mendelssohn also foresaw the coming struggle between ghetto and state. A ghetto ruled by Talmudic Law was akin to a Jewish state within a state, he held, and in the Modern Age there could be only one national state. Taking a leaf from Rousseau, Mendelssohn urged the Jews to dissolve their "contract" with the "ghetto state" in the same way their Christian brethren were dissolving their contracts with the feudal state.

Mendelssohn had appeared none too soon. Before the *kaddish* intoned over his grave faded out of his mourners' memory, the "deluge" Louis XV had invited arrived in the form of the French Revolution that overthrew the monarchy, breached the walls of the ghetto, and brought the Jews face to face with Napoleon who was to ask them the very questions Mendelssohn had raised.

The French Revolution was an event which should not have happened but did, a revolt which Kant predicted would become a European conflagration and Goethe foresaw would ripen into a world cataclysm. Its roots reached back to the seventeenth century, which initiated the splendid decline of the French monarchy that out of sheer boredom gaily sowed the seeds of its own destruction.

The story of France's gentle trot to the guillotine begins with debonair Henry IV, who for political reasons married frowzy, fat, blond Marie de Medici, whom Rubens, as a personal safety precaution, painted as a seductive beauty. After Henry's assassination, Marie took over the regency, intending to rule for a lifetime. But her ungrateful son, Louis XIII, at the age of sixteen, seized control and banished all of his mother's political appointees except one, Cardinal Richelieu, painted by many historians as the real power behind the throne. But Louis XIII, though a stammerer, knew how to say what he wanted, and Richelieu, in whom rationalist philosophy was combined with absolutist government, did his bidding. He shattered the military power of the Huguenots, destroyed the political power of the Hapsburgs, and reduced the social power of the French nobles. France no longer wore the smile of the Renaissance but the iron mask of Richelieu.

King Louis XIII and Cardinal Richelieu died within a year of each other, and a new team, Louis XIV and Mazarin, took their place. A statesman of Italian birth, lover of Anne of Austria, the king's mother, Mazarin endured for a while the hoots and jeers of the nobles then ruthlessly subdued their rebellion known as the Fronde. Whereas Richelieu had clipped the claws of the nobles and made them manageable, Mazarin extracted their teeth and rendered them harmless.

When Mazarin died, France was securely in the hands of Louis XIV. If he did not say "I am the State," it was because it was not necessary. He was the state, the "Sun King," who loved the theater, music, glory, women. He was the royal stallion who serviced a dazzling succession of high-bred mares, among them tart-tongued Madame de Montespan who unofficially "reigned" with him for a decade. His was the classical age of Racine and Molière, La Fontaine and Le Nôtre, Lully and Lebrun. The civilization of France became the civilization of Europe.

More fearful of Protestants than of Jews, Louis XIV banished the Huguenots from France. From their ghetto windows, the Jews watched these weary exiles tread a refugee road they themselves had trod three centuries previously. But this move did not make Louis XIV popular. A quarter century of wars had wearied France. Her people were surfeited with glory. When he died, the French rejoiced and hailed his great-grandson, Louis XV, as monarch. But not for long.

Not having had a Richelieu or Mazarin to teach him, frail, gloomy, and slightly effeminate, Louis XV had never learned the duties of a king. Bored with his wife after having sired ten children "without addressing a word to her," he finally fell into the arms of Madame Pompadour who amused him with her love, and provided for his entertainment the top artists and writers of France. When her body no longer pleased, she procured for him younger courtesans.

Though the French people generally never had it so good as under Louis XV, though he had stamped French court life on the aristocracy of Europe, he died mourned by few at home and abroad. What France needed in her hour of drifting crisis was a king of wisdom. What she got was "an honest blockhead." On the head of his grandson, Louis XVI, who succeeded him, converged the Bourbon deluge.

Louis XVI, chaste, a devout son of the Church, a father who loved his people, tried hard enough to please. But isolated in the splendor of Versailles he did not know how to communicate with his people. A timid man, terrified of his beautiful wife, Marie Antoinette, whose frivolity made her immune to ideas, his chief interests gradually shriveled down to working on locks and hunting. France, bereft of a ruler, drifted to her appointment with terror.

Actually, all of Europe was drifting toward revolt. England had already cast herself adrift from the continent to seek an empire overseas. Germany had initiated a Renaissance that was to lead to her unification in the next century. Rebellion was brewing in Italy. Greek nationalism was stirring. But nothing went as anticipated. In the eighteenth century, the exact reverse of what happened in the twentieth century took place. In the twentieth century, everyone assumed that the communist revolution would take place in an industrially advanced nation like Germany, but instead it took place in Russia, an industrially backward nation. The eighteenth-century bourgeois revolution, expected to take place in one of the economically less advanced nations, took place in France, one of the most advanced. Here good times had generated an atmosphere of better times, and the expectation of more generated a revolution for more. France became Europe's laboratory for a bourgeois revolution that was to give the coup de grâce to the aristocracy.

The French Revolution did not begin with the masses but with the elite, in the world of intellect. The ideas of the *philosophes* and the Encyclopedists were bandied about in the salons of the haute monde, where the sentimental revolution of Rousseau and the rational revolution of Montesquieu were debated with wit, verve, and insincere ardor.

The *philosophes*, the name given to the leaders of the French Enlightenment, saw all knowledge, including the social and natural sciences, as falling within their province. They all believed that the mind, in its own vacuum, could conceive of an ideal state better than experience could. Their idea of progress was a regression back to nature. All of these doctors of social ills believed in the inherent goodness of man, in the grandeur of nature, and in the inevitability of a state of perfect happiness if religion were but dethroned and reason enthroned. All were men of goodwill who abhorred violence. They intended the best, but they reaped the worst. Or, in the words of Madame de Staël, they "inflamed everything but discovered nothing."

The course of the French Revolution is too often obscured by too many facts. Stripped down to vulgar simplicity, the French Revolution engulfed France when the ideas of the *philosophes* trickled from the refined salons to the squalor of the streets where they swelled into a dirty flood. Here these ideas were no longer empty words bandied about by a perfumed aristocracy but loaded slogans shouted by a sweaty proletariat who turned thoughts into deeds.

The Revolution began inconspicuously, with a Constituent Assembly (1789) where Count Mirabeau, champion of the bourgeoisie, defied the king in the name of reason. Within three years that appeal to reason matured into a Reign of Terror that in the name of reason beheaded its opponents. Like furies unleashed, the people stormed and sacked the Bastille.[3] "Is it a riot?" asked the king. "No, sire," replied the courtier, "it is a revolution." The Tuileries was invaded and the Swiss Guard massacred. Men draped in the tricolor stormed the prisons of Paris, and in an explosion of collective sadism murdered 1,200 aristocrats.

This was but a prelude to the terror to come. The monarchy was abolished. France was declared a republic, and the guillotine was elevated to chief justice. Tumbrils loaded with nobles creaked through jeering French mobs to the guillotine, much as a century and a half later freight cars packed with Jews rumbled through jeering German mobs to gas chambers. Like the Jews in the 1940s, who walked to death with dignity, contempt in their eyes for the German murderers, so the French aristocrats in the 1790s

[3]The famous state prison in Paris, built as a château in 1370 and first used as a prison by Louis XI.

faced death with dignity, contemptuous of the French rabble.

Three men have come to symbolize that Reign of Terror —Jean Paul Marat, a Swiss-born Frenchman and disillusioned fanatic, Georges Jacques Danton, the son of a peasant and instigator of the prison massacres, and Maximilien François Robespierre, a male virgin, fearful of women, who rarely practiced any of the virtues he was accused of.

Marat, a sickly doctor, and architect of the policy to terrify the country into submission, was the first of the triumvirate to perish, assassinated in his bathtub by Charlotte Corday for having betrayed the ideals of the Revolution. Danton, whose ugly face was pitted with smallpox, was a prototype for a Nazi concentration camp commandant. An attorney who rose to Minister of Justice, he became a victim of the Terror he helped institute and was guillotined after a farcical trial. Robespierre, a cruel, thin-lipped tyrant with nearsighted green eyes, believed that liberty was achieved by silencing every voice except his own. Known as the "Incorruptible," he was not a sadistic killer like Marat and Danton, but a murderer without guilt who exercised his tyranny in the name of virtue, and was at last himself guillotined by revolutionaries grown tired of that "virtue."

The middle classes (the bourgeoisie) in a burst of revulsion and courage seized power from the lower classes (the proletariat), overthrew the Reign of Terror, and instituted the Directory, a new republican form of government. Sensing an opportunity, nobles who had managed to escape the Reign of Terror launched a royalist counter-Terror, and threatened to take over the new regime. The stage was set for Napoleon Bonaparte (1769–1821), future emperor of the bourgeoisie, who entered the revolutionary drama in a bit part and walked off with the lead. The Directory asked Napoleon, then a young general of the artillery, to quell the incipient insurrection. He ended it with a "whiff of grapeshot," his cannons firing point-blank into the ranks of the royalists who fled in panic. Now followed a series of dazzling victories that were to take Napoleon from general in 1795 to emperor of France in 1804.

History has drawn two portraits of Napoleon, one that of a dictator and enslaver of Europe, the other that of a liberator and benefactor of mankind. Both are equally true, depending on whether one views him through feudal or capitalist eyes.

By 1805, Napoleon had extended the limits of France to her natural frontiers and laid the foundations for a state that was far more rational than any yet devised by man, including the United States. A dynamic liberalism suffused the country, for though Napoleon did not believe in liberty, he believed in equality. Like Cromwell before him, Napoleon institutionalized the new capitalism, doing away with local autonomy and making the nation supreme.

Napoleon's military end came with Waterloo, and his political demise with the Congress of Vienna (1815), where the rulers of Europe came to restore the old order and eradicate such radical notions as equality, fraternity, and liberty. In a sense, the political situation in Europe after Waterloo resembled the political situation after World War II. After World War II, the dominant Western powers —the United States, France, and England—formed an alliance to fight radical political ideas and curtail communist revolutions against the established order. After Waterloo, the dominant powers—Russia, Prussia, Austria, and England—formed a Holy Alliance (and the Metternich System) to restore the façade of the old monarchist Europe and put the lid on any democratic revolutions against the established order. But just as the Western powers could not silence Karl Marx's proletarian hymn to socialism, so the monarchists could not silence Napoleon Bonaparte's bourgeois hymn to capitalism.

The flames of revolt burned their way out of the box of repression, and banners of defiance were unfurled across the continent. Greece declared herself independent of Turkey, and Belgium freed herself from the Dutch. The Austrians sent their reactionaries packing. The French overthrew the monarchy imposed on them by the Holy Alliance. In a series of uprisings, Italy at last was unified. Out of the debris of a shattered Holy Roman Empire rose a new, unified Germany. Riding a wave of nationalism, Europe rolled toward the twentieth century, where it would collide head-on with two cataclysmic events—World Wars I and II—that would rearrange her ideological frontiers.

It was into this century of nationalism (1800–1900) that the ill-prepared Jews were catapulted by the emancipation in the wake of the French Revolution. This emancipation did not come about from any conviction that an injustice had been done. It came about incidently, as a result of the mathematics of rationalism. In the same way that it gave the world the decimal system, the French Revolution gave the Jews citizenship. Not humanity, but logic demanded it. As in the view of the rationalists all human beings had equal rights, and since the Jews were also human beings, ergo, they too had equal rights.

As profoundly as the barbarian invasions had changed the political, social, and economic framework of sixth-century Rome, so the Napoleonic conquest changed the political, social, and economic order of nineteenth-century Europe. Whereas the feudal order that rose in the footsteps of the barbarian advance was the unplanned result of unforeseen institutions cropping up in a political void, the Napoleonic changes were the result of planned policies. After toppling the feudal order in each conquered country, Napoleon entrenched capitalism and democratic institutions, leaving the middle class firmly in power. And as he abolished the feudal state, so he abolished the ghetto.

Though the Christian-instituted ghetto that held the Jews in physical repression was abolished, the ghetto as a Jewish institution holding the Jews in an intellectual repression, remained. Here the Talmud, not the state, ruled. Here rabbis had their own laws, their own courts, their own administration—a Jewish enclave within a Gentile state. But Napoleon had as acute an insight into this ghetto duality as Moses Mendelssohn. He realized that such feudal remnants in the midst of a modern political state would be intolerable, indigestible islands. He demanded that the Jews convoke a Sanhedrin to formally renounce their ghetto Talmudic laws and formally affirm their allegiance to the state and its laws.

Stunned, the Jews convoked a Sanhedrin of Jewish notables, the first such assembly since the destruction of

Jerusalem. With the guidelines so prophetically supplied by Mendelssohn, the French Jews answered the questions posed by Napoleon. These answers in essence reaffirmed earlier Talmudic injunctions that the laws of the host state were the laws of the Jews, provided no law abridged the freedom of religion. With this public affirmation, the tyranny of the "maharils," who clung to ghetto power with iron claws, was broken. In one stroke, Napoleon had created a new status for the Jews. They were no longer a minority Jewish nation within a Christian nation, but citizens, with the same rights and obligations, even though their religion differed from that of the dominant majority. Having performed its function, the artificially convoked Sanhedrin ceased to exist.

With the Modern Age, the social and psychological condition of the Jew in Diaspora society changed drastically. Whereas the medieval world had accepted the Jews as a community, the modern world accepted the Jews as individuals. Whereas the insecure individual Jew in feudal society strove for security, the emancipated Jew in modern society strove for classification. Thus, while more integrated into the Gentile social milieu than the medieval Jew, the Modern Age Jew had less identity.

Freed at last from their three-century imprisonment, however, the Jews spilled en masse into the nineteenth century. They did not wait for a Czar Peter to shave off their beards or cut their caftans; they did it themselves. The ideological corral staked out by Mendelssohn was neither large enough nor strong enough to contain the herd of Jews that stampeded through the ghetto gates to pick up their "passports to civilization"—baptism. In ever greater numbers, they vanished into Christianity, agnosticism, or atheism. A crisis faced Judaism.

Even if the Talmudists had tried, it is doubtful they could have come up with the proper response, for the Talmud itself, as an independent judicial arm of a Jewish government in exile, was no longer needed. The condition that had given rise to the Talmud—self-government for the Jews in the Roman, Sassanid, Islamic, and Feudal ages—had changed. In the new democracies developing in the Western world, the need for self-government seemingly vanished because the new democratic states included the protection of minorities within their realms. Thus, when democracy with its free institutions confronted the Jews in the sixth challenge, the Talmudist neither came to their aid nor was he needed. The trampled-down Mendelssohnian fences were repaired by a new breed of non-Talmudic Diaspora designers who widened the path delineated by Mendelssohn into a comfortable modern highway.

Two separate sets of non-Talmudic Diaspora designers, one Western and the other Eastern in orientation, channeled Jewish youth into a modern enclave of Judaism. The first redefined the Jewish religion and identified Jewish culture with Western values; the second reexamined Jewish philosophy and identified Jewish culture with Jewish values. Both rejected the Talmud as a bulwark in their new frameworks for Judaism.

A trio of German rabbis, Leopold Zunz, Zacharias Frankel, and Abraham Geiger—the Jewish "Zwingli, Calvin, and Knox"—were the main trailblazers of the Western path. Between them they hammered out a new Reform Judaism, each with his own variations on dogma to soothe different degrees of deviations from orthodoxy. Zunz (1794–1886), a pioneer in the history of Jewish literature, made Judaism a respected religion in the eyes of the intellectuals with his works on the "Science of Judaism." Frankel (1801–1875), after shocking Christians and Jews by showing that most early views of the Church Fathers stemmed from the early Talmud, tied the Jewish tradition to the European Enlightenment to show that the two were not incompatible. Geiger (1810–1874), a child prodigy who mastered the Hebrew and German alphabets at three and the Mishna at six, shaped the Reform Judaism that swept through Jewish orthodoxy the way Protestantism had swept through Catholicism.

Essentially, the Jewish Reformation followed the same pattern as the Protestant. Just as the Protestant reformers had thundered against Trinity, sacraments, and image worship, so the Jewish reformers denied the divinity of the Talmud, abolished phylactery worship, and discarded "maharil" rituals. Services were shortened, meaningless Aramaic prayers were deleted, and the vernacular was introduced. They did their job well. The rush to the baptismal fonts was stopped, and young Jews, as in Hellenic times, could again be comfortable as intellectuals within the sphere of Judaism.

In eastern Europe, emancipation from the yoke of ghetto Talmudism took a different course from that in western Europe, because here Jewish history took a different turn. As Napoleon's *grande armée* had been defeated in Russia, the feudal framework in eastern Europe had not been smashed. Here the political status of the Jews was not changed. Here, pitiful Jewish anachronisms still roamed the Pale. Whereas a ready-made Gentile Enlightenment had awaited the emancipated Jews of the West, a Jewish "enlightenment" had to be structured for the unemancipated Jews of the East. This structured enlightenment, which became known as the *Haskala,* was forged by many hands, but basically it was designed by a mixed trio of Jewish scholars—Polish-born Nachman Krochmal (1785–1840), who wrote the first philosophical history of the Jews; Russian-born Isaac Baer Levinsohn (1788–1860), who argued for educational reforms for Russian Jews; and Italian-born Samuel David Luzzatto (1800–1865), who scoffed at Jewish reformers for putting their trust in the Western Enlightenment.

Jewish spirituality, Nachman Krochmal held, could be perceived only through its religious greatness. In his book, *Guide to the Perplexed of the Time,* with its theory that every people has a spirituality all its own that permeates that people's intellectual achievements, Krochmal comes close to a Hegelian concept of Jewish history. This work was to exercise a profound influence on Jewish intellectuals and their future approach to the meaning of Jewish existence.

Unlike Krochmal, who used philosophy, Isaac Baer Levinsohn resorted to satire to break the barrier of ignorance surrounding the *shtetl* Jews. A descendant of wealthy scholars and merchants, Levinsohn was more popular with enlightened Russians than with unenlightened Jews. His most famed work, *House of Judah,* had the dual purpose of rehabilitating Judaism in the eyes of the Russians and pleading with the Jews for acceptance of a new educational plan for elementary, industrial, and agricultural schools for the children of the Pale.

Poverty and misfortune dogged Samuel David Luzzatto all his life. His children died in their teens, his wife went insane, and he became practically blind. But he saw with an inner vision. Fluent in Italian, French, Latin, and Greek, he wrote in Hebrew in order to resurrect it from a language of prayer to one of literary expression. Western civilization with all its beauty and culture could not save mankind, Luzzatto declared. Her science, divorced from humanity, he predicted, would lead man to a vast international cemetery. Only the primary laws of Judaic ethics and morals could save man from such a fate, he exhorted.

The ideas of Krochmal, Levinsohn, and Luzzatto, as well as those of a host of other Jewish humanists, were seized by self-appointed disciples of the Haskala known as *Maskils*, who set out to seduce the children of the Pale by holding up the skirt of the Haskala for a glimpse of her pleasures. But to the Hasids and Talmudists, the Haskala was synonymous with licentiousness and apostasy. Many a pious Jew, on learning that a son was studying medicine or law instead of Torah and Talmud, declared him dead or had him placed under the ban. In the end, the Maskils broke the power of the Hasids, for the pen of literature was to prove stronger than the formula for excommunication.

To gain the attention of *shtetl* Jews, the Maskils began to write escape novels, where the action was laid in the heroic age of Palestine, where Jews fought pagans with valor and the men kissed a woman's breast instead of a Torah breastplate. Seeing that these potboilers were more interesting to the *shtetl* dwellers than Talmudic tractates, Russian Jewish intellectuals exploited that interest by inserting modern ideas in their literary works, moving them into the Pale via two paths. One was the high road of Hebrew, the elegant language of the learned, and the other was the low road of Yiddish, the folk language of the ignorant. Their fiction, poetry, and essays mirrored the drab lives of these *shtetl* Jews, boldly outlined new horizons for their sleeping intellects, and stimulated revolt against that life.

Among the foremost writers marching on the high road of Hebrew were Ahad Ha'Am who, after exchanging his Talmudic orthodoxy for Haskala humanism, wrote brilliant essays on the role of Jewish culture in the emerging Jewish nationalism; Hayyim Bialik, a truant from the Talmud who in scathing poetry entreated Jewish youth to shed the pacifism of ben Zakkai for the militancy of Bar Kochba; Saul Tchernichovsky, a Jewish urchin who after growing up like a pagan on the steppes of the Crimea, settled for a literary career and in impassioned poetry exhorted the Jews to free God from the bonds of the Talmudists and return to their universal destiny.

On the low road of Yiddish marched an even more colorful entourage of writers who hammered away at the masses with fiction imitating life. There was Mendele the Bookseller who, after vomiting his "maharil" education, swallowed new courses in the universities of the West, and in satiric prose inveighed against the narrow dogmatism of overrated *shtetl* life. There was Sholem Aleichem, who spoofed the Jews and their *shtetl* traditions in stories so human and universal that Communist Chinese peasants reading them in translations identify their plight today with that of the Jews of the Pale of yesterday. And there was I. L. Peretz, a lawyer turned literateur, the first Jewish proletarian writer who spoke of the problems of the Jewish worker in the big urbanized cities of eastern Europe, a new phenomenon in Jewish history.

Within a century, the Enlightenment of the West and the Haskala of the East broke the back of Europe's unyielding Orthodox and kept the questioning intellectuals within Judaism. Within one century, the former "children of the ghetto" achieved a Golden Age in Europe that eclipsed in depth, diversity, and brilliance their three-century-long Golden Age in Spain.

The Jews, who in the fourteenth century were standing on the threshold of a breakthrough into modern science, had been shunted into the ghetto and thus prevented from producing Jewish counterparts to a Galileo, Kepler, or Newton. But in the nineteenth century they made up for that absence. Their crucial influence in the fields of physics and medicine alone can be gauged by noting that though the Jews comprised but one half of one percent of the world's population, this tiny minority won over 20 percent of all Nobel Prizes in physics and medicine awarded between the founding of that prize in 1901 and the outbreak of World War II.

Even more noteworthy than the rise of so many Jews to the highest posts European states had to offer and the eminence of so many Jews in science, was the sudden and dramatic entrance of Jews into art, music, and literature. The paintings of Pissarro, Soutine, Modigliani, and Chagall are treasured prizes in modern art collections. The symphonies of Felix Mendelssohn, Gustav Mahler, Saint-Saëns, Arnold Schonberg, and Ernest Bloch are important compositions in the world's repertoire of classical music. Marcel Proust, Franz Kafka, and Stefan Zweig broke new ground in literature.

Just as Halevi, Maimonides, and Crescas epitomized the Jewish Golden Age in Spain, so Baruch Spinoza, Karl Marx, Sigmund Freud, and Albert Einstein epitomized the Jewish Golden Age in modern times. But what, one might ask, is specifically Jewish about Spinoza, the excommunicated agnostic, Marx, the baptized Red prophet, Freud, the alienated intellectual, or Einstein, the skeptical iconoclast?

Though their works contain nothing specifically "Jewish," all four are universalist in their outlook, a thread that runs throughout Jewish thought. Just as in our first act Abraham did away with all idols, and substituted one God, Moses preached one code of ethics for man, and the Prophets proclaimed one brotherhood for mankind, so in our second act these four intellectual giants of the West carried on the same tradition of universality. Spinoza searched for a philosophy that would unite God, nature, and man into one harmonious unity. Marx probed for the one economic system that would do away with poverty and make all men free from want. Freud tried to synthesize every aspect of man—id, ego, and superego, conscious and unconscious—into a psychology of one mind in a universal man. Einstein reached for a physical law that would unify all phenomena on earth and in heaven into one field theory. This concept of unity in all phenomena is strictly Jewish.

Surveying Jewish achievements in the twilight of the second act, we can now perceive a qualitative distinction between the two acts that have thus far transpired. Whereas the first act contained the ideas that gave the Jews their ideological indestructibility—the concepts of monotheism, the Torah, charismatic power, canonization, the ethics of the Prophets—the second has contained no such universal prescriptions. Though the Jews did innovate ideas within each of their six challenges, they were only adornments to the civilizations within which their destiny evolved, primarily responses for their own survival and only secondarily for the benefit of mankind. Thus the Jewish universalist message was forged in the first act, not in the second.

Nevertheless, surveying Jewish achievements in this second act, one might well ask if the Jewish manifest destiny has not arrived with this unique cultural, literary, and scientific climax in the Modern Age, rendering a third act unnecessary? According to the rationalists, with faith abolished and God dethroned, reason should rule, logic prevail, and goodwill toward all men flourish. The millennium should have arrived.

Alas, what so proudly was hailed as the new freedom of man turned into a nightmare of hate. What the rationalists did not realize was that painting a society with the brush of reason does not give it reason, only a deceptive coating. Under this coating of a "pale cast of thought," a subtle social interaction fermented. Soon it blistered the surface of civilization with the nodules of deadly "isms."

The biblical paradise was shattered by a snake that seduced man to knowledge. The "modern paradise" was obliterated by the three-headed hydra of communism, fascism, and anti-Semitism that poisoned man with hate. How did this hydra gain entry into the paradise of rationalism? Not only does God move in mysterious ways his wonders to perform in man's life, but ideas move in even more mysterious ways to wreak havoc in men's minds.

Ideas have a habit of not developing in predicted ways, but behaving like electromagnetic waves. Heinrich Hertz, the German-Jewish physicist, formulated his law of electro-magnetic waves thus: "The consequence of the image will be the image of the consequence." In the social world, this translates as: White creates black. If there were no white people, there would be no black people, only people. Learning creates its image of ignorance, which begets the consequence of social unrest. The counterimage of reason is unreason, and the consequence of unreason became a Romantic movement that in art turned to intuition and in politics to myth. By abolishing the grace of God (brother-hood), the world begot its counterimage, the grace of blood (racism). With the demise of faith, the anti-Jewish-ness of the Church begot its counterimage of the anti-Semitism of the state.

Anti-Semitism was but a symptom of a larger syndrome of the social diseases of communism, fascism, racism—counterimages of the French Revolution. The global car-riers of these deadly strains were two world wars in the twentieth century. In the first half of the twentieth century, communism would conquer a third of the world, and Nazism would murder a third of the Jews. Anti-Semitism would beget its own counterimage—a Jewish state.

The poet Goethe, in predicting a world revolution, was more prescient than the philosopher Kant, who merely predicted a European revolt.

JEWS AND GOD IN THE TWENTIETH CENTURY

At the dawn of the twentieth century, God was in His heaven and all was well with the world. The white race stood at the summit, controlling 85 percent of the surface of the earth. England, France, and Germany had carved off the choicest portions of Africa and Asia for their per-sonal preserves known as "colonies." British settlers had poisoned off most of the natives of Australia to secure that continent as a white island in a colored Pacific. United States Marines kept Central and South America in proper obeisance with bayonet and contempt. The gook knew his place and the nigger his master.

Then in quick succession came two calamities that fractured the world of the WASP, the White Anglo-Saxon Protestant. On the battlefields of two total wars died not only 27,000,000 soldiers but also the ideologies that had shaped Europe. World War I, fought to preserve democracy, shattered it. World War II, fought to preserve the "Four Freedoms," scattered them. Out of the redundance of terror of these two wars rose not democracy and freedom but communism and fascism. The former obliterated the religious frontiers hammered out after the Thirty-Years' War, and the latter corroded the democratic borders erected after the French Revolution.

World War I was a miscalculation conceived by the merger of accident and design. In 1914 people believed that a balance of power would preserve peace in their time, just as people today believe that a balance of terror will preserve peace in our time. But five dynasties and one republic bent on altering the prevailing status quo took Europe to its rendezvous with death. The dynasties were the Hohenzollerns of Germany, the Hapsburgs of Austria, the Romanovs of Russia, the Osmanli of the Ottoman Empire, and the Windsors of the British Empire. The republic was France.

Germany's Kaiser Wilhelm II, ignored by his mother and humiliated by a withered arm, was "neither a Hun nor a monster," only a monarch of limited intellect who mindlessly followed Austria into an unnecessary war. Ferocious in talk, his chief difficulty was that he "approached all questions with an open mouth." But after the war, from his refuge in Holland, he had to silently watch his 300-year-old Hohenzollern inheritance pass into the hands of the Hun Hitler. To the Jews, this demise of the Hohenzollerns spelled disaster. In imperial Germany, they had been an intellectual elite, totally wedded to German *Kultur,* ensconced in cabinet posts and winners of Nobel Prizes. They had filled army ranks from privates to generals, while waving the flag of super-patriotism to a country that soon would betray them.

Kaiser Franz Joseph II, the next to last of the 700-year Hapsburg dynasty, ruler of the Vienna of Waltz, *Schmaltz,* and *Schwermerei,* was every inch a king. Arrogant and enlightened, he ruled a doomed empire beset with too many problems. Life had dealt him a series of defeats— his wife assassinated, his heir murdered, and his son, Rudolf, a suicide. After falling in love with the hauntingly beautiful seventeen-year-old Marie Vetsera, an illegitimate daughter of the emperor, Rudolf had killed her and himself at the hunting lodge of Mayerling upon learning of their kinship. Like Germany, the Austria-Hungarian Empire was a breeding ground for Jewish intellectuals, world-renowned writers, musicians, scientists, and Nobel Prize winners.

Nicholas II, the last czar of the 300-year-old Romanov line, was a gentle, stupid paragon of bourgeois respectability, dominated by his ignorant wife. Whereas Peter I had killed his son, Catherine II her husband, and Alexander I his father, Czar Nicholas killed no one except a few thousand of his subjects. An autocrat by conviction, he possessed a mind "shielded by antimacassars of prejudice." He met his fate—death against a blood-spattered wall— with apathy and dignity. The Romanov Jewish policy, a blend of pogroms and starvation, squeezed two million of Russia's Jews to the United States, where they sparked the first intellectual current in America's intellectually dormant Jewry.

When the Ottoman Empire entered the twentieth century, Abdul Hamid II, the tubercular son of a Circassian slave, sat on the throne. A chronic reactionary, a "prig of despotism," and a cringing coward, his ambition of ruling the Arab world outran his ability. Instead, he contented himself with the massacre of defenseless Armenians, whom he ordered clubbed to death like cattle. Not even his sycophants mourned his death in 1903. His monstrously incompetent successor, his brother, Mohammed VI, took the Ottoman Empire into war on the side of Germany. The Jews in the empire, intellectually dead and socially unacceptable, existed unhistorically like Eskimos, victims of the general oppression that gripped all in a vise of sloth and poverty.

The only "Big Five" dynasty that survived World War I was England's House of Windsor. The decline of the British Empire began with the reign of Queen Victoria, an absurd old woman to whom Disraeli pandered with insincere flattery and to whom Gladstone listened with deferential hypocrisy. There is little that can be said for her son Edward VII and his successor George V. The Jews in England, however, lived in freedom and stultifying middle class life. Since their return to that country in the days of Cromwell, they had contributed no great ideas to Jewish history.

The modern history of France begins with the year 1848, which Arnold Toynbee has defined as a turning point where history failed to turn. The First Republic, born in 1792 with the French Revolution, died in 1799 with the coup d'état of Napoleon I. The Second Republic was even more short-lived. Born in the streets of Paris in the aimless Revolution of 1848, it died at the age of three with the coup d'état of Napoleon III. The Third Republic was born amid the debris of the defeat of France in the Franco-Prussian War of 1870. The third French Republic worked against being drawn into the war in 1914, but ultimately she too was swept into this ancient game of death and prestige. The Jews in France, freed from the ghettos by the French Revolution, lived in two spheres. One was the elegant society of the upper class in which Jews moved with aplomb in a Proustian dream world of decadent aristocracy, isolated from reality by romanticism and wealth. The other was the drab society of the middle class, whose Jews were shaken by the Dreyfus[4] trial into apprehension and doubt.

The deadly game of "ultimatums" that triggered World War I began in 1914 in the colorless Serbian town of Sarajevo, when a tubercular Bosnian teen-age student shot the heir to the Austria-Hungarian crown. Austria tendered Serbia an ultimatum. Russia backed Serbia. Germany backed Austria. France backed Russia. Nobody backed down. Austria declared war on Serbia. Germany marched east into Russia and west into France via Belgium, which was backed by England. World War I, the world's most promiscuous carnage, was on.

The nonwhite world watched incredulously while white,

---

[4] A French Jew falsely accused of treason. The trial set in motion a wave of anti-Semitism in France.

handsome, aristocratic generals sent millions of men like cattle to slaughter; saw them live like moles in trenches of liquid mud mixed with excrement and urine. From the Battle of Verdun in 1916—a climactic madness that exacted a toll of 700,000 dead—to the Battle of the Marne in 1918—a gristmill of death that swallowed half a million casualties—no more than ten miles of ground ever changed hands. When the war came to an end, the soil of Europe cradled ten million dead soldiers, and twenty million mutilated men hobbled home across her blood-drenched body. They had died and been maimed in vain. The "war to end wars" had ripped the unity of Europe, shattered its balance of power, and opened a path to totalitarianism and World War II.

Though France suffered half a million casualties and lost the richest parts of her country, and Belgium lost over half her territory and 40 percent of her field army in the first months of the war, these two countries nevertheless fought on for another three years to final victory. But the moment the Allies broke German lines, the Germans begged for peace. Winston Churchill's phrase, "The Hun is either at your throat or at your feet," correctly appraises the German spirit.

The German generals who lost the war blamed the defeat on a "stab in the back" by Jews and profiteers. But the fact was that the German armed forces had mutinied, unwilling to die for either Kaiser or *Vaterland*. The *Wehrmacht* mutiny did not begin with exhausted soldiers on the front, but with sailors resting in Kiel, where the German Navy had been tucked away ever since its inglorious defeat by the British in 1916. There were no Jews or profiteers on the decks of those German warships, only Aryan Germans hoisting the Red flag of rebellion that spread like a pilonidal cyst through German military colons. Even the Kaiser's most trusted regiments deserted. To save their pride, the generals suggested that the Kaiser rescue the honor of Germany by galloping at the head of a company into enemy fire to find gallant death on the battlefield, a deed that would then grow into heroic legend. But not even the Kaiser was willing to die for the *Vater-*

land. In the dark of night he slipped across the frontier of Holland, begging asylum, and Germany sued for peace.

To Versailles came Woodrow Wilson, President of the United States, to build the peace on the slogans of his Fourteen Points, the "fourteen commandments" that caused Georges Clemenceau to exclaim, "The good Lord had only ten." And on the banks of Lake Leman in Switzerland, the peacemakers founded the League of Nations, doomed to failure from its inception, for though the voice was the voice of Wilson, the hands were the hands of Lloyd George and Clemenceau. Europe was carved up along ideas so lofty that they failed to touch reality. The Austria-Hungarian Empire was dismembered into Czechoslovakia, Poland, Romania, Yugoslavia, Austria, and Hungary—six independent sources for future disaster. Spin-off ethnic parts of the fallen czarist and Ottoman empires were also declared nations and given certificates of independence. This dismemberment gave Europe no more stability than would the carving up of the United States along ethnic, religious, and color lines—Texas to the Mexicans, Mississippi to the Negroes, Massachusetts to the Vatican—give her.

Ideology divorced from reality could not stop the cataclysmic events that soon convulsed Europe. Within one decade, instead of being free and democratic, most of Europe was a prisoner of dictators. Russia, led by the triumvirate of Lenin, Trotsky, and Stalin, marched out of the war in 1917 and into communism in 1918. Italy, seduced by Benito Mussolini, turned to fascism. An assortment of strong men seized Turkey, Hungary, Poland, Portugal, Yugoslavia, Austria, Bulgaria, Greece, and the three Baltic states. Spain, following Francisco Franco, joined the fascist elite. The former Hohenzollern-Hapsburg dynasties seemed like a vanished paradise. And the hopes of the Jews for a better world promised by the rationalists and Wilson's Fourteen Points were dashed as dictators abolished previous civic gains.

When history entered the twentieth century, there were three Diaspora centers, one each in Germany, Russia, and the United States. The German Jews were the brilliant imitators of Western civilization, the social elite; the Russian Jews were the brilliant innovators of the Jewish Enlightenment, but the social parvenus; and the American Jews were the intellectual parvenus, tolerated by the German and Russian Jews because of their economic power. Half a century later, when Jewish history emerged from the wringer of two Christian world wars, the German Jews had vanished, the Russian Jews had been reduced to an impotent mass, and the American Jews had become the leaders of Diaspora Judaism.

To untangle the skein of these intertwining events, let us first delineate the fortunes and adventures of the Jewish people in the North American continent, then examine the social forces that incarcerated the Russian Jews in communist enclaves, and finally assess the barbaric acts of the heirs to the Holy Roman Empire that eliminated the Jews from the European scene.

Jews and God in Capitalist America

Two thousand years ago, the Hellenic drawing room was the laboratory where a new Judaism was hammered out for survival in the second act. Today, the American living room is the laboratory where a new Judaism is being hammered out for survival in the coming third act. But before examining the nature of the Jewish condition in present-day United States, let us review that phase of American history that set Jewish destiny upon a new vector.

The real hero in American history is not man but spirit, a spirit which has unconsciously spun an American manifest destiny as a spider instinctively spins a web. The growth of the American continent from the private hunting ground of Indians to the dominant world power in less than four centuries is an inspiring example of the power of fiction over fact.

American history is a paradox that proceeds like a dream on two levels. On one level, it consists of solemn phrases of peace, uttered with conviction. On the second, it consists of actions completely contradictory to these verbal statements. While piously reciting George Washington's admonition of "no foreign entanglements," the United States has become the chief meddler in world politics. While sincerely preaching that she sought no man's territory, she has erected the largest commercial empire in the history of man. While proclaiming that she was but a small-time hick with no diplomatic skill, she has carted off most of the blue chips from the world's diplomatic gaming tables. While loudly proclaiming a fierce intention to fight for democracy anywhere, she has never entered a war of liberty on behalf of others without being forced to do so by world events or self-defense. Thus, while loudly professing innocence, ineptitude, and virtue, the United States has become the twentieth century's leading world power, as sincerely blind to the disparity between her words and deeds today as she ever was.

Two factors have helped shape America's destiny—the spirit of the frontier and the spirit of the Puritans. From 1607, when the vast American continent was informally opened, until 1890, when it was formally closed, the frontier has been a dominant influence in the shaping of American history. To the European mind, this frontier was a fixed line that delineated the end of influence; to the American mind it was a fluid zone that invited settlement. As explorers followed by trappers fleeing the settlers all trekked to the Pacific, a new frontier, like the Eldorado of the Conquistadores, beckoned from across the Pacific—the vast landmass of Asia.

The spirit of the frontier was merged into a political manifest destiny by the Puritans. Originally seceders from the Reform Church of England in the time of Queen Elizabeth, they were so called because they stood for a more radical purification of Catholic elements than the Anglican Church allowed. The sole authority of the Puritans, like that of the Karaites, was the "pure word of God" without "note or comment." In the seventeenth century, as England entered her period of religious wars, the Puritans, who cursed Anglicans and papists with equal vehemence, were ripe for persecution. They headed for America in search of freedom.

Except for their worship of Jesus, the Puritans were as

Jewish in spirit as Job, who had made his way into the Old Testament as a canonized Gentile. The Puritans in England regarded themselves primarily as Hebraists. They took the Old Testament as their model of government and tried to reshape the Magna Carta in its image. The original Magna Carta did not care about the people or their rights. Its sixty-four dry paragraphs (two of them devoted to how to cheat the Jews) gave concessions to predatory lords. Not until 300 years later, after the English Puritans, inspired by the Old Testament and guided by Talmudic precedents, began to reinterpret the Magna Carta in their struggle for individual rights, did it become a charter of freedom for the people.

The British rulers rightly regarded the Puritans as Jewish fellow-travelers, and when they departed for the Colonies, the British ruling class wrote them off as good riddance. In America, the Puritans modeled their new homeland upon Old Testament principles. When Harvard University was founded in 1636, Hebrew along with Latin was taught as one of the two main languages. Governor Cotton wanted to make the Mosaic Code the law of Massachusetts, and Hebrew at one point almost became the official language of that state.

The principles of the United States Constitution and constitutional law derive from this Puritan heritage. The framers of the Constitution were familiar with the techniques used by the Jews for amending their Torah with Talmud, though they did not envision the body of constitutional law that was to grow out of their Constitution any more than Moses envisioned the body of Talmudic law that was to grow out of his Torah. But the Constitution of the United States came to function in American political life much as the Talmud had functioned in Jewish life. Like the Talmud, it created a spirit of law through the judicial arm rather than the legislative, for whereas Congress makes the laws, the Supreme Court can affirm or nullify those laws with its power to interpret their constitutionality. Just as Hai Gaon in Islamic times expanded the power of the Talmud in every area of Jewish life from commerce to morals, so Chief Justice Marshall in nineteenth-century America expanded constitutional law into every segment of American political and civil life.

The Puritans transformed the Jewish concept of a religious manifest destiny into a political manifest destiny, believing it was God's will that Americans should rule the continent and the seas beyond, a mystique that gave the Colonists ideas of grandeur undeterred by reality. Even while the future United States consisted of but thirteen scraggly colonies, American revolutionaries, not knowing whether a patriot's medal or hangman's noose awaited them, grandiosely named their governing body the "Continental Congress" and their army the "Continental Army." An incident that occurred during the Revolutionary War suggests how thoroughly the Puritans identified themselves with the Spirit of the Old Testament and the spirit of a manifest destiny. When Colonel (later General) Ethan Allen ordered the British commander at Ticonderoga to surrender, the British general haughtily asked, "In whose name?" Allen insouciantly answered, "In the name of the great Jehovah and the Continental Congress."

It was the Liberty Bell, with its inscription from Leviticus (25:10): "Proclaim liberty throughout the land, unto all the inhabitants thereof," that, in the Jewish tradition, rang out for the first reading of the Declaration of Independence. It was this Puritan spirit of initiative and destiny, carried by explorers, traders, and settlers across the continent and embedded in the American consciousness, that left a more enduring imprint on the American character than did the spirit of the frontier. From this minority group of Puritans, not from the majority groups of Anglicans and Catholics, came the main thinking of the leaders of the American Revolution and the founders of American constitutional and legislative thought.

Though the political power of the Puritans was broken in 1800, their ideology became the American ethos. By 1820, the Puritan-inspired politicians had formulated the mystique of an American manifest destiny into political slogans. Two decades later, with the Monroe Doctrine, it took on its international aspects, loftily appointing the United States the guardian of the American continents, long before it had the power to enforce such unilateral provisions.

It was this combined spirit of frontier and Puritanism that greeted the first Jews arriving in Colonial America in the seventeenth century. This Puritan atmosphere of Colonial America has shaped the American Jew as much as Greco-Roman ideology shaped the Hellenistic Jew, the Mohammedan culture the Islamic Jew, and the Western tradition the European Jew.

The Jews reached the United States in three "ethnic" migratory waves from Spain, Germany, and Russia over a span of three centuries. When Spanish and Portuguese navigators discovered America, Jews were in the advance party, settling as early as 1500 in South America. When the Inquisition established branch offices in the New World, the Jews fled north. Thus it came about that Spanish and Portuguese Jews, fleeing from Brazil and the West Indies, settled in the Colonies as early as 1621, a year after the *Mayflower* arrived. Two centuries later came the German Jews, along with German Christians, fleeing the economic, social, and political upheavals in Germany. Toward the end of the nineteenth century came the third ethnic migratory wave. In the four decades between 1880 and 1920, religious persecution and political repression funneled two million Jews from Russia into America. But, though the fabric of American Judaism is woven from these three ancient strands of Judaism, the pattern in the fabric is uniquely American.

Why has American Judaism taken such a different course from that of European Judaism? Four factors explain it. The Spanish Jewish settlers who first came to America had no ghetto tradition and were otherwise undistinguishable in looks from the rest of the American population. They became part of the American scene from the beginning and set the pattern for other Jews to follow. Because the Colonists did away with the European system of nobles, priest, and serf, and themselves constituted the middle class of farmers, tradesmen, and artisans, the Jews, who were the middle classes in feudal Europe, were readily absorbed into the American middle class milieu. As Jews had equal protection under the laws and were part of the country's economic fabric, there was no need for them to form their own "state within a state" as they had had to do in previous challenges. Though American Jews came from the great centers of Talmudic learning in Europe, the Talmud never took root in America, and played but a minor role in the development of American Judaism. Slowly, most European-Jewish institutions vanished on American soil. And lastly, there were no ordained rabbis in America in the first two centuries of American Jewish history. The autocratic rabbinic system of Europe never had a chance to establish itself. When the rabbis did arrive, power had already passed into the hands of the Jewish congregations, in much the same manner that the power of the Anglican Church passed into the hands of the Puritan congregations.

Though the spirit of the American Jew has been forged over a period of three centuries, he lived unhistorically until the twentieth century, when capricious history placed the symbolic scepter of Diaspora Judaism in his willing or unwilling hands. Will this responsibility entrusted to him by the blind permutations of historic forces wilt in a wasteland of anti-intellectualism, or will an American-Jewish renaissance insure this culture a continued growth? Could it be that American Judaism is destined to play the same dominant role in the coming third act as Pharisee Judaism played in the second act and Sadducee Judaism in the first?

The position of the Jew in America today resembles that of the Jew in Palestine 2,000 years ago, when Pharisee Judaism slowly gained ascendance over Sadducee Judaism. Is American Judaism today similarly destined to gain ascendance over the Pharisee Judaism that has been the Judaism of the Diaspora throughout the 2,000 years of the second act?

Everything points to such a takeover. In the waning centuries of the first act, Pharisee Jews undermined and finally did away with the Sadducee cults of sacrifice, Temple, and priesthood. American Jews in the waning centuries of the second act are similarly doing away with the Pharisee symbols of prayer, synagogue, and rabbinate. Pharisee Judaism discreetly discarded those portions of Torah and Talmud that interfered with their mode of worship. American Judaism is openly discarding those parts of Torah and Talmud rendered obsolete by its new modes of observances. Just as 2,000 years ago the Sadducees railed and ranted at the "heresies" of the Pharisees, so today's "Pharisees," the orthodox Jews, rail and rant at the "heresies" of the American Reform innovators who dare tamper with "traditional Judaism." And just as 2,000 years ago the Pharisee institutions that had slowly replaced the Sadducee way of life could not be clearly perceived until several centuries later, so the new American institutions slowly replacing former Pharisee ideologies may not be clearly discerned until a century or so hence. This new American Judaism could become not only the Judaism for the Diaspora in the third act, but for Israel, too.

Jews and God in Communist Russia

The United States, the capitalist and westernmost flank of Western civilization, containing six million Jews, today stands poised for a clash over the hegemony of Asia with Soviet Russia, the communist and easternmost flank of Western civilization, containing three million Jews, the second largest aggregate of Jews in any one country. As the next Diaspora center could be in Russia, we must now briefly review the history of Communist Russia and assess the metahistoric probabilities of the fate of the Jews contained within its vast landmass.

The three decades from World War I to World War II were more momentous to Russian history than the three-century rule of the Romanovs from Czar Michael to Nicholas II. In those three decades communism settled over Russia, transforming her from a fifth-rate power to a contender for world leadership.

Ironically, the communist gospel tailored for the West by the German Jew Karl Marx was bought by the East much as the Christian gospel tailored for the East by the Palestinian Jew Jesus Christ was bought by the West. Christianity, designed for Orientals, was rejected by them but taken up in the West by Roman slaves, barbaric Vandals, Gauls, and Goths, who represented the lowest rungs of Europe's social strata. Communism, designed for the elite states of western Europe, was rejected by them but taken up by the serfs, peasants, and workers of Russia and China, the then social dregs of the East.

Marx held that capitalism would be the protesting midwife to communism because of an ironic inner contradiction. In quest of ever more profits, the communist doctrine held, capitalists would press the wages of workers below the level of subsistence and thus force the proletariat into a revolution against capitalism. Because Marx had diagnosed capitalism as an incurable illness, the communists sat around for half a century waiting for their capitalist patient to expire voluntarily. But capitalism would not cooperate. What Marx had not foreseen was that labor unions would press wages up and labor-saving devices would press costs down so that even as workers received higher wages, capitalists made greater profits. Instead of workers being submerged below the level of subsistence, they crept above it, causing communist leaders to complain that there was a danger of the proletariat becoming bourgeoisie.

The communist line had to change. Instead of waiting for communism to develop of itself in Western industrial states, as prescribed by Marx, a trio of communists decided to force a revolution in Russia, a backward, agrarian country. The Russian Revolution was the product of two Mongols and a Jew—Lenin (born Vladimir Ilyich Ulyanov, 1870–1924), descendant of a Volga Kalmyk, who laid the political foundations for communism in a nonindustrialized country; Trotsky (born Leon Davydovich Bronstein, 1877–1940), the son of a Russian Jewish farmer, who forged the revolutionary armies that thwarted all capitalist efforts to overthrow the state; and Stalin (born Joseph Vissarionovich Djugashvili, 1879–1953), the son of a Georgian cobbler, who transformed the foundering Leninist state into a formidable Stalinist empire.

The fate of this famed trio of Russian revolutionaries uncannily resembles the fate of the famed triad of French revolutionaries. Like Marat, assassinated by Charlotte Corday for having betrayed the ideals of the French Revolution, so Lenin narrowly missed assassination at the hands of Fanya Kaplan for having betrayed the ideals of the Russian Revolution.[5] Like Robespierre, guillotined by his own party for his insufferable ideological virtues, so Trotsky was assassinated by his own party for his dogmatic ideological faith. Like pockmarked Danton, sending men to death in constant fits of fear, so pockmarked Stalin, in constant dread of a conspiracy against his life sent men to their death. But unlike Danton, who died of a severed head on the guillotine, Stalin died of a stroke in bed.

It took the ingenuity of St. Paul to transform the social humanism of Jesus into a religious dogma, and it took the genius of Lenin to transform the economic humanism of Marx into a political dogma. At the Communist Party Congress of 1903 in London, at the proposal of Lenin, the Bolsheviks (the Russian word for majority) voted to do what Marx had thought was impossible—to skip the capitalist phase on the road to communism and go directly from feudalism into communism. Thus it came about that the despised Slavs, whom Marx considered totally unfit for communism because of their backward economy, became the first communist state with Leninism as the midwife.

Perhaps the real midwife of Russian communism, however, was not Leninism but the German military staff, which in 1917 permitted Lenin, then living in exile in Switzerland, to pass through Germany in a sealed train via Helsinki into Russia. The theory was that if Lenin could foment a revolution inside Russia that would remove her from the war, it would permit the Germans to concentrate their forces on the Western Front, and after defeating the Allies in the west, turn on the Russians in the east. Had it worked, the plan would have been brilliant. Instead it turned out to be a disaster.

[5] Shot at in 1918, one bullet lodging in his neck, the other in his shoulder, Lenin lived in pain for six years more, before dying officially from a stroke.

The first part worked out according to schedule. In three brief months, Lenin achieved the impossible. He toppled the democratic Kerensky regime, which assumed power in Russia after the fall of the czar, and signed the humiliating peace treaty of Brest Litovsk with Germany that took Russia out of the war with the loss of most of the territories she had acquired since Peter the Great. However, the German High Command had not figured on the Jew named Trotsky taking the defeated, dejected, and dispirited Russian soldiers and forging them into a triumphant Red Army that would stop all the czarist and interventionist forces hurled at them—the counterrevolutionary armies of Yudenich, Wrangel, and Denikin on its western front, and the interventionist armies of Czechoslovakia, Japan, and America[6] in Siberia. By 1922, the communists were in total possession of Russia's bloody, battered, but Red body. Great though the Bolshevik victory over the White forces was in winning the civil and interventionist wars, the victory in conquering internal anarchy in five short subsequent years was even greater. America had achieved her "empire" with artless innocence; Russia was about to win hers with cunning ruthlessness.

Lenin harnessed the Russian Revolution to Marxism, but in the process, the humanity of Marx hardened into the brutality of "Leninism," the political bridge that reached from feudalism directly into communism. He launched the Red Terror not so much as countermeasure to the White Terror but to eliminate the bourgeoisie and to usher in more quickly the dictatorship of the proletariat. What he begot was chaos. The socialists, still believing in Marxist humanism, denounced Leninism as an "Asiatic perversion of Marxism." When the Red Terror threatened to mire the entire nation in chaos and blood, as the French Revolution had similarly threatened France, Lenin called a halt and instituted a modified communism known as the New Economic Policy, or NEP.

[6]The interventionist force consisted of 72,000 Japanese, 12,000 Czechoslovakians, and 8,000 Americans. General William Sidney Graves, commander of the American force, called the intervention (1918–1920) a failure and recommended America's withdrawal.

Lenin had hoped that Trotsky would succeed him after death, but as Engels once observed, history always keeps a card up its sleeve. Instead of humanistic ex-lawyer Trotsky, secretary of the War Commissariat, Russia inherited a ruthless ex-theological student named Stalin, secretary of the Communist Party.

If history measures greatness by final achievement, irrespective of method, then history will adjudge Stalin "great," for he wrought a Russia which Catherine the Great and Peter the Great dreamt of but never achieved. Single-handedly, he delivered out of the bloody womb of revolutionary Russia a new world state and a new civilization. He inherited a Russia playing at the side of a manure pile and bequeathed his successors a Russia experimenting with an atomic pile. Just as Marxism was the ideology that inspired the Russian Revolution, and Leninism was the political phase that entrenched it, so Stalinism bureaucratized the revolution into the normalcy of everyday life. Whereas Czar Peter's cruelties were sadistic, serving no social good, Stalin's crimes were impersonal, perpetrated solely as a policy of state. With unspeakable cruelty, he disposed of the revolutionary intellectuals and riffraff he had inherited from Lenin, ended the NEP, instituted his first Five Year Plan, and in three decades transformed a primitive Russia into a modern empire.

In much the same way as Christians had taken the religious creed of Jesus and headquartered it in the Vatican, so the Bolsheviks took the economic creed of Marx and headquartered it in the Kremlin. For the Jews there was a second parallel: the Church had deified the Jewish founder of Christianity but villified the Jews; the Kremlin deified the Jewish founder of communism and also villified the Jews. The communist villification of the Jews, however, did not begin as a planned policy; it grew out of unanticipated events. The special hostility against Jews grew out of a general war against religion.

The ancient Jews of Israel had regarded idolatry as an abomination unto God that had to be eradicated ruthlessly, the early Christians had viewed heresy as the enemy of Christ that had to be eradicated mercilessly, and the devout communists regarded religion as an infestation of society that had to be weeded out pitilessly. Religion, to the communists, was a drug which had to be taken away from the people in consonance with Marx's dictum that "Religion is the lament of the oppressed, the soul of a world that has no soul, the hope of a humanity which has lost all hope; it is the opium of the people."

Churches were razed or turned into museums, hospitals, or schools. The priesthood was abolished. Atheism was legalized. Church officials were brought to trial for suspected conspiracy against the state. Religion itself was not suppressed, but without support from the state, organized religion collapsed. Thus, of the 46,500 churches in Russia in 1917, about 4,000 survived after half a century of communism, and out of 1,000 monasteries, but 38 remained. Along with Christianity, Mohammedanism, and all other religious creeds, Judaism, too, was made an enemy of the state. Judaism as a religion received no more protection from the state than any other religion, and synagogues suffered the same fate as churches and mosques.

Upon seizing power, the Soviet Union freed all ethnic minorities from restrictions imposed upon them by czars. Lenin abolished Jewish self-rule, proclaimed that hatred against any minority people was shameful, and vowed that anti-Semitism would be torn out by its roots from the Russian body politic. As in France after the French Revolution, so the Jews in Russia after the Russian Revolution became citizens, and anti-Semitism became a criminal act, vigorously prosecuted by the new state.

Many Jews had fought in the front ranks of the revolution and risen to high party posts, but the mass of the Russian Jews knew nothing of communist aims. All they knew was that they were free from the czarist yoke, and they looked with gratitude on the communists who had given them their freedom. But when Judaism would not die graciously, Jews and communists eventually clashed on the frontiers of politics and religion.

To the vast majority of Russians, mainly feudal peasants and workers, the transition to communism was not great. They simply became communist peasants and workers.

To the Jews, however, chiefly tradesmen, artisans, business-men, and marginal entrepreneurs, the transition was more difficult. Overnight, communism had abolished their capitalist-oriented trades and professions, leaving a large segment of Jews rootless. While Jewish youth attended communist schools and universities, the Soviet Union waited patiently for the older generation of Jews to die and for the younger Jews to grow out of Judaism into communism. Though Jewish youth became communist and were ensconced in high posts, though they did give up orthodox religious notions, they nevertheless retained a spiritual tie to Judaism.

The communists did not know what to do with this high-ly educated, highly intelligent elite minority[7] that still clung to aspects of Judaism when, according to revealed com-munist text, they should have abandoned it for superior Marxist dialectic. The Jews, on the other hand, did not know how to fight this Soviet enemy which punished anti-Semites, gave the Jews equality, left them in physical peace, but took away their synagogues and filled the minds of their children with irreligion.

Until World War II, a stalemate existed, during which time the Soviets thought they would eventually digest the Jewish problem and the Jews thought they would survive the Soviet threat. But World War II and its aftermath begat Russia two new problems which brought unanticipated consequences—Nazi anti-Semitism and political Zionism.

Not four but five apocalyptic horses rode herd with the Nazi armies as they invaded Russia. The fifth horseman was anti-Semitism, the only one welcomed by the populace. But along with this German anti-Semitism was the news of the valiant struggle of the Zionists to create a homeland for disenfranchised Jews in Palestine. Thus, after its victory over the Nazis, the Soviet government found itself con-fronted with what it considered two problems—anti-

[7]Though the Jews in Soviet Russia constitute but 1½ percent of the total population, 12 percent of Russia's top scientists, 15 percent of all doctors, and 10 percent of all Russia's lawyers are Jews. Of the outstanding artists and writers listed in Russia's *Who Is Who* 8 percent are Jewish.

Semitism ravaging anew Russian minds and Zionism seducing Jewish hearts. This time the communists did not attack the anti-Semitism sweeping the land with the same vigor of the postrevolutionary days. Because of Zionism, Judaism now gave the Soviet state a special political headache other religions did not. The Politbureau viewed Zionism as a form of dangerous internationalism, as Cosmopolitanism, that made the Jews in Russia kin to the Jews in Europe, America, Israel and thus, presumably, a threat to Soviet Russia itself.

To eliminate this presumed danger of Zionism, the Communist Party decided upon a "Jewish course" that greatly resembled the "Jewish course" of the Church in the Middle Ages—a state-controlled anti-Jewishness. The Jew was not to be exterminated, but Judaism was to be eradicated, and through it, Zionism. Though Jews were safe from pogroms, they became subject, as in feudal times, to discrimination and exclusion. Jewish cultural activities, once encouraged, were abolished. Jewish schools and theaters were closed. The Jewish press died.

Do these acts make Russia anti-Semitic, as most Jews today contend? Or is Russia merely antireligious, as the communists assert? Russia cannot be compared to Nazi Germany, but neither are its anti-Jewish policies merely an outcome of general hostility to religion. The position of the Jew in Russia today is akin to the position of the Jews in the Spain of Torquemada. In Spain we saw a great assimilation of Jews into Catholicism via the Marranos; in Russia we see a great assimilation of Jews into communism via the educated Jewish elite. Just as Jews in Spain who converted to Catholicism became bishops and archbishops in the Spanish church hierarchy, so Jews in Russia who converted to communism became commissars and Politbureau members in the Communist Party hierarchy. And just as Spanish Catholics were afraid that too many "Jewish Christians" in high church posts would depaganize their Christianity and "Judaize" it, so many Russian communists are afraid that too many "Jewish communists" in high party posts will "de-Leninize" their communism with original "Jewish Marxism." The Catholic Church, under the guidelines of *limpieza de sangre,* dumped its intellectual "Jewish church leaders" for deserving native Catholics; the Communist Party, under its guidelines of anti-Cosmopolitanism, dumped its intellectual "Jewish Party leaders" for deserving Gentile communists. Thus both Church and Party were made *Judenrein,* that is, clean of Jews. Both, however, permitted the Jews full expansion in the sciences and humanities. Eventually, we saw Spain expel the Jews. What Russia will do remains to be seen.

Is Judaism dying in Soviet Russia? Before the revolution, 95 percent of Russia's Jews lived in *shtetls* and "Pales," embraced ghetto orthodoxy, and spoke Yiddish. This *shtetl* Judaism is as dead in Soviet Russia today as it is in the United States. Because *shtetl* Judaism and Yiddish in the United States died natural deaths through indifference and in Soviet Russia by force, will not alter the fact that no nostalgic tears, either in America or Russia, will resurrect a dead Jewish way of life and a dead Yiddish press. The educated Soviet Jew will no more return to the Pharisee symbols of *t'fillin* and Talmud of his grandfathers than will the American Reform Jew.

Historically, the position of the Russian Jew today resembles that of the Jew in eighteenth-century Europe when he stood at the threshold of his emancipation from the ghetto. Just as rationalism emancipated the Jews from Europe's ghettos in that century, so communism emancipated the Jews from Russia's Pales of Settlement in the twentieth century. Just as Europe's emancipated Jews, rejecting ghetto Judaism, needed a Moses Mendelssohn to fence them in on the range of Judaism with a reform movement, so Russia's emancipated Jews today, rejecting their ghetto Judaism, need a Moses Mendelssohn to fashion a modern Judaism that will hold them within the orbit of their faith.

Marx may have been as wrong in thinking of religion as the opium of the people as Freud was in thinking of it as an illusion. In spite of Marx's definition, the religious spirit persists in Russia, not just among the Jews, but among all its people. The moment the antireligious blanket is lifted, the spiritually sensitive Russian people will return to some form of religious expression, as will the Jews. Communism, an economic system, cannot be made to serve the spiritual function of religion any more than religion can be made a substitute for a social system. In the words of Jesus, religion must render unto Caesar that which is Caesar's and unto God that which is God's. Christianity has served the feudal state through Catholicism and the capitalist state through Protestantism. If Russia, or China, can find a religion that will serve its people's spiritual needs without threatening the state, it will adopt such a religion.

Such a religion might be a different variety of Christianity, or a totally new religion. It could very well also be a pantheistic version of Judaism—the doctrine that holds God is everything and everything is God, that the real "trinity" is man, God, and nature. Such a concept was introduced to the world in the seventeenth century by Baruch Spinoza, a God-intoxicated Jew who proved the existence of God in nature with geometric propositions. Such pantheistic Judaism differs no more drastically from the Judaism of today than the spiritual Judaism introduced by the Prophets differed from the anthropomorphic Judaism introduced by Abraham. Just as "a God of intellect" was more acceptable to man in the second act than the "God of the senses" in the first act, so an "ecological God," a God synonymous with nature, may well be more acceptable to man in the third act. This does not imply that God changes, but merely that man's concept of God changes.

Soviet philosophers, searching for a spiritual basis for communism, are looking beyond Marx to Spinoza. Spinoza, they say, was a realist who persistently sought a material basis for the existence of God. His very great role in the history of religion may be

> that having created a profoundly thought-out materialist philosophy he anticipated with genius and formulated with brilliance a whole series of dialectical propositions which found their development in Hegel, and subsequently in those of the great founders of scientific communism . . . He was the first in the

history of science to provide a fully developed philosophical basis for atheism.[8]

Thus Western Christianity and Eastern communism are united in the veneration of a Jewish pantheistic philosopher, whom the former call "God-intoxicated" and the latter "atheist-inspired." Spinoza, instead of Marx, may yet become the messiah of the communists in the third act, and Soviet philosophers may become the new priesthood of communism in the way the rabbis became the "priesthood of" Talmudism.

Jews and God in Fascist Germany

It was in Germany, however, that the most portentous events since the invasion of the Huns took place. In 1933, the Germans abolished the Weimar Republic founded after the flight of the Kaiser, and established the Third Reich under Adolf Hitler. The Junkers, generals, and industrialists, who hated the Republic and longed for an authoritarian regime, mistook Hitler for a fool they could use for their own ends. Hitler's success story is the saga of this underestimation. In the end, it was not they who used Hitler but Hitler who used them in a swift rise to power that carried him from an obscure corporal in 1918 to absolute dictator in 1933. He rose on an orgy of manic oratory, a torrent of erotic hatred, and a tide of quenchless greed. His political gospel was as simple as it was potent—destroy communism, hate the Jews, covet the wealth of your neighbors. Seizing the rule of Germany in a coup d'état, he abolished local autonomy, suppressed all political parties, disenfranchised the Jews, and ushered in a total-

---

[8]As quoted in *Spinoza in Soviet Philosophy* by George L. Kline, p. 42. I. K. Luppol, in an essay entitled "The Significance of Spinoza's Philosophy" in that same book, states: "To say that Marxism is a variety of Spinozism would be quite incorrect. But it is precisely in dialectical materialism that Spinoza's materialism has found its historical and logical fulfillment" (p. 176).

itarian state of mind the infamy of which the world had never before seen. Germany became a force-fed culture. For the Jews, the rise of Hitler was to spell the end of their thousand-year civilization in Europe.

It is difficult for history to take this sallow-faced, black-haired apostle of "blond Aryans" seriously—the lock of hair theatrically pasted on his forehead, the Charlie Chaplin moustache hanging under his nose, the cocksure ignorance, the incredible vulgarity. Yet this modern scourge of God, who murdered his way into history from the gutters of Vienna, cannot be casually dismissed.

Wherein did Hitler's hold on the German people lie? All his ideas—his anti-Semitic tirades, his community of blood theory, his Aryan racial superiority myth, his concept of history as a sexual orgy—all were but secondary elaborations of racist pornography scribbled on the walls of Europe's *pissoirs* for decades before his arrival. Hitler's genius stemmed not from the originality of his ideas but from his uncanny ability to transform forbidden fantasies of sadism and murder into acceptable forms of statesmanship. To carry out his policies he surrounded himself with a coterie of drug addicts like Goering, pederasts like Roehm, sadists, fetishists, and murderers like Heydrich, Frank, and Himmler who, under the cloak of legality, substituted a code of degeneracy for Decalogue and Gospel. Did Germany, like Faust, perceive the cloven hoof of the devil when he laid his hand upon her? Did she willingly follow this mendicant of death into a war with the world? History has already rendered its verdict. She did.

The road to World War II began inconspicuously in 1936 with Germany's remilitarization of the Rhineland. In swift succession followed her intervention in the Spanish Civil War, annexation of Austria, partition of Czechoslovakia, and invasion of Poland—the straw that broke the back of Europe's frail peace.

In the Western view, Communist Russia was the villain who unleashed World War II. Desirous of seeing the West destroyed by Hitler, so the argument goes, Stalin made a secret pact with Hitler whereby Russia and Germany would jointly invade and partition Poland, and thus induce

Hitler to turn West. As proof for this view, the West cites the undeniable fact that after the partition of Poland, Germany did unleash her war machine on the West, devour Denmark and Norway, swallow Belgium and The Netherlands, and invade France.

The Russians, in turn, blame the West, using the same ex post facto argument, only in reverse. World War II had its origin, the Russian theory goes, with the desire of the West to see Germany turn East to destroy Communist Russia. The Western powers did not interfere with Germany's intervention in the Spanish Civil War, and happily watched Germany annex Austria because this moved German divisions that much closer to Russian soil. Furthermore, Poland, with the connivance of the West, refused to permit Russia to cross her frontiers to aid Czechoslovakia, which was betrayed by the West to allow the Nazis to move still closer to Russia's borders. Her pact with Germany on the partition of Poland was an act of self-defense, Russia contends, an effort to put more miles between herself and Germany.

Perhaps both arguments contain more than a grain of truth, for both sides did secretly wish the annihilation of the other, each feeling that it would be able afterward to make itself master of Europe. However, just as the German Junkers and generals had underestimated Hitler, so Russia and the Western powers also underestimated him. In the end, it was Hitler who outmaneuvered them. Both became involved in a war they had not desired because Hitler was intent on dominating not only the European continent but the world. And he almost succeeded.

As part of his plan to conquer Europe, Hitler now set out to implement two of his favorite fantasies into reality. One was to murder all Jews. The other was to exterminate an unneeded portion of the populations of those conquered nations slated to serve as slaves to the German masters after the war.

The world has witnessed innumerable mass killings, but none has sent as deep a shudder of revulsion throughout civilization as did Hitler's introduction of genocide, the wholesale extermination of peoples. Within four years (1941–1945), the Nazis murdered twelve million civilians

—seven million Christians and five million Jews—as a calculated policy of state. In no other country, in no other age except that of the Third Reich, do we find an educated elite drafting blueprints for the mass murder of women and children at the lowest possible unit cost, technological experts working on the logistics of transporting human beings to specially constructed extermination camps, and a supervisory corps training people for mass murder at union wages. In no other culture except that of Nazi Germany have efficiency experts sat down to devise means for the most economic use of the by-products of the dead. Even as the Germans shouted "Hate the Jews," they slept on mattresses stuffed with hair shaved from the heads of mutilated corpses, ate tomatoes fertilized with the ashes of burned cadavers, washed their bodies with soap made of the fatty acids of boiled bodies, and stood in queues outside government outlet stores to buy eyeglasses, shoes, and clothing once worn by the slain.

Many have asked, Where was God during Auschwitz, the most notorious of German death camps? There is no answer to this, since it is not the question. The question is, Where was man? Auschwitz has not merely left a mark of Cain on the German people but a blot of shame on the escutcheon of man. Perhaps not the Jews, but Christianity, died at Auschwitz.

Historians are puzzled by the fact that even as German soldiers died on Russia's winter fronts, the trains needed to supply them with clothes, rations, and weapons were diverted to haul Jews from conquered provinces to concentration camps. The simple fact is that it was more important for the Nazis to have one last fling at murdering Jews before losing the war than help Germany survive. To send uniforms, food, and arms to the front in a lost cause at the expense of giving up their privileges was as irrational to the Nazi mind as taking the opposite course would seem to the rational mind.

We must not forget that these concentration camps were not just murder institutions but a paradise for scatological sadists. Whereas the Romans crucified Christians for sedition, and the Christians burned heretics to save their souls, the Nazis killed for pleasure. The Nazi state gave medals to their votaries who, as they sent naked children into gas chambers, masturbated excitedly while watching through peepholes the agonizing deaths of children being asphyxiated with potassium cyanide fumes.[9] Even when the end of the war seemed inevitable, the paramount question to the Nazi bureaucracy was how to keep its "de Sade show" going in order to extract every last bit of pleasure in the short time available. Even as the Wehrmacht fled under the impact of Allied blows, concentration camp furnaces belched smoke sickly scented with burnt flesh[10] into God's blue sky, and the paid functionaries of pain worked at their jobs until the very day enemy troops arrived before they fled.

But whereas the Germans murdered Jews out of fear of their intellectual superiority, they exterminated Poles, Russians, Ukrainians, Lithuanians, and other Slavs (whom they regarded as subhuman) for their presumed intellectual inferiority. And the Christian world was so hypnotized by the Nazi cry of "Kill the Jews" that it did not note the extermination of seven million Christian civilians deemed unworthy to live by the brown myrmidons of Hitler.

The amazing fact is that of all the millions enslaved and consigned to death by the Germans, only the Jews

[9]Rudolf Höss, commandant of Auschwitz, was a devoted peephole watcher who dressed himself in an immaculate uniform, carried white gloves, and clutched a horsewhip for his peeping engagements.
[10]Nellie Sachs, winner of the Nobel Prize for Literature in 1966, expressed it thus in her poem, "O The Chimneys":

> O the chimneys
> On the ingeniously devised habitations of death
> When Israel's body drifted as smoke
> Through the air—
> Was welcomed by a star, a chimney sweep,
> A star that turned black
> Or was it a ray of sun?
>
> O the chimneys!
> Freedomway for Jeremiah and Job's dust—
> Who devised you and laid stone upon stone
> The road for refugees of smoke?

fought back.[11] There is no record of Christian concentration camp inmates doomed to death by the Nazis ever fighting back. They supinely accepted their fate. The Jews, however, fought back throughout the ghettos of eastern Europe. Many thousands fought their way out of concentration camps to join underground movements, where an amazing transubstantiation took place. The moment a Jew joined an underground movement his Jewish identity vanished. He became a Christian statistic, always classified as a Greek, Russian, Frenchman—never as a Jew.

From August, 1939 to May, 1945, the time span of World War II in the European Theater of Operations, seventeen million soldiers and eighteen million civilians were killed, thirty million men were maimed, and much of the earth reduced to shambles, the price paid by the world to defeat Hitler. In the end, Hitler, like the Kaiser before him, betrayed the Germany he had professed to love. From his Berchtesgaden redoubt, as his people died like lice on the morally scrofulous body of Germany, he shouted, "I will not mourn the German people if they fail this test." And the German people failed the test of dying for him in his hour of need just as they had failed the Kaiser under similar circumstances at the end of World War I. Only this time the German *Herrenvolk* had no Jews to blame. Instead of heroically girding itself for a long siege, as Leningrad and Stalingrad had, Berlin capitulated to the Russians after a scant two weeks of resistance. In his basement bunker under the Reichschancellery, Adolf Hitler, the man all Germany had so jubilantly *heiled*, ignominiously shot himself through the mouth.

The supreme irony is that but for his anti-Semitism, Hitler might have won the war. The very people whom he expelled or murdered could have brought him victory, for among those who fled Europe because they were Jews, were Albert Einstein, Lise Meitner, Nils Bohr, and Edward Teller, the "fathers" of the atomic and hydrogen

---

[11]Such an authoritative work as the five-volume *Yad Vashem Studies on the European and Jewish Catastrophe and Resistance*, based on documentary evidence instead of speculation, has amply dispelled the popularly held belief that the Jews did not fight back.

bombs. And thus it was that the United States, the country that opened its doors to these refugees from Nazi hate, became the first nuclear power.

On the Western Front, the war came to an end with the Nazi whimper for mercy. On the Eastern Front it came to an end with the flash of the atomic bomb that melted the eyes of Japanese children watching the flight of a lone plane in the sky when it dropped its concentrated load of destruction on Hiroshima. Nature tottered and the moral foundations of Western civilization crumbled. The bang of the atomic bomb awakened the sleeping masses of Asia and Africa. China emerged in a communist uniform and cast off its feudal shackles. India shook off her torpor and flung her yoke in the face of Britain. Africa panicked into the twentieth century, crying for liberty and self-determination. The cycle of Europe's streak of luck had come to an end, and the WASP no longer ruled the world. Was World War II a Pyrrhic victory for the West? Some historians have discerned on the wall of Western civilization the same words of warning that appeared in the time of Daniel on the walls of Belshazzar's palace—*mene, mene, tekel, uparshin*—"God hath numbered thy kingdom and finished it" (Daniel 5:26–28).

For the Jews, World War II was a momentous turning point. In the first act, we saw them dispersed throughout one third of the world, encompassed by the Greco-Roman civilization. As the second act progressed, we saw them dispersed into a second third of the world—Europe and the American continents. With the destruction of European Jewry by Hitler, we see a third dispersion of the Jews. This time it is into the last third, the "uncommitted" part of the world, into Asia, Australia, Africa. The Jews now have Diaspora outposts in every continent, in strategic positions for acting out the third act of their manifest destiny.

But before we pursue the Jewish manifest destiny to its next phase, the Zionist Revolution, that will make true Luria's prediction of a return of the "exiled lights" to Zion, we must assess two modern ideological diseases that corroded the Western mind and afflicted Jewish history. One is the scourge of totalitarianism that replaced faith with terror. The other is the aberration of anti-Semitism that replaced the former goal of converting the Jew to Christianity with eliminating him from earth. An examination of the origin and nature of the totalitarian dictatorships and a dissection of the pretensions of racist anti-Semites will give us an understanding of the special relationship of these two political ideologies to Jewish destiny.

FROM ISAIAH TO HITLER

Isaiah

Messiah

JEWISH CONCEPT	CHRISTIAN CONCEPT
Brotherhood on Earth	Judgment Day in Heaven

←——— RESULTS ———→

Failure of Jewish messiah to appear a first time resulted in	Failure of Jesus to appear a second time resulted in
MESSIANIC PRETENDERS	CHILIASTIC PRETENDERS

FIRST CHALLENGE
Religious
Fanatics   (100–500 A.D.)

Sibylline
Oracles   (600–1000 A.D.)

SECOND CHALLENGE
More Religious
Fanatics   (200–700)

Tafurs   (1100–1300)

THIRD CHALLENGE
Political
Visionaries   (700–1200)

Flagellants   (1300–1400)

FOURTH CHALLENGE
Intellectual
Mystics   (1000–1500)

Amoral
Supermen   (1300–1600)

FIFTH CHALLENGE
Heretical
Deviationists (1500–1800)   Anabaptists (1600–1700)

Transformation of   Transformation of
Religious Messiahs   Religious Chiliasm
to Political Nation-   to Political Rationalists resulted   alism resulted
in   (1800–1900)   in   (1700–1800)

Jewish Emancipators—   French Rationalists—
            Reformers   *Philosophes*

The Humanist Revolution—   The French Revolution—
            Haskala   The Terror

SIXTH CHALLENGE
Millennarian   Totalitarian
Visionaries (1800–2000)   Visionaries (1800–2000)

Zionist—Secular Messiahs   Communism   Fascism

                             Class   Racism
State of Israel   Struggle
                                          Anti-
                             Anti-Judaism Semitism

From Isaiah to Hitler

Why have the totalitarians so persistently picked on the Jews as the central villain in their fantasies? Is this anti-Semitism an independent phenomenon, or is it a consequence of the unfolding of the Jewish manifest destiny? We contend that it is not an accident of history but represents the last milestone along an ideological road that meanders throughout Jewish history from the lofty concepts of Isaiah to the degenerate rantings of Hitler.

But how, may we ask, did the Jewish concept of a brotherhood of man, after coursing through twenty-five centuries of Jewish thought, get sidetracked into the dead end of German concentration camps? The evolution of this ideological trend from Isaiah to Hitler, as it relates to the origins of modern anti-Semitism, is not complex.

The Prophets were the first people on earth to conceive the idea of a messiah who through his very appearance would bring about instant social betterment. This messianic expectation traveled two roads through history. One was a Jewish road via the messiah as a messenger of God who would usher in the perfect state upon his first arrival. The other was a Christian road via the messiah as the son of God who would usher in a Judgment Day on his second appearance.

But as the first coming of the Jewish messiah did not materialize any more than did the second coming of the Christian redeemer, both Jews and Christians tried to hurry history by forcing events to fulfill their expectations. Just as Jews for centuries were assaulted by pretender messiahs, so Christians for centuries were gripped by chiliastic—to use the language of theology—expectations, that is, the expectation of a literal and immediate second arrival of Jesus as promised by the Gospels. But whereas Jewish pseudo-messiahs proclaimed they were sent by God to bring about the promised redemption of Jews, the Christian chiliasts announced they were God's elite, chosen to smooth a path for the return of Jesus. The chiliastic expectations evolved through four successive stages into a revolutionary social messianism, which in turn became dress rehearsals for the totalitarian movements of modern times.

The first of these four phases, the purely chiliastic one, was launched in the sixth century when a revised version of the Christian dogma of redemption swept Europe. This new concept was embodied in a series of writings now known as the Sibylline Oracles. The Christian Sibylline fantasy held that the world was divided between the forces of Christ and anti-Christ, and that a leader, an elect of God, would arise who would ruthlessly smite the forces of anti-Christ. This extermination of the wicked would create a vacuum of righteousness. Jesus would then be able to arrive in safety, and the Saints would rule the earth with justice and merriment. Thus the framework for future chiliastic speculations was set—the idea that the world was dominated by a demonic power of evil that had to be exterminated before the millennium could arrive. Within five centuries (1100–1600), four main chiliastic movements—the Tafurs, the Flagellants, the Amoral Supermen, and the Anabaptists—transformed the Sibylline fantasy from a messianic expectation into a social revolution.

The Tafurs were the vagabonds (from which came their name), the paupers, robbers, renegade monks, the scum on the skin of Europe, who converged like jackals on the trail of the Crusaders. They viewed the Crusades not as a war to wrest Jerusalem from Moslem and Jew, but as a holy mission to exterminate the Saracen "sons of whores" and the Jewish "spawn of Satan" who stood between them and the return of Jesus. Stained with the blood of Jewish and Christian victims in their paths, they eventually reached Syria and Palestine. Wielding clubs weighted with lead, hatchets, and hoes, they slaughtered the inhabitants of towns that fell into their hands with such unbelievable cruelty that mere pillage, arson, and rape seemed like acts of contrition. But because their deeds were held to usher in the millennium, the Tafurs became exalted in legend and their massacres deified into holy deeds.

After the Crusades, the purely religious fanaticism of the Tafurs was transferred into the social realm by a new chiliastic movement of self-immolating redeemers known as the Flagellants, who swept across Europe in the fourteenth century. Whereas the Tafurs had been sadists and rapists, the Flagellants were masochists and ascetics who substituted self-flagellation for sexual intercourse. Masses of boys, youths, and men, wearing white robes with a red cross, marched under flying banners. Led by a *Master*, the Flagellants would stop in front of a church, shed their uniforms, and then, clad only in loincloth, start flogging themselves with leather scourges, mercilessly, hours on end. The theory that Christ would thus be moved to arrive with his promised paradise for the true believers.

There was a significant psychological difference between the Tafurs and the Flagellants. The Tafurs had aimed at converting the Jews, viewing only unconverted Jews as anti-Christ. The Flagellants demanded the extermination of all Jews as a prerequisite for the millennium to arrive. When the Flagellants entered Frankfort in 1349, elevating their fantasy into reality by murdering every Jew in that city, the Church placed them under the ban. After several Flagellants were beheaded or hanged by Church and prince, the movement evaporated. But it left an ominous stain on the social fabric of the century.

The sixteenth century was not only a "silken robe smeared with blood," but a coarse sheet spotted with semen. In that century surfaced the Amoral Supermen, the collective name history has given the hodgepodge of mystics and crackpots who ringed the pseudo-intellectual frontiers of Europe's burgeoning towns. Not only did these Amoral Supermen enlarge their arena of enemies by including the feudal prince along with clergy and Jews, but they also enriched chiliastic thought with their philosophy of sex and sadism. As with twentieth-century hippies, promiscuity became a revered ritual with the Amoral Supermen. As with the twentieth-century Nazis, the Amoral Supermen considered themselves above the law, and permitted themselves any act of brutality. Viewing themselves as the "sword of God," charged with cleansing the earth, they showed no reverence for the "establishment." They believed that a rebellion against it would allow history of its own volition to usher in their undefined concept of a perfect state.

As long as the Amoral Supermen did not deviate from dogma, the Church was lenient with them. But when chiliastic voices began to blend with the voices of heresy in the Anabaptist movement of the seventeenth century, the Church took alarm. But by then it was too late. As with the Tafurs, Flagellants, and Amoral Supermen, so Anabaptist chiliasm was also based on the fantasy that only the total extermination of all who did not believe in their cause would immediately cure all social and economic ills. However, to this dogma the Anabaptists added some "communistic" overtones.

The Anabaptists (from the German *Wiederteufer*, "again-baptized," because they believed in a second baptism at maturity) knew the exact time Christ would arrive. On that day, all the ungodly would be annihilated by the "Sword of Christ," and the Anabaptists would rule co-equally with Jesus. Meanwhile, they congregated in communities, sharing wealth and sex, though their leaders enjoyed a larger measure of both. With one of these leaders and founders of the Anabaptist movement, Thomas Münzer (1489–1525), chiliastic expectations were merged with a class war. Extraordinarily learned, intensely intellectual, Münzer started out in life as a preacher and at first joined Luther's heresy. But envisioning himself a leader of a new "Elect," he forsook the Protestant cause to help found Anabaptism. He joined the German Peasants' War (1524–1525), which he thought to exploit for his own purposes.

The villain in the Peasants' War against the nobles was the printing press. The Old and New Testaments, hitherto unavailable to the masses, but now available in print, became true revelation for the first time to most Christians. They learned to their amazement that the Prophets had not merely predicted the coming of a messiah but had also pleaded for social justice. They learned that Jesus had not died on the cross merely to redeem Christians but that in life he had also sided with the poor. The Bible became the social manifesto of the peasants of the seventeenth century who now dreamt of a utopia where the poor might actually share in the bounties of this world instead of waiting for the hereafter.

These yearnings of the peasants for a better life exploded in revolt. But whereas the leaders of this revolt tried to direct it against the oppressive nobility, Münzer's bands of Anabaptists looted, burned, and murdered indiscriminately, to pave a path for the savior. The "godless," claimed Münzer, had no right to live, save by whatever grace was given them by his Anabaptists. This was a direct threat to the Church, and the Anabaptists were put under the ban and hunted like animals. The Peasants' War was put down with a severity that won Luther's approval. The Anabaptists were placed on the rack, roasted on pillars, drawn asunder, or torn with red-hot pincers. Münzer, too, was captured, properly tortured, and beheaded.[1]

With the victory of the Reformation, chiliasm as a religious vocation died. But the core of its doctrine of instant social betterment was taken up by other unexpected voices that ushered in the second stage of the chiliastic evolution, the philosophic. After the Anabaptists, a new set of social prophets, the rationalists, transferred the chiliastic one-cause one-cure explanation of social ills from the religious to the political sphere.

With the eighteenth century, with the massive intellectual barrage of the writings of Montesquieu, Voltaire, Rousseau, and Diderot, the *philosophes* launched the Age of Reason. Reason is a better guide to utopia than faith, said the rationalists. Man himself can construct a better paradise than Christ. Abolish the wicked priesthood, they ad-

---

[1] The present Baptist sects are derivatives of the Anabaptists who have shed their political utopian views for strictly religious visions.

vised, elevate Reason to the throne of God, and human nature will change from evil to good. Man will then create the perfect state because logic will guide him to better solutions than God had.

The French revolutionaries replaced religious ethic with a social ethic, and religious morality with a social morality. Virtue was made synonymous with conformity to the new society. Surely, nobody would be unreasonable enough to question logic. But alas, it did not work out that way. The result was not unity but schism. People refused to be "reasonable," and saw no virtue in blindly accepting someone else's concept of perfection. Reason, it seemed, was as hydra-headed as Faith had been.

The rationalist revolutionaries were in a dilemma. Two diametrically opposite views—that of the liberals and totalitarians—divided their ranks. Should or should not force be used for the good of man? The liberal democrats flinched at the idea of using force and suggested a method of trial and error. With time, they argued, perfection would arise, because man would discard faulty reasoning for better reasoning. The "totalitarian democrats," on the other hand, felt that their ideas for a perfect state justified a little force now to realize a greater good later.

Thus, by the end of the eighteenth century, when society failed to produce the promised perfect state, the French revolutionaries added a postscript of force to the rationalist formula of goodwill. The wicked nobles, who stood in the way of progress and would not yield to reason, would have to be eliminated by force to permit the ideas of the rationalists to work. And thus came about the Terror of the French Revolution—"the tyranny of the just to rule the unjust." In all sincerity, the French revolutionaries carted nobles to the guillotine to help usher in happiness faster, much as the Inquisition had carted heretics to the *autos-da-fé* to hasten the arrival of salvation. Thus Reason led to more bloodshed than Faith had in previous centuries.

In spite of the blood shed by the French Terror, however, the millennium was still delayed, and the rationalists were hard-pressed for an explanation. Into the breach stepped a new "secular messiah," a baptized Jew named Karl Marx (1818–1883), who offered a socialist explanation for the delay in the arrival of the rationalist millennium. With Marx, the chiliastic prescription for all social ills entered its third phase, that of economics.

When Karl Marx was six years old, his father dragged him to a baptismal font to be pronounced a Protestant. The baptism did not take. He renounced his conferred Christianity for the communism he was to invent. At the age of twenty-four, he married the beautiful Jenny von Westphalen, daughter of an aristocratic, wealthy, feudal German family. Their marriage was a love affair that lasted through a stormy life of exile and poverty, defamation and fame, until his death in London.

Though born to wealth, young Marx rebelled against the social inequities he saw around him. But instead of writing novels about man's inhumanity to man, as did his contemporary Charles Dickens, Karl Marx, throughout a long life of exile, poverty, and defamation, wrote economic manifestos that shook the world and converted one billion people to the creed of socialism within a century.

Just as Jews have villified the teachings of Jesus because the Church has corrupted much of what he originally said, so the West has villified the works of Marx because the communists have corrupted most of his doctrines. Karl Marx was basically an idealist concerned with the material welfare of man in the way Jesus was an idealist totally concerned with the spiritual welfare of man.

Whereas the German philosopher Hegel dealt with the philosophy of culture, Marx dealt with the culture of economics. It is not ideology that shapes our material world, he argued, but the material condition that gives rise to our ideologies. The way a society produces and sells its goods also determines what kind of society, religion, and culture it will have. The perfect state failed to arrive in the wake of the French Revolution, explained Marx, because of a cultural drag exerted by the institutions of the past. The villain was not the individual, who was only a by-product of his society, but the economic system that had produced his society. If the capitalist system (based on production by the individual for profit) were deposed and a socialist system (based on production by the state for need) were instituted, said Marx, then the social paradise on earth would be achieved.

Just as Christ's religious gospel of a humanistic brotherhood was seized by the pagans of Europe and propagated as Christianity, so Marx's socialist gospel of humanistic economics was seized by the Slavs of Russia and propagated as Leninism. The Leninist communists were the new "secular chiliasts," with a new prescription for the perfect state. The philosophy of Terror of the French Revolution, they argued, had been correct but misapplied. What was needed was a combination of "Terror" that would exterminate the capitalists, and "surgery" that would remove all capitalist institutions. Thus there would be no capitalists and no cultural drag to prevent the "entry" of the perfect socialist state.

Though the communists could create "history," they could not control it. The communist combination of "Terror and surgery" begot a counterreaction from the capitalist countries, which saw their entire profit system threatened. Their answer to this communist millennium was a countermillennium of their own—fascism, the fourth and last stage in this macabre evolution. Fascism represented capitalist economics without democracy. The concept of racial purity was substituted for religious purity as the one-cause one-cure ingredient in its prescription for social welfare.

We can now perceive the underlying unity between chiliastic and totalitarian thought, for the chiliastic mind is closer to that of the modern dictator than to that of the ancient tyrant. Though a tyrant is ruthless, he generally does not kill if he is not opposed in his arbitrary rule; he is mainly concerned with maintaining his own power and the system of privileges it entails. The dictator, on the other hand, kills in the name of an ideology because he conceives of himself as the harbinger of the perfect state. He kills anyone he thinks will not fit the Procrustean[2]

---

[2]In Greek mythology, Procrustes was an innkeeper who had a bed which any lodger using it had to fit. If the traveler was too tall, his legs were sawed off to the proper length; if too short, he was stretched on a rack to fit it.

blueprint of his state. Those whose ideas extend beyond the blueprint must be chopped down to fit; those who fall short of its ideology must be stretched to size. Thus, in both the chiliastic and totalitarian regimes, people are doomed to death not only for active opposition but for not fitting the framework of an ideology.

The parallels between chiliastic and totalitarian thought can now be brought into sharper focus. In the chiliastic fantasy, the true believers are the self-elected Saints of God; the enemy is the forces of anti-Christ which, if exterminated, would usher in the Christian paradise. In the communist fantasy, the true believers are the self-elected members of the proletariat; the enemy is the capitalist class, whose elimination would herald the arrival of the bolshevik paradise. In the Nazi fantasy, the true believers are the self-elected members of the German race; the enemy is the Jewish people, whose destruction would signal the start of the Aryan paradise.

The "True Believer," then, can be for good or for evil. He can be a follower of a Jesus or a Rousseau or he can be the follower of a Stalin or a Hitler. What unites them is the conviction that only their idea for saving the world is correct, and that killing in the name of their ideologies is not murder but a *mitzvah*—a righteous deed. Thus, though methods have changed, the underlying motivations for the massacres by the Tafurs in the name of Christ and by the French revolutionaries in the name of Rousseau are the same as the extermination policies of the totalitarians in the name of their patron intellectuals.

The totalitarians, however, in order not to go down in history as murdering Huns, create a defense for their extermination policies. Far from being lawless, they claim, they are more lawful than constitutional governments which derive their laws only from their people, whereas they derive their laws from a higher source. Communists claim that the "class struggle" is an immutable law of history and cite Marx to prove that the evolution of society toward communism is an inevitable historical movement. The Nazis claimed that race supremacy follows the laws of nature, and cited Darwin to prove the inevitable survival of superior species over inferior. Therefore, mass exterminations of capitalists as a "dying class" or of Slavs as an "inferior race" hasten the fulfillment of those laws, the totalitarians claim. If they do not kill off those doomed by these "inevitable" laws, history and nature will, more slowly perhaps, but just as inevitably. In a gruesome way, this totalitarian reasoning parallels that of the early Church, which claimed it derived a higher authority over men from God. Just as the totalitarians take life in the name of history, so the early Church took life in the name of Christ.

There is another parallel between the medieval Church and the totalitarian state. In the Church, man feared the wrath of God and His hell; in totalitarianism, man fears the wrath of the Party and its Terror. Just as hell served the Church as a "concentration camp" to keep religious sinners from clogging the paths to heaven for the righteous, so the Terror serves the Party to keep political sinners from obstructing the path of "history." The Terror, by eliminating all opposition, creates a vacuum into which history can race more effectively toward its "inevitable destiny." Thus notions of guilt and innocence have no meaning for the totalitarians. Just as the Tafurs, Flagellants, Amoral Supermen, and Anabaptists did not see themselves as murderers but merely as agents carrying out the will of God, so totalitarians do not see themselves as executioners but as judges carrying out the will of history.

In one aspect, however, the communist ideology is closer to that of the Church than that of the Nazi. Just as the heretic in the Feudal Age could through contriteness be redefined as a true Christian and thus be reinstated into the grace of the Church, so the communist deviationist can through confession of error be reinstated in the grace of the Party. In Nazism, however, once one had been declared guilty of belonging to an "inferior race" there was no grace, no redemption. No act of contrition or confession could raise him to the grace of superior status. Only death could atone for the "sin" of having been born in the wrong classification.

Thus it came about that the Jews, liberated from the ghetto, were propelled from the frying pan of feudal anti-Jewishness into the fire of Nazi anti-Semitism. Having reached an intellectual summit in the Golden Age of medieval Spain, the Jew encountered the phenomenon of *limpieza de sangre* and was expelled. Having reached an intellectual Golden Age in modern western Europe, the Jew encountered the phenomenon of racism and was murdered. The Age of Reason proved more deadly for the Jews than the Age of Faith. Whereas *faith* had pleaded and held out grace, *reason* murdered and denied hope.

We have now come full circle—from the chiliasts to the totalitarians, the "one-cause one-remedy" road to Nirvana. For just as Jesus, preaching a Judgment Day, begot the Church with its anti-Jewishness, so the chiliasts, predicting the arrival of Christ's Day, begot the totalitarian state with its anti-Semitism. Though the world has been aware of the Jews for almost 4,000 years, anti-Semitism was unknown in Jewish history for the first 3,800 years, until it replaced the anti-Jewishness of the Middle Ages in the nineteenth century. The word "anti-Semitism" was first coined in 1879, in Germany.

Anti-Jewishness must not be confused with anti-Semitism, for they differ from each other as fear differs from anxiety and hate differs from prejudice. Whereas fear and hate are rational, anxiety and prejudice are irrational. If we saw a man freeze with terror while crossing a street, and then beheld a rabid dog lunge at him, we would understand his terror and ascribe it to fear, a rational consequence to an external threat. If, on the other hand, we saw that man paralyzed by terror but saw no dog, and learned that his terror was caused by a feeling that if he crossed the street his mother would drop dead, we would ascribe his terror to anxiety, caused by an irrational, internal conflict. Hate, too, is the result of an external threat, whereas prejudice is the result of an internal conflict having no relation to reality. The French hatred of the Germans in 1870, for example, was a result of their humiliating defeat at the hands of Germany. The attitude of some white people against black people, on the other hand, stems not from such an objective hate, for it is not the black man who has dealt grievously with the white man, but vice versa. The white man's actions stem from prejudice, from internal, irrational feelings and attitudes.

Jews were feared and hated prior to 1800. The ancient Greeks vented their spleen on the Jews because the Jews challenged all of their basic assumptions and were contemptuous of Greek customs and morality. Roman reprisals against the Jews stemmed not from prejudice but from apprehension, for the Jews had thrice rebelled against the empire and the punishment they were meted was no different from that given other rebellious peoples. Islamic legislation against Jews differed in no way from legislation against other "infidels." Feudal man was opposed to Judaism as a competitor to Christianity, not to the Jews. Though the Jew in the Middle Ages was discriminated against, as were all non-Christian elements in its midst, he became an honored citizen the moment he converted.

The anti-Semite, however, who appeared after 1800, after the overthrow of God by the rationalists, does not care whether or not the Jew converts to Christianity. He not only fears the Jew but the syndrome of ideas that has become synonymous with Jews. So fearful is the anti-Semite of this syndrome of Jewishness that he believes the Jew must be killed in order to rid the world of the ideas the Jew carries in his mind.

Has the Jewish manifest destiny become a world obsession, totally out of proportion to the small number of Jews? Is there a syndrome of Jewishness? And if so, what is there in such a syndrome that inspires anxieties in the totalitarian mind so awesome that they can be quelled only by the death of all Jews? Is there something in this syndrome of Jewishness that is compatible with the democratic ideal but antithetical to totalitarianism?

History has indeed developed a prototype of Jewishness which like a magnet both attracts and repels. Under the impact of the training program hammered out by God, Prophets, and zealots in the first act, and under the impact of their sojourn in six civilizations in their second, has emerged the image of a universal, cosmopolitan Jew with four recognizable traits shaped by his ideologies. It is the concepts embodied by this symbolic Jew that are either accepted or rejected.

The first characteristic is that Jews are iconoclasts. Iconoclasm is an old Jewish profession, going all the way back to Abraham, who undermined the pagan world when he smashed its idols. This smashing of idols continued with Moses, with the Prophets, with Jesus. It continued with the Tannas, the Amoras, and the Gaons, whose former "heresies" have by now been sicklied over with acceptance. Gershom, Maimonides, and Spinoza jarred the medieval world with their iconoclastic thought as much as Marx, Freud, and Einstein jarred the modern world with theirs. The Jews will not worship idols, be they religious, secular, or scientific.

A consequence of this first characteristic is a second one, that of the Jews as skeptics who never accept the say-so of anyone, not even God. The right to question God and to hold him accountable was canonized in the Old Testament with the Book of Job.

A third, acknowledged characteristic of the Jews is that they are a people of law. They are a people born with a pontificating finger, moral busybodies who are forever telling the world what is right and what is wrong. Ever since the days of Moses, the Jews have been swinging the club of morality and shouting: Thou shalt not force thy daughter into harlotry, thou shalt not commit sodomy, thou shalt not murder, steal, commit perjury. They derided the pagan fun of sodomy, naming it bestiality. They denounced as murder the Greek custom of killing unsightly children in the name of aesthetics. They debunked the custom of holy prostitution, labeling it immorality. They rejected the idea of divine rights of kings and the idea of legalized torture. They formulated the world's first laws against illegal search, and were the first to give the accused the right to confront his accusers. Holding their Ten Commandments aloft like a banner, Jews have marched through the centuries as though they were conquerors, not the conquered.

Finally, Jews have always supported education and general welfare. Scholarship and philanthropy have always been recognized by non-Jews as essentially Jewish qualities. Throughout the ages, Jews have tended to enter those professions and arts that preserved and healed, doctors who alleviated suffering, lawyers who prevented miscarriage of justice, financiers who supported cultural institutions, humanists who spoke for the rights of man.

Viewed collectively, the Jewish ethic is the guardian of humanity, the highest law in the universe. But as the Prophets foresaw with such great prescience, mankind must accept these ideas by itself; they cannot be rammed into one's mind by torture or force. This is why the world has never been able to ignore Judaism, why it has always had to accept or reject its ideas without compromise. Those who have accepted these ideas have tended toward democracy; those who have rejected them have, in the main, drifted toward totalitarianism.

Thus viewed, Judaism places anti-Semitism in a new perspective. Just as Freud showed that the seeming irrationality of insanity was dictated by rational, though unconscious forces, so the seeming irrationality of anti-Semitism has a rationale all its own, also dictated by unconscious forces. The reasons behind the seeming irrationality of anti-Semitism is that it caters to those unconscious instincts which civilization tries to repress, instincts to which the Jewish ethic has declared itself an enemy.

We can now understand the hatred of the Jews by people with totalitarian tendencies. Jew and anti-Semite have become symbols in a great morality play, the "good guys" versus the "bad guys." The Jew stands for the repression of that which is base in man, and the anti-Semite stands for the freedom of man's unconscious drives, aberrations, perversions. In religious terms, it is an acting out of the age-old conflict between good and evil, the struggle between God and Satan. As a psychological drama, it is a conflict of the conscious versus the unconscious, the ego versus the id. It is an Armageddon where the representatives of evil have unerringly centered their hatred on the Jew precisely because he is in the forefront of the battle against evil. The *Götterdämmerung* in the third act will not be between capitalists and communists, or between whites and blacks, but between humanistic universalists versus racist tribalists, between the Judaic ethic versus the Nietzschean Superman.

The Jews have rightfully earned the hatred of totalitarian pimps, sadists, and murderers who rally round any flag that symbolizes the basest in man, while the Jewish ethic rallies round the flag that symbolizes what is noblest in man. Anti-Semitism is not a political movement but a counterrevolution to annul the march of civilization, a last stand of "jungle man" against "culture man." If such ethical ecumenism is the crime anti-Semites accuse the Jews of committing, then the Jews must plead guilty and like Luther exclaim, "Here I stand, I cannot do otherwise."

The march of the Christian chiliasts from the Sibyllines to Münzer uncannily parallels the march of the Jewish pretender messiahs from Theudas to Sabbatai, not only in chronology but in their singularity of purpose. In each century, no matter how varied their fantasies, all chiliasts had one common goal, that of reuniting the Christian with Jesus. So, too, in each challenge, the Jewish messianic pretenders—comic, tragic, pathetic—were also dedicated to one goal, that of reuniting the Jew with Zion. If Jewish history is to continue this eschatological parallel with Christian history, we should expect no religious messiahs in the sixth challenge, but only secular ones. This surmise is correct. Just as the works of the rationalist in the eighteenth century rendered obsolete the religious expectations of the chiliasts, so the works of the Maskils in the nineteenth century rendered obsolete the religious expectations of the pretender messiahs.

Where are our pretender messiahs who hitherto have so enlivened Jewish history with foible and faith? In this sixth challenge so far, we have traversed Jewish history from the fall of the ghetto to the rise of the concentration camp without beholding a single one. Yet they have been there all along, not behind the scenes this time but in the midst of history, disguised. To recognize them in their disguise we must remove the layers of deceptive semantics that hide their true identity. Then we shall behold our old pretender messiahs, no longer wrapped in the folds of faith but draped in the mantle of a new nationalism known as Zionism. Just as the Enlightenment metamorphosed the chiliasts into revolutionary rationalists, so the Haskala metamorphosed the pretender messiahs into revolutionary Zionists.

With the Modern Age, a totally new challenge demanding a totally new response, was hurled at the Jews. The Zionists were the first to recognize that ben Zakkai's response of political surrender at the beginning of Act I was no longer effective. The totalitarians of the Modern Age did not demand the mere political vassalage of the Jews, as did the kings of the feudal times, but their total extermination. Jewish history is now about to reverse itself. The first-century Diaspora designers had yanked the sword from the side of the Masada "man of war," and transformed him into the Jabneh "prince of peace." The twentieth-century Zionists would snatch the olive branch from the hands of this "prince of peace," place a gun on his shoulders, and retransform him into another "man of war."

In spite of their modern dress, however, the Zionists are united in spirit with the messianists through their common aim of reuniting the Jew with Zion. Untrammeled by layers of Diaspora Talmudism, they are destined to achieve the improbable, to lead the Jews back to their ancient homeland after a 2000-year absence. What the messianic pretenders had not been able to achieve, the Zionist revolutionaries will bring about.

The Zionist Revolution

In 1900, after twenty centuries of war, hate, and neglect, Palestine was a barren patch of desert, an unimportant *vilayet* in the vast Ottoman Empire. Five decades later, she was the independent state of Israel, a modern agricultural and industrial nation. In 1900, her 45,000 square miles of soil could barely support 350,000 people—nomadic Bedouins ravaging the countryside, poverty-stricken fellahin living in mud huts, ignorant Hasids come to die in the Holy Land, and predatory Turkish bureaucrats squeezing the last *paras* out of a diseased, starved, and oppressed population. Five decades later, though shrunk through successive partitions to one fifth her former size, she supported over 2,000,000 people. She was the only country born in the aftermath of World War II which, without enslaving other nations, without exploiting a segment of her own population, or without tying her fate to an outside power, succeeded in securing a standard of life, liberty, and law on a par with that of the most advanced Western nation.

How was all this achieved in such a short time, in less than the life span of one generation? How could this small country, ravaged, denuded, and despoiled for 2,000 years by Romans, Byzantines, Sassanids, Arabs, Crusaders, Mamelukes, Turks, and Englishmen, have hoisted herself from serfdom to independence, from beggary to affluence, from cultural poverty to intellectual eminence in five short decades? How was she able to absorb two million Diaspora Jews and create an economic framework to sustain them with groceries and democracy? Where did the capital come from to pay for the industrial plants, for the high standard of living, for her cultural activities? And most incredibly, how was she able to rally Jews round the world to return to their point of origin after a 2000-year absence, to wrest independence from the British, to defeat invading Arab armies, and to continue to defend that independence against all odds in history?

For the task of delivering a new state of Israel, history chose a most unlikely cluster of Jews—disenchanted Talmudists, alienated intellectuals, humanistic agnostics. Imbued with the spirit of a secular messianism known as Zionism, they swept the Jews on a tide of victory across two millennia of statelessness into statehood. What was the nature of this movement that stirred the Jews to the roots of their past?

In *The Rebel*, Albert Camus distinguishes between two forms of rebellion. One is "revolt," which aims at changing a personal relationship between man and man. The other is "revolution," which aims at changing an impersonal relationship between man and society. In a revolt, one man supplants another. In a revolution, one ideology is made to supplant another. The Spartacus rebellion against Rome in the first century B.C. was a "revolt," because it aimed not at overthrowing Roman institutions but merely at ending a relationship between slave and master. The frequent strife between medieval kings and popes were also "revolts," because neither side wished to overthrow feudal institutions but merely to subordinate one contender for power to the other. The American, French, and Russian revolutions, however, were "revolutions," because the Americans eradicated a hereditary monarchy, replacing it with an elective presidency, the French overthrew the ancien régime, substituting for it the bourgeois state, and the Russians drowned in blood an absolute feudal monarchy, exchanging it for an absolute communist dictatorship.

Within this definition, Zionism too was a revolution, for it not only aimed at ousting the British from Palestinian soil but also at substituting Western democracy for Eastern feudalism. Zionism, however, differed in one unique aspect from all other revolutions. The American, French, and Russian revolutions were brought about by Americans, Frenchmen, and Russians who lived and fought in their own respective countries. This was not the case with Zionism. The Jews who precipitated the Zionist Revolution did not live exclusively in Palestine, where the revolution was fought. Most lived in the Diaspora. The Zionist Revolution, therefore, is unique in that its component parts were constructed outside and then assembled in Palestine.

Who were these Zionists who achieved this unique task? If we sand off the patina rubbed over them by their acolytes, we shall discover that they were but a modern version of the dissenters we have seen marching alongside Jewish history ever since the days of Jesus. This time, however, they are not pseudo-messiahs come to establish the Kingdom of God, but secular revolutionaries come to establish a homeland for the Jews.

Historically, the early Zionists were a by-product of both Jewish messianism and French rationalism. The nineteenth-century Jewish intellectuals who so deeply etched Zionist ideology into twentieth-century Jewish consciousness were men who had taken the promises of the Enlightenment at face value. They were emancipated Jews who had forsaken not only ghetto and orthodoxy but most of their Judaism in order to join the world citizenship of Western civilization proffered them by the rationalists. They were convinced that this rational, egalitarian, intellectual world preached by the *philosophes* had overthrown the "tyranny" of prince, priest, and pope, and would open the doors of world society to them. They were convinced that, like any Gentile, they would now enter the paradise of this rationalist civilization in direct proportion to their wealth, intellect, and culture. Here, in this secular paradise, they were convinced that they would be able to retain their new moderate Jewishness like moderate Catholics, Episcopalians, Lutherans, Unitarians, or any other religious sect.

Alas, their image of rationalism was a mirage. What they encountered was not the consequence of the image but the image of the consequence. Instead of finding the door to paradise open, they ran into the anti-Semitic keeper at that door, a doorman who refused to honor their credentials of intellect, wealth, and goodwill. Having rejected the *gefilte* fish milieu of the ghetto, and having been rejected by the *escargot bourguignon* society of the Gentiles, these Jewish intellectual foundlings of the Enlightenment became the modern Cains of the Western world. They became the *no v'nods,* the wanderers between Caro's *Prepared Table* and Rousseau's *Social Contract.*

Realizing they could neither enter the paradise of Western society nor return to the world of Jewish orthodoxy, they decided to open their own all-Jewish club, a secular Jewish state modeled after that from which they had been rejected. They would establish a Jewish national home where they could enjoy the elegant freedom of mind of the most advanced European democracies. To realize that goal, these disenchanted Jewish intellectual founders of Zionism returned not to the letter of Talmudic Judaism but to the spirit of biblical prophecy. They made Jewish history rival to revelation, and launched a Third Zionade. But whereas in the First and Second Zionades, in the fifth century B.C., the godly had led the ungodly back to Zion, in this one, 2,300 years later, the roles were reversed. The ungodly led the godly back to the Promised Land.

History does not always carefully select the men who carry out her dictates, but sometimes catapults the most unlikely personalities into undreamed-of roles, capriciously permitting them success. Just imagining these founders of modern Zionism would have made the gray hair of the makers of the Mishna stand on end. From an orthodox viewpoint, a more horrifying group of *apikorsim*—unbelievers—could hardly be found. There was Moses Hess (1812–1875), a renegade German Jew who, before hitting the Zionist road, turned to communism and married a French whore to show his contempt for Judaism. There was Russian-born Peretz Smolenskin (1842–1885), a truant from Talmud who, at age twelve, tossed his phylacteries out the window and, after living as a bum for a decade, showed up in Vienna for a secular education. There was Judah Pinsker (1821–1891), an overintellectualized Russian-Jewish army officer who preached integration, until he ran into anti-Semites who confused Judaism with Original Sin. And there was Theodor Herzl (1860–1904), the rich, handsome, black-bearded, superbly tailored Viennese "Moses" who, while on a fantasy trip to a baptismal font, found Judaism instead. Yet it was these four refugees from Judaism who mapped the first section of the road back to Zion. Each wrote a slender work whose searing words drove home the necessity for a homeland in Palestine.

Moses Hess, tauntingly called "the communist rabbi" by Karl Marx, could not submerge his Jewish humanism to communist materialism. He broke with the left-wing movement, returned to the periphery of Judaism and, with the insight his alienation from Judaism had given him, wrote his pioneering *Rome and Jerusalem.* In it he advocated a return to Palestine and the creation not only of a physical haven for Jews but also a spiritual center for Judaism. Peretz Smolenskin, in his *The Eternal People,* prophesied that Palestine once again would become a world center where the Jewish spirit could reassert itself, a nation whose humanistic values would one day become the values of the world. Judah Pinsker, in his pamphlet *Auto-Emancipation,* denounced his previous assimilationist stand and preached a return to territorial independence and the formation of a strong Jewish consciousness.

But to most Western nineteenth-century Jews, Hess, Smolenskin, and Pinsker were crackpot voices crying wolf in the night, for the anti-Semite at the door of Western society was as yet discernible only to the eye of the prophet. After all, these three cried out in a world where a Jew like Disraeli was Prime Minister of England, Sir Isaac Rufus was Viceroy of India, Guiseppi Ottolenghi Minister of War in Italy, Ferdinand LaSalle leader of the German Socialists, and Rothschild the greatest name in European banking. Not until the appearance of Theodor Herzl's *The Jewish State,* in 1896, did the message prick the Jews to the quick, for by then they too could see what the prophets of Zionism had seen. Thus anti-Semitism became the unwitting godfather to a new Jewish state.

Theodor Herzl, born of a half-assimilated Jewish family

in Budapest, was brought up in Vienna on a German culture enriched with a little Judaism. But even this haphazard, minimal Jewish education ended with his bar mitzvah at age thirteen. Admitted to the bar of Vienna, Herzl gave up law to become a feuilletonist on a Viennese newspaper. Rebuffed by anti-Semites, he often fancied having himself baptized, but never did. Sent to Paris to cover the trial of Captain Alfred Dreyfus, Herzl heard the ugly sound of "Death to the Jews" reverberating through the streets of Paris. He gave up all thoughts of baptism, returned to Judaism, and wrote *The Jewish State*, the "word" that shook the Jewish world.

In *The Jewish State*, Herzl created a new world out of a dream, substituting honor for indignity:

> The Jews who wish it, will have their own state. We shall live at last as free men on our own soil, die peacefully in our own homes. The world will be freed by our liberty, enriched by our wealth, magnified by our greatness.

These words sent shivers of pride through Jewish hearts. The dream had been boldly stated. Just as Rousseau's *Social Contract* helped incite the French Revolution, as Paine's *Common Sense* fueled the American Revolution, as Marx's *Das Kapital* ignited the Russian Revolution, so Herzl's *The Jewish State* sparked the Zionist Revolution.

His next, most important step took Zionism out of the realm of intellect into the world of politics. Like Napoleon convoking a Sanhedrin to clarify the Jewish relationship to the Gentile state, so Herzl convoked a World Zionist Congress to clarify the relationship of the Diaspora Jew to a Jewish state. In 1897, Zionist delegates—including several Christians—from the world at large met in Basel, Switzerland, to chart a course that would lead to reverberating events in the twentieth century. As Herzl walked slowly, majestically to the podium, a delegate shouted, "Long live the king!" For fifteen minutes the air was saturated with tumultuous applause from the 201 delegates dressed in full evening attire for the occasion. That evening, Herzl wrote in his diary: "In Basel I founded the Jewish state . . .

Maybe in five years, certainly in fifty, everybody will recognize it." He was wrong. It took fifty-one.

Zeal kept Herzl working beyond his strength, and in 1904 a heart attack took him to an early death. With his demise, the first stage of the Zionist Revolution ended and the second stage began.

But what was this second stage? An answer can best be stated by comparing the course of the Zionist Revolution to the course of the American, French, and Russian revolutions—revolutions that have completed their cycles from the womb of the mind to the tomb of history. With the aid of such hindsight, we note that before any of these revolutions could deliver their promised states each had to undergo an intellectual, a political, and an administrative phase.

In the first phase, the ideas of a quartet of English philosophers—Locke, Hobbes, Bacon, and Burke—inseminated the American Revolution. The ideas of a trio of French intellectuals—Rousseau, Voltaire, and Montesquieu—fomented the French Revolution. The duo of Marx and Engels intellectually instigated the Russian Revolution. Similarly, in its first phase, the Zionist Revolution was sparked by the ideas of the Jewish intellectual quartet—Hess, Smolenskin, Pinsker, and Herzl.

In the second phase, the ideas of the intellectuals slowly germinate in the minds of a new set of revolutionary experts, the politicals, who carry the ideological gospel to the people to motivate them to establish a new state, by force if necessary. And force always seems necessary, for no one ever seems willing to give up power voluntarily. In due course, revolutionary politicals in America, France, and Russia seized the ideas of the intellectuals and sired their respective revolutions—Adams, Jefferson, Hamilton, and Madison in America; Danton, Marat, and Robespierre in France; Lenin, Trotsky, and Stalin in Russia.

With the success of the political phase, the third set of experts, the administrators, swing into action, procuring the surplus capital necessary to pilot the new ship of state to a safe fiscal harbor. This third and final phase is crucial, because most revolutions that have been won at the barricades are lost at the bank counters. The American,

French, and Russian administrators were successful because they solved the problem of finding surplus capital to carry their revolutionary states to success.

The Zionist Revolution not only paralleled its three seniors by initiating its revolution with a set of intellectuals, but followed their lead not only with a second step, a set of political experts who took the Zionist revolutionary ideology to the people, but also with a third step, a set of bureaucratic administrators who would procure the necessary surplus capital.

History is made of dreams and men of action. Whereas the first stage of the Zionist revolutionary road was paved with the works of four alienated intellectuals, the second was laid mainly with the deeds of a quartet of dedicated nationalists—bald, gimlet-eyed Menahem Ussishkin, the paternal dictator who shaped the colonization policy of Palestine; polished, sensitive Chaim Weizmann, the "aristocrat with a taste for Tory culture," who was instrumental in inducing a great power to underwrite a guarantee for Palestinian independence; indomitable, implacable Vladimir Jabotinsky, who rattled the need for a Jewish army like a sword of defiance in the face of the world; and tough, fiery, "almost monstrously photogenic" David Ben-Gurion, who set the internal political framework for the then nonexistent state of Israel.

These four architects of the second stage of the Zionist Revolution took up the cries of the alienated intellectuals, and like them discarded their ghetto clothes and *shtetl* Talmudism. But they never doubted the superiority of Jewish humanism over French rationalism, nor were they on a rebound from a Gentile paradise. In them burned ingrained Jewishness. They never thought of assimilation. They always believed fervently in the eternity of Israel. They could not conceive of Moscow, Berlin, London, or New York becoming islands of a Jewish renaissance. In their view, this could come only from Zion, where belonged the Jewish soul. They were, in fact, the true successors of the Haskala. Within one decade, from 1910 to 1920, they erected a Zionist framework so strong that it was able to hold Palestine open to stateless Jews against the coming onslaughts of British imperialism, Arab nationalism, and Vatican hostility.

Menahem Ussishkin (1863–1941), who, with his bald head, granite features, and walrus moustache, more nearly resembled a czarist general than a Zionist revolutionary, realized that a new homeland had to be built with the blood and sweat of colonizers before it would yield food and freedom. His ideal was the United States, because he saw that the greatness of American democracy rested on past ruthlessness. Ussishkin left diplomacy and tact to others. He knew what he wanted, and rammed through his wishes over the heads of friend and foe alike. When speaking for Zionism at Versailles, he spoke in Hebrew to let the world know it was not a dead language. As chairman of the National Jewish Fund, he controlled the heartbeat of Zionism, the funds for its colonization program.

Though the colonization movement received its most important impetus under his leadership, the surge back to Zion started before him. Ironically, it was not the emancipated Reform Jews of western Europe who first heeded the call for a return to Zion but the poor masses of eastern Europe. Stripped of their possessions, their dignity, their homes, they followed the godless in a Zionade that dared shift the mission of leading a return to Palestine from the shoulders of the messiah to the shoulders of the Jews themselves. The poor, the insulted, the injured, flocked to the new banner of the future state—the blue shield of King David on a white field—designed by Herzl himself. To them, Herzl was the king, the prophet, the Jewish "christ," the messiah. The Hasids and Talmudists at first aligned with the Reform Jews in their opposition to Zionism. They cursed it, villified it, spat on it, but in the end joined it.

The most diverse elements in the Diaspora marched down the Zionist colonization road to Jerusalem land. They were led by such movements as the *Hibbat Zion*, whose slogan "On to Palestine" swept youth from the hinterland of the Pale to the valleys of Jordan; the Bilu, which motivated students to exchange books for shovels and the cities of Europe for the plains of Jezreel; the

Hovevei Zion, headed by an orthodox rabbi who dared defy his peers and bid the pale denizens of the *shtetls* to become their own messiahs by heading for the sun of Hebron. American colonizers had loaded their meager belongings onto Conestoga wagons to head west, but these Jewish colonizers packed their belongings in bundles to be carried on their backs as they headed toward Zion. They came not like the pious men of old, with skull cap and phylacteries to pray and die, but with spade and hoe to sow and reap. Their toil had to create the foundation for the future Jewish state. They drove themselves in the blistering sun to make the soil fertile for coming life, the land safe for future generations.

Thus Zionism was born out of the union of two extremes in nineteenth-century Jewry, the ideas of the alienated cosmopolitan intellectuals who had nowhere to go and the toil of the poverty-stricken *shtetl* dwellers who had nothing to lose. The Zionists, however, did not come like European colonists to the Orient, who had the natives do the work for them, but like American settlers, come to do their own hard work. But whereas all other colonization movements had been upward, that of lower classes seeking an escape to higher status, Zionism was the reverse, that of an elite intellectual class deliberately transforming itself into a blue-collar class of farmers and workers. Slowly a new Palestine arose out of the desert in the way a new Russia had sprouted out of the marshlands and a new America had been hewed out of the wilderness.

Like Russian and American colonizers in the past, so the twentieth-century Palestinian settlers were confronted with the problem of what to do with indigent people squatting in squalor on the land. But unlike the Russians who exterminated the native Finno-Ugric population in their path as they appropriated the land from Kiev to Moscow, and unlike the Americans who slaughtered the native Indians in their path as they seized the land from the Atlantic to the Pacific, the Jews purchased the land in the path of their colonization drive from Lebanon to Egypt, and killed none. The Russians and Americans were successful in solving their problems by impersonal extirpation, but the Jews were not equally successful with their method of just compensation.

The money to buy Palestinian land came from the Jewish National Fund, an organization founded in 1901 on a suggestion by Herzl to redeem the land of Israel by popular subscription to enable workers without capital to settle there. Pennies from the poor and gold from the rich poured into the fund. Suddenly, land which for centuries Turk and Arab had regarded as nearly worthless became valuable. Where Turks and Arabs saw only sandy wastes to be sold to Jews at inflated prices, the Jews laid foundations for future farms, towns, and cities.

While the colonization movement gained momentum, the search for a political formula floundered until, in the middle of World War I, a Zionist leader appeared who fused unforeseen events into a springboard for daring action. That leader was Dr. Chaim Weizmann (1874–1952), destined to be the first president of Israel. Born in Motol, a drab townlet in the flat, mournful province of Minsk in White Russia—"mud in the spring, ice in the winter, and dust in the summer"—he was educated until his thirteenth year in a squalid, one-room school ruled by a teacher distinguished by an above-average incompetence. Young Weizmann escaped his dreary surroundings when his family sent him to Germany for an education. Graduating with degrees in chemistry, he was appointed lecturer of biological chemistry in England in 1904, and made director of the British Admiralty Chemical Laboratories in 1916. With this appointment, Zionism and world events were fused into a new political element with Weizmann as the catalyst.

At this point in his career, Weizmann was an ardent Zionist and a famous chemist who had made a discovery that helped England win World War I. German submarines were sinking boats carrying Chilean nitrates to England, its only source of explosives. Weizmann found a way of producing acetone, a rare but essential ingredient in the synthetic manufacture of explosives, and turned his discovery over to the British government.

Through his position in the Admiralty, Weizmann came in contact with the highest personages in the British

ministry, and succeeded in interesting many members in
Zionist aspirations. "Acetone converted me to Zionism,"
Lloyd George, Prime Minister of England, was fond of
stating dramatically. One day, the subject of Zionism came
up at an informal gathering. Lord A. J. Balfour, Foreign
Secretary, casually suggested to Weizmann that Uganda
instead of Palestine be used as a place for Jews to settle.
"If I were to offer you Paris instead of London, would
you take it?" asked Weizmann, to which Balfour, surprised, answered, "But Dr. Weizmann, we have London."
"That's true," replied Weizmann, "but we had Jerusalem
when London was a marsh." This conversation was to have
momentous repercussions. It led to the most famed document in Zionist history, the Balfour Declaration, one of
three involving the future fate of Palestine authored during
World War I by the British.

By the end of 1914, the war had ground to a stalemate,
and by 1915 was going badly for the Allies. But with
characteristic vision, England was drawing blueprints for
structuring a postwar world, with herself as victor. A
Machiavellian plan for victory was shaping up, as England
plunged three diplomatic irons into the political fire—the
McMahon Correspondence of 1915, the Sykes-Picot Treaty
of 1916, and the Balfour Declaration of 1917, each of
which promised all things to all men.

In the first phase of this three-pronged perfidy, Sir
Henry McMahon, British commissioner in Egypt, entered
into secret negotiations with Arab leaders within the Ottoman Empire. He promised that the Turkish province of
Syria would be theirs as an independent state provided
they rebelled against their masters. But he neglected to
state clearly that Palestine was not included in the deal.
In the second part of this trilogy of deceit, Sir Mark Sykes,
for the British, and Georges Picot, for the French, reached
an agreement whereby Syria would be a French-dominated
territory after victory, and Egypt a British-dominated territory, with Palestine carved up between them as buffer
zones. The third deal sent the Zionists into paroxysms of
joy. The British government quietly issued The Balfour
Declaration, a one-sentence masterpiece in diplomatic deceit:

His Majesty's Government view with favor the establishment of a National Home for the Jewish people, and will use their best endeavor to facilitate the achievement of this object, it being clearly understood that nothing shall be done which may prejudice the civil and religious rights of existing non-Jewish communities in Palestine, or the rights of and political status enjoyed by Jews in any other country.

But the British neglected to inform the Jews of the McMahon Correspondence and the Sykes-Picot Treaty, or the Arabs of the Sykes-Picot Treaty and Balfour Declaration. When published, these three documents stirred the sons of Ishmael and the sons of Isaac into revolts that eventually would drive the British and the French out of the Middle East and envelop all Arab nations in strife over Palestine. Though the world did not expect the Jews in Palestine to survive these encounters, they did, because farsighted leadership had prepared them for the perils to come.

Early settlers in Palestine soon found that if they wished to survive they had to add a gun to their agricultural arsenal of hoe, pick, and spade. Twentieth-century Bedouins, as in the days of Mohammed, still lived on plunder, and to them, killing for loot was an incidental bagatelle. The Bedouins were the first to learn that a Jew with a rifle was as formidable as any other opponent similarly armed. Just as the world had underestimated Arab nationalism, so it underestimated the Jewish ability to fight. This reversal of the psychology of the Diaspora was the work of a man so blind to the realities of his day that he saw only the truths of tomorrow. He was Vladimir Jabotinsky, the "Jewish Garibaldi," who preached self-defense long before there was a state to defend.

Short, stocky, ungainly Vladimir Jabotinsky was a remarkable performer, even on the Jewish stage of history. Born in 1880 in Odessa, most cosmopolitan "Jewish city" in Russia, he was a graduate not of a yeshiva but of a gymnasium, a drama critic, and a bohemian member of the Russian intelligentsia. He had to flee Russia, however, for heaping abuse on an Odessa police chief who had had him thrown out of a theater. In 1908, on a visit to Israel, Jabotinsky became an avowed Zionist, seeing in that movement the only hope the Jews had of being masters in their own land.

Jabotinsky's Zionist gospel was simple. Start organizing for self-defense before the threat arrives, for it will arrive soon, he predicted. Act as though you had a state to defend, he exhorted. Begin with a platoon, a company, a battalion, a regiment, and the army will take care of itself. Jabotinsky became the gadfly that disturbed the tranquility of Zionist bureaucracy. When World War I erupted, he agitated the British War Ministry for permission to form Jewish units to fight in the British Army, and succeeded in organizing three Jewish brigades that marched under Allenby to retake Jerusalem from the Turks. As a first lieutenant known as "Jug o' Whiskey," because none knew how to pronounce his name, he led one of these brigades into Galilee in 1918.

When the Balfour Declaration was made public, Jabotinsky was the only voice to warn the Jews that the British would soon repudiate it to accommodate the Arabs. The Zionist world, which had placed its trust in declarations and Englishmen, soon woke up to the reality Jabotinsky had predicted. When the Arabs in 1921 rose in their first anti-Jewish revolt, Jabotinsky led the armed resistance. Arrested by the British for the arrogance of striking back, he received a fifteen-year sentence, but under the mounting pressure of world opinion he was released. The Jews had learned their lesson. They organized themselves into armed units, and the *Haganah*, a sub-rosa Jewish army of defense, became the fighting arm of Palestine. Jabotinsky had done his work well.

Along with the progress made on the Palestinian colonization front under Ussishkin, on the Diaspora political front under Weizmann, and on the self-defense front under Jabotinsky, equally great advances were made on the Palestinian political front. Here, too, thanks to the hands, mind, and heart of the man from Plonsk—David Ben-Gurion—the Zionists were ready with the deed before the need.

Plonsk, a dreary factory town in Poland, recorded the

400 THE INDESTRUCTIBLE JEWS

birth of Ben-Gurion in 1886. Here caftaned Hasids viewed his father as an apostate for daring to wear frock coat and striped trousers. A rabid Zionist from the age of ten, Ben-Gurion hitchhiked to Palestine in 1906, hiring himself out as a farmhand. In 1910 he was in Jerusalem to form a workers' party, and in 1913 matriculated in a Constantinople law school. In 1915 he was expelled from Ottoman territory as an Allied sympathizer, and in 1916 was in New York, enlisting Jews to fight in Palestine. Here he met a young student nurse who a few months later accompanied him to city hall to be married. "I could tell that he was one of the Prophets of the Bible," she said, and never changed her opinion. In 1918, when Adolf Hitler was a corporal in the German Army, David Ben-Gurion was a corporal in one of Jabotinsky's brigades.

After World War I, Ben-Gurion's name became inextricably woven with the Palestinian struggle for independence, as he worked unceasingly to create a party organization that could take over and run the state when freedom arrived. His creed was bold and direct—unlimited immigration into Palestine, the creation of a Jewish army to defend the rights of the colonizers, and the unification of all Palestine into a Jewish state. As one Zionist candidly expressed it, "Whenever the Arabs listened to Weizmann, they heard the drums of Ben-Gurion."

With the colonization program as a base, with the Balfour Declaration as a blueprint, with a well-trained militia for self-defense, and with a political framework for statehood, the four architects of modern Israel had prepared Palestine to withstand coming assaults.

Which view prevails—Carlyle's notion that it is the hero who bends history to his will, or the Marxist contention that events catapult the right man into the right place at the right time? Perhaps it is a blend of both. Nothing, however, guarantees that the right man will appear at the right time in the right place. Many a hero ahead of the need of his time has lost his head on the scaffold, and all too often opportunities have withered for want of a hero. Where none of the messianic pretenders in our previous challenges succeeded, either because they were ahead of their times or because they were not heroes, the secular

Zionists did succeed. History had come up with the right combination of men, times, and events. All the pieces for the coming struggle for power were on the Palestinian checkerboard, ready for the first move, in 1920.

History in action, however, is as crowded as a Brueghel canvas, and must be given coherence by interpretation. If we hammer maverick facts of Palestinian history into a relevant pattern, we will see the struggle between Arabs and Jews as a miniature recapitulation of the struggle between the feudal and capitalist classes in Europe's Middle Ages. Feudal lords had wrapped themselves in the folds of the Catholic flag to put down the threatening capitalist class that had wrapped itself in the Protestant banner. Today, in the Near East, feudal sheiks have likewise wrapped themselves in the banner of Mohammedanism to put down the threat of the Jews who are undermining their feudal power structure with Western capitalist ideas.

The sheiks in Arab lands today are no more ready to yield their power to the new economic forces than the feudal princes had been. Jewish immigration and Jewish enterprise had to be stopped if the status quo was to be maintained. With the arrival of the Zionists, the Arabs in Palestine sprang back to life. Though the Arab birthrate declined in the first four decades of the twentieth century, the Arab population quadrupled between 1900 and 1942. Sanitation methods introduced by the Jews decreased the Arab deathrate by 25 percent, and job opportunities introduced by Jewish investments attracted increasing immigration to Palestine from Arab lands around Palestine.

Thus reinvigorated in number, health, and wealth, new dreams of grandeur expanded Arab ambitions—to reclaim the land they had sold to the Jews and inherit the new prosperity. Arab leaders wrapped themselves in the flag of nationalism and cried that Palestine was Arab, its people Arab, and the Jews intruders.

Who were the Arabs in Palestine? When and how did they get there? Did they hold title to the country by squatter's rights, or as the rightful spoils of conquerors? Was it an ancient inheritance, or a possession deeded them by international law?

History shows that the Arabs were late arrivals in Pales-

tine and brief title-holders. After starting out in life as
the common-law wife of Canaanites, Amorites, Egyptians,
Hittites, Moabites, Philistines, and Jebusites, Palestine became the bride of the Jews in the twelfth century B.C. After
a stormy, seven-century marriage, she was kidnapped by
the Babylonians, who lost her to the Persians, who lost her
to the Greeks, who lost her back to the Jews, who in turn
lost her to the Romans. In the fourth century A.D., when
the unwieldly Roman Empire was split in two, Palestine
went with the Eastern portion, thus becoming part of the
Byzantine Empire. In 614 she fell into the arms of a new
set of conquerors, the Sassanids, who enjoyed her briefly.
In 648 she was swept into the harem of Islam, along with
a multitude of other nations that huddled around the
southern shores of the Mediterranean.

It took the invading Mohammedans several centuries to
"Arabize" the Christians in Palestine, who then constituted
the majority population. When the Crusaders arrived in the
eleventh century, they had to restock the country with
Christians from the West to again give that land a Christian
majority.

Palestine slowly became Moslem-populated under its
next masters, the Mamelukes, former Turkish slaves who
seized power in Egypt and Palestine in the thirteenth
century. For 267 years, forty-seven Mameluke sultans
ruled the realm; a few were insane, many were illiterate,
and most came to the throne by assassination and left the
same way. They succeeded in reducing the population of
Palestine by two-thirds, and the residue into paupers. The
end to Mameluke rule came in the sixteenth century when
their kissing cousins, the Ottoman Turks, conquered the
former Abbasid and Byzantine empires and in one century
gathered under their robes all the lands around the Aegean
Sea from Greece to Egypt, fusing them into the Ottoman
Empire.

During the first two centuries of Ottoman rule (1500–
1700), Jews in great numbers returned to Palestine, invigo-
rating her mind with learning and revitalizing her body
with business. But with the eighteenth century, the Ottoman Empire declined into corruption and poverty as the
royal harem produced ever more dissolute and incompetent

rulers. Palestine's population again dwindled, until by 1850 most who could flee had fled. By 1900, of the 350,000 remaining population, about 50,000 were Jews, another 50,000 were European and Arab Christians, and about 50,000 were nomadic Bedouins. The rest of the population —a conglomerate of 200,000 Mongols, Mamelukes, Syrians, Lebanese, and Turks—bound loosely together, not by language (most spoke not Arabic but an Aramaic patois), but by adherence to different sects of Mohammedanism— were called Arabs only for want of a better name. They were united in misery, oppressed by Arab *effendi*, mulcting Turks, and absentee landlords. Most lived in mud huts or tents with their animals in filth and stench, burned dung for fuel, were covered wtih sores, plagued by trachoma, rickets, and tuberculosis, and enjoyed an average life expectancy of thirty-five years, without hope of a better existence except in the hereafter.

The end of this four-century Turkish rule came in 1917, when a British army, including the three Jewish brigades organized by Jabotinsky, invaded Palestine from Egypt, while Arab horsemen, led by the romantic T. E. Lawrence, rode out of the desert to protect the flank of the advancing British. In December of that year, Jerusalem fell into the hands of the British.

With the divine rights of victors, England and France neatly dismembered the Ottoman Empire, appropriating for themselves former Arab lands held by the Turks. But Palestine could not be annexed outright; Britain could not openly repudiate the Balfour Declaration, which President Woodrow Wilson and the United States Congress had recognized as a valid document. The League of Nations, an instrument of the Western powers, dutifully handed over Palestine to Britain as a mandate, which the British promptly proceeded to rule like a colony. In the three decades of the British Mandate (1920–1948), Palestine resembled a schizophrenic patient, split in two by its irreconcilable Arab and Jewish personalities. Like American democracy, the Jewish state too was to emerge in the course of an anti-British war.

In the first decade of its mandate, the British tried to cure the patient with a "frontier lobotomy." They lopped off (in 1922) some 35,000 square miles of Palestine, about four fifths of its total area, and created with it the Arab state of Transjordan (now Jordan), the first and most dramatic partition of Palestine.[1] But instead of appeasing the Arabs, this surgery inflamed them, resulting in Arab uprisings (in 1929) that revealed the deep schism in Palestine's political libido.

In the second decade, increased Jewish immigration, propelled by the Nazi terror, intensified Arab paranoia into a manic phase that erupted into wanton violence against Jewish settlements. To escape world censure for any drastic moves, the British High Commissioner of Palestine (in 1936) called in a team of specialists from England (the Peel Commission) to render a fresh diagnosis and prescribe a new therapy. After a hard look at Arab intransigence and Jewish desperation, the Peel Commission recommended the unexpected—a partition of the patient into two component parts along ethnic sutures. The Jews reluctantly accepted this recommendation, the Arabs vehemently rejected it, and the British diplomatically ignored it, preferring a schizoid patient to none at all. To tranquilize the Arabs, the British gave the Jews a shock treatment, the White Paper of 1939, which would reduce Jewish immigration to 15,000 a year for five years and then stop it altogether, aiming at freezing the Jews into a permanent minority in the Arab majority. The Jews vehemently rejected this, the Arabs reluctantly accepted it, and the British enthusiastically enforced it.

The third decade of the mandate began with Palestine in a catatonic coma. Arabs and Jews froze their differences for the duration of World War II, the former in the main joining Hitler, the latter the Allies. But upon beholding Hitler's *Festung Europa* invaded, the Arabs betrayed their Nazi friends and switched allegiance (in 1945) to the Allies just in time to gain seats in the United Nations as a reward for their staunch six-month defense of democracy. The war over, Palestine's catatonic stupor exploded in

[1] In 1948, after Jordan had annexed 2,000 more square miles of Israeli territory, 80 percent of her territory consisted of former Palestinian land.

violence, generated by the heat of the White Paper, now again enforced by the British.

In defiance of the White Paper's immigration restrictions, surviving remnants of Hitler's Europe sailed in leaky boats —their Mayflowers of freedom—through illegal channels to Palestine. Anarchy erupted as Jews returned Arab violence with counter-violence. In desperation, the British (in 1947) appealed to the United Nations to send an international team of experts for another round of diagnostic advice. After a six-month study, the United Nations team came up with the same recommendation the 1936 Peel Commission had—partition of Palestine into a Jewish state (55 percent of the land, largely desert), and an Arab state (45 percent of the land, mostly arable), with Jerusalem as an international city.

In November, 1947, with both the United States and Soviet Russia agreeing, the United Nations voted for this partition plan. Britain stated she would withdraw her troops in May, 1948. The Jews announced they would proclaim their independence. The Arabs vowed they would invade the Jewish state, drive the Jews into the sea, and establish a pure Arab state. Thus began the "Long War," consisting of the Pre-Invasion Hot War (1947), the War of Independence (1948), the Sinai Campaign (1956), and the Six-Day War (1967).

In the first phase, the Pre-Invasion Hot War, five Arab armies positioned themselves around Palestine's borders, poised for invasion. Meanwhile irregular forces were sent across the frontiers to disrupt Jewish communications and seize strategic points. Arab commanders proudly proclaimed that their goal was not conquest but total destruction, with no quarter to be given to any Israeli man, woman, or child. All would be driven into the sea or mercifully slaughtered.

Rich Palestinian Arabs fled to their villas on the Riviera; Palestinian Arab political leaders fled to the Arab armies ringing Palestine. Both waited for victory to return and pluck new political plums. Finding themselves leaderless, the Palestinian Arab populace panicked. Over 600,000 Arabs fled in a mass exodus, hastened by fear of sharing the fate they felt awaited the Jews, and sustained by the hope of a quick return to share in the loot.[2]

A crowded agenda choked the hours of Wednesday, May 14, 1948, the day that heralded the beginning of the second phase of the Long War. The British in Palestine[3] hauled down the Union Jack and departed. In an emotion-choked voice, Ben-Gurion declared the creation of the state of Israel. His words leaped across the world to the White House in Washington, where President Harry S Truman recognized the new state within three hours of its creation. Practically every nation rejoiced, including Russia, but not the Vatican, which had been pushed by this event into an embarrassing position. For two millennia the Church had maintained that the exile of the Jews was due to their refusal to recognize the divinity of Jesus, and that they would not return to Zion until such recognition. Now, with the reality of a Zionist victory, even though the Jews were still not convinced of the divinity of Jesus, the Church

---

[2] Jacques Soustelle, former French Minister of Information, assesses the blame for the plight of the refugees on the Arab leaders thus: "The evacuation of Palestine was the work of the Arabs themselves. An uninterrupted flood of radio propaganda was loosed on the Palestine Arabs urging them to leave the country without delay, in order to return shortly in the footsteps of the army of liberation." *The Long March of Israel.*

When Israel refused to readmit those who had fled and betrayed the country in her hour of peril, the Arab states, in revenge, confiscated the property and expelled 700,000 Jews who had lived in these countries since the days of Mohammed. In ten years after World War II, the Arabs also confiscated most of the property of 3,600,000 Christians who fled the way the Finns had fled from the territory annexed by the Russians; 2,200,000 Italians left Libya, 1,700,000 Frenchmen left Tunisia, Morocco, and Algeria, and 700,000 other European nationals fled from Egypt, Iraq, Yemen, and Libya. Whereas the 20,000,000 European refugees in the aftermath of World War II and the 700,000 Jewish and 3,600,000 Christian refugees from Arab lands have all been resettled, the Arabs remain the only ones who have not resettled their people, content to have them subsidized by United Nations handouts and exploit them for political purposes.

[3] There was a total of 100,000 British in Palestine—military and civilian—more than it took to rule all India.

had to change its dogma or pray for an Arab victory to protect its infallibility.

With best wishes for the new state pouring in from leaders round the world came also the promised invasion of Israel by five Arab armies, so confident of victory that they announced the successful conclusion of the war before its start. And indeed, it looked as if Israel would be a twenty-four-hour state. Egyptian forces struck through the Gaza Strip. Jordanians seized Old Jerusalem. Syrians poured in from the Golan Heights. Lebanese pressed down from Acre. The Vatican rejoiced. The United Nations, which had voted for the creation of Israel, now, under new pressures, expressed insincere despair at its inability to do anything and sat *shivah* (held a wake) for the still living, but seemingly doomed, state.

Israel, however, did not have the grace to cooperate with its foes. In swift, brilliant strokes the Jordanians were routed, the Egyptian advance was stemmed, the Syrians smashed, and the Lebanese driven back. A stunned United Nations quickly dispatched Count Folke Bernadotte with truce flags to halt a total Israeli victory. Twice the Arabs broke this truce, thinking their failures were flukes, for certainly eighty million Arabs could not be vanquished by a mere 600,000 Jews. But to no avail. The Arab armies were again routed. However, Jordan and Egypt annexed the territory that was to have been an independent Palestinian Arab state, and Jordan, which had seized Old Jerusalem, managed to keep it.

Prevented by the United Nations from pursuing the enemy and achieving total victory, the Jews looked to that international body to bring the Arabs to the peace table to discuss frontiers. But the Arabs, taking heart at the United Nations intervention in their behalf, refused to recognize Israel and openly announced they would strike again to annihilate it.

The leader in this defiance, whose history from the seventh century B.C. to the present day uncannily parallels the history of Palestine, was Egypt. Like Palestine, Egypt was defeated and devastated by Assyrians and Babylonians, and then passed successively into the hands of Persians, Greeks, Romans, Byzantines, Mohammedans, Crusaders,

Mamelukes, Turks, and Englishmen (1882). Finally, in 1922, after 1,900 years of vassalage, Egypt freed herself from foreign rule to assume the yoke of the inept and lecherous dynasty of King Fuad I, whose pornography collecting son, King Farouk, led Egypt into its disastrous war with Israel in 1948. Egypt was searching for a hero to rescue it from its mire of ossified venality. Tall, handsome, charismatic Gamal Abdel Nasser, a man eminently qualified for leadership, appointed himself to fulfill that role.

Born in 1918 in a small village in Upper Egypt, the son of a minor postal official, Nasser, as an infantry battalion commander, had fought with great personal courage in the war of 1948 against Israel. Perceiving the lecherous corruption of Farouk's regime, he was resolved to overthrow it. More than anything else he wanted to restore dignity to his country, heal the scars of poverty, alleviate the pangs of hunger. The coup came in 1952, and in 1956 Nasser became president of Egypt. The Egyptian people looked upon him as a savior, but, tragically, Nasser abandoned his program of steady social progress for quick military glory.

Instead of pressing upon his brow the crown of Saladin, Nasser clad himself in the robes of Pope Urban II. Just as Urban had decided that a Crusade to wrest Palestine from the Mohammedans would unify the Christian world and solve its economic ills, so Nasser decided to institute a Jihad, the Mohammedan equivalent of a Crusade, to wrest Palestine from the Jews in the hope of unifying the dissident Arab world and solve its economic ills. Convinced of quick victory, he seized the Suez Canal, alienated the West, and turned to Russia for economic and military assistance.

Russia had voted for the state of Israel in the United Nations, hoping to thus dislodge Britain from the Middle East. She also counted on the Jews, who had fathered Marx, to join the communist orbit. But just as the Jews 2,000 years earlier had refused to follow Jesus, so they now refused to follow Marx. And just as the Vatican in the Middle Ages had turned against the Jews for their refusal to follow the Christian line, so the Kremlin in the

Modern Age turned against the Jews for refusing to follow the communist line. Egypt offered the Russians the Middle East foothold Israel denied them, and the Russians gratefully armed the Egyptians with the latest technology of death. The consequences were swift. What began as the third phase of the Long War almost erupted into a third world war.

Israel was again ringed by Arab armies. Nasser closed the Suez Canal to all Israeli shipping, and in October, 1956, publicly proclaimed he would annihilate Israel in a matter of days. Instead, world headlines proclaimed an Israeli victory. Like the French in World War I saving Paris at the first battle of the Marne by taking its army swiftly to the front in taxicabs to stem the German advance, so the Israelis used laundry trucks and commercial vans to get its troops quickly to the edge of the Sinai for its slashing advance across the desert. In one hundred hours the entire Sinai was in Israeli hands; the Egyptian armies were enveloped in a ring of steel and audacity, and the Jews stood along the eastern banks of the Suez from Port Said to Sharm-el-Sheikh. On November 2, the war entered its international phase. French and British bombers attacked strategic points in Egypt. Port Said was occupied. Egypt's case seemed hopeless, her armies annihilated by the Israelis, her territory invaded by France and England.

The collapse of Egypt seemed imminent. But like the heroine in a melodrama rescued by the hero in her hour of peril, so Egypt was rescued in her hour of peril by United Nations oratory. Fearful of a nuclear confrontation with Russia (or irritated by the independent action of Jews, Frenchmen, and Englishmen), the United States, through the United Nations, pressured England, France, and Israel to withdraw, promising all grievances would be ironed out at future peace talks. The French and British[4] departed with their fleets; the Israelis withdrew their forces from the Sinai. And thus it came about that Nasser, though defeated, won the third phase of the Long War. Instead of sitting down to discuss peace, he prepared for a fourth phase, again with Russia's aid.

[4]The Sinai War marked the end of empire for the British in the Middle East.

In 1967, the Egyptians were ready. Jordan, Syria, and Saudi Arabia rallied round Nasser, who demanded that the United Nations security force be withdrawn so he could tear Israel apart. The United Nations obliged. On June 4, Cairo radio blared: "We will wipe Israel off the face of the map and no Jew will remain alive." On June 5, the combined Arab forces of 650,000 men, with 2,700 tanks and 1,090 aircraft at its command, clashed with Israel's force of 300,000 men, 800 tanks, and 400 aircraft. Energy and élan made up for the deficit in men and arms. In six days the Egyptian Army was smashed, the Syrians were in retreat, and the Jordanians screamed for a United Nations cease-fire. It was a victory that stunned the world into admiration for the Jews who had fought with valor and begged no aid.

This time the Israelis refused to evacuate occupied territory, as they had following the Sinai War, unless the Arabs first signed a peace treaty. Once again the Arabs refused. Confident of further protection by the United Nations and once more rearmed by the Russians, the Arabs demanded the return of their territories from which to again invade Israel. Thus came about a situation never before encountered in history—the victors imploring the vanquished to discuss peace, and the vanquished not only refusing to do so, but openly proclaiming they would start another war.

Whatever the future outcome of this Long War, the second stage of the Zionist Revolution came to a conclusion with the proclamation of independence in 1948. With that event, the Zionist Revolution was ready for its third stage, for the administrators to take over the destiny of the new state. But though the Zionist Revolution in its first two stages closely paralleled the American, French, and Russian revolutions, the course of the third stage drastically diverged from that set by its predecessor revolutions.

How did states in the past develop from backward, feudal economies into modern, self-sustaining states? How did countries like France, Germany, England, and the United States hoist themselves from rags to riches? Where had they found the surplus capital to finance their gigantic industrial complexes? Why could not new nations simply emulate them?

Alas, the manipulation of events today is not as simple as in the days of old. The classic pattern of acquiring surplus wealth in previous centuries was exceedingly simple. All one needed was a successful army with which to invade another nation, steal its wealth, and enslave its population. These practical measures created misery for the vanquished but prosperity for the conquerors. It was thus that England, France, and Germany accumulated their initial wealth. They carved up large sections of the American, Asian, and African continents, looting the wealth, stealing the natural resources, and enslaving the people. The United States was no exception. Instead of annexing colonies, she imported slaves. When George Washington was President, 50 percent of the American people were either slaves or indentured servants. By the nineteenth century, when the colonial powers had accumulated enough surplus capital to launch their industrial independence, when they no longer needed these methods of exploitation, they denounced them as un-Christian.

Thus, when the United States and France fomented their revolutions in the late eighteenth century, French and American revolutionary specialists could easily establish their industrial states with the surplus capital liberated by colonialism and slave exploitation. But in the twentieth century, when Russia launched her revolution, her third-stage administrators were faced with a new world morality. Russia dared not invade and enslave other nations, as had been the custom in previous centuries. The midwives of the Russian Revolution realized, however, that unless they did procure the surplus capital with which to raise their nation from feudalism into industrialism the revolution would collapse. To solve this dilemma, the communists modernized the Western precedent. Instead of importing slaves, they arbitrarily enslaved a segment of their own population. Just as England in the seventeenth century, in order to create a needed cheap labor force in the Colonies, sentenced men to twenty years indentured servitude for stealing a sheep, so Russia in the twentieth century, in order to create a cheap labor force, sentenced men to twenty years servitude in Siberia for suspected anti-communist activities. The savings thus effected by the sweat, blood, and death of its own people were used to buy the machinery necessary to start her industrial society. China, when she instituted her revolution after World War II, had no recourse but to emulate the Russian example. But both Russia and China have keenly felt the stigma of world contempt for this ruthless exploitation.

Israel, born too late to emulate the methods of colonialism used by the West, did not resort to that expediency to achieve economic independence. Her religion, her sense of justice, did not permit her to follow the examples of Russia and China in enslaving any part of her own population. Where then did her surplus capital come from to pay for her industrial plants, for the absorption of two million Diaspora Jews and backward Arabs into her economy? United States loans and German reparations helped, but these were of a temporary nature and did not account materially for her economic advance.

The main capital came, of course, from the most vital source, from the Israelis themselves, who voluntarily toiled, saved, and taxed themselves for the weal of all. But the crucial extra capital came from a historically new source, from the Diaspora Jews. Just as Herzl's idea was the motivating force behind the Jewish National Fund to buy land in Palestine with the contributions from Jews all over the world, so the Diaspora Jews extended that idea to include the preservation of the state. There was a universal identification of the Diaspora Jews with the Jews in Israel.

In essence, the third phase of the Zionist Revolution gave birth to a new political concept of man—the concept that a nation can achieve fulfillment not through war, not through exploitation, not through politically inspired grants-in-aid, but through an extension of brotherhood, perhaps one of the greatest contributions of the Jews to the world in this second act.

Though the Long War still continues, and an atmosphere of tension prevails in the Middle East, Israel is a reality, an accomplished fact. But we have seen great empires, great civilizations, strut their brief centuries of glory on a stage of history, only to disappear with a bang, or a whimper, all heirs to the inexorable laws of historical decay. Even assuming that Israel will establish lasting peace with her Arab neighbors, can she survive indefinitely in a world where all nations eventually seem to perish? Can the small nation of Israel defy this "natural" law of death?

When the curtain descended on our first act, we saw the Jews milling in the lobby of history, debating what to do. Should they deny the past, integrate, and continue life under whatever nom de plume history would confer on them? Or should they reaffirm the past, continue as Jews, and follow the labyrinth of their manifest destiny to the brotherhood envisioned by the Prophets?

In the second act, we saw them choose the latter. We saw them confidently confront and successfully respond to their first four challenges, only to wind up in the ghettos of their fifth. Freed from the ghetto in the sixth, we saw them stare in disbelief at the wonders of the Gentile world that had grown around them during their three-century incarceration. We saw them chuck the Talmud that had sustained them for eighteen centuries, and swallow the rationalist catechism, hook, line, and ideology. Discarding their caftans and rabbinics, we saw them stand side by side with their Christian brethren, blessing Reason, Logic, and Science, the trinity of the Modern Age. Then they found that whereas Christian Faith had consigned the Jews to ghettos, rationalist Reason consigned them to concentration camps; that whereas feudal society had been errant in its religious zeal, modern society was sick unto its scientific soul. With the twilight of the second act, we saw the Jews come to a turning point in their destiny, a confrontation that almost took them out of history. Instead, like Christ risen from the Cross, they were resurrected from the ashes of the concentration camps to return, in Lurianic fashion, to Zion, there to create the new state of Israel after a 2,000-year absence.

With the return of the "exiled lights" of Israel, the kabalistic act of *shevirat ha'keilim,* the "antithesis," should be over. But as the curtain closes, we are aware for the first time of an odd progression of Jewish history, a series of unique relationships between Israel and the world. At the end of the first act, we saw the curtain fall on the

Temple in flames, Jerusalem gutted, and the Jews dispersed into the Diaspora. Now, at the end of the second act, we have beheld a reverse action, the triumphant return of the Jews to Zion, Israel reborn, and Jerusalem once again the capital of the Jewish state. Thus in the first act there was a Jewish state but no Diaspora. In the second there was a Diaspora but no Jewish state. And now, as the third act is about to unfold, there is both a Diaspora and a Jewish state.

Is there any significance to this evolution of events? Has the creation of the state of Israel eliminated the need for a Diaspora? Does this simultaneous existence of Israel and Diaspora mean that the Diaspora should be abolished and all Jews emigrate to Israel? Or should they assimilate into the diverse cultures within which they now reside?

Let us now repair to the lobby of history for a brief intermission, and speculate about what may transpire during the next 2,000 years in the destiny of the Jews.

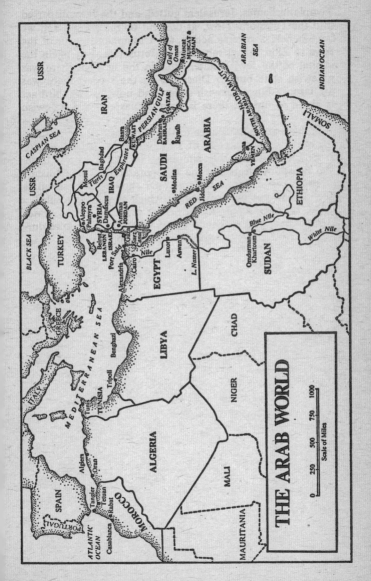

ACT III

THE PARADOX
OF THE
DIASPORA

*Israel, The World, and
The Brotherhood of Man*

(TIME SPAN: FROM BEN-GURION TO THE MESSIAH)

FROM BEN-GURION TO THE MESSIAH

According to Spengler:	Western civilization, having entered its Winter phase, is doomed to death, and the Slavic and Sinic civilizations, having entered their Spring phases, will evolve into their Summer and Autumn growth cycles. New civilizations will in time replace them in the eternal life and death dance of people and cultures.
According to Toynbee:	Though Toynbee, like Spengler, sees the doom of Western civilization, he nevertheless sees a possibility for its regeneration through a return to the religious values that sparked it. But he also foresees the evolution of new civilizations out of the debris of past ones.
According to Luria:	The beginning of the third phase, the *tikkun*, of his metaphysical world history, wherein the redemption of the Jews will herald the redemption of mankind.
According to the author:	The diasporization of man into one world, and a synthesis of the Western, Slavic, and Sinic civilizations into one universal culture having the ethics of the Torah for its moral foundation and Jerusalem as its spiritual center.

The Paradox of the Diaspora

ILLUSION AND REALITY

Viewing the Jewish odyssey through the telescope of hindsight, we see a striking series of parallels in each act. Each has been ushered in by a cataclysm that threatened to obliterate mankind. A physical event, the Flood, threatened to drown the world before the first act began. A psychological obsession, the Judgment Day, threatened to wipe out man just before the second act began. And now, a man-made object, the nuclear bomb, threatens to eradicate mankind before the third-act curtain is raised. Are these meaningless events, or are they dramatic fulfillments? Even if we discount the Flood as legend and Judgment Day as fantasy, the atomic bomb is a reality.

There is also a chilling progression in our parallelism. Whereas this capacity for total destruction was at first possessed only by nature, and then by theology, it is now at the capricious disposal of man. As he stands at this juncture of destiny, holding the ideas of redemption in his mind and the tools of destruction in his hands, to which ideology should he entrust his fate? To totalitarianism—the call of domination, or to universalism—the voice of brotherhood?

We saw our first act proceed with God as the divine author and director of the action, designed to train the Jews for survival in a Diaspora in order to spread the message of the Prophets to all mankind. We saw the second act proceed with the Jew himself as the author of his survival script, while history catapulted him from civilization to civilization, carrying him to the four corners of the world and back to Israel.

Has our kabalistic drama now ended with the return of the Jews to the vortex of their history, or is this only an intermission while we wait for a third act as envisioned by Luria? Are the Jews confronted with that same existentialist choice their ancestors were confronted with 2,000 years ago, after the first act? Should they deny the past, or should they reaffirm it? Have they chased a grand illusion or have they pursued a divine mission? Like their ancestors during the intermission after the first act asking who would write the second-act script, they now ask who will write the script for the third? Will it be God as in the first, or the Jew himself as in the second? Or will it be an ecumenical script, written by God, Jew, and Gentile as a team? Or will an atomic holocaust obliterate man before the script is written?

If the Jews today, like their ancestors, choose not to deny the past but to affirm it, then they too, in true existentialist fashion, will become the prisoners of that choice and be forced by the logic of their decision to carry out their manifest destiny. They thus would be confronted with several questions as to the role of the Diaspora in the future. Has it been merely a refuge for a time of trouble, or is it a permanent citadel? If, as has been asserted, the Diaspora was not a punishment for sins but an exile into freedom, what in the Diaspora has given the Jews their indestructibility? Even if the Diaspora has played a role as a savior of the Jewish people in the second act, will it serve an equally essential role for the Jews in the third? And finally, if the metahistorians are right in their predictions of doom for Western civilization, where will the next Diaspora centers crop up? What will be the eventual relationship between the Diaspora and Israel on one hand and the Diaspora and the world on the other?

Can there be answers to questions for which history has not yet provided facts? Can we fit something that has not happened into a framework that does not exist? Science does not hesitate to do so. With a few known facts, it constructs a theory with which to probe the unknown. A breed of scholars known as metahistorians have similarly formulated speculative insights into the future. Instead of using nations as units, as do objective historians, they use civilizations. Just as the chemist Mendeleev, by constructing a theory based on the property of known elements, could predict the properties of undiscovered elements, so the metahistorian, by constructing a theory of history based on the behavior of known civilizations, tries to predict the behavior of future civilizations.

The genesis of the modern metahistorian began as early as the third century A.D., with Jewish kabalists theorizing on the meaning of history, rather than its content, as did the Greeks and Romans. Though mindful of facts, these early Jewish metahistorians preferred to assess the impact of spirit and ideas in the belief that these, not men and dates, determine the course of history. They perceived Gentile history as cycles of rising and falling empires caused by social and economic factors. But observing that Jews appeared again and again in new Gentile civilizations, they conceived of Jewish history as a divine process of redemption. Attributing the concept of the Jews as the Chosen People to divine causes, their exile to an accident of history, and the Jewish character to natural evolution, the kabalists began to weave these divine, accidental, and natural factors into a thesis of Jewish destiny.

In the sixteenth century, corresponding with the ghetto phase, this Jewish eminence in metahistorical writing began to decline, but the groundwork had been laid. Christian historians gained intellectual ascendance. Until recent times, Christian historians in general ignored Jewish metahistorical speculations, but Christian metahistorians, who took their cue from Jewish kabalists, could not.[1] The logic of their own methodology forced them to admit Jewish history into their systems. Puzzled by this people which persisted in history as if Moses had never died and Jesus had never

[1] So, for instance, Giovanni Battista Vico (1688–1744), an uncouth, choleric Neapolitan born to poverty but not humility, who is usually credited with being the first Christian metahistorian, held that the Jews alone were exempt from the inexorable law of historical decay because they alone were the true possessors of the word of God.

lived, they tried to dispose of the problem of the ever-present Jew by accounting for him either as a minor heartburn in the otherwise healthy metabolism of Western civilization, or as a lingering fossil of history.

THE DIASPORA ESCAPE HATCH

We have already examined the metahistory of Isaac Luria. Let us now focus the historic function of the Diaspora into sharper intellectual visibility by surveying history through the different perspectives of two Christian metahistorians, the German Oswald Spengler, a former high school teacher famed for his iconoclastic *Decline of the West,* and the British Arnold Toynbee, a gentleman scholar renowned for his monumental *A Study of History.*

The early life of Oswald Spengler (1880–1936) was a succession of failures. At thirty, often cold and hungry, he was reduced to living in a slum and eating in slop houses, while writing his *Decline of the West* by candlelight in a dank garret. Completed in 1914, the book gained universal recognition after World War I. The Nazi deified his work. Spengler refused to participate in the persecution of the Jews and died before the Nazis could decide whether to overlook this deficiency in his character or put him in a concentration camp.

Spengler's logic of history forced him to conclude that all civilizations had been and would be victims of the same inevitable historical process of decay. All civilizations follow the same laws, he contended, and their future course is as predictable as the life cycle of an individual. Each cycle in the Spenglerian culture morphology is comparable to human ontology, for civilizations undergo the same stages of conception, birth, growth, and death as does life.

The first stage in the life and death of a civilization, which gives birth to a new religion and a new world outlook, Spengler called *spring.* Spiritually, this phase is reared on mythology. Its people exist in an uncritical, precultural stage, characterized by mystical symbolism and primitive "form-expression." There is as yet no fully formalized philosophy, science, or sophisticated politics.

Next comes *summer*, culminating in the first philosophical systems and new mathematical concepts. This stage heralds the first opposition to *spring* forms of religion. Architecture expresses itself in urban forms. Groups arise with their own "feeling-tones," paving the way for the formation of new nations within one culture. Politically, *summer* is feudalistic, an age of the vassal struggling against the seigneur.

This period is followed by *autumn*, the zenith of intellectual creativeness, the age of great systems. Art, as an individual expression, is centered in urban areas. Power has shifted from country to town, from aristocracy to business, from property to money. It is the age of maturity, the perfection of all forms of intellectual development. According to Spengler, there is only one way to go from here, and that is down.

The final phase is *winter*, the old age of a civilization, characterized by materialism, a cult of science, degradation of abstract thinking, and a dissolution of old norms. It is a dying culture, characterized by nerve excitement, meaningless luxuries, outlets in sports, rapidly changing fashions. The people become the monster "massman," dominated by money and pandered to by politicians. It is the age of Caesarism, the era of great powers and annihilation wars. The West, said Spengler in 1914, was in its *winter*, its death phase, whereas the new Slavic and Sinic civilizations in Russia and China were in their *spring* phases.

Arnold Toynbee (born 1889), like Spengler, holds that the unit of historical study is not a nation but a civilization. But whereas Spengler's concept of history is cyclical, Toynbee's is zigzagical. Where Spengler views civilizations as independent totalities succeeding each other, Toynbee sees them as representing an evolution from lower to higher forms. Though Toynbee, like Spengler, sees doom in every civilization, including his own, he also notes what Spengler did not. He sees Western civilization saved from doom by none other than the White Anglo-Saxon Protestant.

The son of distinguished parents, Toynbee was properly educated at Oxford in Latin, Greek, and the Gospels, and had the proper background for a British gentleman scholar as a delegate to the 1919 Paris Peace Conference. Thus his *A Study of History* (ten volumes, 1934–1939) has the proper slant.

According to Toynbee, a new civilization comes into being through a burst of creative energy from a small group of idea men called the creative minority. A new civilization, he says, is sparked if the uncreative majority voluntarily adapts the views of the creative minority, either by undergoing the same experience (mimesis) or by mechanically imitating its actions. In practice, only the second alternative has ever worked, except for one people, the Jews. They underwent the same emotional, psychic, and spiritual experience at Mount Sinai as their leaders did.

Once a civilization has been launched, says Toynbee, it must continually respond to challenges hurled at it by chance and circumstance, and the path of history is strewn with the corpses of aspiring civilizations that did not make it. Some civilizations respond to initial challenges but fail to come up with answers to new ones, and become what Toynbee calls "arrested civilizations." Others, falling victim to self-idolization, refuse to change with changing times and become ossified cliff-hangers as history passes them by. Still others just vanish, too thin-skinned to fight the battle of survival.

Disintegration of an entire civilization sets in, according to Toynbee, when the creative minority ceases to create. It begins to rule by force and establishes a Universal State, that is, totalitarianism. When this happens, the uncreative majority stops following and becomes an Internal Proletariat in search of a new religion. If the Internal Proletariat of a dying civilization can spark a new religion in the body of the dying Universal State, then a new civilization will be born.

If it is a religion that sparks a civilization, says Toynbee, then the dying Western civilization could regenerate itself by returning to the origins of Christianity that gave it its life. But how far back into its religious origins should Western civilization go to regenerate itself? If it were to go all the way back, it would have to reembrace Judaism, which is not Toynbee's objective. Therefore, he stops his backward trek to the soul of Western civilization just at the point where Christianity dissociated itself from Judaism. At this crossroad of history and faith, Toynbee neatly nails the Jews to the cliff of history, as fossils who failed to respond to the challenge of the New Testament, while Christianity triumphantly marched on.

Though he is often wrong about the details of Jewish history, Toynbee has a remarkable grasp of its total flow. He rightly perceives the religious progress represented by the ideas of Abraham, Moses, the Prophets, and Jesus. He rightly realizes that from the sixteenth century onward the Protestant movement "furnishes a clear example of a powerful and popular renaissance of Judaism." But he denies the Jews a place on the pinnacle of destiny as the final rescuers of Western civilization, reserving that spot for the White Anglo-Saxon Protestant.

Yet, even if we grant Toynbee his view of Christianity as the savior of an otherwise disintegrating Western world, it does not exclude the larger concept of Judaic ideas as the savior of an otherwise doomed mankind. In fact, Spengler's and Toynbee's own arguments demonstrate that it is the Judaism of Abraham, Moses, the Prophets, and the "Jewish Jesus" that form the main spokes in the wheels of a redemption chariot destined to carry the world to a universal brotherhood.

The Jews began their historic existence in the full Spenglerian sense, with a new religion and a new way of thought. In Toynbeean terms, they responded to the successive challenges of nomadic existence, enslavement, and subsequent freedom. They responded to the challenge of survival in Babylonian captivity and to the challenge of rebuilding Jerusalem upon their return. From about 1000 to 300 B.C., they evolved into their Spenglerian summer phase. Enriched with the ethics and morals of the Prophets and the science and philosophy of the Greeks, they successfully responded to the challenge of Hellenism and entered their intellectual autumn phase. In spite of this successful response and survival, both Spengler and Toynbee deny the Jews membership in their metahistoric civilizations, Spengler because they do not represent a civilization and Toynbee because they represent a fossilized one.

It was at the turn of the first century A.D. that the Jews began to disappoint and confound Spengler and Toynbee. Why? Because they failed to progress to their winter phase, says Spengler. Because they failed to respond to the challenge of Christianity, says Toynbee. Spengler omitted them from his "club" because to include them would admit an exception to his theory. Toynbee, needing a resurrection of Christianity to save his otherwise disintegrating West, relegated them to cliff-hanger status so they would not be seriously considered as future world saviors.

With the hindsight history gives us, we can only applaud these failures. Spengler's and Toynbee's reasons for excluding the Jews are the very reasons the Jews survived. If we accept as equally true their contradictory assertions that Judaism is not a civilization and that it is an arrested civilization, we could define Judaism as a culture. There is a difference between these two concepts. Culture predominates in young societies and is essentially trailblazing. It "implies original creation and new values, new intellectual and spiritual structures, new sciences, new legislation, new moral codes."[2] Civilization, on the other hand, is the crystallization of a preceding culture. It is uncreative, sterile, living on its parent culture like a parasite. Civilization "aims at the gradual standardization of men within a rigidly controlled framework—masses of common men who think alike, feel alike, thrive on conformism, men in whom a social instinct predominates over the creative individual."[3]

Culture, then, corresponds to Spengler's spring, summer, and autumn, but his winter is the parasitic "civilization" that feeds on the parent culture. In Toynbee's terms, "culture" corresponds to his concept of the rule of the creative minority, and "civilization" corresponds to his concept of the Universal State and its subsequent disintegration.

[2]Amaury de Riencourt, *The Coming Caesars*. A frightening, brilliant study of the symbolic meaning of the parallelism between Greco-Roman history on the one hand and present-day Western history on the other.

[3]*Ibid.*

Both Toynbee and Spengler say in essence that the Jews never made it "to the top," that they never made the transition from a "trailblazing intellectual culture" to a "sterile, parasitic civilization." They were left outside, stuck with "culture." But this "retarded growth" turned out to be a blessing. By failing to enter Spengler's winter and Toynbee's Universal State, the Jews were saved from death as a "civilization."

What event in history conferred this "indestructibility" on them? Spengler himself provides the answer by attributing Jewish indestructibility to the exile imposed on them by the Romans in the first century A.D. But he failed to understand the full impact of the liberating role this exile played in subsequent Jewish survival. Defying all historical precedent, the Jews did not disappear like other nations when exiled from their homeland. No longer tied to the soil of a specific country, they became exempt from the "laws" of Spengler and Toynbee which apply to people living within national boundaries and not to those in the world at large.

In the first century A.D., when the Romans destroyed the Second Temple and dispersed the Jews, the Jews carried with them a highly developed culture packaged for export by Prophets and later adjusted for Diaspora life by Talmudists. Thus the Jews were intellectually and pragmatically prepared for life in all varieties of strange civilizations. So, for instance, if the host civilization was in its spring phase when history catapulted them into it, as in the early Middle Ages, Jews were the avant-garde intellectuals. If the host civilization was in its autumn phase when they entered it, as when they stepped from the medieval ghetto into the Modern Age, the Jews were stimulated to new heights of achievement. If a civilization was in its dying winter phase, as in the declining years of the Islamic civilization, the Jews in its midst also stagnated. If a civilization failed to respond to new challenges and became an arrested civilization, as in the Ottoman Empire, the Jews in that civilization also faltered.

Two thousand years of the Diaspora have crystallized three of its unique aspects. If its function was to bring the Jews in contact with other civilizations in order to universalize them, it has certainly achieved this. Each Diaspora interaction enriched Judaism, giving it a new virility, verisimilitude, and a broader spectrum of intellectual activity. But its inner core always remained distinctly Jewish. No matter how much the Jews borrowed, they did not doubt the superiority of Judaism itself. The Greeks did not dazzle them, the Romans did not awe them, the Sassanids did not impress them, the Arabs did not overpower them, the Europeans did not seduce them. They borrowed, thanked, and went on as Jews.

But this universalization of the Jews was only one function of the Diaspora. Not only did the Jews feel the impact of Gentile civilizations, but the Gentile civilizations also felt the impact of the Jews. With each new challenge, with each successive enlargement of the Diaspora, Judaic ideas were indelibly imprinted on each host civilization. This "Judaization" of the world that has imperceptibly coursed below the surface of history in our second act is destined to surface in the third.

The third most unique feature of the Diaspora is that the Jews, in spite of their brilliance, have never originated a new civilization. There is a logic in this. If the Jews are destined to help the world achieve universal brotherhood, they must not yield to the temptation of creating a new civilization, for a new one might not have the same mission as the old one.

By fitting Jewish history into the frameworks of Spengler's and Toynbee's metahistories, we see that the Diaspora is an absolutely essential ingredient in the Jewish manifest destiny. If not for the Diaspora the Jews might have become an extinct people, like other peoples who lived and died within the boundaries of their states, or simply vanished when transplanted into alien cultures. The Diaspora not only saved the Jews from extinction, it placed them in the midst of history. Because of the Diaspora, the Jews did not die culturally when a host civilization died. There were always Jews in other civilizations to give perpetuity to the Judaic heritage. Wittingly or unwittingly, the Diaspora designers in the second act transformed a temporary political exile into a permanent ideological Diaspora, which for the Jews became their escape hatch from death as a civilization, leading them to "eternal life" as a culture.

We have seen how twice in history the Jews were exiled from their homeland—once at the hands of the Babylonians and again at the hands of the Romans. Each time it was Diaspora Jews who not only preserved Judaism in exile but eventually restored the Jewish state. The leaders who restored the destroyed Kingdom of Judah in the fifth century B.C.—Sheshbazzar, Zerubbabel, Jeshua, Ezra, Nehemiah—were all born in the Diaspora. The Zionist leaders who restored the state of Israel in the twentieth century A.D.—Herzl, Ussishkin, Weizmann, Jabotinsky, Ben-Gurion—were also all born in the Diaspora. Without a Diaspora to preserve a reservoir of Jews there would have been no Jews 2,500 years ago or today to rebuild the ancient homeland as an independent state.

Do these events hold a meaning for the Jews in the future? If all Jews in the Diaspora were to emigrate to Israel, could they survive within that state's geographic boundaries as a people for another millennia or two? If someday, God forbid, a military calamity were to disperse them from their land for a third time, what would happen if there were no Diaspora to absorb them? If the Jews were to liquidate their Diaspora and bind the fate of Judaism to one nation, would they not also pass into their winter phase, the death phase of a civilization? If they were to nurse but one culture, tied to one plot of geography, like all other nations, might they not also stagnate and die? If they were to give up the Diaspora, the one physical condition which differentiates Jewish history from that of all other histories, could they continue to count on being exempt from the normal historical process of decay and death?

To escape death as a civilization, the Jews must therefore continue to cultivate their Diaspora. If they choose to reaffirm their past, and fulfill their destiny, they must enter the third act with both a Jewish humanist citadel in Israel and Jewish ideological outposts in the Diaspora. Each must nurture the other, because each is dependent on the other. The world needs both.

THE DIASPORA AND THE WORLD

If Spengler is right in his prediction of the death of Western civilization within a century or so, what will happen to the Diaspora Jews now overwhelmingly centered in that civilization? According to precedent, we would expect them to sink with Western civilization. But again, according to precedent, we should also expect them to reemerge in a new civilization.

According to Spengler, the new tidal waves of civilizations should be those of Russia and China. It should be no more impossible for the Jews to establish viable Diaspora centers in Russia and China than it has been in other lands, other cultures. Having shown their ability to establish Diaspora centers in such diverse social, economic, and religious societies as Babylonia, Persia, Greece, Rome, Parthia, Sassania, the Islamic Empire, as well as in the Catholic and Protestant Christendoms, why not Russia and China?

One thing history teaches us is that we cannot count on the present to perpetuate itself. Countries that were once pro-Jewish have turned against the Jews bitterly, and vice versa. The Hadrianic repressions of the Jews in second-century Rome turned into universal citizenship for the Jews in the third. Spain, once the spawning ground for a Jewish Golden Age, became the land of Inquisition and expulsion. So, too, present-day anti-Jewishness in Russia could vanish with an abrupt change in the Party line. The paucity of Jews in China today should not preclude the possibility of a Diaspora center taking root there, just as in the past Diaspora centers have risen in countries where previously there had been no Jews.

Future Jewish history in Russia could take one of four courses. Under the impact of antireligious propaganda, the Jews could be totally assimilated within a century; the Communist Party line could take an abrupt about-face and permit a return to religion; there could be, as once in Spain, a mass expulsion; or there could be a vast migration of Jews out of Russia.

If the Communist Party line were to change and religion be permitted, then Russia's three million Jews could nucleate a formidable intellectual Diaspora center in Soviet Russia. In case of an expulsion or exodus, however, where could the Jews go? Could Israel, because of its small size, absorb them all? Would the immigration policies of Western nations permit them to enter? China, in need of a trained scientific elite, might welcome a significant number, just as other underdeveloped nations have in the past.

Once before in history the Jews had an outpost in China. In the eighth century, Jews settled in Chang Ku Feng, in central China, where, for a thousand years, they maintained a Jewish enclave. Though cut off from Jewish learning, the Chinese Jews nevertheless held out until, around 1800, they finally disappeared.

Ideologically, China could be a fertile civilization for a Diaspora center, because the Chinese of today are even more "Judaized" than were the Puritans of Colonial America. Though the Chinese may not make obeisance to a Jewish heritage, though they may not know a Jew from a Christian, their ideology is more "Jewish" in origin than that of Western civilization. According to the meta-historians, new civilizations are sparked by a combination of a new world religion, a new concept of nature, and a new outlook of man. In China today, the influences of Confucianism, Buddhism, Taoism are being replaced by new religious, scientific, and psychological thought. Just as the Bible is the motivating ideology behind the world's one billion Christians, so *Das Kapital* is the motivating ideology behind the world's one billion Chinese. China's "religion" is the economic doctrine of a Jew, Karl Marx. Her science is the theoretical physics of a Jew, Albert Einstein. Her psychology of man is that of a Jew, Sigmund Freud.

History could, of course, deal other alternatives. The present-day flourishing Jewish communities of South America and South Africa could erupt as Diaspora centers. According to precedent, however, Diaspora centers seem to spring to life in civilizations that are in their spring, summer, or autumn phases, not in their winter phase. Technically speaking, both South America and South Africa are by-products of the already doomed Western civilization. A more likely place might be India, for though there are few Jews in India today, a new civilization is more likely to arise there and thus attract a Diaspora nucleus. After all, the first act transpired in a Semitic Age and the second in an Aryan Age. The third act might well transpire in the as yet uncommitted Mongolian third of the world.

The geographic location for a new Diaspora center is not as important as the fact that the Diaspora is here to stay, with a significance not only for the Jews but for mankind. Judaism may be performing a function in the development of both a universal religion and a universal Diaspora for a new-world citizen. If the Space Age should make the national state obsolete, we can foresee the formation of new, more meaningful aggregates, for which the Diaspora has already established a pattern.

If once again we step out to our vantage point in the universe, we will behold three stages in the development of man from the dawn of prehistory to the present, one past, the second vanishing, and a third emerging.

In the first stage, that of pre-civilization, we see man as a food-gathering hunter following the game, a rootless man, living within no geographic boundaries. With the dawn of civilization, he enters his second stage, the agricultural phase, which in time ties him to individual parcels of land that grow into villages, then into cities, into provinces, into nations, into empires, entities all based on geography.

With the Space Age, we see a third stage emerging, a new society, where technological wonders transgress national boundaries and create new loyalties that exceed those of national interest. Industrialization has freed man from the soil, and in a sense has again made him rootless. Technology, not man, produces the world's food today. Instead of following the wild game, instead of being tied to a plot of ground to eke out his daily bread, he follows the availability of work created by machines. The common market of Europe has taken Italians to France and Germany. The world economy has taken Americans to Europe, and Japanese to America. Industrialization has taken Kalmyks to the Crimea and Tibetans to Siberia. These migrations, in Toynbee's language, are the equivalents of the external proletariats of disintegrating civilizations in search of a new religion. Such migratory waves are setting new fluid world population patterns. The world is now becoming one vast "diaspora" and man himself is on his way to being "diasporized."

If the Space Age renders national slogans meaningless, then diasporized man living in a diasporized world will be compelled to search for a new ideology that will give his life meaning. Why could not Jerusalem, now the spiritual homeland for the Diaspora Jew, become the spiritual world center for diasporized man? Will that be the future function of Israel? If so, will that not also imply a universal need for Judaism as an ethical creed for man in the third act?

Perhaps Western civilization is not dying, as predicted by Spengler, but merely undergoing an evolution from its Christian parochial phase to a Judaized universalist phase, much as the Greek Hellenic idea evolved into a universalist Hellenism. Under the communist skirt of Russia and China we still behold the body of Western civilization. What is more natural than that monotheism, Christianity, Mohammedanism, capitalism, socialism, communism—all spun by Jewish brains—should find a universal abode in Jewish humanism.

Toynbee, villified by Jews because he branded them fossils, has perceived the true function of Judaism more clearly than the Jews themselves. At a lecture delivered to the World Jewish Congress in 1959, Toynbee reconsidered his earlier appraisal of the Jews, stating "The future of Judaism is to convert the world. It is an extraordinary thing that twice before in history the Jews have allowed outsiders to run away with their religion, and spread it over the world . . . does not the real future of Jews and Judaism lie in spreading Judaism, in its authentic form, over the whole world?"

Though the world seems unaware of it, or reluctant to admit it, Judaism is already one of the most successful

spiritual forces influencing and shaping the mind of ma
today. It is still the fashion to denigrate Judaism becaus
it is the creed of but twelve million souls. Yet history
judges not by quantity but by quality. Great ideas are
usually held in contempt, at first. But those who deride
them die and are forgotten, whereas the ideas they derided
live to shape destiny. Jesus was ignobly crucified by the
Romans, but his ideas lived to shape the world's most
magnificent civilization. Mohammed died illiterate at the
bosom of his child bride, but his ideas wrought the re-
splendent Islamic world. Marx lived exiled and despised,
yet his ideas sparked the momentous ideologies of Russia
and China. Incubation periods for ideas vary, unrelated
to their future magnitude. For Christianity it was a thousand years, for Mohammedanism and Marxism it was but
one century. Judaism, which has already existed for 4,000
years, may take another century or two before its full
impact will be felt.

All the great religions that once conquered worlds are
crumbling today. The sword of Constantine and the
scimitar of Mohammed have passed to Marx. Today, the
200 million Slavs of Russia profess this new faith; Red
China has converted to the Sickle as Charlemagne did to
the Cross; the dark millions of Africa are acquiring it.
Hundreds of millions of Moslems, Hindus, and Buddhists
are wavering between their ancient faiths and this current
creed.

The pendulum is now swinging from empty scientism
to prophetic humanism, because Marxism is an economic
creed, not a spiritual gospel. Behold the pagans of Africa,
catapulted from their Stone Age into the twentieth-century
Atomic Age, bewildered by their loss of tribe and faith.
Behold India's half a billion souls in search of a religion
that will neither drown them in mythology nor smother
them with materialism. Behold the Chinese, a spiritually
sensitive people, suddenly bereft of a religion. Behold
the Russians, taught atheism for half a century, yet still
seeking a religion that will satisfy their spiritual urge. And
behold the Christian world itself, proclaiming God is dead,
yet groping for new values. Are the people of the world
as ready to embrace Judaism today as the pagans in the

Empire were ready to accept Christianity? Can
step into the breach at this crucial juncture of
ialist wealth and disintegrating spirit? Can this tiny,
rphous, ethnic group known as Jews achieve what all
great "isms" have been unable to achieve?

Does rationalism, communism, nazism, fascism, or
racism hold greater promise than the ethics of Judaism?
Has not the Old Testament shown itself superior to the
philosophies of Plato, Hegel, or Kant? Do we feel safer
with the finger of the scientist or the finger of God on the
trigger of the hydrogen bomb?

Will it be the destiny of the Jews in the third act to
proselytize the universalistic aspect of their faith to a
diasporized world sick unto its scientific soul, ready, perhaps, at last, to accept their prophetic message? Is it
possible that Christianity, Mohammedanism, communism
have been but stepping-stones to make it easier for
diasporized man to cross over into a universal Judaism?

Just as Christianity is a Jewish religious stepping-stone
for a spiritual brotherhood, so Marxism may be a Jewish
secular stepping-stone to a social brotherhood. This may
be difficult for some to accept, because they view Christianity against a 2,000-year development, whereas Marxism
is viewed against a distance of only one hundred years.
But if we compare the first few centuries of Christianity
with the first century of communism, we can see re-
semblances. Christianity was more abhorrent to the Romans
in the second century than communism is to the capitalists
in the twentieth. Just as Jesus never foresaw the crimes
and follies of the early Christian sects, so Marx never
envisioned the crimes and follies of the early communist
parties. But just as time has dissolved the barbarism of
the early Christians, so time will in all probability soften
the inhumanity of today's communists. Just as the Gospels
survived in spite of the Christians, so *The Communist
Manifesto* may survive in spite of the communists, because
the message in both is greater than the people proclaiming
them. In the future, perhaps, the spiritual message of
Judaized Christianity and the economic message of Judaized
socialism may fuse with the morality of the Jewish Prophets

and the ethics of the Jewish patriarchs to bring about a secular millennium.

At the end of the first act, Jesus proclaimed a religious brotherhood of man in heaven. At the end of the second act, Marx proclaimed an economic brotherhood for man on earth. What will be proclaimed at the end of the third act? Will the Christian Jesus reappear as promised by the Gospels, or will a Jewish messiah appear as promised by the Prophets? What if both predictions are fulfilled? Will it be two different messiahs, or one and the same messiah?

It is said that man selects a hero to save him, but that God selects a people to save mankind. The Christians selected Jesus as their hero to save them. Did God select the Jews to save man? In Jesus, the Jewish "Word" was made "flesh" by the Christians, but rejected by the Jews. Will the Christian "flesh" eventually be transformed back into the Jewish "Word" in the third act? Perhaps in the third act there will be no messiah as a person, but only as an idea. The message will be more important than the messenger.

Thus, in the third act, man himself will be faced with an existentialist choice. Should he choose the Christian paradise in heaven, with an avenging Jesus returning to end mankind with a Judgment Day, or should he choose the Jewish paradise on earth brought about by a messianic concept of brotherhood?

THE FUNCTION OF ISRAEL

We stated earlier that the Zionists were the twentieth-century's secular messiahs who did what the theological messiahs should rightfully have done. The rationalist twentieth-century Jew, though he has abandoned the theological idea of the messiah, still has a vision of that messianic concept—the redemption of the Jew through the soil of Palestine. In the end, therefore, the motivating force behind Zionism was the 2,000-year existence of messianism, the mystique of the Prophets. No philosophy,

438   THE INDESTRUCTIBLE JEWS

no logic, no science has altered this Jewish belief in the ancient idea of a prophetic manifest destiny. The distant past is closer to the heart of the Jew than recent history. Nothing, not anti-Semitism, not communism, not fascism, can uproot this attachment to his past or blind his vision of the future.

But how could these forthright Zionist agnostics claim to be heirs to the messianic ideal? How could they deny God and yet proclaim the chosenness of the Jewish people? Perhaps Ben-Gurion best resolved this dilemma when he said:

> My concept of the messianic idea is not a metaphysical but a social-cultural one . . . I believe in our moral and intellectual superiority, in our capacity to serve as a model for the redemption of the human race . . . The glory of the Divine Presence is within us, in our hearts, and not outside us.[4]

Zionist writers have recognized that Israel must be more than a haven for Jews hopscotching the globe, one step ahead of anti-Semitism. Israel, they have warned, must never be just another nation among nations. She must never imitate nor tie her fate to any existing civilization or ideology, for if she does she, too, will die. Her salvation, they exhort, is in becoming a universalist state, a symbol of peace, a sanctuary of the prophetic ideal. In the words of Martin Buber:

> There is no reestablishing Israel, there is no security for it save one: It must assume the burden of its uniqueness; it must assume the yoke of the kingdom of God.[5]

But what Buber declaimed in cadenced prose in the twentieth century, the Prophets exhorted in sublime poetry

---

[4] *The Zionist Ideal*, by Arthur Hertzberg, p. 94.
[5] From an essay "The Jew in the World," in *Israel and the World*, by Martin Buber.

two and a half millennia ago. In the first millennia B.C., the Prophets warned Israel against compromising its spirit, insisting that there was no security for Israel except in her uniqueness. The Prophets knew that if Israel existed only as a political structure, she would perish, and that only by standing fast as a chosen messenger of God could she survive. They were the first to call upon Israel to enter world history as a prototype of an ethical-religious community and be an example for mankind.

Just as Christian metahistorians think of an aggregate of nations forming a civilization as the real unit for the study of history, and Jewish kabalists think of a cluster of civilizations as the proper unit for the study of destiny, so the Prophets held that mankind itself was the only unit for the study of existence.

The ancient Jews realized that the Prophets spoke allegorically. They understood that in predicting doom for the people of Assyria and Babylonia, the Prophets were also warning the world of the formation of totalitarian states that would threaten the liberties of all men. Instead of seeing history as an impersonal flux of fate, as do historians, the Prophets saw history as the unfolding of a divine plan. Isaiah expresses in poetic language the ideas used by Luria and Hegel. Only the terminology is different. His words could be cast in a three-act play that encapsulates the total drama—past, present, and future—of world history.

The first act of the Isaiahn drama, corresponding to Luria's *tzimzum*, and Hegel's "thesis," is Isaiah's Day of Wrath. The Prophet visualized the Universal State (any oppressive superstate) as being the instrument of God's anger. No people, Isaiah declares, Jew or Gentile, can escape the oppression or destruction of the superstate out to dominate the world.

The second act, the *shevirat ha'keilim* of Luria and the "antithesis" of Hegel, is Isaiah's Day of Judgment. The Lord's anger will be turned against the superstate and He will destroy it. The yoke of the oppressed nations will be lifted and man freed.

The third act, Luria's *tikkun* and Hegel's "synthesis,"

is Isaiah's Age of Salvation which will follow in the wake of the destruction of the Universal State, at which time a universal brotherhood will replace the former totalitarianism. This vision of Isaiah can best be expressed in his own words:

> He shall judge among the nations,
> and shall rebuke many people;
> and they shall beat their swords into plowshares,
> and their spears into pruning hooks;
> nations shall not lift up sword against nation,
> neither shall they learn war any more.

Almost three millennia after they were uttered, Isaiah's words still express the longing of men of all faiths, the universal hope of mankind.

The twentieth-century Jews, standing in the lobby of history waiting for the third act to start, will soon have to make their existentialist choice. If they, like their ancestors after the first act, choose not to deny the past, they too will have to reaffirm the belief in their manifest destiny and devise new responses for continued survival in history as Jews.

If the first act proceeded like a Greek predestination drama, and the second like a French existentialist drama, the third act might well begin like a drama of the absurd. To quote the Prophets in an age when science and computers determine ethics and morality, to call for a brotherhood of man at a time when mankind is racing toward Caesarism, is the quintessence of absurdity, the mad undertaking of a Sisyphus.

In Greek legend, Sisyphus, founder of Corinth, was doomed by Zeus to eternally roll a stone up a slope. Each time he neared the top, the stone would slip from his hands to roll to the bottom, and the wearisome task would begin all over again.

Is the Jew the Sisyphus of the world, destined forever to roll the millstone of a brotherhood nearly to the pinnacle of man's professed aspirations, only to behold his efforts and hopes dashed time and again? The Greeks were pes-